WORDSWORTH CLASSICS
OF WORLD LITERATURE

General Editor: Tom Griffith

THREE PLAYS

D0720845

Racine
Three Plays

Andromache, Phaedra,
Athaliah

The French text, with a new
Translation by Tim Chilcott

With an Introduction by
Michael Hawcroft

WORDSWORTH CLASSICS
OF WORLD LITERATURE

This edition published 2000 by Wordsworth Editions Limited
Cumberland House, Crib Street, Ware, Hertfordshire SG12 9ET

ISBN 1 84022 112 7

Typeset by Antony Gray
Printed and bound in Great Britain by
Mackays of Chatham, Chatham, Kent

CONTENTS

CONTENTS

INTRODUCTION

Between the mid-sixteenth century and the early nineteenth, many hundreds of five-act verse tragedies were written in French, all with a striking family resemblance. But the eleven tragedies of Jean Racine (1639-99) stand out from the rest and make their author the undisputed master of tragic drama in France. The plays translated in this volume, *Andromaque*, *Phèdre* and *Athalie*, are among his best-known, and amply demonstrate those qualities that grant them classic status: powerful passions are both depicted and aroused, but through a supremely restrained form; issues of guilt and innocence, freedom and responsibility, are explored in all their delicate complexity. Taking a genre he had inherited, Racine produced works more theatrically compelling and more subtly suggestive than any by his predecessors or successors.

Racine's dramatic career

Racine's dramatic career began in 1664 with *La Thébaïde ou les Frères ennemis*. The play was a direct challenge to the established dramatist Pierre Corneille, treating, as it does, the enmity between the sons of Oedipus: Corneille had represented the story of Oedipus himself in his *Œdipe* of 1659. Racine followed this with *Alexandre le grand* in 1665, an unambiguous attempt to attract the attention of Louis XIV, whose interest in Alexander was evidenced by his commission to the artist Le Brun for a series of tapestries depicting scenes from Alexander's life.

His first two plays are less often read and performed today than his third, *Andromaque*, staged for the first time in a private performance at court for Henriette d'Angleterre on 17 November 1667 before its public performances at the Hôtel de Bourgogne, one of the three principal theatres in Paris at the time. The gazetteer

Robinet describes the performance he saw thus: 'I have seen the new play about Andromaque, widow of Hector, who many centuries after her death reappears appetizingly in the form of an actress [Mademoiselle Du Parc], a great temptress of men, who, filled with ceremonial grief, plays her role admirably well, using voice, gesture and eyes. Pyrrhus keeps her in his court, a prisoner of war and love. And this Prince, who loves the widow without being loved in return, is represented powerfully by that much vaunted actor, to whom few can compare, called Floridor. Oreste comes to ask for Astyanax, and this frenetic Oreste is played by Montfleury, who does better than the deceased Mondory. There is also a certain Hermione [Mademoiselle Des Œillets] at Pyrrhus' court, who loves Pyrrhus wildly.' Robinet is struck primarily by the compelling love intrigue and by the performance of the actors. The comparison between Montfleury, who played Oreste, and the dead actor Mondory is both telling and prophetic. Mondory had played the role of King Herod with such gusto in Tristan l'Hermite's *Mariane* of 1636 that he had an apoplectic fit, which left him paralysed. Montfleury played Oreste so frenziedly that after a few weeks he too had a fit and died. Writing later in 1668, the critic Gabriel Guéret put the following words into the mouth of the deceased Montfleury, an excellent, even if comically exaggerated, indication of the passion with which tragic actors performed: 'I wore out my lungs in those violent fits of jealousy, love and ambition. I had to keep looking around furiously, rolling my eyes wildly like a madman, inspiring horror with my grimaces, imprinting on my brow the colours of indignation and frustration, alternating them with the pallor of fear and surprise, expressing the transports of rage and despair, shouting as if possessed, and so dismantling all the limbs in my body to make it supple for these different expressions. If anyone wants to know what I died of, let him not ask if it was of fever, dropsy or gout, tell him I died of *Andromaque*.' When faced with the learned sources advertised by Racine in his preface – the third book of Virgil's *Aeneid*, Euripides' *Andromache*, Seneca's *Troades* – we might find it salutary to remember the practical work of the actors and actresses who brought movingly and terrifyingly to life the passions of his suffering, agitated characters.

Although Racine had found a highly successful formula in

Andromaque – Greek setting, the destruction wrought by love – and although critics often discuss his plays as if they are all cast in the same mould, *Andromaque* was followed by a series of experiments which showed his flexibility and versatility as a dramatist. In 1668 his only comedy, *Les Plaideurs*, was performed, a lively farce satirising the legal profession. In the 1660s Molière reigned supreme in the comic genre. His plays were indebted simultaneously to the tradition of the Roman dramatists Plautus and Terence and to the more recent traditions of French and Italian farce. By writing a comedy based on Aristophanes' *The Wasps*, it was as if Racine was now trying to rival Molière by turning to Greek comic sources, as he had already rivalled Corneille by exploiting Greek tragic sources. For his following experiments he returned to tragedy. Corneille was known for his skill at bringing ancient Rome to life on the tragic stage. In 1669 Racine set his intensely political drama, *Britannicus*, in the court of the emperor Nero. Corneille was also known for his reliance on intricately complex plots to sustain the audience's interest. In 1670 Racine created his Roman play *Bérénice* out of a conflict between only three main characters. Corneille's rival play, *Tite et Bérénice*, was performed at a different theatre at the same time, with a much busier plot. In 1672 Racine turned, exceptionally, to a modern historical event set in seventeenth-century Constantinople. *Bajazet* showed him trying his hand at a conspiracy plot of Cornelian complexity. *Mithridate* (1673) reverts to the ancient world and deals with attitudes towards rebellion against the Romans, as Corneille had done in *Nicomède* (1651), whilst *Iphigénie* (1674) marks Racine's return to Greek sources.

    Phèdre builds explicitly on the triumph of *Iphigénie*, which was so successful at making audiences weep that a contemporary Parisian satire even claims the price of handkerchiefs shot up. Like *Iphigénie*, *Phèdre* has a Greek setting and is so constructed, according to the preface, as to maximize the audience's emotional involvement. The play was first performed on 1 January 1677 at the Hôtel de Bourgogne. Racine's inferior rival Pradon wrote a *Phèdre et Hippolyte* which was performed at the same time in a different theatre. For a time there seemed to be public confusion about which play was whose, and it looked as if Racine's would not do well. But the confusion was soon cleared up, and Racine's was the play that made a lasting impression. Whatever he wrote in his preface about the useful lessons the play can teach needs to be set in the context of the play's obviously daring theme. *Phèdre* is about adultery and incest. Euripides' *Hippolytus* does not show the main character declaring her incestuous love to her stepson, as Seneca's *Phaedra* does. Racine's French contemporaries who treated the subject – Gilbert in 1645, Bidar in 1675, as well as Pradon – all toned down the moral implications of the story by depicting Phèdre not as the wife of Thésée, but as his fiancée. Racine's extraordinary daring was to depict a married woman declaring her passion to her husband's son. This all-consuming passion, which, in different ways, ruins Phèdre and those around her, is not attenuated by the depiction of the gently timorous love of Hippolyte and Aricie; it is thrown into bold contrast by it. The powerful tragic emotions engendered by the play and the audacity of its subject make *Phèdre*, for many critics, the pinnacle of Racine's achievement.

After *Phèdre*, Racine gave up writing for the theatre, married, became a good family man and devout Christian, and dutifully performed his joint role with Boileau as writer of the king's history. The two plays he subsequently wrote, *Esther* (1689) and *Athalie* (1691), were composed at the request of Madame de Maintenon, the king's wife, for very special circumstances. In 1686 she had founded at Saint-Cyr, not far from Versailles, a school for the education of the daughters of impoverished aristocrats. Boys' schools, especially those of the Jesuits, had always stressed the importance of theatrical performance in the curriculum. Boys typically performed edifying plays in Latin penned by their masters. The girls of Saint-Cyr were to perform plays as well. But those written by the headmistress, Madame de Brinon, were not a success. It was decided that the girls would perform Corneille's *Cinna* and Racine's *Andromaque*. But the girls played their roles too successfully for the likes of Madame de Maintenon. She wrote to Racine: 'Our girls have just performed *Andromaque* and have played it so well that they will never play it again, nor any of your plays'.

The solution was for Racine to write a specially edifying play and the result was *Esther*, in which Esther's prevention of the massacre of the Jews is presented in a form suitable for schoolgirls. There are three acts, each with its own splendid setting; and there is a chorus of girls singing music composed specially for the occasion by Jean-Baptiste Moreau. It was performed at Saint-Cyr with great success before a court audience including Louis XIV. Madame de Sévigné was thrilled to be there and gave the following account in a letter to her daughter: 'I cannot tell you how exceedingly delightful this play is. It is something not easy to perform and it will never be imitated. It is a mixture of music, poetry, song and characters, so perfect and so complete that it leaves nothing to be desired. The girls playing kings and other characters seem made for the task. One's attention is held, and the only disappointment is to see such a lovely play come to an end. Everything is simple, innocent, sublime and moving. The fidelity to the biblical story inspires respect. All the songs, which perfectly suit the words, taken from the *Psalms* or the *Book of Wisdom*, are just right for the subject and so beautiful that one cannot help but weep'.

Athalie was set to repeat the success of *Esther*. Indeed it should have been even more successful. It was a more substantial play, with five acts, music again by Moreau, and ample opportunity for spectacle in the representation of the temple of Solomon. But there was trouble. There were those who had been shocked to see schoolgirls taking part in the lavish entertainment that *Esther* certainly was. And by the 1690s devotion had so taken hold of the court that their anxieties prevailed. Court performances of *Athalie* were cancelled. The play was given what would today be called a concert performance on one or two occasions (the first on 5 January 1691), without décor, without costumes, and with a much reduced audience. It was only in 1702 that it was performed at court in its full splendour, and then, exceptionally, the performers were neither schoolgirls nor actors, but courtiers. Finally, in 1716, the year after Louis's death, *Athalie* received its first public performance on the Paris stage at the Comédie-Française, but shorn of its choruses. It is a difficult and expensive play to stage. But some have thought it a magnificent achievement, not least Voltaire. Though out of sympathy with the religious fanaticism it depicts, he still thought it 'perhaps the masterpiece of the human spirit'. Racine wrote nothing else for the stage before his death in 1699.

Racine's reputation

Some reputations are made only after an artist has died. But both
Racine and Molière enjoyed enormous success during their lifetime,
and they were the models, in tragedy and comedy respectively,
throughout the eighteenth century. Whereas both have been
revered in France ever since, Molière's comedies have always been
accepted more readily in the English-speaking world than Racine's
tragedies. Molière had an immediate impact on the English comic
dramatists of the Restoration period and continues to be frequently
translated, adapted and performed on the English stage; but outside
France Racine still has the reputation of being difficult, an acquired
taste. His plays seem rooted in distant worlds: Greek mythology,
ancient Rome, the Old Testament. English expectations of tragedy
are based on the plays of Shakespeare. Racine's plays are different
from Shakespeare's; they are superficially less theatrical and less
exciting, shorter, with fewer characters, no variation of tone, no
intricate sub-plots, no luxuriant language, and allegedly little visual
interest. These apparent obstacles to appreciation, however, deserve
critical scrutiny.

Erudition

Racine is himself partly to blame for his reputation as a difficult
writer. When he published his plays, he presented them as erudite
achievements. His prefaces explain and justify them with reference
to the terminology with which Aristotle had discussed tragedy in
the 4th century BC, and he defends his plots and characterization
with reference to the works of ancient historians and poets, who
are often quoted in Latin and Greek. He prefaced collected
editions with a frontispiece depicting an allegory of tragedy accompanied by an explanatory legend in Greek: 'phobos kai eleos'
(fear and pity).

   Why did Racine package his plays in such learned wrapping
paper? Certainly not in order to intimidate readers with his schol-
arship. In part he did it because reference to established and revered
authorities seemed a good way of defending himself against the
attacks of his jealous rivals. In part he did it in the spirit of what
today would be called a publicity campaign. Racine's biographers
agree that he was an extremely ambitious man. Born in 1639 of
bourgeois stock, he was orphaned within four years and then had

the good fortune to be educated at the school associated with the convent of Port-Royal. The convent was known for its sympathies with the cause of the Jansenists (believers in justification by faith, predestination and moral austerity) and for the excellent grounding in Greek, as well as Latin, on offer to the pupils. Now, the clever young intellectual wanting to be noticed in Paris in the 1660s could scarcely do better than to write for the stage, which would bring his name before the urban public and the court. And Racine's thorough training in Greek at Port-Royal offered him a way of outshining his rivals.

Whilst writing plays similar in many ways to those with which other dramatists found success, Racine often chose Greek subjects and claimed to be reviving Greek tragedy on the French stage. It was a theme that ran throughout his career as a writer for the public stage, even to the extent of undertaking a partial translation of Aristotle's *Poetics*. When Racine read the Greek tragedians, he made notes in the margins of his books on the language and dramaturgy of the ancients, and we are fortunate that these books with their annotations still survive. Racine's publicity campaign, afforced by the evident quality of his plays, paid off. After *Phèdre*, in 1677, when he was appointed to the post of historiographer to the king, he wrote no more plays for the public stage: he no longer needed to.

Tragedy

Even whilst proclaiming the erudition of his achievement, Racine knew full well that his success before an audience was due less to his learning than to his theatrical skills. All those features of his plays which, at first glance, can make them seem alien to a modern non-French audience can be explained with reference to the conventions within which he worked and which he, singularly, knew how to exploit to heighten the pleasure of his spectators. He wanted to secure and hold the attention of his audience by means of an exciting dramatic action; more than that, he wanted to engage his audience's emotions and make them feel pity and fear for the characters on stage. These were the expectations of tragic drama in seventeenth-century France and they are admirably summed up by the observant writer La Bruyère towards the end of the century: 'A tragedy wrings your heart at the very beginning and, throughout, barely leaves you freedom to breathe or time to recover, or, if it allows you some respite, it is only to plunge you afresh into the depths of distress. It leads you through pity to terror or, conversely, through terror to pity, and fills you with tears, sobs, suspense, hope, fear, surprise and horror until the final catastrophe.'

Modern readers might be surprised that tragedy as understood in seventeenth-century France had nothing to do with the gods, fate, or supernatural forces. Neither Racine nor any of his contemporaries thought that the tragic dramatist's task was to present human beings and the gods 'as flies to wanton boys'. It is true that some of Racine's plays lend themselves to an appreciation along these lines. In *Andromaque* Oreste thinks himself the victim of destiny. Phèdre blames her illegitimate passion, and the suffering it causes her, on the goddess Venus, who had cursed her family ever since the Sun-God, Phèdre's grandfather, had revealed her flirtation with Mars. But to locate the tragic nature of Racine's plays in his depiction of transcendental forces would lead to the conclusion that some of his plays are not tragic at all. The gods play no overt role in his Roman plays, *Britannicus*, *Bérénice* and *Mithridate*, where catastrophes are wrought by the clash of purely human motives of amorous and political ambitions. The God of *Athalie* is no wanton boy. One way of interpreting the play, and almost certainly the way in which Racine intended his original devout court audience to interpret it, is as the triumph of divine Providence. Even in *Andromaque* and *Phèdre*, fate and the gods can be seen as figments of the characters' imaginations or as a necessary part of the mythological background which adds to the poetry of the plays. Only the arrival of the sea-monster in *Phèdre*, the result of Thésée's prayer to Neptune, can be seen as direct supernatural intervention; and, in comparison with his ancient predecessors, Racine has done a good deal to tone down the creature's supernatural origins.

Racine's prefaces, learned though they are, bear constant witness to his fundamental aim of arousing the emotions of the theatre audience. He tells us that he has conceived the character of Andromaque so as to increase the audience's pity for her. In the dedicatory epistle of the play, he specifically mentions the tears which the dedicatee, Henriette d'Angleterre, sister-in-law of Louis XIV, wept on seeing a performance. In the preface to *Iphigénie*, based on Euripides' *Iphigenia in Aulis*, he praises himself and flatters his Parisian audience: 'My spectators were moved by the same things which, in ancient times, caused the most learned people in Greece to shed tears and which led to the saying that among poets Euripides was extremely tragic, which is to say that he was marvellous at exciting pity and fear, which are the true effects of tragedy.' He particularly singled out the character of Phèdre as a tragic success, because she illustrates perfectly the nature of the tragic heroine as identified by Aristotle. According to Aristotelian theory, the heroes likely to arouse pity and fear most effectively should be morally ambiguous, neither entirely good nor entirely bad. The suffering of a good character would evoke outrage; that of a bad character, delight. Phèdre's moral ambiguity lies on the one hand in her illegitimate passion for her stepson, which she declares to him, and in her collusion with Œnone, who wrongfully accuses him, and on the other hand in her acute and painful awareness of her crime, as she fights against it and eventually takes her own life in expiation of it. So when Racine chose to depict an allegory of tragedy as the frontispiece of his collected plays and identify it with the Greek words for pity and fear, he was not only showing off his erudition. He was making it visibly plain to potential readers what kind of pleasure was on offer. And in the preface to *Bérénice*, he kindly exempts his critics from struggling with Aristotle: 'They should entrust to me the tedious task of explaining the difficulties in Aristotle's *Poetics*, and reserve for themselves the pleasure of weeping and being moved.'

Heroes

The allegorical depiction of tragedy in Racine's frontispiece with its ancient columns, costumes and crowns highlights one of the features that potentially alienates audiences from these plays: the characters' distance from the spectators. Seventeenth-century and modern audiences differ enormously in what they bring to the plays, but the characters' distance is meant to be part of the experience of any audience. For most characters, this distance is historical, geographical and social.

Andromaque and *Phèdre* are both based on Greek mythology. *Andromaque* depicts an episode from the aftermath of the Trojan War and is set in the palace of Pyrrhus, King of Epirus. Pyrrhus is betrothed to Hermione, the Greek princess, but is in love with his own captive, Andromaque, the widow of Hector, son of Priam, King of Troy. Oreste, son of king Agamemnon, cousin but also suitor of Hermione, comes on a mission to hasten the politically convenient marriage between Pyrrhus and Hermione. *Phèdre* is set in Troezen, a town in the Peloponnese, in the palace of Thésée, king of Athens. His queen, Phèdre, is half-divine, the daughter of Minos, King of Crete, and Pasiphaé, whose ancestors include Jupiter and the Sun-God. Now dead, Minos sits in the under-world, judging all new arrivals. The secret love between Thésée's son, Hippolyte, and Aricie is illicit because Aricie is Thésée's enemy, the only survivor of the royal family of Athens, which Thésée had massacred in order to usurp power. *Athalie* is a dynastic drama, set in the temple of Jerusalem. It depicts the overthrow of queen Athalie, worshipper of Baal, at the hands of the priests and Levites who restore the only remaining rightful ruler, the little boy Joas, to the throne of David. For non-believers, it is perfectly possible to interpret *Athalie* as a theocratic revolution. Audiences at these plays see before them kings and queens, princes and prin-cesses, and high priests, facing crucial matters of state in far-away places in the distant past.

In seventeenth-century France there was a closely observed hierarchy of literary genres, and tragedy along with epic poetry was at the top of the ladder. This position required the genre to be a dignified one. The protagonists' noble status and their temporal and geographical distance contributed substantially to that dignity. In one of his plays, *Bajazet*, Racine chose, however, to represent an action that had taken place in seventeenth-century Constantinople. He justifies himself in his second preface to the play. 'We must look at tragic heroes differently from the way we look at characters who are close to us. One might say that the respect one feels for the heroes increases the further removed from us they are . . . Geographical distance in some measure makes up for the too great temporal proximity . . . This explains how the Turkish characters, however modern they may be, retain dignity on our stage.'

The characters' distance and dignity, however, are not absolute. The very fragility of their dignity contributes compellingly to the tragic impact. The kings and queens of tragedy turn out to be very much like the rest of humanity when it comes to the life of the emotions. Not all theorists in the seventeenth century were happy that sexual attraction should have a prominent place in tragedies. But, except in his final two plays, both on biblical themes, Racine made his depiction of love central to his tragic mechanism. Whatever their social standing, whatever urgent political concerns bear down upon them, his characters are brought low by basic human emotions.

The famed King Pyrrhus, victor of the Trojan War, is reduced to blackmailing his prisoner Andromaque: either she must marry him or her son will be handed over to the Greeks and certain death. Andromaque has to weep and kneel before the haughty Hermione to ask for her help in approaching Pyrrhus and is cruelly rebuffed by her. Love of Hermione makes the ambassador Oreste commit regicide, and Racine depicts his subsequent derangement. Phèdre's love for her stepson is so overwhelming that it consumes her life. She is a picture of physical decay when we first see her. Whilst aware that her lust cannot be satisfied, she drifts helplessly into a declaration of it and then, guilt-ridden, asks Hippolyte to kill her. To avoid discovery, she lets her nurse Œnone weave a tissue of lies, so implicating herself further in the moral quagmire. Athalie's weakness is not sexual desire. She is a great queen, but is reduced to a state of anxiety by a dream which makes her afraid of a little boy; and she is the victim of a carefully calculated trick, whereby she is lured into the temple of Solomon only to see the restoration of power to the rightful ruler acted out before her very eyes.

Some critics have interpreted Racine's characters as allusions to real people in the French court. But Racine was an ambitious courtier and his rulers are portrayed too unflatteringly for them to be intended as references to real individuals. It is none the less probable that part of the pleasure for Racine's original audiences was the illusion that they were peeping into the corridors of power. What they saw was mighty rulers a prey to destructive passions.

Plots

Spectators also saw the re-enactment of stories with which at least the better educated amongst them would have been quite familiar. The actions that Racine chose to depict in most of his plays were well-known episodes from Greek mythology and ancient or biblical history. Yet it was not only men who had been to good schools who would have read these stories in the ancient texts or translations of them. Women spectators too would have had some knowledge. Madame de Sévigné, whose voluminous correspondence demonstrates her fondness for the theatre (though she preferred Corneille to Racine), read copiously among the ancient writers and particularly enjoyed the historians, including Tacitus.

Some critics have therefore assumed that Racine and other contemporary dramatists could not have been interested in the theatrical excitement that a suspenseful plot might engender. The argument goes that if audiences are familiar with the stories there could be no surprise or suspense for them. But the argument is flawed. Racine changes, adds to, and subtracts from the stories on which he draws, and so creates ample scope for suspense. Those spectators of *Andromaque* familiar with Euripides' *Andromache* would be surprised to discover that in Racine's version Hermione is only engaged to Pyrrhus: in Euripides she is his wife. This change allows Racine to keep the audience on tenterhooks by making Pyrrhus propose marriage alternately to Andromaque and to Hermione. The introduction of the new character Aricie in *Phèdre* gives Hippolyte a love interest, which in turn makes possible Phèdre's fit of painful jealousy, the climactic moment in Act 4. Moreover, even when the dramatic action is consonant with the spectators' expectations, spectators unlike critics easily succumb to the tension of the present moment. We may know that Athalie will be defeated and that little Joas will be crowned king, but we still share successive moments of anxiety as Athalie and her evil minister Mathan work to undermine the efforts of the high priest Joad to protect the child and defend the line of David. Racine achieved what Corneille too aimed for: 'securing the audience's interest in the dramatic action moment by moment'. The anxieties caused by his manipulation of plot are part and parcel of the dramatic effect.

Speech

Although different from the highly coloured and varied language of Shakespeare, speech in Racinian tragedy is carefully calculated to combine aesthetic and theatrical considerations to an unusually compelling degree. Given the prevailing illusionistic theory of drama in seventeenth-century France, it was accepted by all dramatists that the characters could not utter elaborate similes and metaphors: that would destroy the illusion that they were real people and make them seem instead like self-conscious poets. Even so, Racine draws on the stock of common images and, while remaining faithful to convention, breathes new poetic life into them. For instance, the image of the monster recurs in *Phèdre*. It is the literal monster, the Minotaur, the product of the union between Phèdre's mother, Pasiphaé, and Jupiter disguised as a bull. But Phèdre also imagines herself as a monster and invites Hippolyte to slay her, as his father had slain the Minotaur. Then again, the simple image of treasure in *Athalie* leads to the exciting climax, when Athalie is lured into the temple to look at Joad's treasure, never thinking, until it is too late, that the treasure is the metaphorical treasure represented by Joas.

Dryden commented unfavourably on the speeches he saw performed by French actors: 'Their actors speak by the hour-glass, as our parsons do. Nay, they account it the grace of their parts and think themselves disparaged by the poet, if they may not twice or thrice in a play entertain the audience with a speech of a hundred or two hundred lines.' This comment is, however, quite misleading in the case of Racine. The principle dominating Racinian dialogue is one of almost constant persuasive interaction. This is determined by the conventional structure of French drama in the period. In order to maintain the illusion of real life on the stage, it was accepted that the action should evolve within a twenty-four hour span: theorists had little faith that audiences would believe in lapses in dramatic time that were significantly greater than the two or so hours of performance time. The same consideration required that the action evolve within one space: changing scenery would advertise the artifice and destroy the illusion. It follows that the action must therefore involve a small number of characters who know each other well and who, in a limited space and time, reach decisions and perform actions that bring their story to a close. In this perspective, it is reasonable to call seventeenth-century French tragedy crisis drama. All the main characters are motivated in ways that are incompatible. Each character therefore needs to speak in terms that will ensure his or her success.

Hence, persuasive interaction. The excitement for the audience lies in observing closely the strategies deployed by the characters as they try to get their way. They can be ingeniously devious. Oreste has two conflicting roles. As ambassador, he wants Pyrrhus to marry Hermione and hand over Andromaque's son. But as suitor of Hermione, he wants Pyrrhus to break his engagement and to refuse to hand over the child. So when he speaks as ambassador, he makes what, on the surface, are the appropriate claims, but he exaggerates them so much that he irritates Pyrrhus and sees his embassy fail. This is precisely the outcome that Oreste, as suitor, desires. Mathan employs equally devious arguments when he speaks to Josabet ostensibly on Athalie's behalf, persuading her to hand over Joas for safe-keeping. Mathan has persuaded Athalie to let him come on this mission, and he has further persuaded her to agree that, should they be refused the child, her troops will ransack the temple. Mathan has every interest in ensuring the failure of his mission: he has a long-standing hatred of the high priest Joad. His speech to Josabet is consequently made up of weasel words. Grandiloquence is in fact rare in Racine. The characters are too busy speaking in pursuit of their own self-interest.

Yet, whatever momentary successes the characters win, there are no real victories in these plays. Pyrrhus is murdered, Hermione commits suicide, Oreste goes mad, Andromaque is left alone with her son, the widow of a man she had desperately not wanted to marry. Hippolyte dies, the victim of his father's ill-judged curse, Œnone drowns herself, Phèdre drinks poison, leaving two mutual enemies, Thésée and Aricie, bereft of those they loved. Even the appearance of a Jewish victory in *Athalie* turns out to be rather an insecure one. Racine inspires some sympathy for the Jews' enemy, Athalie, who is not painted in unremittingly black colours. She is a victim of both Joad's trick and her own unscrupulous counsellor Mathan. Moreover, the triumph of Joas is only temporary. Athalie correctly prophesies his bloody future and his own profanation of the temple of Solomon. Throughout the plays, characters struggle relentlessly to satisfy their passions and their ambitions. This is what gives dramatic momentum to their dialogue. In *Andromaque* and *Phèdre* their efforts lead to scenes of bereavement and despair; and a dark cloud passes over the coronation of Joas in *Athalie*.

Spectacle

Critical stress on the verbal struggles of Racine's characters, depicted in such limited spatial and temporal confines, has often led to a vision of Racinian tragedy as almost pure disembodied speech. The numerous and colourful characters of Shakespearian tragedy who move from place to place, fight battles, have banquets, and address crowds are, in Racine, pared down to a small number of protagonists who, critical convention has often held it, are physically static in their unchanging and nondescript antechamber.

This view does scant justice to Racine's theatrical eye. Far more than his contemporaries, he was interested in the visual impact of his plays in performance and wrote into his text indications about visual effects that contribute significantly to the arousal of the tragic emotions. Racine retained this interest despite some unpropitious performance conditions. Parisian theatre troupes were small compared to the groups of players for whom Shakespeare wrote. Theatres like the Hôtel de Bourgogne, where most of Racine's plays were performed, were long and narrow with a raised stage at one end. Although audiences were less mixed than Shakespeare's (not least because seats were quite expensive), they still included valets and soldiers and they were still quite noisy. Performances took place in the afternoon by candlelight. Audiences had to identify the actors as best they could amidst those spectators who sat actually on stage, in the most expensive seats of all. The conditions of performance go some way to explaining the relatively subdued visual effects to be found in Racine's plays. Yet these effects remain important.

Andromaque is set in the palace of Pyrrhus and has a backdrop depicting the sea and ships, a constant reminder for the audience of Oreste's desire to sail back to Greece with Hermione. *Phèdre* is set in the palace of Thésée in a space which opens onto daylight. Phèdre is afraid of the daylight, despite being the granddaughter of the Sun-God, and even imagines that the vaulted walls are about to cry out her guilt. When she first comes on stage, she is so weak that she can hardly stand and has to sit down, and so distracted that she tugs at her veil and hair (so the text strongly implies). The height of her degradation is conveyed visually, when she wrests Hippolyte's sword from its sheath with the intention of killing herself. The language with which Racine communicates to his audience is also visual as well as verbal. His visual language was probably most effective in the more lavish circumstances of court performances. It was for performance at court that his last two plays, *Esther* and *Athalie*, were written, and even though *Athalie* was never performed in his lifetime in the way he had intended, the text makes plain the total spectacle that he had envisaged: choruses singing to musical accompaniment, stage properties (holy book, sword, and diadem) invested with symbolic and dramatic significance, and a set representing the room of the high priest. The most spectacular moments occur in Act 5. When Joad pulls open a curtain, the enthroned Joas is revealed, and immediately afterwards the back of the set gives way to show us the inner temple and Levites bearing swords, lances and shields who arrest Athalie on stage and then murder her off stage. Racine was very much a man of the theatre.

Lessons

Racine finely tuned all the resources of the dramatist's art so that he could brilliantly achieve what his prefaces repeatedly tell us he wanted to achieve, namely to give his audiences the pleasure of intense emotional involvement. His characters are proud, ambitious, suspicious, lustful, jealous, bloodthirsty, quick to anger. They are controlled, and undone, by their passions. Whatever their historical or geographical setting, they exhibit recognizable patterns of human behaviour, and this is why they so readily move us. But the emotional involvement is all the more pleasurable (especially for those who can read Racine's French) because of the extraordinary poise and elegance with which the seething emotional turmoil is expressed.

Does Racine offer us any more than this combination of aesthetic and emotional pleasure? Corneille never intended to do so, nor did Racine, at least until he wrote the preface for *Phèdre*. Here he performs a volte-face and tells us that the true purpose of tragedy is to combine pleasure with useful instruction. He even suggests how the play might usefully instruct us. It warns us against vicious passions by depicting the misery to which they give rise. He could have made the same argument for each of his earlier plays, but he didn't. Biography can offer some explanation as to why he chose to use this argument now. When he became a dramatist, he fell out with his former masters from Port-Royal, who held a view common among churchmen that the theatre was of its very nature immoral. The publication of *Phèdre* coincides with Racine's success at court, with his appointment as historiographer royal, and with his return to devotion. It is therefore understandable that he should gloss his most recent work in a way that best suited his new status.

It was over ten years later that he was persuaded by the king's wife, Madame de Maintenon, to write two further plays, but both were for performance by schoolgirls, both were on biblical subjects, and neither was intended for public performance. So in writing *Esther* and *Athalie* his abandonment of the public theatre was not compromised. Indeed in the few years before his death in 1699, he became even less compromising. In a letter of 3 June 1695, he expressly forbids his son to see opera and plays at court. The volte-face was complete. Few dramatists of genius can have so decisively turned against the profession that made their name. Paradoxically, it seems that Racine continued to revise the text of his plays for the last collected edition that appeared in 1697. Perhaps he thought that it was only in powerful performance that they were a danger to the public. But the dramatist had already inscribed the powerful performance into the text.

MICHAEL HAWCROFT
Keble College, Oxford

TRANSLATOR'S PREFACE

Three hundred years after Jean Racine's death, the best reason for offering a new translation of his work may also seem the most ironic: that his plays continue to appear untranslatable. Indeed, there could be few better summaries of his current position within the English-speaking world than the opening words of L. P. Hartley's *The Go-Between*: 'The past is a foreign country: they do things differently there.' Between Racine and us, the countless separations of time, of place, of human perception and behaviour, seem to generate a sense of cultural remoteness that is almost unbridgeable. On the one hand, the scrupulous structures and controls of literary expression in seventeenth-century France; on the other, the erosion of all pattern and shape in a post-modernist world accelerating towards a millennium. If ever there were an illustration to prove the impossibility of all translation, this might well be it. In that foreign country – France – in that other time – the 1660s to 1690s – they did things differently.

Many of the features that contribute towards this sense of distance, even alienness, have already been identified in the general introduction. Yet the question remains: how to translate such a world, as it moves between decorous surface and primitive depths, into an English that is imaginatively persuasive to a contemporary audience and readership? The pitfalls are obvious. An undue stress upon the stylisation and formalities of Racine's expression may lead to a rendering that is self-consciously 'literary' – a style of polished cadence and knowing fluency, rather than direct urgency and reality. Conversely, an over-emphasis upon the simple, lived force of his utterance may lead to a translation that has contemporary and even colloquial relevance, but that lacks any sense of historical context or positioning. Even a diplomatic compromise between these extremes may fail, producing an unconvincing hybrid style that lurches between the 'formal' and the 'ordinary' from line to line. But if these are the difficulties, what kind of English does this new translation embrace?

Five specific features of Racine's language (rhyme, rhythm, syntax, diction and image) are worth exploring in response to the question.

Rhyme

One immediate and major feature to be confronted in translating Racine is whether to retain or discard the rhyming couplets in which his plays are written. Certainly, there are a number of advantages in retaining such a rhyme-scheme. The sound-world evoked clearly signals that the plays are indeed a historical, and not a contemporary, utterance; and the drama is unambiguously positioned within past time. The couplets draw attention, also, to the shaped *form* of the expression, which can often be tellingly counterpointed against content that is tense with uncertainty or irresolution. In Richard Wilbur's words, 'irrational leaps of the self-deceiving mind' can often be sharply highlighted by the 'contrasting coherence of the form, which embodies an ideal of high and orderly consciousness'. Then again, the rhyming couplet, in Racine's hands, evokes subtle effects of suspension and advance, containment and movement. The ear is temporarily held within the sound-world of each rhyme (fidèle/nouvelle, adouci/ici, funeste/Oreste, perdu/rendu), but is also drawn forward in anticipation of the next rhyme, and so on. Nor is such a pattern entirely inflexible. Although *enjambement* is rare, lines and rhymes can be broken up between characters to achieve an almost colloquial register, as for instance in the conversations between Phèdre and Œnone, or Athalie and Joas.

For all these advantages, though, the handicaps are more substantial. The English language is not rich in rhymes; and whether in conscious or unconscious recognition of this, English tragedy has never adopted rhyme as a natural aural tradition. The distinctive strengths of the rhyming couplet have always been most tellingly deployed for satiric and comedic effects, and in poetry rather than drama. It is difficult, too, to avoid the feeling of 'jog-trot' – of an emphatic sound pattern being repeated time after time. Then again, even in the best of such translations, it is hard not to sense moments of contrivance, even palpable artificiality, as syntax or meaning is wrenched by the exigencies of rhyme. Perhaps most damaging, though, is the erosion of tonal consistency that can accompany the rhyming couplet:

> Where are you going? What's your hurry for?
>
> To speak with Hector at his sepulchre.

If it's true she's lifted to the throne of Caesar,
If Titus *has* spoken, *has* chosen, I'll . . . leave her.

And how he heard me! How, with many a shift,
The brute pretended not to catch my drift!

It is undoubtedly unjust to extract such couplets so baldly from the translations of which they are a part. Yet their appearance (and they are not the only examples) in recent rhymed versions by three distinguished writers shows how easily hard-won tonal effects can be weakened. The decision to adopt an unrhymed scheme in this translation, therefore, is an attempt to capitalise upon a natural dramatic tradition in English, where flexibility, richness and appropriateness in the choice of the end-word for each line are paramount. The absence of rhyme, indeed, serves only to foreground more important aural effects, notably the rhythm and metre of the verse.

Rhythm

Racine's plays are famously written in alexandrines, twelve-syllable lines that were first used in the late twelfth-century epic *Le Roman d'Alexandre,* and that later became the standard metrical form for French neo-classical tragedy. In addition to end-rhymes, the alexandrine also contains a caesura, normally corresponding with some measure of phrasal pause, and generally occurring in mid-line after the sixth syllable. There is consequently a sense of balance between the two halves of the line (*hémistiches*). The alexandrine is not unaccented: but it is the syllabic count that fashions the metrical pattern, and that differentiates the pulse so markedly from the strongly accented nature of much English verse. In terms of overall aural impact, the line generates a sense of control and regularity, without strong stress, yet with scope for expansiveness in its twelve-syllable length.

However, although two recent translations (by C. H. Sisson and Robert David MacDonald) have sought to reproduce this expansiveness (with an eleven-syllable and a hexameter line, respectively), few versions have followed the example. Pope's well-known comment continues to bite ('A needless Alexandrine ends the song,/ That, like a wounded snake, drags its slow length along'). The weight and ponderousness of the metre in English are a substantial disadvantage, evoking as they do a stately *largo di molto* rather than any more vibrant pulse. As a result, this translation adopts an iambic pentameter line, with very occasional contractions to a tetrameter or expansions to a hexameter when metrical variety, dramatic effect, or unusually compacted meaning in the original seemed to warrant it. The pentameter not only distils and concentrates Racine's lines yet further, but also speaks to the force of native aural tradition. Just as the alexandrine is the fundamental voice of French neo-classical tragedy, English drama is no less embedded in the pulse and rhythms of blank verse.

Syntax

Racine's syntax embraces a striking range between simplicity and complexity. At one extreme, there are direct, declarative sentences that would pass unnoticed in ordinary, modern speech: 'que veut-il?', 'il n'est plus temps', 'je ne la cherchais pas', 'c'en est trop', 'qu'ont-ils fait!', 'j'entends'. Slightly more formal, though still retaining a basic simplicity of construction, are a number of lines where repetition of a crucial introductory word – pronoun, conjunction or preposition – creates an effect of accumulating power and urgency (as, to take a single instance, in Hermione's passionate reminder to Pyrrhus of her sacrifices: 'j'ai dédaigné. . . je t'ai cherché . . . j'y suis encor[e] . . . je leur ai commandé . . . j'attendais . . . j'ai cru . . . je t'aimais'). Slightly more formal, though still clear in pattern, are those lines where oppositions and contrasts are presented in syntactic balance: 'épouser ce qu'il haït, et perdre ce qu'il aime', 'prête à partir, et demeurant toujours', 'il faut ou périr ou régner', 'ils ne se verront plus / ils s'aimeront toujours!' In terms of translation into English, it is relatively easy to express these repetitions and balances in a similarly transparent sentence construction. More problematic, however, are the many complex expressions of subordination, where parataxis gives way to shifting and often subtle relationships between different phrases and clauses. Consider for a moment the way in which Josabet discusses her planned escape with the boy-king Joas:

> Je suis prête: je sais une secrète issue
> Par où, sans qu'on le voie, et sans être aperçue,
> De Cédron avec lui traversant le torrent,

> J'irai dans le désert où jadis en pleurant,
> Et cherchant comme nous son salut dans la fuite,
> David d'un fils rebelle évita la poursuite.
>
> *(Athalie* 3, 6)

After the syntactic simplicity of 'je suis prête', this modulates into a complicated and highly-wrought sentence in which subordinate clause is piled upon subordinate clause, normal word order is inverted, and main verb forms are replaced by present participles. It would of course be possible to render such complication into English:

> I am ready. I know a secret way out,
> By which, without them seeing him, undetected,
> Crossing the torrent of Cedron, taking him with me,
> I will go into the desert where, once, weeping,
> And like us seeking to find safety in flight,
> David escaped from a rebellious son.
>
> (trans. C. H. Sisson)

This is faithful to Racine's syntax, no doubt, but it raises several questions about the cost of such fidelity for the rhythmic fluency and intelligibility of the rendering. Wherever passages like these occur – and there are many examples in *Andromaque, Phèdre* and *Athalie* – the solution offered in this translation is to 'naturalise' the expression by drawing upon the force of shorter sentences, the urgency of main verb forms:

> I am prepared. I know a secret way –
> We won't be noticed, seen at all –
> We'll cross the torrent Cedron hand in hand
> And reach the desert where king David wept.
> He looked for safety in his flight – like us –
> In order to escape his rebel son.

The diction and especially the biblical allusions here ensure that the relative formality of the tone is not lost; but it is expressed through a simpler and more direct sentence structure. In this way, the wide variations between ease and studiedness in Racine's syntax are translated into a broad but single compass of English, where uncomplicated construction prevails.

Diction

It has long been recognised that Racine draws upon a noticeably restricted lexicon in his plays. Shakespeare, it is calculated, deploys nearly 30,000 different words in his complete work; the Authorised Version about 6,500. By contrast, Racine's entire works comprise only just over 4,000 – and of these, nearly 500 are classified in the concordance as 'mots du théâtre tragique', in other words specialised, 'literary' terms with little or no currency outside French neo-classical drama. The three plays in this volume have a range of between 1,400 and 1,700 different words. Diction is consequently concentrated within a relatively narrow compass of key motifs, terms that accrue in emphasis both through ceremonial repetition and through the shifting contexts of meaning in which they are placed. The effects are subtle. On the one hand, words such as 'gloire', 'amour', 'cœur', 'ciel', 'jour', 'charme', 'yeux', 'sang', 'cruel', generate a sense of a primary and primal language, a vocabulary of fundamental conditions. These are the bedrock terms that anchor human response, articulating characters' concerns with an almost ritualistic inevitability. But however basic such words, they are not invulnerable to change. Indeed, they are terms that are subject to constant opposition, dissimulation, misperception, and varied construction. 'Les yeux', to take a single instance, both see and do not see, both betray and are betrayed, generate both sight and insight, or alternatively sight and blindness. It is Phèdre's eyes that are dazzled and then blurred by the sight of Hippolyte ('je le vis . . . je pâlis à sa vue . . . mes yeux ne voyaient plus'), only later to prove blind to the love between him and Aricie ('par quel charme ont-ils trompé mes yeux?') For the lovers, however, seeing is a liberation, a confirmation ('ils se voyaient avec pleine licence'), even in a place ('le fond des forêts') that is ostensibly dark and 'unseeing'. In these and similar ways, the key words in Racine both stabilise and undermine, and never more than when they speak of elemental things.

In the translation of these basic terms, modern English has one incomparable resource: its rich stock of simple, vigorous, almost always monosyllabic, words that are derived from Old English and Germanic roots. The stock addresses primary experience: love, birth, see, go, blood, death, hand, live, lips, man, wife, and so forth. Drawing upon the force of such vocabulary, this translation seeks to convey the solidity of Racine's utterance, the concrete, specifically-experienced details of his characters' lives. Recourse to this kind of expression is particularly necessary when dealing with the key terms, the *mots précieux,* of his *langue galante*. Rarely can words like 'gloire', 'honneur', 'cœur', 'âme', be translated literally and at the same time effectively. 'Glory', for instance, needs to be more specifically rendered: into 'name' or 'good name', 'reputation', 'renown', 'fame', 'prestige'. Not all such translations can depend upon Old English derivatives, of course; but they all draw abstract or generic terms into a more specified and solidified world. And far from eroding the formalised qualities of Racine's style, such specification serves only to highlight the tension between surfaces and depths that haunts his work. Against the polished, fluent surfaces of civilised behaviour – the known and accepted generalities of 'gloire' or 'honneur' or 'âme' – there is always the persistent pull downwards, towards a deeper and more individual anarchy.

Image

Just as the relative restrictedness of Racine's lexicon has been widely recognised, so too has the relative dearth of imagery in his work. The world he evokes is one that is coolly lit, with little sensuous richness or colour. Even where simile and metaphor occur, they tend to be of a conventional kind (love as a fire, a fruit, a battle, a hunt, and so forth). Confronted with these difficulties, several modern translations have sought to leaven a spare, undecorated style with imported imagery. Where such inventions are carefully fashioned, seeming part of a natural and irresistible extension of expression, they may perhaps be justified. But only too easily, they can take on an independent imaginative life, discernibly removed from the original. Consider a single example:

> Eh bien! Filles d'enfer, vos mains sont-elles prêtes?
> Pour qui sont ces serpents qui sifflent sur vos têtes?
> À qui destinez-vous l'appareil qui vous suit?

> Aha, Infernal Daughters! Quite prepared?
> Who are your snakes for, ladies? Who gets snared
> By all these creatures bringing up the rear,
> Your promenading beasts, your zoo of fear?
>   (trans. Douglas Dunn)

As a rendering of Orestes' maddened words at the end of *Andromaque,* the image of 'promenading beasts' and the metaphor of the 'zoo of fear' have undoubted poetic life; but whether that life is Racinian is more questionable. And this one illustration could be multiplied many times, in translations that decorate and embellish, whether intermittently or sustainedly, rather than hold the original text in steady, unrefracted gaze.

Recognising the dangers of such elaboration, this translation tries to convey the spare, economic use that Racine makes of image, metaphor and symbol. Indeed, the very fastidiousness of his treatment serves only to enhance the effectiveness of the imagery that does occur. Sometimes, it is contained within one or two lines:

> Look . . . the temple roof is whitening with the dawn.

> Amid the banners burns the glow of fires.

> I see the urn of doom slip from your hands

> I only see its towers walled up with ash,
> A river red with blood, deserted fields,
> A boy in chains.

More often, though, some of the key words discussed earlier (light, darkness, blood, fire) form networks of association, image-clusters that radiate from the physical to the metaphoric, and from outer to inner worlds. Light, to take the most famous example, draws together *jour/lumière/soleil/clarté/ciel/éclaircir/flamme,* as well as its opposite *nuit/ombre/nuage/mort.* Racine's spareness, in other words, does not inhibit resonance, and a major feature of this translation is the attempt to achieve that subtle verbal balance between austerity and reverberation.

These major features of rhyme, rhythm, syntax, diction and image are, of course, only part of the complex totality that is Racine's language. It is a language that embraces extraordinary range: from the coolly statuesque to the intensely passionate, from transparency to opaqueness, from simple declarative modes of utterance to complex interrogative modes that subvert and undermine. If there is an English into which this world could be translated, I have believed it to be an English that is a-historical, even timeless, in its directness and simplicity. It is a language of hard yet resonant clarity. It is free both of incongruous colloquialism and of unconvincing archaism. It strikes a middle path between ordinariness and formality. Wherever possible, it elects the mono- rather than the multi-syllable, the Old English root before the Latinate or Romance, the iambic before the trochaic or any other metre. It chooses the end-stopped line of noun, verb and object in preference to *enjambement* and sophisticated hypotaxis. Above all, it is an English grounded in the rhythms and cadences of the human voice, as it celebrates its loves or simply breaks in pain. The infinite subtleties with which even a single line can be spoken (discriminations of pitch and tone, accent and pause, speed and intensity) are of course far beyond the written word to convey, though they will be known instinctually to all good actors and readers. Nevertheless, every line in this translation has been written to be *spoken* and *heard*. On a practical level, this emphasis will explain the frequent contractions between pronoun and verb (I'm, she'll, we're), which may appear slightly colloquial to the eye, yet which in fact sound natural and unforced to the ear. But on a much larger scale, the speaking and hearing of Racine's lines point to one of his abiding concerns, a concern that draws him into a contemporary context with unequivocal force. Voice, and the death of voice, are supreme issues for him. It is speech that defines human reality. Through the speaking of words, or through listening to the silence that always lies in wait, his characters confront central issues of power and authority, of love, passion and infatuation, of simple human survival in the face of pitiless odds. And for all the deflections and dissimulations that words afford, the perception that finally persists is both clear-eyed and unflinching. There are no escape routes offered, no facile conclusions, no murmured easy redemption to assuage the common pain. Of all French, possibly of all European, tragedians, Racine is the one who stares into the whiteness of the sun, and who never blinks.

In the course of translating these plays, I have been very conscious of my indebtedness to those translators who have paved the way, not only by indicating paths to follow but – equally important – by signalling what have seemed less profitable routes. It is always invidious to select particular names for mention, many of whom are listed in the suggestions for further reading; but the late John Cairncross' translations yielded many insights, to the extent of providing several phrases and, occasionally, even whole lines that could not be bettered. An article by Kevin Jackson in *The Independent* (3 February 1990), to which Neil Bartlett, Sian Evans, Alan Hollinghurst and Eric Korn contributed different versions of a passage from *Phèdre,* provided an invaluable starting-point. Other debts go even further back. I hope that the shade of the late Lloyd Davies would approve how a certain adolescent's view of the arch-Romantic Hugo as infinitely preferable to the classical Racine has now matured. Peter Cobb will recall sessions tutoring the same adolescent in translating Jules Romains. Christopher Gill gave a vital push as final drafts were completed, and Gaylord Meech was a constant partner. More recently, Michael Hawcroft provided much helpful advice; and Tom Griffith proved an exemplary general editor, efficient and supportive in all that he did.

TIM CHILCOTT
Brighton, Sussex

1639   Born, the son of a minor civil servant, in La Ferté-Milon, some sixty miles east of Paris. Baptised on 22 December.

1641   His mother dies, 28 January.

1642   His father remarries, only to die three months later, on 6 February. Racine and his sister are cared for by their paternal grandmother, Marie des Moulins.

1643   Enters the abbey of Port-Royal, where his aunt, Agnes des Moulins, is a nun, and begins to be instructed in the doctrines of Jansenism.

1649   Begins studies at the Petites Écoles de Port-Royal.

1653–5   Continues studies at the Collège de Beauvais, which has strong links with Port-Royal.

1658–9   Completes studies at the Collège d'Harcourt in Paris. Begins to turn away from religion and to become involved in literary affairs. Meets La Fontaine.

1661   Disappointed by the rejection of two pieces for the theatre, goes to stay with his uncle, a vicar-general in Uzès, hoping to be offered a church living. Hopes gradually fade.

1663   Returns to Paris. Granted an official state allowance in recognition of his *Ode sur la Convalescence du Roi*, Louis XIV. Is now able to live independently. Becomes acquainted with the critic Boileau, the beginning of a long friendship.

1664   Gains the support of Molière, whose theatre company produces his first play, *La Thébaïde*, though without great success.

1665   Second play, *Alexandre le Grand*, produced in Molière's theatre, but then transferred by Racine to a rival company, who perform it to great acclaim. Serious argument and split with Molière.

1667   *Andromaque* performed in November, and is a huge

success. Secretly marries the actress who plays the
lead, Mlle du Parc.

1668   *Les Plaideurs*, his only comedy, is performed, but fails.
Mlle du Parc found poisoned.

1669   *Britannicus* produced, meeting with hostility from
Corneille.

1670   *Bérénice*, presented within a week of Corneille's *Tite et
Bérénice*, but to far greater acclaim.

1672   *Bajazet*.

1673   *Mithridate*. Elected to the Académie Française.

1674   *Iphigénie*.

1677   *Phèdre*.
Marries Catherine de Romanet, for financial advantage
rather than for love. Jointly appointed with Boileau as
Historiographer Royal to Louis XIV. Officially
reconciled with religion, and with Port-Royal and
Jansenism in particular.

1678–87 Accompanies the king and the army on a number of
journeys – to Ypres, Alsace, Luxemburg.

1688   Commissioned by Madame de Maintenon to write a
play suitable for the girls of Saint-Cyr, a school under
her patronage.

1689   *Esther* performed.

1691   *Athalie* performed privately before Louis XIV and
Madame de Maintenon by the girls of Saint-Cyr.

1691–3 Accompanies the king to the sieges of Mons and
Namur.

1692   His seventh and last child, Louis, born on 2 November.

1695–7 Writes a history of Port-Royal.

1697–8 Relations with the king and with Madame de
Maintenon appear to cool, for uncertain reasons.

1699   Dies in Paris on 21 April. Is buried at Port-Royal.

1711   Racine's ashes transferred to Saint-Étienne-du-Mont.

NOTE ON THE TEXT

The text of Racine's plays reproduced here is that of the last edition published during Racine's lifetime (1697), though spelling and punctuation are modernised and obvious typographical errors corrected. Each play had been published separately after its first performance: *Andromaque* in 1668 and 1673, *Phèdre* in 1677, and *Athalie* in 1691 and 1692. In addition there were collected editions of his plays to date in 1676 and 1687. Variants mostly concern points of style, except in the case of *Andromaque*. In the original edition, there was a scene in Act 5 in which Andromaque reappears on stage as Pyrrhus's widow; it was later suppressed, no doubt to maintain dramatic tension.

A NOTE ON PRESENTATION

Racine divides each of his plays into the conventional five acts, and also follows the French neo-classical convention of beginning a new scene whenever there is a change of characters on stage. These divisions of act and scene are followed in the translation. However, to enhance clarity and fluency, simple stage directions (*Athaliah enters, Orestes leaves*, and so forth) are added in the translation to minimise any uncertainty about exits and entrances. Line numbering is provided for both original and translation; and it is worth noting that, for each play, the total number of lines in the translated version is the same as in the original.

FURTHER READING

Editions

Racine, *Théâtre complet*, eds Jacques Morel and Alain Viala, 2nd edn, Garnier, Paris 1995; introduction in French.

Racine, *Andromaque*, eds R. C. Knight and H. T. Barnwell, Droz, Geneva 1977; reproduces the text of the first edition of the play (1668); introduction in French.

Racine, *Athalie*, ed. Peter France, Clarendon Press, Oxford 1966; introduction in English.

Racine, *Phèdre*, ed. Richard Parish, Bristol Classical Press 1996; introduction in English.

Translations

Among contemporary versions of Racine's work in English, the following selected translations of Andromache, Phaedra *and* Athaliah *are of specific interest:*

Robert Bruce Boswell, *Phaedra*, Players Press 1993.

John Cairncross, *Iphigenia, Phaedra, Athaliah*, Penguin Classics 1963; and *Andromache, Britannicus, Berenice*, Penguin Classics 1967.

Douglas Dunn, *Andromache*, Faber and Faber, London 1990.

Ted Hughes, *Phèdre*, Faber and Faber, London 1998.

R. C. Knight, *Four Greek Plays* [Andromache, Iphigenia, Phaedra, Athaliah], Cambridge University Press 1982.

Eric Korn, *Andromache* [Old Vic Theatre Collection, Vol. 1], Applause Theatre Book Publications 1989.

Robert Lowell, *Phaedra*, Faber and Faber, London 1963.

R. D. MacDonald, *Phaedra*, in *Landmarks of French Classical Drama*, ed. David Bradby, Methuen, London 1991.

C. H. Sisson, *Britannicus, Phaedra, Athaliah*, Oxford University Press 1987.

Richard Wilbur, *Andromache*, Harcourt Brace, New York 1984; and *Phaedra*, 1987.

Life and theatre

Four biographies of Racine can be recommended:

Geoffrey Brereton, *Jean Racine*, 2nd edn, Barnes and Noble, London 1973; in English.

Raymond Picard, *La Carrière de Jean Racine*, Gallimard, Paris 1961; the most scholarly and best documented biography; in French.

Jean Rohou, *Racine entre sa carrière, son œuvre et son Dieu*, Fayard, Paris 1992; in French.

Alain Viala, *Racine: La Stratégie du caméléon*, Seghers, Paris 1990; lively and entertaining; in French.

Recent criticism in English has concentrated on the plays as dramatic structures. The following can all be recommended:

H. T. Barnwell, *The Tragic Drama of Corneille and Racine: An Old Parallel Revisited*, Clarendon Press, Oxford 1982.

Peter France, *Racine's Rhetoric*, Clarendon Press, Oxford 1965.

Michael Hawcroft, *Word as Action: Racine, Rhetoric and Theatrical Language*, Clarendon Press, Oxford 1992.

David Maskell, *Racine: A Theatrical Reading*, Clarendon Press, Oxford 1991.

Odette de Mourgues, *Racine or the Triumph of Relevance*, Cambridge University Press 1967.

Richard Parish, *Racine: The Limits of Tragedy*, Papers in French Seventeenth-Century Literature, Paris-Seattle-Tübingen 1993.

Henry Phillips, *Racine: Language and Theatre*, University of Durham 1994.

P. J. Yarrow, *Racine*, Basil Blackwell, Oxford 1978; a useful introductory study of Racine's career and plays.

For students, there are introductory critical guides in English to each of the plays in this volume:

J. Dryhurst, *Racine: 'Athalie'*, Grant and Cutler, London 1994.

Peter France, *Racine: 'Andromaque'*, University of Glagow French and German Publications 1990; originally published by Edward Arnold 1977.

Edward James and Gillian Jondorf, *Racine: 'Phèdre'*, Cambridge University Press 1994.

J. P. Short, *Racine: 'Phèdre'*, Grant and Cutler, London 1983.

Readers of French will find the following critical works stimulating:

Jean-Louis Backès, *Racine*, Seuil, Paris 1981; suggestive comments on Racine's verbal skill.

Roland Barthes, *Sur Racine,* Seuil, Paris 1963; a work that approaches Racine's world from the perspective of structuralist anthropology and that, when it appeared, put Racine's plays at the very centre of debates about modern theoretical approaches to literature.

Lucien Goldmann, *Le Dieu caché: Étude sur la vision tragique*, Gallimard, Paris 1955; a Marxist approach, stressing Racine's links with Jansenism.

Charles Mauron, *L'Inconscient dans l'œuvre et la vie de Racine,* Editions Ophrys, Gap 1957; a psychoanalytical approach.

Jean Rohou, *L'Évolution du tragique racinien*, SEDES, Paris 1991; chapters explore Racine's evolution play by play.

Jacques Scherer, *Racine et/ou la cérémonie*, Presses Universitaires de France, Paris 1982; sensitive readings of the tragic, dramatic and poetic qualities of the plays through the notion of ceremony.

Background reading

Jean-Marie Apostolidès, *Le Prince sacrifié: Théâtre et politique au temps de Louis XIV*, Éditions de Minuit, Paris 1985; explores links between royal authority and dramatic production.

Christian Delmas, *La Tragédie de l'âge classique (1553–1770)*, Seuil, Paris 1994; a short and lavishly illustrated account of the genre Racine practised.

John Lough, *Seventeenth-Century French Drama: The Background*, Clarendon Press, Oxford 1979; theatres, playwrights, companies, audiences and dramatic conventions.

The general reader might be particularly interested in other works dealing with the same subjects as Racine. The plays of Euripides and Seneca are readily available in modern translations:

Euripides, *Andromache* in *Electra and Other Plays*, translated by John Davie, introduction by Richard Rutherford, Penguin Books, London 1998

Euripides, *Hippolytus* in *Alcestis and Other Plays*, translated by John Davie, introduction by Richard Rutherford, Penguin Books, London 1996.

Seneca, *Phaedra* in *Four Tragedies and Octavia*, translated by E. F. Watling, Penguin Books, London 1966.

The biblical account of Athaliah can be read in 2 Kings xi and 2 Chronicles xxii–xxiii.

Racine's plays have a fascinating posterity. Not only are there translations and adaptations into many languages, and infinitely varied productions on stage. There are transpositions into other art forms. Zola thought of his novel *La Curée* (1871), which explores sexual corruption in the Paris of the Second Empire, as a new *Phèdre*. Music lovers can see what happened to *Phèdre* in Jean-Philippe Rameau's opera *Hippolyte et Aricie* (1733) and Benjamin Britten's cantata *Phaedra* (1976) (settings, written for Janet Baker, of extracts from Robert Lowell's translation of the play). Rossini composed an operatic version of *Andromaque – Ermione* (1819) – and Handel the dramatic oratorio *Athaliah* (1733). Excellent recordings are available of all these works.

ANDROMACHE

1667

A MADAME

Madame,

Ce n'est pas sans sujet que je mets votre illustre nom à la tête de cet ouvrage. Et de quel autre nom pourrais-je éblouir les yeux de mes lecteurs, que de celui dont mes spectateurs ont été si heureusement éblouis? On savait que Votre Altesse Royale avait daigné prendre soin de la conduite de ma tragédie; on savait que vous m'aviez prêté quelques-unes de vos lumières pour y ajouter de nouveaux ornements; on savait enfin que vous l'aviez honorée de quelques larmes dès la première lecture que je vous en fis. Pardonnez-moi, Madame, si j'ose me vanter de cet heureux commencement de sa destinée. Il me console bien glorieusement de la dureté de ceux qui ne voudraient pas s'en laisser toucher. Je leur permets de condamner l'*Andromaque* tant qu'ils voudront, pourvu qu'il me soit permis d'appeler de toutes les subtilités de leur esprit au cœur de Votre Altesse Royale.

Mais, Madame, ce n'est pas seulement du cœur que vous jugez de la bonté d'un ouvrage, c'est avec une intelligence qu'aucune fausse lueur ne saurait tromper. Pouvons-nous mettre sur la scène une histoire que vous ne possédiez aussi bien que nous? Pouvons-nous faire jouer une intrigue dont vous ne pénétriez tous les ressorts? Et pouvons-nous concevoir des sentiments si nobles et si délicats qui ne soient infiniment au-dessous de la noblesse et de la délicatesse de vos pensées?

On sait, Madame, et Votre Altesse Royale a beau s'en cacher, que, dans ce haut degré de gloire où la Nature et la Fortune ont pris plaisir de vous élever, vous ne dédaignez pas cette gloire obscure que les gens de lettres s'étaient réservée. Et il semble que vous ayez voulu avoir autant d'avantage sur notre sexe, par les connaissances et par la solidité de votre esprit, que vous excellez

TO MADAME
[Henrietta of England, Duchess of Orleans]

MADAME,

It is not without good cause that I place your renowned name at the head of this work. With what other name could I dazzle my readers' eyes than the one with which my audiences have been so happily dazzled? It was known that Your ROYAL HIGHNESS had deigned to participate in the making of my tragedy. It was known that you had given me several insights so as to add fresh ornamentation to it. It was known, lastly, that you had honoured it with some tears at my first reading it to you. Forgive me, Madame, if I dare boast of this happy beginning to its fortune. It is a wonderful consolation for the severity of those who would not let themselves be moved by it. I will allow them to condemn Andromache as much as they want, provided I am allowed to appeal against all their quibbling to YOUR ROYAL HIGHNESS's heart.

But, MADAME, it is not only with the heart that you judge the quality of a work. It is with an intelligence that cannot be deceived by false appearances. Could we stage a story that you did not know as thoroughly as us? Could we make up a plot whose motivations you would not fathom? Could we create such noble and sensitive feelings that were not infinitely beneath the nobility and sensitivity of your own thoughts?

It is known, MADAME, and YOUR ROYAL HIGHNESS cannot keep this secret, that in the high and glorious rank to which nature and fortune have been pleased to raise you, you do not look down on the obscure reputation that men of letters have kept as their own preserve. And you seem to have wished to outshine our sex as much by your knowledge and sound judgment as by all the outstanding graces that surround yours. The Court regards you as the arbiter of everything that is pleasant and tasteful. And we, who work to please

dans le vôtre par toutes les grâces qui vous environnent. La cour vous regarde comme l'arbitre de tout ce qui se fait d'agréable. Et nous qui travaillons pour plaire au public, nous n'avons plus que faire de demander aux savants si nous travaillons selon les règles. La règle souveraine est de plaire à VOTRE ALTESSE ROYALE.

Voilà sans doute la moindre de vos excellentes qualités. Mais, MADAME, c'est la seule dont j'ai pu parler avec quelque connaissance; les autres sont trop élevées au-dessus de moi. Je n'en puis parler sans les rabaisser par la faiblesse de mes pensées, et sans sortir de la profonde vénération avec laquelle je suis,

MADAME,

    DE VOTRE ALTESSE ROYALE,

    Le très humble, très obéissant, et très fidèle serviteur,

RACINE.

the public, no longer have to ask the scholars whether we work according to the rules. The sovereign rule is to please YOUR ROYAL HIGHNESS.

No doubt this is the least of your excellent qualities. But, MADAME, it is the only one I can speak of with some knowledge. The others are far above me. I cannot speak of them without diminishing them by the poverty of my thought, and without departing from the deep respect with which I am,

MADAME,

YOUR ROYAL HIGHNESS'S

Most humble, obedient and faithful servant

RACINE.

PREMIÈRE PRÉFACE

Virgile au troisième livre de l'*Énéide* (c'est Énée qui parle):

> Littoraque Epiri legimus, portuque subimus
> Chaonio, et celsam Buthroti ascendimus urbem . . .
> Solemnes tum forte dapes, et tristia dona . . .
> Libabat cineri Andromache, Manesque vocabat
> Hectoreum ad tumulum, viridi quem cespite inanem,
> Et geminas, causam lacrymis, sacraverat aras . . .
> Dejecit vultum, et demissa voce locuta est:
> 'O felix una ante alias Priameia virgo,
> Hostilem ad tumulum, Trojae sub mœnibus altis,
> Jussa mori, quae sortitus non pertulit ullos,
> Nec victoris heri tetigit captiva cubile!
> Nos, patria incensa, diversa per aequora vectae,
> Stirpis Achilleae fastus, juvenemque superbum,
> Servitio enixae tulimus, qui deinde secutus
> Ledaeam Hermionem, Lacedaemoniosque hymenaeos . . .
> Ast illum, ereptae magno inflammatus amore
> Conjugis, et scelerum Furiis agitatus, Orestes
> Excipit incautum, patriasque obtruncat ad aras.'

Voilà, en peu de vers, tout le sujet de cette tragédie. Voilà le lieu de la scène, l'action qui s'y passe, les quatre principaux acteurs, et même leurs caractères. Excepté celui d'Hermione dont la jalousie et les emportements sont assez marqués dans l'*Andromaque* d'Euripide.

Mais véritablement mes personnages sont si fameux dans l'antiquité, que, pour peu qu'on la connaisse, on verra fort bien que je les ai rendus tels que les anciens poètes nous les ont donnés. Aussi n'ai-je pas pensé qu'il me fût permis de rien changer à leurs mœurs. Toute la liberté que j'ai prise, ç'a été d'adoucir un peu la férocité de Pyrrhus, que Sénèque, dans sa *Troade*, et Virgile, dans le second de

In the third book of the *Aeneid*, Virgil writes (Aeneas is speaking):

We sailed along the coast of Epirus, until we reached
The port of Chaonia, and climbed up to the city of Buthrotes . . .
Andromache was pouring out her offerings of grief
In ritual sacrifice to Hector's ashes. She called
Upon his spirit at his empty tomb on a green mound,
Where she had sanctified two altars, as a place to mourn . . .
She looked downcast, and quietly said:
'Happiest of women must Priam's virgin daughter be,
Sentenced to die upon an enemy's grave beneath the towering
Battlements of Troy. She did not have to bear the choice
of lottery,

Nor satisfy a conqueror's lust as captive slave.
Yet I have left my home in flames, have sailed across the seas
In harshest slavery, to suffer all the arrogance
Of Achilles' young son, who soon left me to wed
A Spartan called Hermione, the grand-daughter of Leda . . .
Orestes, though, still tortured by the Furies for his crime,
Burned hot with passion for the wife that Pyrrhus had borne off.
He caught him by surprise, and killed him at the altar of
his home.

(ll. 292-332, trans. TJC)

Here, in a few lines, is the entire subject of this tragedy. Here is the
setting, the events that occur, the four main actors, and even their
characters – apart from Hermione, whose jealousy and passions are
fairly clearly defined in Euripides' *Andromache*. But really my
characters are so well known from antiquity that, however little you
know them, it will be obvious that I have depicted them as the
poets of old have handed them down to us. I have not felt

l'*Énéide*, ont poussée beaucoup plus loin que je n'ai cru le devoir faire.

Encore s'est-il trouvé des gens qui se sont plaints qu'il s'emportât contre Andromaque, et qu'il voulût épouser une captive à quelque prix que ce fût. J'avoue qu'il n'est pas assez résigné à la volonté de sa maîtresse, et que Céladon a mieux connu que lui le parfait amour. Mais que faire? Pyrrhus n'avait pas lu nos romans. Il était violent de son naturel, et tous les héros ne sont pas faits pour être des Céladons.

Quoi qu'il en soit, le public m'a été trop favorable pour m'embarrasser du chagrin particulier de deux ou trois personnes qui voudraient qu'on réformât tous les héros de l'antiquité pour en faire des héros parfaits. Je trouve leur intention fort bonne de vouloir qu'on ne mette sur la scène que des hommes impeccables mais je les prie de se souvenir que ce n'est point à moi de changer les règles du théâtre. Horace nous recommande de peindre Achille farouche, inexorable, violent, tel qu'il était, et tel qu'on dépeint son fils. Aristote, bien éloigné de nous demander des héros parfaits, veut au contraire que les personnages tragiques, c'est-à-dire ceux dont le malheur fait la catastrophe de la tragédie, ne soient ni tout à fait bons ni tout à fait méchants. Il ne veut pas qu'ils soient extrêmement bons, parce que la punition d'un homme de bien exciterait plutôt l'indignation que la pitié du spectateur; ni qu'ils soient méchants avec excès, parce qu'on n'a point pitié d'un scélérat. Il faut donc qu'ils aient une bonté médiocre, c'est-à-dire une vertu capable de faiblesse, et qu'ils tombent dans le malheur par quelque faute qui les fasse plaindre sans les faire détester.

authorised to change anything in their behaviour. The only liberty I have taken is to tone down Pyrrhus' fierceness a little, which Seneca in *The Troades*, and Virgil in the second book of the *Aeneid*, depicted much more strongly than I thought I ought to do. Some people, though, have complained that he loses his temper with Andromache and that he wanted to marry a captive whatever the price. I admit he is not responsive enough to his mistress's wishes, and that Celadon knew 'perfect love' better than him. But what can one do? Pyrrhus had not read our novels. He was naturally violent. And all heroes are not cut out to be Celadons.

Whatever the truth, public reaction has been too favourable for me to worry about the personal distress of two or three individuals who would like to reform all the heroes of antiquity and make them perfect heroes. It is a fine intention to want only faultless men portrayed on the stage; but I ask these critics to remember that it is not for me to change the rules of the theatre. Horace recommends us to depict Achilles as fierce, inexorable, violent – just as he was, and just as his son is portrayed. And Aristotle, far from asking for perfect heroes, asks on the contrary that tragic characters (that is, those whose misfortunes make up the catastrophe of the tragedy) should be neither totally good, nor totally wicked. He does not want them to be completely good, because punishing a virtuous man would excite indignation rather than pity in the audience. Nor should they be entirely evil, because nobody can feel pity for a wicked man. They should therefore be of average goodness – that is, their virtues should be open to weakness, and they should fall into misfortune through some flaw that makes them pitiable rather than detestable.

SECONDE PRÉFACE

Virgile au troisième livre de l'*Énéide* (c'est Énée qui parle):

> Littoraque Epiri legimus, portuque subimus
> Chaonio, et celsam Buthroti ascendimus urbem . . .
> Solemnes tum forte dapes, et tristia dona . . .
> Libabat cineri Andromache, Manesque vocabat
> Hectoreum ad tumulum, viridi quem cespite inanem,
> Et geminas, causam lacrymis, sacraverat aras . . .
> Dejecit vultum, et demissa voce locuta est :
> 'O felix una ante alias Priameia virgo,
> Hostilem ad tumulum, Trojae sub mœnibus altis,
> Jussa mori, quae sortitus non pertulit ullos,
> Nec victoris heri tetigit captiva cubile!
> Nos, patria incensa, diversa per aequora vectae,
> Stirpis Achilleae fastus, juvenemque superbum,
> Servitio enixae tulimus, qui deinde secutus
> Ledaeam Hermionem, Lacedaemoniosque hymenaeos . . .
> Ast illum, ereptae magno inflammatus amore
> Conjugis, et scelerum Furiis agitatus, Orestes
> Excipit incautum, patriasque obtruncat ad aras.'

Voilà, en peu de vers, tout le sujet de cette tragédie, voilà le lieu de la scène, l'action qui s'y passe, les quatre principaux acteurs, et même leurs caractères, excepté celui d'Hermione dont la jalousie et les emportements sont assez marqués dans l'*Andromaque* d'Euripide.

C'est presque la seule chose que j'emprunte ici de cet auteur. Car, quoique ma tragédie porte le même nom que la sienne, le sujet en est cependant très différent. Andromaque, dans Euripide, craint pour la vie de Molossus, qui est un fils qu'elle a eu de Pyrrhus et qu'Hermione veut faire mourir avec sa mère. Mais ici il ne s'agit point de Molossus : Andromaque ne connaît point d'autre mari qu'Hector, ni d'autre fils qu'Astyanax. J'ai cru en cela me conformer à l'idée que nous avons maintenant de cette princesse. La plupart de ceux qui ont entendu parler d'Andromaque ne la connaissaient guère que pour la veuve d'Hector et pour la mère

SECOND PREFACE – 1676

In the third book of the *Aeneid*, Virgil writes (Aeneas is speaking):

We sailed along the coast of Epirus, until we reached
The port of Chaonia, and climbed up to the city of Buthrotes . . .
Andromache was pouring out her offerings of grief
In ritual sacrifice to Hector's ashes. She called
Upon his spirit at his empty tomb on a green mound,
Where she had sanctified two altars, as a place to mourn . . .
She looked downcast, and quietly said:
'Happiest of women must Priam's virgin daughter be,
Sentenced to die upon an enemy's grave beneath the towering
Battlements of Troy. She did not have to bear the choice
                                                     of lottery,

Nor satisfy a conqueror's lust as captive slave.
Yet I have left my home in flames, have sailed across the seas
In harshest slavery, to suffer all the arrogance
Of Achilles' young son, who soon left me to wed
A Spartan called Hermione, the grand-daughter of Leda . . .
Orestes, though, still tortured by the Furies for his crime,
Burned hot with passion for the wife that Pyrrhus had borne off.
He caught him by surprise, and killed him at the altar of
                                                     his home.

                                        (ll. 292-332, trans. TJC)

Here, in a few lines, is the entire subject of this tragedy. Here is
the setting, the events that occur, the four main actors, and even
their characters – apart from Hermione, whose jealousy and
passions are fairly clearly defined in Euripides' *Andromache*.
   This is practically the only feature that I have borrowed from this
writer. Although my tragedy has the same title as his, the subject
matter is entirely different. In Euripides, Andromache fears for the
life of Molossus, a son she had borne Pyrrhus and whom Hermione
wished to kill, together with his mother. Here, though, Molossus
does not enter the picture. Andromache has had no other husband
but Hector, and no other son but Astyanax. In depicting her so, I
felt I was conforming to the idea that we have of this princess

d'Astyanax. On ne croit point qu'elle doive aimer ni un autre mari, ni un autre fils; et je doute que les larmes d'Andromaque eussent fait sur l'esprit de mes spectateurs l'impression qu'elles y ont faite, si elles avaient coulé pour un autre fils que celui qu'elle avait d'Hector.

Il est vrai que j'ai été obligé de faire vivre Astyanax un peu plus qu'il n'a vécu; mais j'écris dans un pays où cette liberté ne pouvait pas être mal reçue. Car, sans parler de Ronsard, qui a choisi ce même Astyanax pour le héros de sa *Franciade*, qui ne sait que l'on fait descendre nos anciens rois de ce fils d'Hector, et que nos vieilles chroniques sauvent la vie à ce jeune prince, après la désolation de son pays, pour en faire le fondateur de notre monarchie?

Combien Euripide a-t-il été plus hardi dans sa tragédie d'*Hélène*! il y choque ouvertement la créance commune de toute la Grèce : il suppose qu'Helene n'a jamais mis le pied dans Troie, et qu'après l'embrasement de cette ville, Ménélas trouve sa femme en Égypte, d'où elle n'était point partie; tout cela fondé sur une opinion qui n'était reçue que parmi les Egyptiens, comme on le peut voir dans Hérodote.

Je ne crois pas que j'eusse besoin de cet exemple d'Euripide pour justifier le peu de liberté que j'ai prise. Car il y a bien de la différence entre détruire le principal fondement d'une fable et en altérer quelques incidents, qui changent presque de face dans toutes les mains qui les traitent. Ainsi Achille, selon la plupart des poetes, ne peut être blessé qu'au talon, quoique Homère le fasse blesser au bras, et ne le croie invulnérable en aucune partie de son corps. Ainsi Sophocle fait mourir Jocaste aussitôt après la reconnaissance d'Œdipe; tout au contraire d'Euripide qui la fait vivre jusqu'au combat et à la mort de ses deux fils. Et c'est à propos de quelques contrariétés de cette nature qu'un ancien commentateur de Sophocle remarque fort bien 'qu'il ne faut point s'amuser à chicaner les poètes pour quelques changements qu'ils ont pu faire dans la fable; mais qu'il faut s'attacher à considérer l'excellent usage qu'ils ont fait de ces changements, et la manière ingénieuse dont ils ont su accommoder la fable à leur sujet.'

nowadays. Most of those who have heard of Andromache hardly know her other than as Hector's widow and Astyanax' mother. We do not believe she should love another husband or another son. And I doubt her tears would have made the impression they did on my audiences, had they been shed for a son other than the one she bore Hector.

It is true that I have had to make Astyanax live a little longer than he did. But I write in a country where such a liberty could not be taken amiss. Quite apart from Ronsard, who chose this same Astyanax as the hero of his *Franciade*, everyone knows that our kings of old are meant to be descended from this son of Hector, and that our ancient chronicles save the life of this young prince, after his country is laid waste, so as to make him founder of our monarchy.

How much bolder Euripides was in his tragedy *Helena*. There, he openly flouts the common belief of all of Greece. He supposes Helen never set foot in Troy – that after the city was set on fire, Menelaus finds his wife in Egypt, which she had never left. And all this based on a view that was accepted only by the Egyptians, as can be seen in Herodotus.

I do not think I need this example from Euripides to justify the slight liberty I have taken. There is a world of difference between destroying the very foundations of a story and changing some of the incidents, which are in any case altered by everyone who portrays them. So Achilles, according to most poets, can be wounded only in the heel, although Homer depicts him wounded in the arm, and never considers any part of his body invulnerable. Sophocles has Jocasta dying immediately after Oedipus' realisation, totally opposite from Euripides, who keeps her alive until the fight between her two sons and their death. It is because of differences like this that an old commentator on Sophocles justly remarks: 'we should not delight in quibbling with poets about the few changes they may have made to the story; we ought to concentrate on the excellent use they have made of these changes, and the ingenious way they have adapted the story to their subject.'

ACTEURS

ANDROMAQUE, veuve d'Hector, captive de Pyrrhus

PYRRHUS, fils d'Achille, roi d'Épire

ORESTE, fils d'Agamemnon

HERMIONE, fille d'Hélène, accordée avec Pyrrhus

PYLADE, ami d'Oreste

CLÉONE, confidente d'Hermione

CÉPHISE, confidente d'Andromaque

PHŒNIX, gouverneur d'Achille, et ensuite de Pyrrhus

SUITE D'ORESTE

La scène est à Buthrot, ville d'Épire, dans une salle du palais de Pyrrhus.

CAST

ANDROMACHE, Hector's widow, captive of Pyrrhus

PYRRHUS, son of Achilles, king of Epirus

ORESTES, son of Agamemnon

HERMIONE, Helen's daughter, betrothed to Pyrrhus

PYLADES, friend of Orestes

CLEONE, Hermione's confidante

CEPHISA, Andromache's confidante

PHOENIX, mentor of Achilles, and subsequently of Pyrrhus

ORESTES' RETINUE

The scene is set at Buthrotes, a town in Epirus, in a room in Pyrrhus' palace.

ANDROMAQUE

ACTE 1 SCÈNE 1

Oreste, Pylade

ORESTE

Oui, puisque je retrouve un ami si fidèle,
Ma fortune va prendre une face nouvelle;
Et déjà son courroux semble s'être adouci
Depuis qu'elle a pris soin de nous rejoindre ici.
Qui l'eût dit, qu'un rivage à mes vœux si funeste
Présenterait d'abord Pylade aux yeux d'Oreste?
Qu'après plus de six mois que je t'avais perdu,
A la cour de Pyrrhus tu me serais rendu?

PYLADE

J'en rends grâces au ciel qui, m'arrêtant sans cesse,
Semblait m'avoir fermé le chemin de la Grèce   10
Depuis le jour fatal que la fureur des eaux
Presque aux yeux de l'Épire écarta nos vaisseaux.
Combien, dans cet exil, ai-je souffert d'alarmes!
Combien à vos malheurs ai-je donné de larmes,
Craignant toujours pour vous quelque nouveau danger
Que ma triste amitié ne pouvait partager!
Surtout je redoutais cette mélancolie
Où j'ai vu si longtemps votre âme ensevelie.
Je craignais que le ciel, par un cruel secours,
Ne vous offrît la mort que vous cherchiez toujours.   20
Mais je vous vois, Seigneur; et si j'ose le dire,
Un destin plus heureux vous conduit en Épire :
Le pompeux appareil qui suit ici vos pas
N'est point d'un malheureux qui cherche le trépas.

ORESTE

Hélas! qui peut savoir le destin qui m'amène?
L'amour me fait ici chercher une inhumaine.
Mais qui sait ce qu'il doit ordonner de mon sort,
Et si je viens chercher ou la vie ou la mort?

ANDROMACHE

ACT 1 SCENE 1

Orestes, Pylades [with Orestes' retinue]

ORESTES

Pylades, oh my dear, dear friend. You're here.
My fortune has begun to change.
At last its anger seems to be less fierce;
It's taken pains to reunite us here.
Who would have thought I'd find you – and so soon –
And in a place so hostile to me now.
To think that you've been lost for six long months,
And now come back to me at Pyrrhus' court.

PYLADES

I thank the gods. They would not let me pass,
And seemed to close the road to Greece – all since   10
That fateful day when raging seas within
The sight of Epirus made our ships part.
I felt so anxious while I was away.
I kept on grieving for your wretchedness,
Always afraid of some new danger facing you
That my poor friendship could not share.
But most of all, I feared that dark, sad mood
In which I've seen your mind caught up so long.
I was afraid the gods would cruelly help
And let you have the death you've always sought.   20
But you are here, my lord. And dare I say
A brighter fortune brings you now to Epirus.
The pomp and splendour of this retinue
Do not suggest a man who wants to die.

ORESTES

Who can foretell where destiny may lead?
Love for a cruel woman draws me here.
Who knows what fate that love may bring
Or if I come to find my life or death?

PYLADE

Quoi? votre âme à l'amour en esclave asservie
Se repose sur lui du soin de votre vie?
Par quel charme, oubliant tant de tourments soufferts,   30
Pouvez-vous consentir à rentrer dans ses fers?
Pensez-vous qu'Hermione, à Sparte inexorable,
Vous prépare en Épire un sort plus favorable?
Honteux d'avoir poussé tant de vœux superflus,
Vous l'abhorriez; enfin vous ne m'en parliez plus.
Vous me trompiez, Seigneur.

ORESTE   Je me trompais moi-même!
Ami, n'accable point un malheureux qui t'aime.
T'ai-je jamais caché mon cœur et mes désirs?
Tu vis naître ma flamme et mes premiers soupirs.   40
Enfin, quand Ménélas disposa de sa fille
En faveur de Pyrrhus, vengeur de sa famille,
Tu vis mon désespoir; et tu m'as vu depuis
Traîner de mers en mers ma chaîne et mes ennuis.
Je te vis à regret, en cet état funeste,
Prêt à suivre partout le déplorable Oreste,
Toujours de ma fureur interrompre le cours,
Et de moi-même enfin me sauver tous les jours.
Mais quand je me souvins que parmi tant d'alarmes
Hermione à Pyrrhus prodiguait tous ses charmes,   50
Tu sais de quel courroux mon cœur alors épris
Voulut en l'oubliant punir tous ses mépris.
Je fis croire et je crus ma victoire certaine;
Je pris tous mes transports pour des transports de haine.
Détestant ses rigueurs, rabaissant ses attraits,
Je défiais ses yeux de me troubler jamais.
Voilà comme je crus étouffer ma tendresse.
En ce calme trompeur j'arrivai dans la Grèce,
Et je trouvai d'abord ses princes rassemblés,
Qu'un péril assez grand semblait avoir troublés.   60
J'y courus. Je pensai que la guerre et la gloire
De soins plus importants rempliraient ma mémoire;
Que mes sens reprenant leur première vigueur,
L'amour achèverait de sortir de mon cœur.
Mais admire avec moi le sort dont la poursuite

PYLADES

How can your mind be so enslaved by love
To make the main care of your life of it?
What spell could make you so forget its pain   30
And once again agree to be its slave?
Hermione in Sparta would not yield.
You think she'll act more favourably in Epirus?
You were ashamed of making all those vows in vain.
You came to loathe her, would not speak of her.
You have deceived me.

ORESTES   I've deceived myself.
My dearest friend, don't overwhelm me now.
When did I hide my heart's desires from you?
You saw my love at birth, the yearning so.   40
And then, when Menelaus gave his daughter's hand
To Pyrrhus, who'd avenged his family,
You witnessed my despair. You've seen me since,
Dragging my chain of grief from sea to sea.
In this dark mood, I saw you were prepared –
Against my will – to stay with me throughout,
To break up all those fits of rage,
And save me from myself each day.
When I remembered, in that turmoil then,
Hermione give Pyrrhus all her charms,   50
You know the rage that overwhelmed my heart.
I tried for vengeance by forgetting her.
I made myself believe that I had won.
I took each frenzy as a fit of hate.
I damned her rigidness, disparaged all her charm,
And challenged her to trouble me again.
My tenderness was stifled, so I thought.
The calm deceived. I came to Greece.
Straightway, I found her princes gathering,
Troubled, it seemed, by dangers of great weight.   60
I joined their cause. I thought that war and fame
Would fill my mind with greater things –
That once my senses were restored to health,
Love would at last have vanished from my heart.
But marvel at the ways of fate. It hounded me

Me fit courir alors au piège que j'évite.
J'entends de tous côtés qu'on menace Pyrrhus;
Toute la Grèce éclate en murmures confus;
On se plaint qu'oubliant son sang et sa promesse
Il élève en sa cour l'ennemi de la Grèce,   70
Astyanax, d'Hector jeune et malheureux fils,
Reste de tant de rois sous Troie ensevelis.
J'apprends que pour ravir son enfance au supplice
Andromaque trompa l'ingénieux Ulysse,
Tandis qu'un autre enfant, arraché de ses bras
Sous le nom de son fils fut conduit au trépas.
On dit que peu sensible aux charmes d'Hermione
Mon rival porte ailleurs son cœur et sa couronne.
Ménélas, sans le croire, en paraît affligé
Et se plaint d'un hymen si longtemps négligé.   80
Parmi les déplaisirs où son âme se noie,
Il s'élève en la mienne une secrète joie :
Je triomphe; et pourtant je me flatte d'abord
Que la seule vengeance excite ce transport.
Mais l'ingrate en mon cœur reprit bientôt sa place :
De mes feux mal éteints je reconnus la trace;
Je sentis que ma haine allait finir son cours,
Ou plutôt je sentis que je l'aimais toujours.
Ainsi de tous les Grecs je brigue le suffrage.
On m'envoie à Pyrrhus; j'entreprends ce voyage,   90
Je viens voir si l'on peut arracher de ses bras
Cet enfant dont la vie alarme tant d'États.
Heureux si je pouvais, dans l'ardeur qui me presse,
Au lieu d'Astyanax, lui ravir ma princesse!
Car enfin n'attends pas que mes feux redoublés
Des périls les plus grands puissent être troublés.
Puisque après tant d'efforts ma résistance est vaine
Je me livre en aveugle au destin qui m'entraîne.
J'aime : je viens chercher Hermione en ces lieux,
La fléchir, l'enlever, ou mourir à ses yeux.   100
Toi qui connais Pyrrhus, que penses-tu qu'il fasse?
Dans sa cour, dans son cœur, dis-moi ce qui se passe.
Mon Hermione encor le tient-elle asservi?
Me rendra-t-il, Pylade, un bien qu'il m'a ravi?

Right to the trap I wanted to avoid.
I hear that Pyrrhus now is threatened from all sides.
All Greece explodes with murmuring and doubt.
He has forgotten, they complain, both blood and vows,
And brings up in his court the enemy of Greece.   70
Astyanax is Hector's young, unhappy son,
The last of many kings now buried under Troy.
To save the boy from death, I'm told
Andromache deceived the cunning Ulysses.
Another child was snatched up from her arms,
And taken for her son, and killed.
It's said that Pyrrhus shuns Hermione
And that he takes his heart and crown elsewhere.
Her father doubts it still, and yet seems grieved,
Complains about a wedding day so long delayed.   80
Her mind seems drowned in so much hurt,
And yet a secret joy floods up in mine.
I've won. At first, I erringly believed
Revenge alone had made for such delight.
But in my heart, she soon regained her place.
I saw the mark of love that would not die.
I felt my hate had run its course
Or rather . . . knew I loved her still.
And so I canvassed all the Greeks; I'm named
Ambassador to Pyrrhus. I've come to see   90
If I can take away from him that boy
Whose mere existence troubles many states.
And yet, my love is so intense I want
To take Hermione before the child.
And it's increased. You can't expect to find
It threatened by the greatest dangers now.
I've tried so hard. But holding out is vain.
I give myself up blindly to this ecstasy.
I love Hermione. I've come to find, to move,
To take her off, or die in front of her.   100
You know Pyrrhus. What will he do, you think.
Tell me what's happening in his court, his heart.
Does my Hermione still capture him?
Will he give back the good thing that he took?

PYLADE

Je vous abuserais si j'osais vous promettre
Qu'entre vos mains, Seigneur, il voulût la remettre.
Non que de sa conquête il paraisse flatté;
Pour la veuve d'Hector ses feux ont éclaté;
Il l'aime. Mais enfin cette veuve inhumaine
N'a payé jusqu'ici son amour que de haine;   110
Et chaque jour encore on lui voit tout tenter
Pour fléchir sa captive, ou pour l'épouvanter.
De son fils qu'il lui cache il menace la tête,
Et fait couler des pleurs qu'aussitôt il arrête.
Hermione elle-même a vu plus de cent fois
Cet amant irrité revenir sous ses lois,
Et de ses vœux troublés lui rapportant l'hommage,
Soupirer à ses pieds moins d'amour que de rage.
Ainsi n'attendez pas que l'on puisse aujourd'hui
Vous répondre d'un cœur si peu maître de lui :   120
Il peut, Seigneur, il peut, dans ce désordre extrême,
Épouser ce qu'il hait, et punir ce qu'il aime.

ORESTE

Mais dis-moi de quel œil Hermione peut voir
Son hymen différé, ses charmes sans pouvoir.

PYLADE

Hermione, Seigneur, au moins en apparence,
Semble de son amant dédaigner l'inconstance,
Et croit que trop heureux de fléchir sa rigueur
Il la viendra presser de reprendre son cœur.
Mais je l'ai vue enfin me confier ses larmes;
Elle pleure en secret le mépris de ses charmes.   130
Toujours prête à partir, et demeurant toujours,
Quelquefois elle appelle Oreste à son secours.

ORESTE

Ah! si je le croyais, j'irais bientôt, Pylade,
Me jeter . . .

PYLADE   Achevez, Seigneur, votre ambassade.
Vous attendez le roi : parlez, et lui montrez
Contre le fils d'Hector tous les Grecs conjurés.

PYLADES

    I would deceive you if I dared to say
    That he will ever give her up to you.
    Not that his conquest has not charmed him much.
    Andromache has kindled all his fire;
    He loves her. But till now she's been unmoved.
    She's answered all his love with hate.   110
    And yet each day he risks his all
    To woo his captive or to frighten her.
    He keeps her son from her, threatens his life,
    And makes her cry such tears . . . which he then stops.
    Hermione herself has seen this angry man
    Come back to her a hundred times.
    He'll bring the tokens of a troubled heart,
    Sigh at her feet, yet more with rage than love.
    So don't expect a prompt response
    From one so little master of himself.   120
    His frenzies go so far, he could, my lord,
    Could wed the one he hates, and lose his love.

ORESTES

    But tell me how Hermione looks at
    Her marriage now. Her charm has lost its power.

PYLADES

    Hermione, at least to public view,
    Seems to despise his broken promises.
    She thinks he'll be so glad to be less cruel,
    He'll come and beg her take his love again.
    But she's confided me with all her tears.
    She cries in secret – her charm is spurned –   130
    Ready to leave, but always staying on.
    Sometimes she calls Orestes to her aid.

ORESTES

    If I thought that, I'd go at once, my friend,
    I'd throw myself . . .

PYLADES   Complete your mission here, my lord.
    Wait for the king. Speak to him. Show him now
    How all the Greeks cast Hector's son aside.

Loin de leur accorder ce fils de sa maîtresse,
Leur haine ne fera qu'irriter sa tendresse.
Plus on les veut brouiller, plus on va les unir.
Pressez, demandez tout, pour ne rien obtenir.   140
Il vient.

ORESTE   Eh bien! va donc disposer la cruelle
A revoir un amant qui ne vient que pour elle.

SCÈNE 2

Pyrrhus, Oreste, Phœnix

ORESTE

Avant que tous les Grecs vous parlent par ma voix,
Souffrez que j'ose ici me flatter de leur choix,
Et qu'à vos yeux, Seigneur, je montre quelque joie
De voir le fils d'Achille et le vainqueur de Troie.
Oui, comme ses exploits nous admirons vos coups :
Hector tomba sous lui, Troie expira sous vous;
Et vous avez montré, par une heureuse audace,
Que le fils seul d'Achille a pu remplir sa place.   150
Mais, ce qu'il n'eût point fait, la Grèce avec douleur
Vous voit du sang troyen relever le malheur,
Et vous laissant toucher d'une pitié funeste,
D'une guerre si longue entretenir le reste.
Ne vous souvient-il plus, Seigneur, quel fut Hector?
Nos peuples affaiblis s'en souviennent encor.
Son nom seul fait frémir nos veuves et nos filles,
Et dans toute la Grèce il n'est point de familles
Qui ne demandent compte à ce malheureux fils
D'un père ou d'un époux qu'Hector leur a ravis.   160
Et qui sait ce qu'un jour ce fils peut entreprendre?
Peut-être dans nos ports nous le verrons descendre,
Tel qu'on a vu son père embraser nos vaisseaux,
Et, la flamme à la main, les suivre sur les eaux.
Oserai-je, Seigneur, dire ce que je pense?

Far from securing them the boy,
Their hatred will arouse his tenderness.
The more they're set at odds, the more they'll be as one.
Press your demands – so that they'll be refused.   140
He's coming.

ORESTES   Go. Prepare Hermione
To see me soon. I only came for her.

               [*Pylades leaves. Pyrrhus and Phoenix enter*

SCENE 2

Pyrrhus, Orestes, Phoenix

ORESTES   Pyrrhus,
Before I speak to you for all of Greece –
And I am proud that they have chosen me –
I ought to say how glad I am to see
Achilles' son, the conqueror of Troy.
We marvel at his exploits, and your deeds.
Hector brought down by him, and Troy by you.
And you have shown, by wondrous daring deeds,
Only Achilles' son could take his place.   150
And yet he did not do what Greece now sadly
Sees you do: restore the destiny of Troy.
You've let yourself show pity for the dead
And keep an orphan from that war alive.
You do recall, my lord, who Hector was.
Our poor, weak people still remember him.
His very name still makes our widows, young girls, shake.
There are no families the breadth of Greece
Who won't demand his wretched son explain
The fathers and the husbands that were killed.   160
And who knows what this son will do one day?
Perhaps we'll see him sail upon our ports,
Just as we saw his father burn our ships
And drive them out to sea, fire in his hand.
So shall I dare to tell you what I think?

Vous-même de vos soins craignez la récompense,
Et que dans votre sein ce serpent élevé
Ne vous punisse un jour de l'avoir conservé.
Enfin de tous les Grecs satisfaites l'envie,
Assurez leur vengeance, assurez votre vie;   170
Perdez un ennemi d'autant plus dangereux
Qu'il s'essaiera sur vous à combattre contre eux.

PYRRHUS

La Grèce en ma faveur est trop inquiétée.
De soins plus importants je l'ai crue agitée,
Seigneur, et sur le nom de son ambassadeur,
J'avais dans ses projets conçu plus de grandeur.
Qui croirait en effet qu'une telle entreprise
Du fils d'Agamemnon méritât l'entremise;
Qu'un peuple tout entier, tant de fois triomphant
N'eût daigné conspirer que la mort d'un enfant?   180
Mais à qui prétend-on que je le sacrifie?
La Grèce a-t-elle encor quelque droit sur sa vie?
Et seul de tous les Grecs ne m'est-il pas permis
D'ordonner d'un captif que le sort m'a soumis?
Oui, Seigneur, lorsqu'au pied des murs fumants de Troie
Les vainqueurs tout sanglants partagèrent leur proie,
Le sort, dont les arrêts furent alors suivis
Fit tomber en mes mains Andromaque et son fils.
Hécube près d'Ulysse acheva sa misère;
Cassandre dans Argos a suivi votre père;   190
Sur eux, sur leurs captifs, ai-je étendu mes droits?
Ai-je enfin disposé du fruit de leurs exploits?
On craint qu'avec Hector Troie un jour ne renaisse;
Son fils peut me ravir le jour que je lui laisse :
Seigneur, tant de prudence entraîne trop de soin;
Je ne sais point prévoir les malheurs de si loin.
Je songe quelle était autrefois cette ville
Si superbe en remparts, en héros si fertile,
Maîtresse de l'Asie; et je regarde enfin
Quel fut le sort de Troie, et quel est son destin.   200
Je ne vois que des tours que la cendre a couvertes,
Un fleuve teint de sang, des campagnes désertes,

You fear the recompense for all your care:
That one fine day, this poison you've brought up
Will punish you for keeping him alive.
Answer the longing of all Greece.
Ensure their vengeance, and secure your life.   170
You'll kill an enemy. He's dangerous.
He'll plan his strike on you by fighting them.

PYRRHUS

The Greeks are too much worried for my sake.
I thought they were concerned with greater cares,
My lord. And their ambassador's renown
Made me expect much grander, weightier plans.
Who would have thought that such an enterprise
Would need the help of Agamemnon's son?
That a whole people, crowned with victory,
Would stoop to plot against a young child's life?   180
Who do they say that I should hand him to?
Does Greece still have some say upon his life?
Am I, alone among the Greeks, not now allowed
To keep a prisoner given me by fate?
Oh yes, my lord. Beneath the smoking walls of Troy,
The blood-caked conquerors shared out their spoils.
The will of fate was carried through.
It gave me Andromache and her son.
Ulysses drew Hecuba, at her sorrow's end.
Cassandra went to Argos with your father.   190
Did I extend my claims to them, their prisoners,
And try to eat the fruit of all their deeds?
You fear that Hector's son will one day rebuild Troy,
Will take from me the life I've given him.
My lord, such prudence shows too much concern.
I cannot see troubles so far ahead.
I dream of what that city was in time
Gone by, her soaring ramparts, heroes numberless,
Mistress of Asia. And now I look at what
The fate of Troy will be, its destiny.   200
I only see its towers walled up with ash,
A river red with blood, deserted fields,

Un enfant dans les fers; et je ne puis songer
Que Troie en cet état aspire à se venger.
Ah! si du fils d'Hector la perte était jurée,
Pourquoi d'un an entier l'avons-nous différée?
Dans le sein de Priam n'a-t-on pu l'immoler?
Sous tant de morts, sous Troie, il fallait l'accabler.
Tout était juste alors : la vieillesse et l'enfance
En vain sur leur faiblesse appuyaient leur défense;   210
La victoire et la nuit, plus cruelles que nous,
Nous excitaient au meurtre, et confondaient nos coups.
Mon courroux aux vaincus ne fut que trop sévère.
Mais que ma cruauté survive à ma colère?
Que malgré la pitié dont je me sens saisir,
Dans le sang d'un enfant je me baigne à loisir?
Non, Seigneur : que les Grecs cherchent quelque autre proie;
Qu'ils poursuivent ailleurs ce qui reste de Troie :
De mes inimitiés le cours est achevé;
L'Épire sauvera ce que Troie a sauvé.   220

ORESTE

Seigneur, vous savez trop avec quel artifice
Un faux Astyanax fut offert au supplice
Où le seul fils d'Hector devait être conduit.
Ce n'est pas les Troyens, c'est Hector qu'on poursuit.
Oui, les Grecs sur le fils persécutent le père;
Il a par trop de sang acheté leur colère,
Ce n'est que dans le sien qu'elle peut expirer,
Et jusque dans l'Épire il les peut attirer.
Prévenez-les.

PYRRHUS   Non, non. J'y consens avec joie!
Qu'ils cherchent dans l'Épire une seconde Troie;   230
Qu'ils confondent leur haine, et ne distinguent plus
Le sang qui les fit vaincre et celui des vaincus.
Aussi bien ce n'est pas la première injustice
Dont la Grèce d'Achille a payé le service.
Hector en profita, Seigneur; et quelque jour
Son fils en pourrait bien profiter à son tour.

A boy in chains. I cannot think
That Troy will dream of vengeance in that state.
If death for Hector's son was sworn indeed,
Why has it been delayed a whole long year?
You could have killed him then – at Priam's breast –
And covered him with all the dead of Troy.
All things then were just. Old people, children,
Relied upon their frailty in vain.   210
The victory, the night – they were more cruel than us –
Excited us to random, murderous blows.
My rage against the vanquished was too harsh.
But that my cruelty should outlast that rage,
That I should feel some pity taking hold
Yet bathe at leisure in a young child's blood –
No, my lord. The Greeks must find some other prey.
Let them pursue the dregs of Troy elsewhere.
My enmities have run their course.
Epirus will keep alive what Troy has saved.   220

ORESTES

My lord, you know too well the trick by which
A false Astyanax was tortured to the death
That had been kept for Hector's son alone.
It is not Troy, it's Hector Greece pursues.
We're visiting the father's sins upon
His son. He's bought our wrath from so much blood,
A wrath his blood alone can make subside.
He still can draw the Greeks to Epirus . . .
Prevent a war.

PYRRHUS   Oh no, I welcome it.
Let them all seek another Troy in Epirus.   230
Their hatred's all confused. They'll not sort out
The blood of conquered men from conquerors.
This, after all, is not the only time
That Greece has ill repaid Achilles' deeds.
Hector once turned that to account, my lord.
One day his son may do the same.

ORESTE

Ainsi la Grèce en vous trouve un enfant rebelle?

PYRRHUS

Et je n'ai donc vaincu que pour dépendre d'elle?

ORESTE

Hermione, Seigneur, arrêtera vos coups :
Ses yeux s'opposeront entre son père et vous.   240

PYRRHUS

Hermione, Seigneur, peut m'être toujours chère,
Je puis l'aimer, sans être esclave de son père;
Et je saurai peut-être accorder quelque jour
Les soins de ma grandeur et ceux de mon amour.
Vous pouvez cependant voir la fille d'Hélène :
Du sang qui vous unit je sais l'étroite chaîne.
Après cela, Seigneur, je ne vous retiens plus,
Et vous pourrez aux Grecs annoncer mon refus.

SCÈNE 3

Pyrrhus, Phœnix

PHŒNIX

Ainsi vous l'envoyez aux pieds de sa maîtresse?

PYRRHUS

On dit qu'il a longtemps brûlé pour la princesse.   250

PHŒNIX

Mais si ce feu, Seigneur, vient à se rallumer?
S'il lui rendait son cœur, s'il s'en faisait aimer?

PYRRHUS

Ah! qu'ils s'aiment Phœnix! J'y consens. Qu'elle parte.
Que charmés l'un de l'autre ils retournent à Sparte!
Tous nos ports sont ouverts et pour elle et pour lui.
Qu'elle m'épargnerait de contrainte et d'ennui!

ORESTES

So Greece should find in you a fractious child?

PYRRHUS

Did I win battles to depend on Greece?

ORESTES

My lord, Hermione will stop you still . . .
She'll stand between you and her father now.   240

PYRRHUS

Hermione, my lord, can still be close to me.
I need not be her father's slave for that.
And some day I may find a way to match
The call of glory with the claims of love.
You may however see Queen Helen's child.
I know how close your blood-ties are.
That done, my lord, I shall not hold you here.
Tell all the Greeks that I've said no.
     [*Orestes leaves, with his retinue. Pyrrhus and Phoenix remain*

SCENE 3

Pyrrhus, Phoenix

PHOENIX

So then, you've sent him to his mistress' feet.

PYRRHUS

He's yearned for her a long while, so they say.   250

PHOENIX

And if the fire should burn again, my lord?
If he should give his heart, become beloved . . . ?

PYRRHUS

Then let them love, Phoenix. She may leave. Agreed.
Let them go back to Sparta arm in arm.
Our ports are open to them both.
How much constraint and worry I'd be spared . . .

PHŒNIX

Seigneur . . . .

PYRRHUS   Une autre fois je t'ouvrirai mon âme :
Andromaque paraît.

SCÈNE 4

Pyrrhus, Andromaque, Céphise

PYRRHUS   Me cherchiez-vous, Madame?
Un espoir si charmant me serait-il permis?

ANDROMAQUE

Je passais jusqu'aux lieux où l'on garde mon fils.
Puisqu'une fois le jour vous souffrez que je voie   260
Le seul bien qui me reste et d'Hector et de Troie,
J'allais, Seigneur, pleurer un moment avec lui :
Je ne l'ai point encore embrassé d'aujourd'hui.

PYRRHUS

Ah, Madame! les Grecs, si j'en crois leurs alarmes,
Vous donneront bientôt d'autres sujets de larmes.

ANDROMAQUE

Et quelle est cette peur dont leur cœur est frappé,
Seigneur? Quelque Troyen vous est-il échappé?

PYRRHUS

Leur haine pour Hector n'est pas encore éteinte.
Ils redoutent son fils.

ANDROMAQUE   Digne objet de leur crainte!   270
Un enfant malheureux qui ne sait pas encor
Que Pyrrhus est son maître, et qu'il est fils d'Hector.

PYRRHUS

Tel qu'il est, tous les Grecs demandent qu'il périsse.
Le fils d'Agamemnon vient hâter son supplice.

PHOENIX
My lord . . .

PYRRHUS   Another time I'll tell you everything.
Andromache is coming.

            [*Andromache and Cephisa enter*

SCENE 4

Pyrrhus, Andromache, Cephisa

PYRRHUS   My lady . . . ? so would
It be too much to hope you looked for me?

ANDROMACHE
I'm on my way to where my son is kept.   260
Since you allow one sight of him a day –
The single good I'm left of Hector's Troy –
I go, my lord, to cry with him a while.
I haven't held him yet today.

PYRRHUS
If their alarm can be believed, the Greeks
Will soon provide you further cause for tears.

ANDROMACHE
What is this fear that strikes their hearts,
My lord? Some Trojan has escaped from you . . . ?

PYRRHUS
Their enmity for Hector has not died.
They fear his son.

ANDROMACHE   A fitting cause for dread . . . !   270
A poor young boy who doesn't even know
That Hector is his father, you his lord.

PYRRHUS
For what he is, all Greece demands his death.
Orestes is here to hasten it on.

ANDROMAQUE

Et vous prononcerez un arrêt si cruel?
Est-ce mon intérêt qui le rend criminel?
Hélas! on ne craint point qu'il venge un jour son père;
On craint qu'il n'essuyât les larmes de sa mère.
Il m'aurait tenu lieu d'un père et d'un époux;
Mais il me faut tout perdre, et toujours par vos coups.   280

PYRRHUS

Madame, mes refus ont prévenu vos larmes.
Tous les Grecs m'ont déjà menacé de leurs armes,
Mais dussent-ils encore, en repassant les eaux,
Demander votre fils avec mille vaisseaux,
Coutât-il tout le sang qu'Hélène a fait répandre,
Dussé-je après dix ans voir mon palais en cendre,
Je ne balance point, je vole à son secours.
Je défendrai sa vie aux dépens de mes jours.
Mais parmi ces périls où je cours pour vous plaire,   290
Me refuserez-vous un regard moins sévère?
Haï de tous les Grecs, pressé de tous côtés,
Me faudra-t-il combattre encor vos cruautés?
Je vous offre mon bras. Puis-je espérer encore
Que vous accepterez un cœur qui vous adore?
En combattant pour vous, me sera-t-il permis
De ne vous point compter parmi mes ennemis?

ANDROMAQUE

Seigneur, que faites-vous, et que dira la Grèce?
Faut-il qu'un si grand cœur montre tant de faiblesse?
Voulez-vous qu'un dessein si beau, si généreux,
Passe pour le transport d'un esprit amoureux?   300
Captive, toujours triste, importune à moi-même,
Pouvez-vous souhaiter qu'Andromaque vous aime;
Quels charmes ont pour vous des yeux infortunés
Qu'à des pleurs éternels vous avez condamnés?
Non, non; d'un ennemi respecter la misère,
Sauver des malheureux, rendre un fils à sa mère,
De cent peuples pour lui combattre la rigueur,
Sans me faire payer son salut de mon cœur,

ANDROMACHE

And you'll decree such cruelty? His death?
Is it because of me he's made a criminal?
It's not his father's vengeance that they fear.
They fear one day he'll dry his mother's tears.
He would have been a father, husband, to me – both.
But I must lose the world, and still because of you.   280

PYRRHUS

I have said no, my lady, to prevent
Your tears. All Greece has threatened me with war.
But were they now to cross the seas again
And with a thousand ships demand your son,
Were it to cost each drop of blood that flowed
For Helen, and ten years, my palaces ablaze –
I would not hesitate. I would help him.
I would defend his life before my own.
I face these dangers for your sake,   290
So might you look on me with gentler eyes?
I'm hated by all Greece, attacked on every side.
Must I fight off your cruelties as well?
I offer you my hand. Might I still hope
You would accept a man who worships you?
I fight your cause. I ask to be allowed
Never to count you with my enemies.

ANDROMACHE

My lord, what do you do? What will Greece say?
So great a heart, and yet such weaknesses . . . ?
You want so fine, so generous a plan
To seem the fancy of a man in love?   300
I am a captive – mournful, anxious in myself –
How can you want me to return this love?
What magic can you find in these sad eyes
That you've condemned to everlasting tears?
No, no. Respect the sorrow of an enemy.
Save those in need, and give me back my son.
A hundred nations will be cruel to him, fight that.
But do not make me buy his safety with my heart.

Malgré moi, s'il le faut, lui donner un asile :
Seigneur, voilà des soins dignes du fils d'Achille.   310

PYRRHUS

Hé quoi! votre courroux n'a-t-il pas eu son cours?
Peut-on haïr sans cesse? et punit-on toujours?
J'ai fait des malheureux, sans doute; et la Phrygie
Cent fois de votre sang a vu ma main rougie;
Mais que vos yeux sur moi se sont bien exercés!
Qu'ils m'ont vendu bien cher les pleurs qu'ils ont versés!
De combien de remords m'ont-ils rendu la proie!
Je souffre tous les maux que j'ai faits devant Troie.
Vaincu, chargé de fers, de regrets consumé,
Brûlé de plus de feux que je n'en allumai,   320
Tant de soins, tant de pleurs, tant d'ardeurs inquiètes . . .
Hélas! fus-je jamais si cruel que vous l'êtes?
Mais enfin, tour à tour, c'est assez nous punir :
Nos ennemis communs devraient nous réunir.
Madame, dites-moi seulement que j'espère,
Je vous rends votre fils, et je lui sers de père;
Je l'instruirai moi-même à venger les Troyens;
J'irai punir les Grecs de vos maux et des miens.
Animé d'un regard, je puis tout entreprendre :
Votre Ilion encor peut sortir de sa cendre;   330
Je puis, en moins de temps que les Grecs ne l'ont pris,
Dans ses murs relevés couronner votre fils.

ANDROMAQUE

Seigneur, tant de grandeurs ne nous touchent plus guère.
Je les lui promettais tant qu'a vécu son père.
Non, vous n'espérez plus de nous revoir encor,
Sacrés murs que n'a pu conserver mon Hector!
A de moindres faveurs des malheureux prétendent,
Seigneur : c'est un exil que mes pleurs vous demandent.
Souffrez que, loin des Grecs, et même loin de vous,
J'aille cacher mon fils, et pleurer mon époux.   340
Votre amour contre nous allume trop de haine.
Retournez, retournez à la fille d'Hélène.

Give him a refuge now, in spite of me.
These are the proper duties of Achilles' son.   310

PYRRHUS

So then, your anger hasn't run its course . . .
Can hatred be unceasing . . . punish for all time?
I've made men scream; and Phrygia has seen
My hands drenched in your blood a hundred times.
But how well trained your eyes have been on me.
How much they've cost me all the tears they've shed.
How much remorse has preyed on me through them.
I've suffered all the pain I caused to Troy.
Destroyed, weighed down in chains . . . and such regrets . . .
And burning with more fires than I once lit.   320
So many cares, and tears, and troubled love . . .
I never was as cruel as you are now.
We've taken turns enough in punishing.
Our common enemies should join us close.
Tell me no more than . . . I may hope. I'll give
You back and be a father to your son.
I'll teach him how to take revenge for Troy.
I'll punish Greece for all your pain and mine.
Lit by your glance, I can take on the world.
Your Ilium can rise from ashes still.   330
In less time than the Greeks demolished it,
I'll build its walls again, and crown your son.

ANDROMACHE

Such noble things can scarcely touch me now.
I promised them to him before his father died.
The sacred walls that Hector could not save
Must not now hope to look on us again.
Unhappy people ask for smaller gifts,
My lord. I plead with you for banishment.
Let me go far from Greece, and far from you,
And hide my son and mourn my husband's death.   340
Your love will bring us too much hate.
Go back. Go back to Helen's daughter now.

PYRRHUS

Et le puis-je, Madame? Ah! que vous me gênez!
Comment lui rendre un cœur que vous me retenez?
Je sais que de mes vœux on lui promit l'empire;
Je sais que pour régner elle vint dans l'Épire;
Le sort vous y voulut l'une et l'autre amener :
Vous, pour porter des fers, elle, pour en donner.
Cependant ai-je pris quelque soin de lui plaire?
Et ne dirait-on pas, en voyant au contraire   350
Vos charmes tout-puissants, et les siens dédaignés,
Qu'elle est ici captive et que vous y régnez?
Ah! qu'un seul des soupirs que mon cœur vous envoie,
S'il s'échappait vers elle y porterait de joie.

ANDROMAQUE

Et pourquoi vos soupirs seraient-ils repoussés?
Aurait-elle oublié vos services passés?
Troie, Hector, contre vous, révoltent-ils son âme?
Aux cendres d'un époux doit-elle enfin sa flamme?
Et quel époux encore! Ah! souvenir cruel!
Sa mort seule a rendu votre père immortel;   360
Il doit au sang d'Hector tout l'éclat de ses armes,
Et vous n'êtes tous deux connus que par mes larmes.

PYRRHUS

Eh bien, Madame, eh bien! il faut vous obéir :
Il faut vous oublier, ou plutôt vous haïr.
Oui, mes vœux ont trop loin poussé leur violence
Pour ne plus s'arrêter que dans l'indifférence;
Songez-y bien : il faut désormais que mon cœur,
S'il n'aime avec transport, haïsse avec fureur.
Je n'épargnerai rien dans ma juste colère :
Le fils me répondra des mépris de la mère;   370
La Grèce le demande, et je ne prétends pas
Mettre toujours ma gloire à sauver des ingrats.

ANDROMAQUE

Hélas! il mourra donc. Il n'a pour sa défense
Que les pleurs de sa mère et que son innocence.
Et peut-être après tout, en l'état où je suis,

PYRRHUS

How can I, lady? Oh, you torture me.
How can I give her back the heart you've won?
I know I promised she'd command my every wish.
I know she came to Epirus to rule.
Fate willed you both to come together here,
For you to be in chains that she'd put on.
But have I taken pains to pleasure her?
Would you not say the opposite is true –   350
Your charm all powerful, hers disdained,
That she is captive here, and you are queen?
Oh, if one single sigh my heart sends you
Escaped to her, what joy she'd feel.

ANDROMACHE

So why should all your wooing be repulsed?
Has she forgotten everything you've done?
Do Troy and Hector make her blame you so,
Her husband's ashes still demand her love?
And what a husband . . . Memory is cruel.
Your father's immortality came from his death.   360
He owed his warrior's renown to Hector's blood.
The two of you are known now only through my grief.

PYRRHUS

And so, my lady, so I must obey.
I must forget you – better, start to hate.
My needs have been too violent, gone too far
To come to rest in mere indifference.
Think carefully. From now, my heart denied
The ecstasies of love, must hate in rage.
I will spare nothing from this rightful wrath.
Your son will answer for his mother's scorn.   370
Greece wants him. So. I do not mean to use
My fame in saving thankless people's lives.

ANDROMACHE

So he will die. He has his mother's tears,
His innocence alone, to save him now.
But in my state . . . perhaps when all is done

Sa mort avancera la fin de mes ennuis.
Je prolongeais pour lui ma vie et ma misère;
Mais enfin sur ses pas j'irai revoir son père.
Ainsi, tous trois, Seigneur, par vos soins réunis,
Nous vous . . .

PYRRHUS   Allez, Madame, allez voir votre fils.   380
Peut-être, en le voyant, votre amour plus timide
Ne prendra pas toujours sa colère pour guide.
Pour savoir nos destins j'irai vous retrouver.
Madame, en l'embrassant, songez à le sauver.

His death will hasten on the end of grief.
I've gone on living, hurting so, for him.
But now I'll see his father in his steps.
And then all three of us, united by your care,
My lord, we'll . . .

PYRRHUS   Go, lady. See your son.   380
The sight of him may make your love less fierce –
It won't take anger always as its guide.
I'll come back soon to learn our fate.
But think to save him as he cuddles in your arms.

ACTE 2 SCÈNE 1

Hermione, Cléone

HERMIONE

Je fais ce que tu veux. Je consens qu'il me voie.
Je lui veux bien encore accorder cette joie.
Pylade va bientôt conduire ici ses pas;
Mais si je m'en croyais, je ne le verrais pas.

CLÉONE

Et qu'est-ce que sa vue a pour vous de funeste?
Madame, n'est-ce pas toujours le même Oreste
Dont vous avez cent fois souhaité le retour,   390
Et dont vous regrettiez la constance et l'amour?

HERMIONE

C'est cet amour payé de trop d'ingratitude
Qui me rend en ces lieux sa présence si rude.
Quelle honte pour moi, quel triomphe pour lui,
De voir mon infortune égaler son ennui!
Est-ce là, dira-t-il, cette fière Hermione?
Elle me dédaignait; un autre l'abandonne.
L'ingrate, qui mettait son cœur à si haut prix,
Apprend donc à son tour à souffrir des mépris?
Ah dieux!   400

CLÉONE   Ah! dissipez ces indignes alarmes :
Il a trop bien senti le pouvoir de vos charmes.
Vous croyez qu'un amant vienne vous insulter?
Il vous rapporte un cœur qu'il n'a pu vous ôter.
Mais vous ne dites point ce que vous mande un père?

HERMIONE

Dans ses retardements si Pyrrhus persévère,
A la mort du Troyen s'il ne veut consentir,
Mon père avec les Grecs m'ordonne de partir.

CLÉONE

Eh bien, Madame, eh bien! écoutez donc Oreste.
Pyrrhus a commencé, faites au moins le reste.   410

ACT 2 SCENE 1

Hermione, Cleone

HERMIONE

   I'll do, then, what you want. I will see him.
   Indeed, I'm glad to give such joy to him.
   Pylades will soon bring him here . . . and yet
   If I thought more, I should not speak to him.

CLEONE

   But why should seeing him bring any harm?
   So is this not the same Orestes still,   390
   For whose return you've yearned a hundred times,
   Whose love and constancy you so much missed?

HERMIONE

   It's just that love for which I gave small thanks
   That makes his being here so hard to bear.
   The shame for me, and triumph now for him,
   That my small hurts should equal his distress.
   Is this the proud Hermione? he'll ask.
   She spurned me once; and now she's spurned.
   She was untouched and overprized her love,
   And now she's learning how to suffer scorn.   400
   Oh god . . .

CLEONE   Stop all these fears. They're not deserved.
   He's felt too well the power your magic holds.
   You think a lover comes to laugh at you?
   He brings a love to you he can't shake off.
   What has your father ordered, though? Please say.

HERMIONE

   If Pyrrhus perseveres in his delays
   And won't allow the Trojan boy to die,
   My father orders me to leave with Greece.

CLEONE

   So then, Orestes should be listened to.
   You must at least complete what Pyrrhus has begun.   410

Pour bien faire il faudrait que vous le prévinssiez.
Ne m'avez-vous pas dit que vous le haïssiez?

HERMIONE

Si je le hais, Cléone! Il y va de ma gloire,
Après tant de bontés dont il perd la mémoire;
Lui qui me fut si cher, et qui m'a pu trahir,
Ah! je l'ai trop aimé pour ne le point haïr!

CLÉONE

Fuyez-le donc, Madame; et puisqu'on vous adore . . .

HERMIONE

Ah! laisse à ma fureur le temps de croître encore.
Contre mon ennemi laisse-moi m'assurer.
Cléone, avec horreur je m'en veux séparer.   420
Il n'y travaillera que trop bien, l'infidèle!

CLÉONE

Quoi? vous en attendez quelque injure nouvelle?
Aimer une captive, et l'aimer à vos yeux,
Tout cela n'a donc pu vous le rendre odieux?
Après ce qu'il a fait, que saurait-il donc faire?
Il vous aurait déplu, s'il pouvait vous déplaire.

HERMIONE

Pourquoi veux-tu cruelle, irriter mes ennuis?
Je crains de me cónnaître en l'état où je suis.
De tout ce que tu vois tâche de ne rien croire;
Crois que je n'aime plus, vante-moi ma victoire;   430
Crois que dans son dépit mon cœur est endurci,
Hélas! et, s'il se peut, fais-le moi croire aussi.
Tu veux que je le fuie? Eh bien! rien ne m'arrête :
Allons; n'envions plus son indigne conquête :
Que sur lui sa captive étende son pouvoir.
Fuyons . . . Mais si l'ingrat rentrait dans son devoir!
Si la foi dans son cœur retrouvait quelque place;
S'il venait à mes pieds me demander sa grâce;
Si sous mes lois, Amour, tu pouvais l'engager!
S'il voulait . . . Mais l'ingrat ne veut que m'outrager.   440
Demeurons toutefois pour troubler leur fortune,

To do it well, you must forestall him now.
Have you not said how much you hated him?

HERMIONE

Hate him – the honour of my name demands no less.
So many kindnesses he now forgets . . .
He was so dear to me, and then betrayed . . .
I loved him far too much to stop my loathing now.

CLEONE

Avoid him then. And since Orestes yearns . . .

HERMIONE

Oh, give my anger time to grow still more.
Let me be sure against this enemy.
I want to part from him quite horrified.   420
His faithlessness must work its power.

CLEONE

So are you waiting for some further hurt?
He loves a prisoner, before your eyes.
Does that not make him odious enough?
What else is needed after all he's done?
He would have hurt you more if he'd known how.

HERMIONE

This cruelty . . . why do you torture me?
I fear to see myself . . . the state I'm in.
Each thing you see, try not to trust.
Believe I've ceased to love, and cry out 'victory'.   430
Believe my heart is stone, despite itself,
And if you can, make me believe it too.
You want me to avoid him? Nothing keeps me here.
Let's cease to envy victories so ill-deserved,
And let his prisoner extend her power.
Let's leave . . . If, though, he felt his conscience prick,
If honesty could find some place in him,
If he could ask forgiveness on his knees,
If love could bind him so to my desire,
If he but wished . . . He wants to outrage me.   440
So why not stay to spoil their happiness?

Prenons quelque plaisir à leur être importune;
Ou, le forçant de rompre un nœud si solennel,
Aux yeux de tous les Grecs rendons-le criminel.
J'ai déjà sur le fils attiré leur colère;
Je veux qu'on vienne encor lui demander la mère.
Rendons-lui les tourments qu'elle m'a fait souffrir :
Qu'elle le perde, ou bien qu'il la fasse périr.

CLÉONE

Vous pensez que des yeux toujours ouverts aux larmes
Se plaisent à troubler le pouvoir de vos charmes,   450
Et qu'un cœur accablé de tant de déplaisirs
De son persécuteur ait brigué les soupirs?
Voyez si sa douleur en paraît soulagée.
Pourquoi donc les chagrins où son âme est plongée?
Contre un amant qui plaît pourquoi tant de fierté?

HERMIONE

Hélas! pour mon malheur, je l'ai trop écouté.
Je n'ai point du silence affecté le mystère :
Je croyais sans péril pouvoir être sincère.
Et sans armer mes yeux d'un moment de rigueur,
Je n'ai pour lui parler consulté que mon cœur.   460
Et qui ne se serait comme moi déclarée
Sur la foi d'une amour si saintement jurée?
Me voyait-il de l'œil qu'il me voit aujourd'hui?
Tu t'en souviens encor, tout conspirait pour lui :
Ma famille vengée, et les Grecs dans la joie,
Nos vaisseaux tout chargés des dépouilles de Troie,
Les exploits de son père effacés par les siens,
Ses feux que je croyais plus ardents que les miens,
Mon cœur, toi-même enfin de sa gloire éblouie,
Avant qu'il me trahît, vous m'avez tous trahie.   470
Mais c'en est trop, Cléone, et quel que soit Pyrrhus,
Hermione est sensible, Oreste a des vertus;
Il sait aimer du moins, et même sans qu'on l'aime,
Et peut-être il saura se faire aimer lui-même.
Allons. Qu'il vienne enfin.

CLÉONE   Madame, le voici.

Let's find some pleasure being troublesome,
Force him to break a holy bond,
Make him a criminal in all Greeks' eyes.
I have already drawn their anger on
The son. Now let them seek his mother too.
I'll give her back the pain she's made me bear.
Let her kill him, or he lead to her death.

CLEONE

Her eyes are always full of tears – will she
Delight to undermine your charm and power?   450
You think a heart so overwhelmed with cares
Will crave her persecutor's pain?
See if her sadness is relieved by that.
Why the despair in which her mind is sunk?
Why does her lover meet with so much pride?

HERMIONE

I've listened to him – to my grief too much.
I didn't feign the mystery of quiet,
But thought I could be honest without harm.
Not for one moment did I look aloof.
I spoke to him directly, from the heart.   460
Who would have not confessed like me
On love's great faith so honourably sworn?
Did he then see me as he sees me now?
You still remember it – the world was his:
My family avenged, Greece overjoyed,
Our ships weighed down with all the spoils of Troy,
His father's exploits quite eclipsed by his,
His passion that I thought burned fiercer than my own,
My heart, and you, too, dazzled by his fame . . .
Before his treachery, you'd all betrayed me too.   470
It's all too much, Cleone. Whatever Pyrrhus is,
Orestes has his virtues, I'm aware.
He isn't loved, but knows what love can be.
Perhaps he'll find the way to be beloved.
So let him come.

CLEONE   My lady, he is here.

HERMIONE

Ah! je ne croyais pas qu'il fût si près d'ici.

SCÈNE 2

Hermione, Oreste, Cléone

HERMIONE

Le croirai-je, Seigneur, qu'un reste de tendresse
Vous fasse ici chercher une triste princesse?
Ou ne dois-je imputer qu'à votre seul devoir
L'heureux empressement qui vous porte à me voir?   480

ORESTE

Tel est de mon amour l'aveuglement funeste.
Vous le savez, Madame, et le destin d'Oreste
Est de venir sans cesse adorer vos attraits,
Et de jurer toujours qu'il n'y viendra jamais.
Je sais que vos regards vont rouvrir mes blessures,
Que tous mes pas vers vous sont autant de parjures :
Je le sais, j'en rougis; mais j'atteste les dieux,
Témoins de la fureur de mes derniers adieux,
Que j'ai couru partout où ma perte certaine
Dégageait mes serments et finissait ma peine.   490
J'ai mendié la mort chez des peuples cruels
Qui n'apaisaient leurs dieux que du sang des mortels :
Ils m'ont fermé leur temple; et ces peuples barbares
De mon sang prodigué sont devenus avares.
Enfin je viens à vous, et je me vois réduit
A chercher dans vos yeux une mort qui me fuit.
Mon désespoir n'attend que leur indifférence :
Ils n'ont qu'à m'interdire un reste d'espérance.
Ils n'ont, pour avancer cette mort où je cours,
Qu'à me dire une fois ce qu'ils m'ont dit toujours.   500
Voilà depuis un an le seul soin qui m'anime.
Madame, c'est à vous de prendre une victime
Que les Scythes auraient dérobée à vos coups,
Si j'en avais trouvé d'aussi cruels que vous.

HERMIONE

I did not think he was so close to us.

[*Orestes enters*

SCENE 2

Hermione, Orestes, Cleone

HERMIONE

My lord . . . should I believe that some last tenderness
Makes you seek out a princess in her pain?
Should I ascribe to conscience alone
This joyful eagerness to meet me here?   480

ORESTES

It is the deadly blindness of my love –
As well you know, my lady. I'm fated
To keep returning to adore your charm
And keep on swearing that I'll not come back.
I know your glance will open up the wounds,
That every step to you is strewn with treachery.
I know. I blush. And yet I call the gods
As witness to my frenzied, last good-bye.
I ran to every place where certain death
Would free me from my vows and end my pain.   490
I begged for death from those most pitiless,
Whose gods were calmed by human blood alone.
The heathens closed their shrines to me, became
Like misers with the blood I offered them.
I've come at last to you, reduced
To seeking in your look the death that slips me by.
Indifference is all my wretchedness expects.
Your eyes have just to banish each last hope.
To hasten on the death I crave, they need
Just say once more what they have always said.   500
A year, you've been the only one to rouse my heart.
It's now for you to take a victim's life
The Scythians would have hidden from your blows,
Had I found them as merciless as you.

HERMIONE

   Quittez, Seigneur, quittez ce funeste langage.
   A des soins plus pressants la Grèce vous engage.
   Que parlez-vous du Scythe et de mes cruautés?
   Songez à tous ces rois que vous représentez.
   Faut-il que d'un transport leur vengeance dépende?
   Est-ce le sang d'Oreste enfin qu'on vous demande?   510
   Dégagez-vous des soins dont vous êtes chargé.

ORESTE

   Les refus de Pyrrhus m'ont assez dégagé,
   Madame : il me renvoie, et quelque autre puissance
   Lui fait du fils d'Hector embrasser la défense.

HERMIONE

   L'infidèle!

ORESTE   Ainsi donc, tout prêt à le quitter,
   Sur mon propre destin je viens vous consulter.
   Déjà même je crois entendre la réponse
   Qu'en secret contre moi votre haine prononce.

HERMIONE

   Hé quoi? toujours injuste en vos tristes discours,
   De mon inimitié vous plaindrez-vous toujours?   520
   Quelle est cette rigueur tant de fois alléguée?
   J'ai passé dans l'Épire où j'étais reléguée :
   Mon père l'ordonnait; mais qui sait si depuis
   Je n'ai point en secret partagé vos ennuis?
   Pensez-vous avoir seul éprouvé des alarmes?
   Que l'Épire jamais n'ait vu couler mes larmes?
   Enfin, qui vous a dit que malgré mon devoir
   Je n'ai pas quelquefois souhaité de vous voir?

ORESTE

   Souhaité de me voir! Ah! divine Princesse . . .
   Mais, de grâce, est-ce à moi que ce discours s'adresse?   530
   Ouvrez vos yeux : songez qu'Oreste est devant vous,
   Oreste si longtemps l'objet de leur courroux.

HERMIONE

   Oui, c'est vous dont l'amour, naissant avec charmes,

HERMIONE

Please stop, my lord. Please stop this talk of death.
All Greece now needs you for more grave concerns.
Why speak of Scythia and my cruelty?
Think of the many kings you represent.
Must all their vengeance rest on fits of love?
Is it your blood they ask you for?   510
You must discharge the duties that you have.

ORESTES

Pyrrhus said no. That is discharge enough,
Lady. He sends me back. Some other force
Makes him take up defence of Hector's son.

HERMIONE

The treachery . . .

ORESTES   And so, I'm ready now to leave.
I came to talk about . . . my life . . . to you.
Already, though, I seem to hear the words
Your hatred speaks against me, secretly.

HERMIONE

This heavy-hearted talk is so unjust.
You still complain that I'm your enemy.   520
What is this hurt alleged so many times?
I went in banishment to Epirus.
My father ordered it. Who knows if since
I've not in secret shared your pain?
You think that you alone have been distressed,
And that I never wept in Epirus?
Who told you, then, there were not times
I hoped to see you, despite my conscience?

ORESTES

You hoped to see me . . . ah Hermione . . .
Are those words really meant for me? Tell me.   530
Open your eyes, and look who stands here now –
This is Orestes. They've raged at me so long.

HERMIONE

Oh yes. Your love was born beneath their spell.

Leur apprit le premier le pouvoir de leurs armes;
Vous que mille vertus me forçaient d'estimer;
Vous que j'ai plaint, enfin que je voudrais aimer.

ORESTE

Je vous entends. Tel est mon partage funeste :
Le cœur est pour Pyrrhus, et les vœux pour Oreste.

HERMIONE

Ah! ne souhaitez pas le destin de Pyrrhus :
Je vous haïrais trop.

ORESTE   Vous m'en aimeriez plus.   540
Ah! que vous me verriez d'un regard bien contraire!
Vous me voulez aimer, et je ne puis vous plaire;
Et l'amour seul alors se faisant obéir,
Vous m'aimeriez, Madame, en me voulant haïr.
O dieux! tant de respects, une amitié si tendre . . .
Que de raisons pour moi, si vous pouviez m'entendre!
Vous seule pour Pyrrhus disputez aujourd'hui,
Peut-être malgré vous, sans doute malgré lui :
Car enfin il nous hait; son âme ailleurs éprise
N'a plus . . .

HERMIONE   Qui vous l'a dit, Seigneur, qu'il me méprise?   550
Ses regards, ses discours vous l'ont-il donc appris?
Jugez-vous que ma vue inspire des mépris,
Qu'elle allume en un cœur des feux si peu durables?
Peut-être d'autres yeux me sont plus favorables.

ORESTE

Poursuivez : il est beau de m'insulter ainsi.
Cruelle, c'est donc moi qui vous méprise ici?
Vos yeux n'ont pas assez éprouvé ma constance?
Je suis donc un témoin de leur peu de puissance?
Je les ai méprisés? Ah! qu'ils voudraient bien voir
Mon rival comme moi mépriser leur pouvoir!   560

HERMIONE

Que m'importe, Seigneur, sa haine, ou sa tendresse?
Allez contre un rebelle armer toute la Grèce;
Rapportez-lui le prix de sa rébellion;

You made them understand the power they had.
Your countless virtues forced me to respect.
I pitied you . . . but then I wished to love.

ORESTES

So now I see. This is my share of grief.
Your heart says Pyrrhus and your reason me.

HERMIONE

Oh do not yearn for Pyrrhus and his fate.
I'd hate you far too much.

ORESTES   You'd love me more.   540
You'd look at me with far, far different eyes.
You want to love me, and yet I cannot please.
But love can make itself obeyed alone.
You'd love me even as you tried to hate.
Dear God, so much esteem, such tenderness . . .
Reason is on my side, if you would hear.
You are alone in fighting Pyrrhus' cause,
Despite yourself perhaps, no doubt despite him too.
Deep down he hates you. His mind is now
Elsewhere . . .

HERMIONE   Who says he's lost regard for me?   550
His looks, his words – have they then told you that?
You think the sight of me inspires such scorn,
It's kindled in his heart so brief a fire?
But other men may see me differently . . .

ORESTES

Go on. A fine response to taunt me so.
What cruelty . . . it's me who's scorned you, then?
Haven't your eyes seen proof of constancy?
Aren't I a witness to their blindness now?
Have I despised them? How they'd love to see
My rival, if he scorned their power like me.   560

HERMIONE

Whether he loves or hates, I do not care.
Go. Arm all of Greece against this rebel.
Bring home the price of his revolt to him.

Qu'on fasse de l'Épire un second Ilion.
Allez. Après cela direz-vous que je l'aime?

ORESTE

Madame, faites plus, et venez-y vous-même.
Voulez-vous demeurer pour otage en ces lieux?
Venez dans tous les cœurs faire parler vos yeux.
Faisons de notre haine une commune attaque.

HERMIONE

Mais, Seigneur, cependant, s'il épouse Andromaque?   570

ORESTE

Hé, Madame!

HERMIONE   Songez quelle honte pour nous,
Si d'une Phrygienne il devenait l'époux.

ORESTE

Et vous le haïssez? Avouez-le, Madame,
L'amour n'est pas un feu qu'on renferme en une âme;
Tout nous trahit, la voix, le silence, les yeux,
Et les feux mal couverts n'en éclatent que mieux.

HERMIONE

Seigneur, je le vois bien, votre âme prévenue
Répand sur mes discours le venin qui la tue,
Toujours dans mes raisons cherche quelque détour,
Et croit qu'en moi la haine est un effort d'amour.   580
Il faut donc m'expliquer; vous agirez en suite.
Vous savez qu'en ces lieux mon devoir m'a conduite;
Mon devoir m'y retient; et je n'en puis partir
Que mon père ou Pyrrhus ne m'en fasse sortir.
De la part de mon père allez lui faire entendre
Que l'ennemi des Grecs ne peut être son gendre.
Du Troyen ou de moi faites-le décider :
Qu'il songe qui des deux il veut rendre, ou garder;
Enfin qu'il me renvoie, ou bien qu'il vous le livre.
Adieu. S'il y consent, je suis prête à vous suivre.   590

Let Epirus be made a second Troy.
Will you still say I love him after that?

ORESTES

Do more, my lady. Come to Greece yourself.
You want to stay a hostage in this place?
Come, let your eyes speak out to every heart.
Let's fuse our hatred in a joint attack.

HERMIONE

But what if he should wed Andromache?   570

ORESTES

What?

HERMIONE   Think of the disgrace for us
If he now took a Phrygian as his wife.

ORESTES

And you hate him? Admit it, my lady.
Love's not a flame that's locked within the soul.
Each thing betrays us — silence, voice, the eyes.
A fire half-covered must burst out the more.

HERMIONE

I see things very well. Your mind's made up.
You pour the poison killing you on all my words.
You always try to twist the things I say.
You think the hate in me is fuelled by love.   580
So then, I must explain. Then you can act.
You know that duty brought me to this place.
Duty now keeps me here. I cannot leave
Unless permitted by my father or the king.
So in my father's name, make Pyrrhus understand
No enemy of Greece can be his son-in-law.
He must decide — the Trojan boy or me.
Which does he want to keep, and which to lose?
He has to send me back, or give the boy to you.
Good bye. If he agrees, I'll follow you.   590

[*Hermione and Cleone leave*

SCÈNE 3

ORESTE [seul]

Oui, oui, vous me suivrez, n'en doutez nullement;
Je vous réponds déjà de son consentement.
Je ne crains pas, enfin, que Pyrrhus la retienne :
Il n'a devant les yeux que sa chère Troyenne;
Tout autre objet le blesse; et peut-être aujourd'hui
Il n'attend qu'un prétexte à l'éloigner de lui.
Nous n'avons qu'à parler : c'en est fait. Quelle joie
D'enlever à l'Épire une si belle proie!
Sauve tout ce qui reste, et de Troie, et d'Hector,   600
Garde son fils, sa veuve, et mille autres encor,
Épire, c'est assez qu'Hermione rendue
Perde à jamais tes bords et ton prince de vue.
Mais un heureux destin le conduit en ces lieux.
Parlons. A tant d'attraits, Amour, ferme ses yeux!

SCÈNE 4

Pyrrhus, Oreste, Phœnix

PYRRHUS

Je vous cherchais, Seigneur. Un peu de violence
M'a fait de vos raisons combattre la puissance,
Je l'avoue; et depuis que je vous ai quitté,
J'en ai senti la force et connu l'équité.
J'ai songé comme vous qu'à la Grèce, à mon père,
A moi-même, en un mot, je devenais contraire,   610
Que je relevais Troie, et rendais imparfait
Tout ce qu'a fait Achille, et tout ce que j'ai fait.
Je ne condamne plus un courroux légitime,
Et l'on vous va, Seigneur, livrer votre victime.

ORESTE

Seigneur, par ce conseil prudent et rigoureux,
C'est acheter la paix du sang d'un malheureux.

SCENE 3

ORESTES [*alone*]

Oh yes, you'll follow me, beyond a doubt.
I can already tell you he'll agree . . .
I'm not afraid of Pyrrhus holding her.
His eyes are only for Andromache –
All other things cause pain. Today perhaps,
A pretext's all he wants to cast her off.
We only have to speak. Then done. The joy
To steal so fine a prey from Epirus.
Oh Epirus, protect what's left of Hector's Troy,   600
And keep his son and widow, thousands more . . .
It is enough Hermione comes back
And never sees your shores or king again.
But there he is – good luck has brought him here.
I'll speak. To all her charms, love, close his eyes.

[*Pyrrhus and Phoenix enter*

SCENE 4

Pyrrhus, Orestes, Phoenix

PYRRHUS

I've looked for you, my lord. Yes, I admit . . .
I was too stubborn – tried to fight the power
Of reasoned arguments. I've felt the force
Of them since leaving you – their equity.
Like you, I thought that I'd begun to fight
All Greece, my father, and indeed myself.
I was rebuilding Troy, and spoiling all   610
That Achilles had done, all that I'd done myself.
Your anger was deserved. You're not to blame.
The Trojan boy will soon be given you.

ORESTES

These counsels are both wise and rigorous, my lord.
You've bought the peace, but with a poor boy's blood.

PYRRHUS

Oui, mais je veux, Seigneur, l'assurer davantage :
D'une éternelle paix Hermione est le gage;
Je l'épouse. Il semblait qu'un spectacle si doux
N'attendît en ces lieux qu'un témoin tel que vous :
Vous y représentez tous les Grecs et son père,   620
Puisqu'en vous Ménélas voit revivre son frère.
Voyez-la donc. Allez. Dites-lui que demain
J'attends, avec la paix, son cœur de votre main.

ORESTE

Ah dieux!

SCÈNE 5

Pyrrhus, Phœnix

PYRRHUS   Eh bien, Phœnix, l'amour est-il le maître?
Tes yeux refusent-ils encor de me connaître?

PHŒNIX

Ah! je vous reconnais, et ce juste courroux,
Ainsi qu'à tous les Grecs, Seigneur, vous rend à vous.
Ce n'est plus le jouet d'une flamme servile :
C'est Pyrrhus. C'est le fils et le rival d'Achille,   630
Que la gloire à la fin ramène sous ses lois,
Qui triomphe de Troie une seconde fois.

PYRRHUS

Dis plutôt qu'aujourd'hui commence ma victoire.
D'aujourd'hui seulement je jouis de ma gloire,
Et mon cœur, aussi fier que tu l'as vu soumis,
Croit avoir en l'amour vaincu mille ennemis.
Considère, Phœnix, les troubles que j'évite,
Quelle foule de maux l'amour traîne à sa suite,
Que d'amis, de devoirs, j'allais sacrifier;
Quels périls . . . Un regard m'eût tout fait oublier.   640
Tous les Grecs conjurés fondaient sur un rebelle;
Je trouvais du plaisir à me perdre pour elle.

PYRRHUS

Quite so. I want, though, to secure it more.
Hermione's the guarantee of lasting peace.
We're marrying. It seemed so sweet a sight
Would only need a witness such as you.   620
You'll represent all Greece, her father too,
Since Menelaus will see his brother live in you.
So go and see her then. Tell her I expect
Tomorrow, from your hand, her heart – and peace.

ORESTES

Dear God . . .

[*he leaves*

SCENE 5

Pyrrhus, Phoenix

PYRRHUS   So Phoenix, am I ruled by love?
You still refuse to see me as I am?

PHOENIX

I recognise you, yes. Your rage – so just –
Restores you to yourself and all the Greeks.
You're not the plaything of some fawning love.
You're Pyrrhus now – Achilles' rival and his son –   630
You've been brought back to glory's power.
You'll triumph over Troy a second time.

PYRRHUS

Say rather that my victory begins today.
I revel in that glory only now.
You've seen my heart so patient. Now it's proud.
I feel I've crushed a thousand enemies in love.
Just think, Phoenix, the troubles I'll avoid,
The host of pains that love brings in its train,
The friends, the duties I'd have sacrificed,
The risks . . . and all forgotten by a single glance,   640
All Greece's plots hurled down upon this rebel king.
I did delight at losing all for her.

PHŒNIX

　　Oui, je bénis, Seigneur, l'heureuse cruauté
　　Qui vous rend . . . .

PYRRHUS　　　　　　　　　Tu l'as vu, comme elle m'a traité.
　　Je pensais, en voyant sa tendresse alarmée,
　　Que son fils me la dût renvoyer désarmée.
　　J'allais voir le succès de ses embrassements :
　　Je n'ai trouvé que pleurs mêlés d'emportements.
　　Sa misère l'aigrit; et toujours plus farouche
　　Cent fois le nom d'Hector est sorti de sa bouche.　　　　650
　　Vainement à son fils j'assurais mon secours :
　　C'est Hector, disait-elle, en l'embrassant toujours;
　　Voilà ses yeux, sa bouche, et déjà son audace;
　　C'est lui-même; c'est toi, cher époux, que j'embrasse.
　　Et quelle est sa pensée? attend-elle en ce jour
　　Que je lui laisse un fils pour nourrir son amour?

PHŒNIX

　　Sans doute. C'est le prix que vous gardait l'ingrate.
　　Mais laissez-la, Seigneur.

PYRRHUS　　　　　　　　Je vois ce qui la flatte :
　　Sa beauté la rassure, et malgré mon courroux,
　　L'orgueilleuse m'attend encore à ses genoux.　　　　660
　　Je la verrais aux miens, Phœnix, d'un œil tranquille.
　　Elle est veuve d'Hector, et je suis fils d'Achille :
　　Trop de haine sépare Andromaque et Pyrrhus.

PHŒNIX

　　Commencez donc, Seigneur, à ne m'en parler plus.
　　Allez voir Hermione, et content de lui plaire,
　　Oubliez à ses pieds jusqu'à votre colère.
　　Vous-même à cet hymen venez la disposer.
　　Est-ce sur un rival qu'il s'en faut reposer?
　　Il ne l'aime que trop.

PYRRHUS　　　　　　　　Crois-tu, si je l'épouse,
　　Qu'Andromaque en son cœur n'en sera pas jalouse?　　　　670

PHŒNIX

　　Quoi! toujours Andromaque occupe votre esprit?

PHOENIX

    My lord, I bless the timely cruelty
    That brings you back . . .

PYRRHUS   Look how she treated me.
    I saw I'd roused a mother's fears. I thought
    Her son would send her back to me disarmed.
    I went to see her joy in cuddling him,
    And all I found were tears and fits of rage.
    She was embittered by her pain. She raved – more wild –
    And shouted Hector's name a hundred times.   650
    I undertook to help her son – but all in vain.
    'It's Hector,' she would say, and hold him tight.
    'There are his eyes, his lips, that daring look of his.
    It's him . . . it's you, dear husband, I hold now.'
    What thoughts race through her mind? Does she expect
    I'll let her keep her son to feed her love?

PHOENIX

    Of course. That is the price ingratitude will ask.
    Leave her, my lord.

PYRRHUS   I see what flatters her.
    Her beauty reassures. Despite my rage,
    She's proud. She still expects me at her feet.   660
    I'd see her fall at mine quite unperturbed.
    She's Hector's widow. I'm Achilles' son.
    We're separated by a sea of hate.

PHOENIX

    Then make a start. Don't talk of her again.
    Go to Hermione. Please her. Be glad.
    Forget your anger, even, at her feet.
    You should prepare her to be wed.
    You cannot trust that task to a rival
    Who's deep in love . . .

PYRRHUS   If I wed her, you think
    Andromache will not be jealous deep at heart?   670

PHOENIX

    Andromache! She's always in your mind.

Que vous importe, ô dieux! sa joie, ou son dépit?
Quel charme, malgré vous, vers elle vous attire?

PYRRHUS

Non, je n'ai pas bien dit tout ce qu'il lui faut dire :
Ma colère à ses yeux n'a paru qu'à demi;
Elle ignore à quel point je suis son ennemi.
Retournons-y. Je veux la braver à sa vue,
Et donner à ma haine une libre étendue.
Viens voir tous ses attraits, Phœnix, humiliés.
Allons.

PHŒNIX Allez, Seigneur, vous jeter à ses pieds. 680
Allez, en lui jurant que votre âme l'adore,
A de nouveaux mépris l'encourager encore.

PYRRHUS

Je le vois bien, tu crois que prêt à l'excuser
Mon cœur court après elle et cherche à s'apaiser.

PHŒNIX

Vous aimez, c'est assez.

PYRRHUS Moi l'aimer? une ingrate
Qui me hait d'autant plus que mon amour la flatte?
Sans parents, sans amis, sans espoir que sur moi;
Je puis perdre son fils, peut-être je le doi;
Etrangère . . . que dis-je? esclave dans l'Épire,
Je lui donne son fils, mon âme, mon empire, 690
Et je ne puis gagner dans son perfide cœur
D'autre rang que celui de son persécuteur?
Non, non, je l'ai juré, ma vengeance est certaine :
Il faut bien une fois justifier sa haine.
J'abandonne son fils. Que de pleurs vont couler!
De quel nom sa douleur me va-t-elle appeler!
Quel spectacle pour elle aujourd'hui se dispose!
Elle en mourra, Phœnix, et j'en serai la cause.
C'est lui mettre moi-même un poignard dans le sein.

PHŒNIX

Et pourquoi donc en faire éclater le dessein? 700
Que ne consultiez-vous tantôt votre faiblesse?

Her joys, her heartaches – God, why should you care?
What magic draws you to her still, despite yourself?

PYRRHUS

I've not yet said to her all I must say.
She's only seen a half of all this rage.
She does not know how much I am her enemy.
Let us go back. I'll brave her to her face
And give my hatred freer range.
Come, Phoenix. See. I'll humble her, her charms . . .

PHOENIX

So throw yourself before her feet, my lord.   680
Go. Swear the homage of your heart to her,
And spur her on to still more fits of scorn.

PYRRHUS

I understand. You think my heart forgives
Too readily, tries to placate, runs after her.

PHOENIX

You are in love. That is enough.

PYRRHUS   Love her?
The more I love, the more she hates. She has
No parents, friends – no hope apart from me.
I could destroy her son. Perhaps I should.
A foreigner in Epirus . . . a slave . . .
I offer her her son, my love, my very throne,   690
And yet her trustless heart won't let me win
A nobler rank than that of torturer.
Oh no . . . I've sworn that my revenge will come.
I need for once to justify her hate.
Her son shall be abandoned. Ah, what tears
There'll be, what names she'll call me in her grief.
How great a scene is being set up now.
It will kill her, Phoenix . . . I'll be the cause.
I will have stabbed the dagger through her heart.

PHOENIX

But why announce the plan so publicly?   700
Why aren't you guided by how weak you've been?

PYRRHUS

Je t'entends. Mais excuse un reste de tendresse.
Crains-tu pour ma colère un si faible combat?
D'un amour qui s'éteint c'est le dernier éclat.
Allons. A tes conseils, Phœnix, je m'abandonne.
Faut-il livrer son fils? faut-il voir Hermione?

PHŒNIX

Oui, voyez-la, Seigneur, et par des vœux soumis,
Protestez-lui . . .

PYRRHUS   Faisons tout ce que j'ai promis.

PYRRHUS

You're right. You must forgive the afterglow.
You fear my anger makes too weak a fight.
This is the final brilliance of a dying love.
So come, Phoenix. I'm in your hands . . . shall I
Give up the boy? And see Hermione?

PHOENIX

Yes, see her. And in your heart's humility,
Vow to her . . .

PYRRHUS   What I've promised, I will do.

ACTE 3 SCÈNE 1

Oreste, Pylade

PYLADE

Modérez donc, Seigneur, cette fureur extrême.
Je ne vous connais plus; vous n'êtes plus vous-même. 710
Souffrez . . .

ORESTE   Non, tes conseils ne sont plus de saison,
Pylade; je suis las d'écouter la raison.
C'est traîner trop longtemps ma vie et mon supplice :
Il faut que je l'enlève, ou bien que je périsse.
Le dessein en est pris, je le veux achever.
Oui, je le veux.

PYLADE   Eh bien! il la faut enlever.
J'y consens. Mais songez cependant où vous êtes.
Que croira-t-on de vous, à voir ce que vous faites?
Dissimulez : calmez ce transport inquiet;
Commandez à vos yeux de garder le secret. 720
Ces gardes, cette cour, l'air qui vous environne,
Tout dépend de Pyrrhus, et surtout Hermione.
A ses regards surtout cachez votre courroux.
O dieux! en cet état pourquoi la cherchiez-vous?

ORESTE

Que sais-je? De moi-même étais-je alors le maître?
La fureur m'emportait, et je venais peut-être
Menacer à la fois l'ingrate et son amant.

PYLADE

Et quel était le fruit de cet emportement?

ORESTE

Et quelle âme, dis-moi, ne serait éperdue
Du coup dont ma raison vient d'être confondue? 730
Il épouse, dit-il, Hermione demain;
Il veut pour m'honorer la tenir de ma main.
Ah! plutôt cette main dans le sang du barbare . . .

ACT 3 SCENE 1

Orestes and Pylades

PYLADES

    You must restrain this awful rage, my lord.
    I do not know you. You're beside yourself.   710
    Just let . . .

ORESTES   The time for your advice has gone,
    Pylades. I'm tired of hearing reason.
    The pain . . . my life . . . they've dragged on much too long.
    I must elope with her, or else I'll die.
    My mind's made up. I mean to see it through.
    I will do it.

PYLADES   Well then, elope you must.
    Agreed. But meanwhile, think of where you are.
    What will they think to see you act like this?
    Pretend. This frenzied rage . . . Calm down.
    And force your eyes to keep their secrets close.   720
    These guards, this court, the air you breathe, depend
    On Pyrrhus, even more Hermione.
    Conceal your rage from her above all else.
    Why did you look for her in such a state?

ORESTES

    Who knows? Could I control myself that time?
    Some . . . rage swept over me. Perhaps I went
    To threaten both of them – her, her sweetheart . . .

PYLADES

    Some . . . rage – what was the point?

ORESTES   Name me
    A man who'd not be left distraught
    At such a blow. My reason reels from it.   730
    Tomorrow, so he says, he'll wed Hermione.
    He'll honour me and take her from my hand.
    Sooner my hand in his barbaric blood . . .

PYLADE

Vous l'accusez, Seigneur, de ce destin bizarre;
Cependant tourmenté de ses propres desseins,
Il est peut-être à plaindre, autant que je vous plains.

ORESTE

Non, non, je le connais, mon désespoir le flatte,
Sans moi, sans mon amour, il dédaignait l'ingrate;
Ses charmes jusque-là n'avaient pu le toucher :
Le cruel ne la prend que pour me l'arracher. 740
Ah dieux! c'en était fait : Hermione gagnée
Pour jamais de sa vue allait être éloignée,
Son cœur, entre l'amour et le dépit confus,
Pour se donner à moi n'attendait qu'un refus,
Ses yeux s'ouvraient, Pylade. Elle écoutait Oreste,
Lui parlait, le plaignait. Un mot eût fait le reste.

PYLADE

Vous le croyez.

ORESTE   Hé quoi? ce courroux enflammé
Contre un ingrat . . .

PYLADE   Jamais il ne fut plus aimé.
Pensez-vous, quand Pyrrhus vous l'aurait accordée,
Qu'un prétexte tout prêt ne l'eût pas retardée? 750
M'en croirez-vous? Lassé de ses trompeurs attraits,
Au lieu de l'enlever, fuyez-la pour jamais.
Quoi? votre amour se veut charger d'une furie
Qui vous détestera, qui toute votre vie,
Regrettant un hymen tout prêt à s'achever,
Voudra . . .

ORESTE   C'est pour cela que je veux l'enlever.
Tout lui rirait, Pylade, et moi, pour mon partage,
Je n'emporterais donc qu'une inutile rage?
J'irais loin d'elle encor tâcher de l'oublier?
Non, non, à mes tourments, je veux l'associer. 760
C'est trop gémir tout seul. Je suis las qu'on me plaigne.
Je prétends qu'à mon tour l'inhumaine me craigne,
Et que ses yeux cruels, à pleurer condamnés,

PYLADES

> My lord, you blame him for this twist of fate,
> And he is tortured by his own designs.
> Perhaps he should be pitied, just like you.

ORESTES

> I know him . . . No, he's gratified by my despair.
> He'd throw her off if not for me – my love.
> She's cast no magic over him, not once.
> He woos her just to take her from me now.   740
> Dear God, what fate . . . had she been won, she would
> Have gone for ever from his sight.
> Her heart was muddled by both love and scorn,
> Was waiting for his 'no' to come to me.
> Her eyes were opening. She listened to me,
> Talked, and pitied . . . there needed just one word.

PYLADES

> You think so?

ORESTES   Why her blazing rage against
> The cold he showed . . . ?

PYLADES   She never loved him more.
> If he'd have let her go, you think some pale
> Pretext would not have kept her back?   750
> Trust me . . . you should grow tired of her deceptive charm.
> Rather than take her, shun her for all time.
> If not, this love of yours will take a shrew
> Who'll loathe you all your life, regret
> She did not grasp this marriage now,
> And want . . .

ORESTES   That's why I want to take her now.
> If not, the world will smile at her; but me –
> I'll take away a futile rage, and go
> Far, far from her to seek forgetfulness.
> Oh no. I want her to be part of all my pain.   760
> Suffering alone's too much. I'm tired of pity.
> I want her heartlessness to fear me too,
> Those callous eyes to be condemned to weep

Me rendent tous les noms que je leur ai donnés.

PYLADE

Voilà donc le succès qu'aura votre ambassade :
Oreste ravisseur !

ORESTE   Et qu'importe, Pylade?
Quand nos États vengés jouiront de mes soins,
L'ingrate de mes pleurs jouira-t-elle moins?
Et que me servira que la Grèce m'admire,
Tandis que je serai la fable de l'Épire?
Que veux-tu? Mais s'il faut ne te rien déguiser,   770
Mon innocence enfin commence à me peser.
Je ne sais de tout temps quelle injuste puissance
Laisse le crime en paix, et poursuit l'innocence.
De quelque part sur moi que je tourne les yeux,
Je ne vois que malheurs qui condamnent les dieux.
Méritons leur courroux, justifions leur haine,
Et que le fruit du crime en précède la peine.
Mais toi, par quelle erreur veux-tu toujours sur toi
Détourner un courroux qui ne cherche que moi?   780
Assez et trop longtemps mon amitié t'accable :
Évite un malheureux, abandonne un coupable.
Cher Pylade, crois-moi, ta pitié te séduit.
Laisse-moi des périls dont j'attends tout le fruit.
Porte aux Grecs cet enfant que Pyrrhus m'abandonne.
Va-t'en.

PYLADE   Allons, Seigneur, enlevons Hermione.
Au travers des périls un grand cœur se fait jour.
Que ne peut l'amitié conduite par l'amour?
Allons de tous vos Grecs encourager le zèle.
Nos vaisseaux sont tout prêts, et le vent nous appelle.   790
Je sais de ce palais tous les détours obscurs;
Vous voyez que la mer en vient battre les murs.
Et cette nuit sans peine une secrète voie
Jusqu'en votre vaisseau conduira votre proie.

ORESTE

J'abuse, cher ami, de ton trop d'amitié.
Mais pardonne à des maux dont toi seul as pitié;

And give me back the names I gave them once.

PYLADES

So this is how your embassy will end –
Orestes, kidnapper.

ORESTES   So what of that?
If Greece enjoyed the vengeance that I brought,
Would she enjoy my tears the less?
And Greece's loud applause – how would that serve
If people jeered at me in Epirus?   770
What should I do? I'll hide the truth no more.
This innocence begins to weigh me down.
I do not know what unjust power in every age
Leaves crime in peace yet hunts down innocence.
Wherever in my life I turn my eyes,
I only see the pain that damns the gods.
So why not earn their anger, justify their hate
And have the fruits of crime before its punishment?
But you keep turning on yourself
The rage that's meant for me. You wrong yourself.   780
My friendship's weighed you down enough – too long.
Leave me to all my sadness and my guilt.
Pity has won you over, dear Pylades.
Leave me these dangers. I'm prepared for them.
Take to the Greeks this boy that Pyrrhus has.
Go now.

PYLADES   Oh no, let's go and take Hermione.
Best courage is revealed when most's at risk.
What cannot friendship do when led by love?
Let's go and fire the hearts of all your Greeks.
Our ships are ready, the winds are calling.   790
I know each secret winding in this place.
You see the waves crash down against its walls.
Tonight, with ease, a secret passageway
Will take your prey aboard your ship.

ORESTES

You're much too good a friend. I'm using that.
Forgive this pain that you alone show pity for.

Excuse un malheureux, qui perd tout ce qu'il aime,
Que tout le monde hait, et qui se hait lui-même.
Que ne puis-je à mon tour dans un sort plus heureux . . .

PYLADE

Dissimulez, Seigneur, c'est tout ce que je veux.   800
Gardez qu'avant le coup votre dessein n'éclate :
Oubliez jusque-là qu'Hermione est ingrate;
Oubliez votre amour. Elle vient, je la voi.

ORESTE

Va-t'en. Réponds-moi d'elle, et je réponds de moi.

SCÈNE 2

Hermione, Oreste, Cléone

ORESTE

Eh bien? mes soins vous ont rendu votre conquête.
J'ai vu Pyrrhus, Madame, et votre hymen s'apprête.

HERMIONE

On le dit; et de plus on vient de m'assurer
Que vous ne me cherchiez que pour m'y préparer.

ORESTE

Et votre âme à ses vœux ne sera pas rebelle?

HERMIONE

Qui l'eût cru, que Pyrrhus ne fût pas infidèle?   810
Que sa flamme attendrait si tard pour éclater?
Qu'il reviendrait à moi, quand je l'allais quitter?
Je veux croire avec vous qu'il redoute la Grèce,
Qu'il suit son intérêt plutôt que sa tendresse,
Que mes yeux sur votre âme étaient plus absolus.

ORESTE

Non, Madame, il vous aime, et je n'en doute plus.
Vos yeux ne font-ils pas tout ce qu'ils veulent faire?
Et vous ne vouliez pas sans doute lui déplaire.

Pardon a wretched man who ruins all he loves,
Whom everybody hates, who hates himself.
In happier times, what could I not have done . . . ?

PYLADES

Pretend, my lord, that's all I ask. Take care   800
Your plan's not known before you strike. Forget
Hermione's ungratefulness till then.
Forget your love. Ah, I see her coming.

ORESTES

Then go. Answer for her. I'll answer for myself.
                    [*Pylades leaves. Hermione and Cleone enter*

SCENE 2

Hermione, Orestes, Cleone

ORESTES

So then, my efforts give you Pyrrhus back,
My lady. I've seen him. Your wedding night draws close.

HERMIONE

So I am told. What's more, I am assured
You sought me out only to tell me so.

ORESTES

And you will not resist what he desires?

HERMIONE

Who wouldn't think he wasn't treacherous   810
When love has held so long to blossom forth,
And he comes back as I am leaving him?
Like you, I want to think he fears the Greeks,
Led by self-interest more than tenderness –
But that I have a greater hold upon his heart.

ORESTES

He is in love with you, I have no doubt.
Haven't your eyes done all they wished to do?
You could not want to give displeasure now . . .

HERMIONE

Mais que puis-je, Seigneur? On a promis ma foi.
Lui ravirai-je un bien qu'il ne tient pas de moi?   820
L'amour ne règle pas le sort d'une princesse :
La gloire d'obéir est tout ce qu'on nous laisse.
Cependant je partais, et vous avez pu voir
Combien je relâchais pour vous de mon devoir.

ORESTE

Ah! que vous saviez bien, cruelle . . . Mais, Madame,
Chacun peut à son choix disposer de son âme.
La vôtre était à vous. J'espérais; mais enfin
Vous l'avez pu donner sans me faire un larcin.
Je vous accuse aussi bien moins que la fortune.
Et pourquoi vous lasser d'une plainte importune?   830
Tel est votre devoir, je l'avoue; et le mien
Est de vous épargner un si triste entretien.

SCÈNE 3

Hermione, Cléone

HERMIONE

Attendais-tu, Cléone, un courroux si modeste?

CLÉONE

La douleur qui se tait n'en est que plus funeste.
Je le plains d'autant plus qu'auteur de son ennui,
Le coup qui l'a perdu n'est parti que de lui.
Comptez depuis quel temps votre hymen se prépare;
Il a parlé, Madame, et Pyrrhus se déclare.

HERMIONE

Tu crois que Pyrrhus craint? Et que craint-il encor?
Des peuples qui dix ans ont fui devant Hector?   840
Qui cent fois effrayés de l'absence d'Achille,
Dans leurs vaisseaux brûlants ont cherché leur asile,
Et qu'on verrait encor, sans l'appui de son fils,

HERMIONE

What can I do? My faithfulness is pledged.
Should I now steal from him a gift I did not give?   820
Princesses' fates are not resolved by love.
Obedience – that crown – is all that's left to us.
And yet I was to leave with you . . . You saw
How easily my sense of duty failed . . .

ORESTES

How much you understand . . . you torture me . . .
Our love can be bestowed at our own choice.
Your love was yours. I hoped, but in the end
You gave him it. I didn't have to steal.
I blame you much, much less than fate.
So why upset you now with these complaints?   830
You have your duty. I know that. Mine is
To spare you all this painful talk.

[he leaves

SCENE 3

Hermione, Cleone

HERMIONE

Did you expect, Cleone, such mild rage?

CLEONE

The grief that does not speak is full of death.
I pity him. The more so since he's caused his pain.
The blow that's brought him down he struck alone.
Think how much time your wedding's been prepared.
Orestes talks . . . Pyrrhus makes up his mind.

HERMIONE

Could Pyrrhus have his fears, you think? What of?
People who fled from Hector ten whole years,   840
Who trembled countless times when Achilles was gone,
And sought a sanctuary in their burning ships?
Who'd still be seen, without his son's support,

Redemander Hélène aux Troyens impunis?
Non, Cléone, il n'est point ennemi de lui-même,
Il véut tout ce qu'il fait, et s'il m'épouse, il m'aime.
Mais qu'Oreste à son gré m'impute ses douleurs :
N'avons-nous d'entretien que celui de ses pleurs?
Pyrrhus revient à nous. Eh bien, chère Cléone,
Conçois-tu les transports de l'heureuse Hermione?   850
Sais-tu quel est Pyrrhus? T'es-tu fait raconter
Le nombre des exploits . . . mais qui les peut compter?
Intrépide, et partout suivi de la victoire,
Charmant, fidèle, enfin, rien ne manque à sa gloire.
Songe . . .

CLÉONE   Dissimulez. Votre rivale en pleurs
Vient à vos pieds sans doute apporter ses douleurs.

HERMIONE

Dieux! ne puis-je à ma joie abandonner mon âme?
Sortons : que lui dirais-je?

SCÈNE 4

Andromaque, Hermione, Cléone, Céphise

ANDROMAQUE   Où fuyez-vous, Madame?
N'est-ce pas à vos yeux un spectacle assez doux
Que la veuve d'Hector pleurante à vos genoux?   860
Je ne viens point ici, par de jalouses larmes,
Vous envier un cœur qui se rend à vos charmes.
Par une main cruelle, hélas! j'ai vu percer
Le seul où mes regards prétendaient s'adresser.
Ma flamme par Hector fut jadis allumée;
Avec lui dans la tombe elle s'est enfermée.
Mais il me reste un fils. Vous saurez quelque jour,
Madame, pour un fils jusqu'où va notre amour;
Mais vous ne saurez pas, du moins je le souhaite,
En quel trouble mortel son intérêt nous jette,   870
Lorsque de tant de biens qui pouvaient nous flatter,

Asking again for Helen from unpunished Troy?
No. His only enemy is himself.
What he wants he does. If he weds me, he loves me.
Orestes is free to blame his grief on me.
But must we always talk abut his woes?
So Pyrrhus will come back to me. Oh Cleone,
You can't conceive the soaring joy I feel.   850
You know who Pyrrhus is. You must have heard
How many deeds . . . but who can count them all?
Fearless, followed by constant victory,
Charming, and faithful to the end. A stainless name.
Think . . .

CLEONE   Disguise your mood. Look, your rival's here
In tears, no doubt to bring her grief to you.

HERMIONE

So can't I now be lost in all this joy?
Let's leave. What should I say to her?
                                   [*Andromache and Cephisa enter*

SCENE 4

Andromache, Hermione, Cleone, Cephisa

ANDROMACHE   You're going then . . . ?
Isn't this sweet enough a sight for you,
With Hector's widow weeping at your feet?   860
I've not come here with tears of jealousy,
To envy you a heart that you have charmed.
I've seen a vicious hand strike down
The only man I ever wished to see.
My love was lit by Hector long ago.
It's with him now, shut up inside his tomb.
But yet my son is left. One day you'll know
How very far a mother's love will go.
And yet, I hope at least you'll never know
The anguish I've been made to feel for him.   870
So many things could give me joy, but he's

C'est le seul qui nous reste, et qu'on veut nous l'ôter.
Hélas! lorsque lassés de dix ans de misère,
Les Troyens en courroux menaçaient votre mère,
J'ai su de mon Hector lui procurer l'appui.
Vous pouvez sur Pyrrhus ce que j'ai pu sur lui.
Que craint-on d'un enfant qui survit à sa perte?
Laissez-moi le cacher en quelque île déserte;
Sur les soins de sa mere on peut s'en assurer,
Et mon fils avec moi n'apprendra qu'à pleurer. 880

HERMIONE

Je conçois vos douleurs. Mais un devoir austère
Quand mon père a parlé, m'ordonne de me taire.
C'est lui qui de Pyrrhus fait agir le courroux.
S'il faut fléchir Pyrrhus, qui le peut mieux que vous?
Vos yeux assez longtemps ont régné sur son âme;
Faites-le prononcer : j'y souscrirai, Madame.

SCÈNE 5

Andromaque, Céphise

ANDROMAQUE

Quel mépris la cruelle attache à ses refus!

CÉPHISE

Je croirais ses conseils, et je verrais Pyrrhus.
Un regard confondrait Hermione et la Grèce . . .
Mais lui-même il vous cherche.

The one good left they want to take away.
When ten long years of war had worn Troy down
And maddened it to seek your mother's life,
I knew I could rely on Hector's help for her.
You can win Pyrrhus now as I did him.
Why fear a living child when Hector's dead?
Please, let me hide him on some desert isle.
You can rely upon the care I'll give.
All he can learn from me is how to weep.   880

HERMIONE

I feel your pain. But when my father speaks,
Duty's restraints demand that I keep quiet.
He is the one who's kindled Pyrrhus' rage.
If Pyrrhus must be swayed, who better now
Than you? You've ruled his heart a long, long while.
Make him decide. I will abide by that.

[*she leaves with Cleone*

SCENE 5

Andromache, Cephisa

ANDROMACHE

The scorn she pours as she says no!

CEPHISA

I'd trust her counsel. Try to see the king.
One look from you would rout her and all Greece.
Ah see . . . he's looking for you now.

[*Pyrrhus enters, accompanied by Phoenix*

SCÈNE 6

Pyrrhus, Andromaque, Phœnix, Céphise

PYRRHUS [*à Phœnix*]   Où donc est la princesse?   890
Ne m'avais-tu pas dit qu'elle était en ces lieux?

PHŒNIX

Je le croyais.

ANDROMAQUE [*à Céphise*]   Tu vois le pouvoir de mes yeux!

PYRRHUS

Que dit-elle, Phœnix?

ANDROMAQUE   Hélas! tout m'abandonne.

PHŒNIX

Allons, Seigneur, marchons sur les pas d'Hermione.

CÉPHISE

Qu'attendez-vous? Rompez ce silence obstiné.

ANDROMAQUE

Il a promis mon fils.

CÉPHISE   Il ne l'a pas donné.

ANDROMAQUE

Non, non, j'ai beau pleurer, sa mort est résolue.

PYRRHUS

Daigne-t-elle sur nous tourner au moins la vue?
Quel orgueil!

ANDROMAQUE   Je ne fais que l'irriter encor.
Sortons.

PYRRHUS   Allons aux Grecs livrer le fils d'Hector.   900

ANDROMAQUE

Ah! Seigneur, arrêtez! Que prétendez-vous faire?
Si vous livrez le fils, livrez-leur donc la mère.
Vos serments m'ont tantôt juré tant d'amitié!

SCENE 6

Pyrrhus, Andromache, Phoenix, Cephisa

PYRRHUS [*to Phoenix*]   Where is she then?   890
Hermione – you told me she was here.

PHOENIX
I thought she was.

ANDROMACHE [*to Cephisa*]   You see my eyes have power.

PYRRHUS
What does she say, Phoenix?

ANDROMACHE   Oh no, now all is lost.

PHOENIX
Let's go and find Hermione, my lord.

CEPHISA
Why are you waiting? Break the silence. Speak.

ANDROMACHE
He promised me my son.

CEPHISA   But hasn't given him.

ANDROMACHE
No, no. I cry in vain. His death is fixed.

PYRRHUS
So won't she deign to look at me, at least?
The pride . . .

ANDROMACHE   I only make him angrier.
Let's go.

PYRRHUS   Then let's surrender Hector's son to Greece.   900

ANDROMACHE
No, stop, my lord. What is it that you'd do?
If you give up my son, give me up too.
Just now, you swore such friendship to me. Swore!

Dieux! ne pourrai-je au moins toucher votre pitié?
Sans espoir de pardon m'avez-vous condamnée?

PYRRHUS

Phœnix vous le dira, ma parole est donnée.

ANDROMAQUE

Vous qui braviez pour moi tant de périls divers!

PYRRHUS

J'étais aveugle alors; mes yeux se sont ouverts.
Sa grâce à vos désirs pouvait être accordée;
Mais vous ne l'avez pas seulement demandée :   910
C'en est fait.

ANDROMAQUE   Ah! Seigneur, vous entendiez assez
Des soupirs qui craignaient de se voir repoussés.
Pardonnez à l'éclat d'une illustre fortune
Ce reste de fierté, qui craint d'être importune.
Vous ne l'ignorez pas : Andromaque, sans vous,
N'aurait jamais d'un maître embrassé les genoux.

PYRRHUS

Non, vous me haïssez et dans le fond de l'âme
Vous craignez de devoir quelque chose à ma flamme.
Ce fils même, ce fils, l'objet de tant de soins,
Si je l'avais sauvé, vous l'en aimeriez moins.   920
La haine, le mépris, contre moi tout s'assemble;
Vous me haïssez plus que tous les Grecs ensemble.
Jouissez à loisir d'un si noble courroux.
Allons, Phœnix.

ANDROMAQUE   Allons rejoindre mon époux.

CÉPHISE

Madame . . .

ANDROMAQUE   Et que veux-tu que je lui dise encore?
Auteur de tous mes maux, crois-tu qu'il les ignore?
Seigneur, voyez l'état où vous me réduisez.
J'ai vu mon père mort et nos murs embrasés,
J'ai vu trancher les jours de ma famille entière,

Can I not touch some pity now, at least . . .
Have you condemned me quite? No hope of pardon then?

PYRRHUS

Phoenix will tell you. I have given my word.

ANDROMACHE

You were to brave so many risks for me . . .

PYRRHUS

Then I was blind. My eyes are open now.
He could have well been saved, as you desired.
And yet you didn't even ask for it.　　　　　　　910
The judgment's made.

ANDROMACHE　　　　　　You understood too well.
I was afraid my grief would be repulsed.
Forgive this remnant from a glorious past,
This legacy of pride that will not beg.
You are aware that, but for you,
I never would have kissed a master's foot.

PYRRHUS

Oh no, you hate me. Deep down in your heart,
You fear to owe my love one single thing.
Even your son, the boy you love so much –
If I had saved him, you would love him less.　　　920
Hatred, contempt – against me all unite.
You hate me much more than the whole of Greece.
Savour at leisure such majestic wrath!
Phoenix?

ANDROMACHE　　Let's go to where my husband is.

CEPHISA

My lady . . .

ANDROMACHE　　What more can I say to him?
You think he doesn't know my pain. He made it.
My lord, you see now what you've brought me to?
I've seen my father die, our walls ablaze,
I've seen each member of my family cut down,

Et mon époux sanglant traîné sur la poussière,   930
Son fils seul avec moi réservé pour les fers.
Mais que ne peut un fils? Je respire, je sers.
J'ai fait plus : je me suis quelquefois consolée
Qu'ici plutôt qu'ailleurs le sort m'eût exilée;
Qu'heureux dans son malheur, le fils de tant de rois,
Puisqu'il devait servir, fût tombé sous vos lois.
J'ai cru que sa prison deviendrait son asile.
Jadis Priam soumis fut respecté d'Achille :
J'attendais de son fils encor plus de bonté.
Pardonne, cher Hector, à ma crédulité.   940
Je n'ai pu soupçonner ton ennemi d'un crime;
Malgré lui-même enfin je l'ai cru magnanime.
Ah! s'il l'était assez pour nous laisser du moins
Au tombeau qu'à ta cendre ont élevé mes soins;
Et que finissant là sa haine et nos misères,
Il ne séparât point des dépouilles si chères!

PYRRHUS

Va m'attendre, Phœnix.

SCÈNE 7

Pyrrhus, Andromaque, Céphise

PYRRHUS [*continue*]   Madame, demeurez.
On peut vous rendre encor ce fils que vous pleurez.
Oui, je sens à regret qu'en excitant vos larmes
Je ne fais contre moi que vous donner des armes.   950
Je croyais apporter plus de haine en ces lieux.
Mais, Madame, du moins tournez vers moi les yeux :
Voyez si mes regards sont d'un juge sévère,
S'ils sont d'un ennemi qui cherche à vous déplaire.
Pourquoi me forcez-vous vous-même à vous trahir?
Au nom de votre fils, cessons de nous haïr.
A le sauver enfin c'est moi qui vous convie.

My bleeding husband dragged out through the dust,   930
His only son kept now in chains for me.
But sons have strength. I've lived a slave for him —
And done much more: even consoled myself
That fate had brought me here and not elsewhere,
That if he had to serve, this son of kings
Would find some fortune as your slave.
I thought his prison might become a sanctuary.
The pleas of Priam won Achilles' ear.
I hoped for yet more kindness from his son.
Forgive, dear Hector, such credulity.   940
I couldn't think your enemy so criminal.
I thought him great of heart despite himself.
If only he would let us stay at least
Beside the tomb my love has built for you.
He'd end his hatred and our pain
If he would let our bodies mingle there.

PYRRHUS
Phoenix, go now and wait.

                                                    [*Phoenix leaves*

SCENE 7

Pyrrhus, Andromache, Cephisa

PYRRHUS   My lady, stay.
The son you mourn may still be given back.
I fear that rousing you to tears
Will simply arm you more against me now.   950
I'd thought to bring here greater hate.
At least, my lady, look at me.
How far now do I seem a callous judge,
An enemy who seeks to do you harm?
Why force me to betray you in this way?
Let's stop the hatred, in your son's own name.
It's me who pleads with you to save him now.

Faut-il que mes soupirs vous demandent sa vie?
Faut-il qu'en sa faveur j'embrasse vos genoux?
Pour la dernière fois, sauvez-le, sauvez-vous.   960
Je sais de quels serments je romps pour vous les chaînes,
Combien je vais sur moi faire éclater de haines.
Je renvoie Hermione, et je mets sur son front,
Au lieu de ma couronne, un éternel affront.
Je vous conduis au temple où son hymen s'apprête.
Je vous ceins du bandeau préparé pour sa tête.
Mais ce n'est plus, Madame, une offre à dédaigner :
Je vous le dis, il faut ou périr ou régner.
Mon cœur, désespéré d'un an d'ingratitude,
Ne peut plus de son sort souffrir l'incertitude.   970
C'est craindre, menacer et gémir trop longtemps.
Je meurs si je vous perds, mais je meurs si j'attends.
Songez-y : je vous laisse, et je viendrai vous prendre
Pour vous mener au temple, où ce fils doit m'attendre.
Et là vous me verrez soumis, ou furieux,
Vous couronner, Madame, ou le perdre à vos yeux.

SCÈNE 8

Andromaque, Céphise

CÉPHISE

Je vous l'avais prédit, qu'en dépit de la Grèce
De votre sort encor vous seriez la maîtresse.

ANDROMAQUE

Hélas! de quel effet tes discours sont suivis?
Il ne me restait plus qu'à condamner mon fils.   980

CÉPHISE

Madame, à votre époux, c'est être assez fidèle :
Trop de vertu pourrait vous rendre criminelle;
Lui-même il porterait votre âme à la douceur.

So must my pleas now beg you for his life?
Must I now kneel to you for his own sake?
For the last time, save him now, save yourself.   960
I'm breaking vows for you, vows with strong chains –
I know the hatred that will tumble down.
I'll send Hermione away, set on her head
Not my royal crown but everlasting shame.
I'll take you to the shrine – her wedding is prepared –
I'll place her wedding band around your head.
You cannot scorn this offer, my lady.
No more. I tell you, either die or reign.
My heart despairs – a year's ingratitude –
I can no longer bear uncertainty.   970
It's been too long for fears and threats and groans.
I'll die if I lose you. But I'll die if I wait.
Remember that. I'll leave you now. I'll come
To take you to the temple where your son will wait.
And there you'll find me, quiet or wild with rage.
I'll either crown you, or kill him in your sight.

      [*he leaves. Andromache and Cephisa remain*

SCENE 8

Andromache, Cephisa

CEPHISA

I told you you'd control your destiny
Again, in spite of all the Greeks.

ANDROMACHE

And what's the dreadful outcome of your words . . . ?
I can do nothing but condemn my son.   980

CEPHISA

It is enough to honour Hector's name.
But too much virtue could become a crime.
Hector himself would counsel carefulness.

ANDROMAQUE

Quoi, je lui donnerais Pyrrhus pour successeur?

CÉPHISE

Ainsi le veut son fils, que les Grecs vous ravissent.
Pensez-vous qu'après tout ses mânes en rougissent?
Qu'il méprisât, Madame, un roi victorieux,
Qui vous fait remonter au rang de vos aïeux;
Qui foule aux pieds pour vous vos vainqueurs en colère,
Qui ne se souvient plus qu'Achille était son père,   990
Qui dément ses exploits et les rend superflus?

ANDROMAQUE

Dois-je les oublier, s'il ne s'en souvient plus?
Dois-je oublier Hector privé de funérailles,
Et traîné sans honneur autour de nos murailles?
Dois-je oublier son père à mes pieds renversé,
Ensanglantant l'autel qu'il tenait embrassé?
Songe, songe, Céphise, à cette nuit cruelle
Qui fut pour tout un peuple une nuit éternelle;
Figure-toi Pyrrhus les yeux étincelants,
Entrant à la lueur de nos palais brûlants;   1000
Sur tous mes frères morts se faisant un passage,
Et de sang tout couvert échauffant le carnage;
Songe aux cris des vainqueurs, songe aux cris des mourants,
Dans la flamme étouffés, sous le fer expirants;
Peins-toi dans ces horreurs Andromaque éperdue :
Voilà comme Pyrrhus vint s'offrir à ma vue,
Voilà par quels exploits il sut se couronner,
Enfin voilà l'époux que tu me veux donner.
Non, je ne serai point complice de ses crimes;
Qu'il nous prenne, s'il veut, pour dernières victimes.   1010
Tous mes ressentiments lui seraient asservis.

CÉPHISE

Eh bien, allons donc voir expirer votre fils :
On n'attend plus que vous. Vous frémissez, Madame?

ANDROMAQUE

Ah! de quel souvenir viens-tu frapper mon âme!

ANDROMACHE

And give him Pyrrhus to succeed him? No.

CEPHISA

Your son the Greeks will take would want it so . . .
Would Hector's ghost blush so if that should be?
Would he despise a king in victory
Who raised you back to your ancestral rank?
Who trod your angry conquerors underfoot,
Forgot he was Achilles' son,   990
Denied his exploits, made them meaningless?

ANDROMACHE

Should I forget them if they've slipped his mind?
Should I forget that Hector, without burial,
Was dragged dishonoured round our walls? Should I
Forget my father falling at my feet
And bloodying the altar that he clutched?
Remember, Cephisa . . . that dreadful night
That was perpetual night for our whole race.
Imagine Pyrrhus then, his eyes ablaze,
His path lit up by palaces of fire,   1000
Picking his way through all my brothers . . . dead . . .
Inciting yet more carnage, drenched in blood.
Think of the victors' shouts, the screams of men
Choked by the flames, and dying by the sword.
Imagine me among this horror, crazed.
This is how Pyrrhus first appeared to me.
These are the acts that made him king.
This is the husband that you offer me.
I will not be accomplice to his crimes.
We'll be the final victims if he wants   1010
And all my anger can be chained by him.

CEPHISA

Then we must go to watch your young son die.
They're waiting just for you . . . You shudder . . .

ANDROMACHE   Oh,

With what a memory you've moved my soul,

Quoi, Céphise, j'irai voir expirer encor
Ce fils, ma seule joie, et l'image d'Hector?
Ce fils que de sa flamme il me laissa pour gage?
Hélas! je m'en souviens, le jour que son courage
Lui fit chercher Achille, ou plutôt le trépas,
Il demanda son fils, et le prit dans ses bras :   1020
Chère épouse, dit-il en essuyant mes larmes,
J'ignore quel succès le sort garde à mes armes;
Je te laisse mon fils pour gage de ma foi :
S'il me perd, je prétends qu'il me retrouve en toi.
Si d'un heureux hymen la mémoire t'est chère,
Montre au fils à quel point tu chérissais le père.
Et je puis voir répandre un sang si précieux?
Et je laisse avec lui périr tous ses aïeux?
Roi barbare, faut-il que mon crime l'entraîne?
Si je te hais, est-il coupable de ma haine?   1030
T'a-t-il de tous les siens reproché le trépas?
S'est-il plaint à tes yeux des maux qu'il ne sent pas?
Mais cependant, mon fils, tu meurs si je n'arrête
Le fer que le cruel tient levé sur ta tête.
Je l'en puis détourner, et je t'y vais offrir?
Non, tu ne mourras point, je ne le puis souffrir.
Allons trouver Pyrrhus. Mais non, chère Céphise,
Va le trouver pour moi.

CÉPHISE   Que faut-il que je dise?

ANDROMAQUE

Dis-lui que de mon fils l'amour est assez fort . . . .
Crois-tu que dans son cœur il ait juré sa mort?   1040
L'amour peut-il si loin pousser sa barbarie?

CÉPHISE

Madame, il va bientôt revenir en furie.

ANDROMAQUE

Eh bien, va l'assurer . . .

CÉPHISE   De quoi? de votre foi?

Cephisa. I go to see my young son die,
Sweet Hector's image, and my only joy . . .
The son he gave as token of his love.
That memory . . . the day he bravely went
To find Achilles, but instead found death.
He asked to see his son. He hugged him tight.   1020
He dried my tears and said, 'My darling wife,
I cannot know what fate will do to me.
I leave my son as token of my faith.
If I am killed, he must recover me in you.
If you keep sweet remembrance of our life as one,
Show to my son how much you cherished me.'
How can I see such precious blood be shed
And let his forebears die with him? So must
My crime drag him down too, you barbarous king?
If I hate you, is he made guilty too?   1030
Has he condemned you for his family's death?
Has he complained of pain he does not feel?
And yet, my son, you'll die unless I stop
The sword that animal hangs over you.
I could prevent it. But I give you up . . .
You will not die. I could not bear your death.
We must find Pyrrhus. No, no . . . Cephisa,
You find him for me now.

CEPHISA   What should I say?

ANDROMACHE

You tell him that I love my son enough . . .
You think that in his heart he's sworn his death?   1040
Could love take barbarousness so far?

CEPHISA

He'll soon come back, my lady, mad with rage.

ANDROMACHE

Go and assure him then.

CEPHISA   Of what? Your promises?

ANDROMAQUE

Hélas! pour la promettre est-elle encore à moi?
O cendres d'un époux! ô Troyens! ô mon père!
O mon fils, que tes jours coûtent cher à ta mère!
Allons.

CÉPHISE   Où donc, Madame, et que résolvez-vous?

ANDROMAQUE

Allons sur son tombeau consulter mon époux.

ANDROMACHE

It's still for me to promise him?
My husband's ashes . . . oh Trojans . . . father . . .
How dearly then I buy your life, my son.
I'll go.

CEPHISA   But where, my lady? What have you resolved?

ANDROMACHE

I'll go to speak to Hector in his tomb.

ACTE 4 SCÈNE 1

Andromaque, Céphise

CÉPHISE

Ah! je n'en doute point : c'est votre époux, Madame,
C'est Hector qui produit ce miracle en votre âme.   1050
Il veut que Troie encor se puisse relever,
Avec cet heureux fils, qu'il vous fait conserver.
Pyrrhus vous l'a promis. Vous venez de l'entendre,
Madame : il n'attendait qu'un mot pour vous le rendre.
Croyez-en ses transports : père, sceptre, alliés,
Content de votre cœur, il met tout à vos pieds.
Sur lui, sur tout son peuple il vous rend souveraine.
Est-ce là ce vainqueur digne de tant de haine?
Déjà contre les Grecs plein d'un noble courroux
Le soin de votre fils le touche autant que vous.   1060
Il prévient leur fureur, il lui laisse sa garde;
Pour ne pas l'exposer, lui-même il se hasarde.
Mais tout s'apprête au temple. Et vous avez promis.

ANDROMAQUE

Oui, je m'y trouverai. Mais allons voir mon fils.

CÉPHISE

Madame, qui vous presse? Il suffit que sa vue
Désormais à vos yeux ne soit plus défendue.
Vous lui pourrez bientôt prodiguer vos bontés,
Et vos embrassements ne seront plus comptés.
Quel plaisir d'élever un enfant qu'on voit croître
Non plus comme un esclave élevé pour son maître,   1070
Mais pour voir avec lui renaître tant de rois!

ANDROMAQUE

Céphise, allons le voir pour la dernière fois.

CÉPHISE

Que dites-vous? O dieux!

ANDROMAQUE   O ma chère Céphise,
Ce n'est point avec toi que mon cœur se déguise.

ACT 4 SCENE 1

Andromache, Cephisa

CEPHISA

My lady, there can be no doubt. Hector
Has worked this miracle within your heart.   1050
He wishes Troy to rise again in strength,
And with your favoured son whom he keeps safe.
Pyrrhus has sworn. You heard him speak yourself.
He only waits one word to give him back.
Believe his rapture. Father, allies, crown –
He'll put them at your feet for joy of you.
He'll make you empress of himself, his realm.
Is this a victor who deserves such hate?
He's full of anger now against the Greeks.
He cares as much about your son as you.   1060
He sees their rage ahead, leaves him his guard.
He puts himself at risk to shield the boy.
The temple's all prepared. You gave your word . . .

ANDROMACHE

I will be there. But first I'll see my son.

CEPHISA

But why the hurry? Isn't it enough
That now he won't be kept from seeing you.
Soon you can pour your tenderness on him,
Not have to count each time you cuddle him.
The joy to raise a child and see him grow,
Not subject to a master as a slave,   1070
But as a rebirth of so many kings!

ANDROMACHE

Let's go to see him for the final time.

CEPHISA

What are you saying? Oh God . . .

ANDROMACHE   My dear Cephisa,
I've never tried to hide my heart from you.

Ta foi, dans mon malheur, s'est montrée à mes yeux;
Mais j'ai cru qu'à mon tour tu me connaissais mieux.
Quoi donc? as-tu pensé qu'Andromaque infidèle
Pût trahir un époux qui croit revivre en elle,
Et que de tant de morts réveillant la douleur,
Le soin de mon repos me fit troubler le leur?   1080
Est-ce là cette ardeur tant promise à sa cendre?
Mais son fils périssait; il l'a fallu défendre.
Pyrrhus en m'épousant s'en déclare l'appui;
Il suffit : je veux bien m'en reposer sur lui.
Je sais quel est Pyrrhus : violent, mais sincère,
Céphise, il fera plus qu'il n'a promis de faire.
Sur le courroux des Grecs je m'en repose encor :
Leur haine va donner un père au fils d'Hector.
Je vais donc, puisqu'il faut que je me sacrifie,
Assurer à Pyrrhus le reste de ma vie;   1090
Je vais en recevant sa foi sur les autels,
L'engager à mon fils par des nœuds immortels.
Mais aussitôt ma main, à moi seule funeste,
D'une infidèle vie abrégera le reste,
Et sauvant ma vertu, rendra ce que je doi,
A Pyrrhus, à mon fils, à mon époux, à moi.
Voilà de mon amour l'innocent stratagème;
Voilà ce qu'un époux m'a commandé lui-même;
J'irai seule rejoindre Hector, et mes aïeux.
Céphise, c'est à toi de me fermer les yeux.   1100

CÉPHISE

Ah! ne prétendez pas que je puisse survivre.

ANDROMAQUE

Non, non, je te défends, Céphise, de me suivre.
Je confie à tes soins mon unique trésor.
Si tu vivais pour moi, vis pour le fils d'Hector.
De l'espoir des Troyens seule dépositaire,
Songe à combien de rois tu deviens nécessaire.
Veille auprès de Pyrrhus; fais-lui garder sa foi :
S'il le faut, je consens qu'on lui parle de moi;
Fais-lui valoir l'hymen où je me suis rangée;
Dis-lui qu'avant ma mort je lui fus engagée,   1110

Through all my pain, you've shown your faithfulness.
And yet I thought you knew me better. Yes.
So did you think I'd turn unfaithful now,
Betray a husband who's alive in me?
Would I wake up the grief of countless dead
And gain my peace of mind by haunting theirs?   1080
Is that the love I promised to his ghost?
His son though will soon die. I have to guard . . .
By marrying me, Pyrrhus becomes his shield.
That is enough. I put my trust in him.
I know what Pyrrhus is: hot-headed but sincere.
He will do more than he has promised to.
I can rely on Greece's violent rage.
Their hate will give a father to my son.
And so I have to sacrifice myself
And pledge my life to Pyrrhus till I die.   1090
When he has sworn his solemn vows to me,
I'll bind him to my son by ties that outlast time.
And then, when I'm alone, I'll kill myself.
I'll cut the rest off of my faithless life.
I'll save my honour, pay back what I owe
To Pyrrhus, son, and husband, and to me.
This is the simple plan I've made – through love.
It's what my husband ordered me to do.
I'll go to Hector and my forbears quite alone.
Cephisa, you will have to close my eyes.   1100

CEPHISA

You shouldn't think I could survive . . .

ANDROMACHE

I will not have you follow me.
I place my greatest treasure in your care.
You've lived for me. Now live for Hector's son.
You'll be the only guardian of all Troy's hopes.
Just think how many kings have need of you.
Watch over Pyrrhus. Make him keep his word.
But speak to him of me, if that must be,
And stress the worth our marriage had.
Tell of my pledge to him before I died,   1110

Que ses ressentiments doivent être effacés,
Qu'en lui laissant mon fils, c'est l'estimer assez.
Fais connaître à mon fils les héros de sa race;
Autant que tu pourras, conduis-le sur leur trace :
Dis-lui par quels exploits leurs noms ont éclaté,
Plutôt ce qu'ils ont fait que ce qu'ils ont été;
Parle-lui tous les jours des vertus de son père,
Et quelquefois aussi parle-lui de sa mère.
Mais qu'il ne songe plus, Céphise, à nous venger :
Nous lui laissons un maître, il le doit ménager.   1120
Qu'il ait de ses aïeux un souvenir modeste :
Il est du sang d'Hector, mais il en est le reste;
Et pour ce reste enfin j'ai moi-même, en un jour,
Sacrifié mon sang, ma haine, et mon amour.

CÉPHISE

Hélas!

ANDROMAQUE   Ne me suis point, si ton cœur en alarmes
Prévoit qu'il ne pourra commander à tes larmes.
On vient. Cache tes pleurs, Céphise, et souviens-toi
Que le sort d'Andromaque est commis à ta foi.
C'est Hermione. Allons, fuyons sa violence.

SCÈNE 2

Hermione, Cléone

CLÉONE

Non, je ne puis assez admirer ce silence.   1130
Vous vous taisez, Madame, et ce cruel mépris
N'a pas du moindre trouble agité vos esprits?
Vous soutenez en paix une si rude attaque,
Vous qu'on voyait frémir au seul nom d'Andromaque?
Vous qui sans désespoir ne pouviez endurer
Que Pyrrhus d'un regard la voulût honorer?
Il l'épouse, il lui donne avec son diadème
La foi que vous venez de recevoir vous-même;

So his resentment may be quelled. I've prized
Him well enough to leave my son with him.
Make my son learn the heroes of his race
And try to make him follow in their steps.
Tell him the deeds that glorify their names,
And rather what they did than who they were.
Speak of his father's goodness every day
And tell him sometimes of his mother too.
But never let him dream of avenging us.
He'll have a master. He must handle him.   1120
Don't let him boast about his ancestors.
He is of Hector's blood, last of his line;
And for that line, within a single day,
I've sacrificed my blood, my hate, my love.

CEPHISA

No, no . . .

ANDROMACHE   Don't follow me. You're too upset.
You know you can't control your tears.
Someone is coming. Don't cry. Remember
I trust my life to your good care. It is
Hermione. Avoid her anger. Come.
          [*Andromache and Cephisa leave. Hermione and Cleone enter*

SCENE 2

Hermione, Cleone

CLEONE

I am astonished at your silence now.   1130
You do not speak. His cruelty, contempt –
They've not upset your spirits in the least.
You bear his harsh attacks so peaceably,
And yet the name Andromache still makes you shake.
You couldn't stand that Pyrrhus honoured her
With one brief glance without despair.
He's marrying her, giving with his diadem
The pledge that you have just received yourself.

Et votre bouche encor muette à tant d'ennui,
N'a pas daigné s'ouvrir pour se plaindre de lui?   1140
Ah! que je crains, Madame, un calme si funeste!
Et qu'il vaudrait bien mieux . . .

HERMIONE   Fais-tu venir Oreste?

CLEONE

Il vient, Madame, il vient. Et vous pouvez juger
Que bientot à vos pieds il allait se ranger;
Prêt à servir toujours sans espoir de salaire,
Vos yeux ne sont que trop assurés de lui plaire.
Mais il entre.

SCÈNE 3

Oreste, Hermione, Cléone

ORESTE   Ah! Madame! est-il vrai qu'une fois
Oreste en vous cherchant obéisse à vos lois?
Ne m'a-t-on point flatté d'une fausse espérance?
Avez-vous en effet souhaité ma présence?   1150
Croirai-je que vos yeux à la fin désarmés
Veulent . . .

HERMIONE   Je veux savoir, Seigneur, si vous m'aimez.

ORESTE

Si je vous aime? ô dieux! mes serments, mes parjures,
Ma fuite, mon retour, mes respects, mes injures,
Mon désespoir, mes yeux de pleurs toujours noyés,
Quels témoins croirez-vous, si vous ne les croyez?

HERMIONE

Vengez-moi, je crois tout.

ORESTE   Eh bien! allons, Madame :
Mettons encore un coup toute la Grèce en flamme;
Prenons, en signalant mon bras, et votre nom,
Vous la place d'Hélène, et moi d'Agamemnon.   1160

And still your lips are dumb at so much pain.
Will they not open and complain of him?   1140
But I'm afraid . . . so ominous a calm.
It would be better . . .

HERMIONE   Orestes – you've sent for him?

CLEONE

He's on his way, my lady. And you see
How eagerly he comes to kneel to you.
He'll serve you constantly, without reward.
Your eyes are all too sure of pleasing him.
He's here.

                    [*Orestes enters*

SCENE 3

Orestes, Hermione, Cleone

ORESTES   My lady, is it true for once
That I have met your wish by coming here?
I haven't been deceived by cheating hope?
Do you indeed now want my company?   1150
Can I believe that you're disarmed at last
And want . . .

HERMIONE   I want to know, my lord, if you love me.

ORESTES

If I love you . . . Dear God, the oaths, the treacheries,
My flight, return, respect, my injuries,
Despair, these eyes for ever weeping tears –
What evidence will you believe, if not all this?

HERMIONE

Avenge me – I'll believe it all.

ORESTES   Then come.
Let's strike a blow to set all Greece on fire.
Let's shout my strength and your renown aloud.
You will be Helen, Agamemnon me.   1160

De Troie en ce pays réveillons les misères,
Et qu'on parle de nous ainsi que de nos pères.
Partons, je suis tout prêt.

HERMIONE   Non, Seigneur, demeurons :
Je ne veux pas si loin porter de tels affronts.
Quoi! de mes ennemis couronnant l'insolence,
J'irais attendre ailleurs une lente vengeance,
Et je m'en remettrais au destin des combats,
Qui peut-être à la fin ne me vengerait pas?
Je veux qu'à mon départ toute l'Épire pleure.
Mais si vous me vengez, vengez-moi dans une heure.   1170
Tous vos retardements sont pour moi des refus.
Courez au temple. Il faut immoler . . .

ORESTE   Qui?

HERMIONE   Pyrrhus.

ORESTE

Pyrrhus, Madame?

HERMIONE   Eh quoi! votre haine chancelle?
Ah! courez, et craignez que je ne vous rappelle.
N'alléguez point des droits que je veux oublier;
Et ce n'est pas à vous à le justifier.

ORESTE

Moi, je l'excuserais? Ah! vos bontés, Madame,
Ont gravé trop avant ses crimes dans mon âme.
Vengeons-nous, j'y consens. Mais par d'autre chemins :
Soyons ses ennemis, et non ses assassins;
Faisons de sa ruine une juste conquête.   1180
Quoi! pour réponse aux Grecs porterai-je sa tête?
Et n'ai-je pris sur moi le soin de tout l'Etat,
Que pour m'en acquitter par un assassinat?
Souffrez, au nom des dieux, que la Grèce s'explique,
Et qu'il meure chargé de la haine publique.
Souvenez-vous qu'il règne, et qu'un front couronné . . .

HERMIONE

Ne vous suffit-il pas que je l'ai condamné?

We'll waken all Troy's sufferings in this land.
They'll speak of us as of our ancestors.
Let's go. I'm all prepared.

HERMIONE   No, stay, my lord.
I'd not take such affronts so far afield.
I'd crown my enemies' insulting pride
By waiting for a slow revenge elsewhere.
I might expose myself to risks of war
Which might not in the end leave me avenged.
When I depart, I want all Epirus to mourn.
If you'll avenge me, do it now – this hour.   1170
If you delay, you have rejected me.
Run to the temple. We must sacrifice . . .

ORESTES   Who?

HERMIONE   Pyrrhus.

ORESTES
  Pyrrhus?

HERMIONE   What's that? Your hatred's wavering?
  Run there. Fear lest I call you back.
  Don't now make claim to rights I would forget.
  It's not for you to justify his life.

ORESTES
  Would *I* excuse him? Your kindnesses, my lady,
  Have carved his crimes too deeply in my heart.
  Avenge ourselves, agreed, but in another way.
  Let's be his enemies, not murderers.   1180
  He can be overthrown by just defeat.
  Should I respond to Greece by killing him?
  Have I assumed a mission from the state
  Only to pay it off by murdering?
  In the gods' names, let Greece explain its case.
  Then let him die weighed down with public hate.
  Remember that he's king; his head is crowned . . .

HERMIONE
  It's not enough for you I've damned him, then?

Ne vous suffit-il pas que ma gloire offensée
Demande une victime à moi seule adressée;   1190
Qu'Hermione est le prix d'un tyran opprimé,
Que je le hais, enfin, Seigneur, que je l'aimai?
Je ne m'en cache point : l'ingrat m'avait su plaire,
Soit qu'ainsi l'ordonnât mon amour ou mon père,
N'importe; mais enfin réglez-vous là-dessus.
Malgré mes vœux, Seigneur, honteusement déçus,
Malgré la juste horreur que son crime me donne,
Tant qu'il vivra, craignez que je ne lui pardonne.
Doutez jusqu'à sa mort d'un courroux incertain :
S'il ne meurt aujourd'hui, je puis l'aimer demain.   1200

ORESTE

Eh bien, il faut le perdre, et prévenir sa grâce;
Il faut . . . Mais cependant que faut-il que je fasse?
Comment puis-je si tôt servir votre courroux?
Quel chemin jusqu'à lui peut conduire mes coups?
A peine suis-je encore arrivé dans l'Épire,
Vous voulez par mes mains renverser un empire;
Vous voulez qu'un roi meure, et pour son châtiment
Vous ne donnez qu'un jour, qu'une heure, qu'un moment.
Aux yeux de tout son peuple, il faut que je l'opprime?
Laissez-moi vers l'autel conduire ma victime.   1210
Je ne m'en défends plus; et je ne veux qu'aller
Reconnaître la place où je dois l'immoler.
Cette nuit je vous sers. Cette nuit je l'attaque.

HERMIONE

Mais cependant ce jour il épouse Andromaque.
Dans le temple déjà le trône est élevé.
Ma honte est confirmée, et son crime achevé.
Enfin qu'attendez-vous? Il vous offre sa tête :
Sans gardes, sans défense il marche à cette fête;
Autour du fils d'Hector il les fait tous ranger;
Il s'abandonne au bras qui me voudra venger.   1220
Voulez-vous malgré lui prendre soin de sa vie?
Armez avec vos Grecs tous ceux qui m'ont suivie;
Soulevez vos amis. Tous les miens sont à vous :
Il me trahit, vous trompe, et nous méprise tous.

Not enough my name has been insulted,
Looks for a victim killed for me alone?   1190
That I am now the prize of stifling tyranny,
That I now loathe the man I once adored?
I won't pretend. He gave me great delight.
Whether my heart, my father, is to blame —
No matter now. Decide that for yourself.
Despite the shameful way I've been betrayed,
Despite the horror that his crime excites,
While he still lives, fear lest I pardon him.
Suspect this wavering anger till he's died.
If he's not dead today, tomorrow I may love . . .   1200

ORESTES

He must be killed before your pardon, then.
He must . . . And yet what must I do? How best
To help your anger here and now?
How can I strike directly at him now?
I've barely just arrived in Epirus
And you want me to overthrow a state.
You want a king to die; and for this death,
A day, an hour, a moment's all you give.
He must be killed before his people's eyes.
So let me lead him to the shrine.   1210
I shall resist no more. I only want
To go and see the place where I must kill.
Tonight I'll serve you well, and strike him down.

HERMIONE

But yet today he weds Andromache.
The throne's already raised up in the shrine.
My shame is known by everyone. His crime's complete.
What are you waiting for? He offers you his head.
He goes to his great feast . . . no guards, defence . . .
He'll make them all draw up round Hector's son.
He'll give in to the power of my revenge.   1220
Will you protect his life in spite of him?
Arm with your Greeks all those who've followed me.
Collect your friends. All mine are on your side.
Me he's betrayed, you deceived — he's despised us all.

Mais quoi? Déjà leur haine est égale à la mienne :
Elle épargne à regret l'époux d'une Troyenne.
Parlez : mon ennemi ne vous peut échapper.
Ou plutôt, il ne faut que les laisser frapper.
Conduisez, ou suivez une fureur si belle;
Revenez tout couvert du sang de l'infidèle;   1230
Allez : en cet état soyez sûr de mon cœur.

ORESTE

Mais, Madame, songez . . .

HERMIONE   Ah! c'en est trop, Seigneur.
Tant de raisonnements offensent ma colère.
J'ai voulu vous donner les moyens de me plaire,
Rendre Oreste content; mais enfin je vois bien
Qu'il veut toujours se plaindre, et ne mériter rien.
Partez : allez ailleurs vanter votre constance,
Et me laissez ici le soin de ma vengeance.
De mes lâches bontés mon courage est confus,
Et c'est trop en un jour essuyer de refus.   1240
Je m'en vais seule au temple, où leur hymen s'apprête,
Où vous n'osez aller mériter ma conquête.
Là, de mon ennemi je saurai m'approcher.
Je percerai le cœur que je n'ai pu toucher,
Et mes sanglantes mains, sur moi-même tournées,
Aussitôt, malgré lui, joindront nos destinées,
Et tout ingrat qu'il est, il me sera plus doux
De mourir avec lui que de vivre avec vous.

ORESTE

Non, je vous priverai de ce plaisir funeste,
Madame : il ne mourra que de la main d'Oreste.   1250
Vos ennemis par moi vont vous être immolés,
Et vous reconnaîtrez mes soins, si vous voulez.

HERMIONE

Allez. De votre sort laissez-moi la conduite,
Et que tous vos vaisseaux soient prêts pour notre fuite.

Already now, their hate's as strong as mine.
They're loath to spare a Trojan woman's lord.
So speak. My enemy cannot escape.
In fact you only have to let them strike.
Just lead or follow all their frenzied rage
And come back covered in the traitor's blood.   1230
Go, then you can be certain of my love.

ORESTES

But think, my lady . . .

HERMIONE   This is too much, my lord.
Your reasons, reasons, reasons insult me.
I've tried to find you ways of pleasing me,
And making you content. But now I see
You'll always be complaining, worth nothing.
So go. Boast of your constancy elsewhere
And leave me here to take my own revenge.
My mind's awash with feeble kindnesses;
It can't be cleaned up in a single day.   1240
I'll walk alone then to the wedding shrine
Where you daren't go to win my hand.
I know how best to go up to my enemy
And stab the heart that I could never touch.
I'll turn my blood-drenched hands against myself
At once. Our destinies will join in spite of him.
Cruel though he is, it will be sweeter far
To die with Pyrrhus than to live with you.

ORESTES

No, I'll relieve you of that deathly joy,
My lady. He'll die by my hand alone.   1250
No one but me will kill your enemies.
You may then recognise my service, if you care.

HERMIONE

Then go. Leave me to steer your destiny.
And have your ships be ready for our flight.

[*Orestes leaves*

SCÈNE 4

Hermione, Cléone

CLÉONE

Vous vous perdez, Madame. Et vous devez songer . . .

HERMIONE

Que je me perde ou non, je songe à me venger.
Je ne sais même encor, quoi qu'il m'ait pu promettre,
Sur d'autres que sur moi si je dois m'en remettre :
Pyrrhus n'est pas coupable à ses yeux comme aux miens,
Et je tiendrais mes coups bien plus sûrs que les siens.   1260
Quel plaisir de venger moi-même mon injure,
De retirer mon bras teint du sang du parjure,
Et pour rendre sa peine et mes plaisirs plus grands,
De cacher ma rivale à ses regards mourants!
Ah! si du moins Oreste, en punissant son crime,
Lui laissait le regret de mourir ma victime!
Va le trouver : dis-lui qu'il apprenne à l'ingrat
Qu'on l'immole à ma haine, et non pas à l'État.
Chère Cléone, cours : ma vengeance est perdue
S'il ignore en mourant que c'est moi qui le tue.   1270

CLÉONE

Je vous obéirai. Mais qu'est-ce que je vois?
O dieux! qui l'aurait cru, Madame? C'est le roi.

HERMIONE

Ah! cours après Oreste; et dis-lui, ma Cléone,
Qu'il n'entreprenne rien sans revoir Hermione!

SCENE 4

Hermione, Cleone

CLEONE

You face defeat, my lady. You must think . . .

HERMIONE

Defeat or not, I dream now of revenge.
He promises – and yet I'm still not sure
If I can trust in others than myself.
Pyrrhus is not so guilty in his eyes as mine,
And I would strike more surely than would he.   1260
The pleasure to avenge my injury myself,
To draw my hand back, soaked in traitor's blood,
And then increase my pleasure and his pain
And keep my rival from his dying eyes.
As he kills him, Orestes must at least
Leave him the sorrow that he died my prey.
Find him. Tell him to let the traitor know
My hatred's burying him, not the state's.
Cleone, run. My vengeance is quite lost
Unless he knows that I have murdered him.   1270

CLEONE

I'll do that, yes. But what is that – oh God . . .
Who would have thought, my lady? It's the king.

HERMIONE

Run to Orestes. Tell him, Cleone,
Not to do a thing until he's seen me.

                          [*Cleone leaves. Pyrrhus enters*

SCÈNE 5

Pyrrhus, Hermione, Phœnix

PYRRHUS

Vous ne m'attendiez pas, Madame, et je vois bien
Que mon abord ici trouble votre entretien.
Je ne viens point armé d'un indigne artifice
D'un voile d'équité couvrir mon injustice :
Il suffit que mon cœur me condamne tout bas,
Et je soutiendrais mal ce que je ne crois pas.   1280
J'épouse une Troyenne. Oui, Madame, et j'avoue
Que je vous ai promis la foi que je lui voue.
Un autre vous dirait que dans les champs troyens
Nos deux pères sans nous formèrent ces liens,
Et que sans consulter ni mon choix ni le vôtre,
Nous fûmes sans amour engagés l'un à l'autre;
Mais c'est assez pour moi que je me sois soumis.
Par mes ambassadeurs mon cœur vous fut promis;
Loin de les révoquer, je voulus y souscrire :
Je vous vis avec eux arriver en Épire,   1290
Et quoique d'un autre œil l'éclat victorieux
Eût déjà prévenu le pouvoir de vos yeux,
Je ne m'arrêtai point à cette ardeur nouvelle;
Je voulus m'obstiner à vous être fidèle :
Je vous reçus en reine, et jusques à ce jour
J'ai cru que mes serments me tiendraient lieu d'amour.
Mais cet amour l'emporte. Et par un coup funeste
Andromaque m'arrache un cœur qu'elle déteste.
L'un par l'autre entraînés nous courons à l'autel
Nous jurer, malgré nous, un amour immortel.   1300
Après cela, Madame, éclatez contre un traître,
Qui l'est avec douleur, et qui pourtant veut l'être.
Pour moi, loin de contraindre un si juste courroux,
Il me soulagera peut-être autant que vous.
Donnez-moi tous les noms destinés aux parjures :
Je crains votre silence, et non pas vos injures,
Et mon cœur soulevant mille secrets témoins
M'en dira d'autant plus que vous m'en direz moins.

SCENE 5

Pyrrhus, Hermione, Phoenix

PYRRHUS

You weren't expecting me. I see
My being here has interrupted you.
I haven't come to mouth some worthless sham,
To veil my hurtful deeds with justice now.
Enough my heart's condemned me to the pit,
And I could ill maintain a thing I did not think.   1280
I'm marrying a Trojan wife. Yes, I confess
I've given her the promises I made to you.
But some might say that, on the plains of Troy,
Our fathers forged those bonds without us there.
Your wishes were not sought, nor mine.
The pact that joined us did not speak of love.
Yet I agreed to it – and that's enough.
My heart was promised you by my ambassadors.
Far from disowning, I endorsed their words.
I saw you come with them to Epirus.   1290
By then, another woman had won me –
A foretaste of the power that you would hold.
I did not cling, though, to that latest love.
I tried to will myself to faithfulness.
I welcomed you as queen, and until now,
I thought my vows could take the place of love.
But love has carried all. By deadly fate,
Andromache has won a heart she loathes.
We run swept up together to the shrine
To swear eternal love despite ourselves.   1300
So burst out now against my treachery.
I grieve at it, and yet I wish it so.
Don't hold the anger back – it's just –
I'll be relieved perhaps as much as you.
Fling all the names for perjurers at me.
I fear your silence, not the words of hate.
Conscience will call a thousand secret witnesses
And tell me all the more, the less you say.

HERMIONE

Seigneur, dans cet aveu dépouillé d'artifice,
J'aime à voir que du moins vous vous rendiez justice, 1310
Et que voulant bien rompre un nœud si solennel,
Vous vous abandonniez au crime en criminel.
Est-il juste après tout qu'un conquérant s'abaisse
Sous la servile loi de garder sa promesse?
Non, non, la perfidie a de quoi vous tenter
Et vous ne me cherchez que pour vous en vanter.
Quoi? Sans que ni serment ni devoir vous retienne
Rechercher une Grecque, amant d'une Troyenne?
Me quitter, me reprendre, et retourner encor
De la fille d'Hélène à la veuve d'Hector? 1320
Couronner tour à tour l'esclave, et la princesse,
Immoler Troie aux Grecs, au fils d'Hector la Grèce?
Tout cela part d'un cœur toujours maître de soi,
D'un héros qui n'est point esclave de sa foi.
Pour plaire à votre épouse, il vous faudrait peut-être
Prodiguer les doux noms de parjure, et de traître.
Vous veniez de mon front observer la pâleur,
Pour aller dans ses bras rire de ma douleur.
Pleurante après son char vous voulez qu'on me voie;
Mais, Seigneur, en un jour ce serait trop de joie; 1330
Et sans chercher ailleurs des titres empruntés,
Ne vous suffit-il pas de ceux que vous portez?
Du vieux père d'Hector la valeur abattue
Aux pieds de sa famille expirante à sa vue,
Tandis que dans son sein votre bras enfoncé
Cherche un reste de sang que l'âge avait glacé;
Dans des ruisseaux de sang Troie ardente plongée,
De votre propre main Polyxène égorgée
Aux yeux de tous les Grecs indignés contre vous,
Que peut-on refuser à ces généreux coups? 1340

PYRRHUS

Madame, je sais trop à quels excès de rage
La vengeance d'Hélène emporta mon courage.
Je puis me plaindre à vous du sang que j'ai versé;
Mais enfin je consens d'oublier le passé.

HERMIONE

So you confess, my lord — and honestly.
I'm glad you can do justice to yourself, at least.   1310
You're now set firm to break a solemn bond
And take up crime just like a criminal.
Why after all should conquerors bow down
Beneath that slavish law of keeping faith?
No, something in treachery beckons you.
You came here just to boast of it to me.
So . . . neither vow nor duty holds you back . . .
You love a Trojan, seek a Grecian's hand.
You leave me, take me back, and then return
From Helen's daughter to Hector's widow;   1320
You'll crown the slave, the princess, turn by turn,
Deliver Troy to Greece, then Greece to Hector's son —
This shows a man who's master of himself,
A hero, slave to nothing like his word.
To please your bride, perhaps I ought to add
The dear, sweet names of traitor, perjurer.
You came to see the whiteness in my face,
Then run into her arms and mock my grief.
You want to see me weeping by her chariot.
That would be too much joy, though, for one day.   1330
Need you seek titles borrowed from elsewhere?
Aren't those you've won enough for you?
Hector's old father — honour, name destroyed
Before his family, dying as they watched.
You plunged your sword deep in his chest,
Searching some drop of blood long chilled by age.
And Troy ablaze, engulfed in streams of blood.
Polyxenes — his throat cut out by you
In front of all the outraged Greeks. How could
The greatness of these deeds be put in doubt?   1340

PYRRHUS

I know only too well the insane rage
That vengeance for Helen carried me to.
I could reproach you with the blood I've shed,
But I am willing to forget the past.

Je rends grâces au ciel que votre indifférence
De mes heureux soupirs m'apprenne l'innocence.
Mon cœur, je le vois bien, trop prompt à se gêner,
Devait mieux vous connaître et mieux s'examiner.
Mes remords vous faisaient une injure mortelle.
Il faut se croire aimé pour se croire infidèle.
Vous ne prétendiez point m'arrêter dans vos fers :
Je crains de vous trahir peut-être je vous sers.
Nos cœurs n'étaient point faits dépendants l'un de l'autre;
Je suivais mon devoir et vous cédiez au vôtre;
Rien ne vous engageait à m'aimer en effet.

HERMIONE

Je ne t'ai point aimé, cruel? Qu'ai-je donc fait?
J'ai dédaigné pour toi les vœux de tous nos princes,
Je t'ai cherché moi-même au fond de tes provinces.
J'y suis encor, malgré tes infidélités,
Et malgré tous mes Grecs honteux de mes bontés.
Je leur ai commandé de cacher mon injure;
J'attendais en secret le retour d'un parjure;
J'ai cru que tôt ou tard, à ton devoir rendu,
Tu me rapporterais un cœur qui m'était dû.
Je t'aimais inconstant, qu'aurais-je fait fidèle?
Et même en ce moment, où ta bouche cruelle
Vient si tranquillement m'annoncer le trépas,
Ingrat, je doute encor si je ne t'aime pas.
Mais, Seigneur, s'il le faut, si le ciel en colère
Réserve à d'autres yeux la gloire de vous plaire,
Achevez votre hymen, j'y consens; mais du moins
Ne forcez pas mes yeux d'en être les témoins.
Pour la dernière fois je vous parle peut-être.
Différez-le d'un jour, demain vous serez maître.
Vous ne répondez point? Perfide, je le voi,
Tu comptes les moments que tu perds avec moi.
Ton cœur, impatient de revoir ta Troyenne,
Ne souffre qu'à regret qu'un autre t'entretienne.
Tu lui parles du cœur, tu la cherches des yeux.
Je ne te retiens plus, sauve-toi de ces lieux,
Va lui jurer la foi que tu m'avais jurée,

1350

1360

1370

1380

I thank the gods that your indifference
Has made my sweetest yearnings innocent.
I see my heart's too quick to blame itself.
It should have known you better, known myself.
And my remorse offends you mortally.
To think yourself betrayed, you must think you're loved. 1350
You never claimed to hold me like a slave.
I feared betraying you. Perhaps I helped you there.
Our hearts were never made to join.
I did my duty. You did yours.
Nothing ever forced you to give me love.

HERMIONE

Me give you love? What do you think I've done?
I scorned the hands of all our kings for you.
I sought you out myself, deep in these lands.
I am still here, despite your faithlessness,
Despite the Greeks, ashamed at my humility. 1360
I ordered them to hide my injury.
I waited for a perjurer's return.
I thought that, one day soon, duty would call
And you would bring me back the heart that's mine.
I loved you faithless. What would I not have done
If you'd kept faith? Your callous lips pronounce
My death with such a calm. Yet even now,
I doubt I do not love you still.
But if it must be so, if heaven's rage
Gives others now the glory of your love, 1370
Be married then. I will consent. Don't force
Me, though, at least, to witness it.
This is the last time that we'll speak, perhaps.
Wait just a day. You will be master then . . .
You don't respond . . . I see your treachery.
You count the minutes that you've lost on me.
You cannot wait to see your Trojan love again.
You cannot bear to hear another's words.
You speak your heart to her, your eyes seek hers.
I'll hold you back no more. Leave this place now. 1380
Go, swear to her the vow you swore to me.

Va profaner des dieux la majesté sacrée.
Ces dieux, ces justes dieux n'auront pas oublié
Que les mêmes serments avec moi t'ont lié.
Porte au pied des autels ce cœur qui m'abandonne.
Va, cours; mais crains encor d'y trouver Hermione.

SCÈNE 6

Pyrrhus, Phœnix

PHŒNIX

Seigneur, vous entendez. Gardez de négliger
Une amante en fureur, qui cherche à se venger.
Elle n'est en ces lieux que trop bien appuyée :
La querelle des Grecs à la sienne est liée;
Oreste l'aime encore. Et peut-être à ce prix . . .   1390

PYRRHUS

Andromaque m'attend. Phœnix, garde son fils.

Profane the great gods' sacred majesty.
Those gods, those righteous gods will not forget
That once the selfsame vows bound you to me.
Take to the shrine the heart that leaves me now.
Go quickly now. Fear lest you find me there.

[she leaves

SCENE 6

Pyrrhus, Phoenix

PHOENIX

You heard, my lord. Don't underestimate
A lover scorned who looks for her revenge.
She's much too well supported in this place.
The cause of Greece is tied with hers.   1390
Orestes still loves her. Perhaps that price . . .

PYRRHUS

Andromache is waiting. Guard her son.

ACTE 5 SCÈNE 1

HERMIONE [*seule*]

Où suis-je? Qu'ai-je fait? Que dois-je faire encore?
Quel transport me saisit? Quel chagrin me dévore?
Errante, et sans dessein, je cours dans ce palais.
Ah! ne puis-je savoir si j'aime, ou si je hais?
Le cruel! de quel œil il m'a congédiée!
Sans pitié, sans douleur au moins étudiée.
L'ai-je vu se troubler et me plaindre un moment?
En ai-je pu tirer un seul gémissement?   1400
Muet à mes soupirs, tranquille à mes alarmes,
Semblait-il seulement qu'il eût part à mes larmes?
Et je le plains encore? Et pour comble d'ennui
Mon cœur, mon lâche cœur s'intéresse pour lui?
Je tremble au seul penser du coup qui le menace?
Et prête à me venger, je lui fais déjà grâce?
Non, ne révoquons point l'arrêt de mon courroux :
Qu'il périsse. Aussi bien il ne vit plus pour nous.
Le perfide triomphe, et se rit de ma rage :
Il pense voir en pleurs dissiper cet orage;   1410
Il croit que toujours faible et d'un cœur incertain,
Je parerai d'un bras les coups de l'autre main.
Il juge encor de moi par mes bontés passées.
Mais plutôt le perfide a bien d'autres pensées :
Triomphant dans le temple, il ne s'informe pas
Si l'on souhaite ailleurs sa vie, ou son trépas.
Il me laisse, l'ingrat! cet embarras funeste.
Non, non, encore un coup, laissons agir Oreste.
Qu'il meure, puisque enfin il a dû le prévoir,
Et puisqu'il m'a forcée enfin à le vouloir.   1420
A le vouloir? Hé quoi? C'est donc moi qui l'ordonne?
Sa mort sera l'effet de l'amour d'Hermione?
Ce prince, dont mon cœur se faisait autrefois,
Avec tant de plaisir, redire les exploits,
A qui même en secret je m'étais destinée
Avant qu'on eût conclu ce fatal hyménée,
Je n'ai donc traversé tant de mers, tant d'États,

ACT 5 SCENE 1

HERMIONE [*alone*]
Where am I? What have I done? Shall I do?
What's holding me? What pain eats through at me?
I dart all through the palace, aimlessly.
So don't I know now if I love or hate?
I've been cast off – that cruelty in his eyes –
No pity, grief – not even feigned. And did
I see him soften for a moment – care?
Did I draw out one single groan from him?   1400
I cried distressed. He stood there, dumb, unmoved.
He did not seem to share my grief at all.
And I still pity him! But there's worse pain.
My heart, my cowardly heart, still takes his side.
I tremble just to think . . . that deathly blow . . .
Revenge is now so close. Will I still pardon him?
I won't revoke the aim of all this rage.
Let him now die. He's not alive to me.
The traitor triumphs, mocks and scorns my hurt.
He thinks he'll see this storm dissolve in tears.   1410
He thinks me always wavering and weak,
That with one hand I'll stop the other's blows.
He judges me by kindnesses now past.
But no . . . he'll take a different view, for sure.
He triumphs at the shrine. What does he care
If life or death is wished on him elsewhere?
He leaves me, devil, with that ghastly choice.
No, just one strike more. Let Orestes act,
And let him die. He must have known, have seen
It all. He forced me into willing it . . .   1420
To *willing* it? Have *I* commanded it?
So will the end of all my love be death?
Pyrrhus . . . in other times, my heart would fill
With such an ecstasy to hear his deeds.
I felt that I was his, even if secretly,
Before my fatal marriage was arranged.
I've crossed so many seas, so many lands,

Que pour venir si loin préparer son trépas,
L'assassiner, le perdre? Ah! devant qu'il expire . . .

SCÈNE 2
Hermione, Cléone

HERMIONE

Ah! qu'ai-je fait, Cléone? Et que viens-tu me dire?　　　　1430
Que fait Pyrrhus?

CLÉONE　　　　　　　　Il est au comble de ses vœux,
Le plus fier des mortels, et le plus amoureux.
Je l'ai vu vers le temple, où son hymen s'apprête,
Mener en conquérant sa nouvelle conquête,
Et d'un œil où brillaient sa joie et son espoir,
S'enivrer, en marchant, du plaisir de la voir.
Andromaque, au travers de mille cris de joie,
Porte jusqu'aux autels le souvenir de Troie.
Incapable toujours d'aimer et de haïr,
Sans joie, et sans murmure elle semble obéir.　　　　1440

HERMIONE

Et l'ingrat? Jusqu'au bout il a poussé l'outrage?
Mais as-tu bien, Cléone, observé son visage?
Goûte-t-il des plaisirs tranquilles et parfaits?
N'a-t-il point détourné ses yeux vers le palais?
Dis-moi, ne t'es-tu point présentée à sa vue?
L'ingrat a-t-il rougi lorsqu'il t'a reconnue?
Son trouble avouait-il son infidélité?
A-t-il jusqu'à la fin soutenu sa fierté?

CLÉONE

Madame, il ne voit rien. Son salut, et sa gloire
Semblent être avec vous sortis de sa mémoire.　　　　1450
Sans songer qui le suit, ennemis ou sujets,
Il poursuit seulement ses amoureux projets.
Autour du fils d'Hector il a rangé sa garde,
Et croit que c'est lui seul que le péril regarde.

Have come so far – just to prepare his death.
To murder, kill him. Oh, before he dies . . .

            [*Cleone enters*

SCENE 2

Hermione, Cleone

HERMIONE

What have I done, Cleone? what have you come   1430
To say? Is Pyrrhus now . . .

CLEONE   He's at the height
Of joy, proudest of men, most deep in love.
I saw him lead his conquest as a conqueror
Towards the temple where his marriage was prepared.
His eyes were bright with joy and hope,
Made drunk with happiness to see her there.
Amid a thousand shouts of joy, Andromache
Took to the shrine the memory of Troy.
She cannot love, but neither can she hate.
She followed joyless, uncomplainingly.   1440

HERMIONE

And Pyrrhus pressed the outrage to the end?
So did you carefully observe his face?
Did he enjoy a peaceful, perfect bliss?
Didn't he glance towards the palace once?
Tell me, didn't you show yourself to him?
Did he not blush on recognising you?
His faithlessness caused some distress . . . ?
Or did he keep his arrogance to the end?

CLEONE

He does not see at all. His safety, fame,
Seem to have fled his memory with you.   1450
He doesn't know who's with him – friend or foe –
He's set his mind on thoughts of love alone.
He's placed his guard round Hector's son,
He thinks that danger eyes the boy alone.

Phœnix même en répond, qui l'a conduit exprès
Dans un fort éloigné du temple et du palais.
Voilà, dans ses transports, le seul soin qui lui reste.

HERMIONE

Le perfide! Il mourra. Mais que t'a dit Oreste?

CLÉONE

Oreste, avec ses Grecs, dans le termple est entré.

HERMIONE

Hé bien? à me venger n'est-il pas préparé? 1460

CLÉONE

Je ne sais.

HERMIONE   Tu ne sais? Quoi donc? Oreste encore,
Oreste me trahit?

CLÉONE   Oreste vous adore.
Mais de mille remords son esprit combattu
Croit tantôt son amour, et tantôt sa vertu.
Il respecte en Pyrrhus l'honneur du diadème;
Il respecte en Pyrrhus Achille, et Pyrrhus même;
Il craint la Grèce, il craint l'univers en courroux.
Mais il se craint, dit-il, soi-même plus que tous.
Il voudrait en vainqueur vous apporter sa tête;
Le seul nom d'assassin l'épouvante et l'arrête. 1470
Enfin il est entré, sans savoir dans son cœur
S'il en devait sortir coupable, ou spectateur.

HERMIONE

Non, non, il les verra triompher sans obstacle,
Il se gardera bien de troubler ce spectacle.
Je sais de quels remords son courage est atteint :
Le lâche craint la mort, et c'est tout ce qu'il craint.
Quoi? sans qu'elle employât une seule prière,
Ma mère en sa faveur arma la Grèce entière?
Ses yeux pour leur querelle, en dix ans de combats,
Virent périr vingt rois qu'ils ne connaissaient pas? 1480
Et moi je ne prétends que la mort d'un parjure,
Et je charge un amant du soin de mon injure,

Phoenix has care of him. He's taken him
On orders to some fort far from this place.
In his great ecstasy, that is his one concern.

HERMIONE

The treachery . . . he'll die. What did Orestes say?

CLEONE

He went into the temple with his Greeks.

HERMIONE

He's ready to avenge me then . . . ?   1460

CLEONE

I can't say . . .

HERMIONE   You cannot say! Orestes . . .
Will he betray me too?

CLEONE   He worships you.
His mind, though, rages with a thousand doubts.
He trusts now in love, now in virtuousness.
In Pyrrhus, he reveres the kingly crown,
Reveres Achilles in him, and the man himself.
He fears the Greeks; he fears the whole world's wrath.
But most of all, he says he fears himself.
He wants to triumph, bring you Pyrrhus' head.
A single word – 'assassin' – makes him shrink.   1470
He went in finally, not knowing in his heart
If he would leave a guilty man, or innocent.

HERMIONE

He'll not prevent their triumph. No, he'll take
Good care not to disturb the scene.
I know with what remorse his heart is filled.
The coward fears death, and that is all he fears.
Without a single plea, my mother roused
The whole of Greece to arms, to fight her cause.
In ten long years of war, she saw some twenty kings
She did not know die in that fight. And I,   1480
I only want a treacherous man to die.
I ask a lover to redress my wrong.

Il peut me conquérir à ce prix, sans danger,
Je me livre moi-même, et ne puis me venger?
Allons : c'est à moi seule, à me rendre justice.
Que de cris de douleur le temple retentisse;
De leur hymen fatal troublons l'événement,
Et qu'ils ne soient unis, s'il se peut, qu'un moment.
Je ne choisirai point dans ce désordre extrême :
Tout me sera Pyrrhus, fût-ce Oreste lui-même.   1490
Je mourrai; mais au moins ma mort me vengera,
Je ne mourrai pas seule, et quelqu'un me suivra.

SCÈNE 3

Oreste, Hermione, Cléone

ORESTE

Madame, c'en est fait, et vous êtes servie :
Pyrrhus rend à l'autel son infidèle vie.

HERMIONE

Il est mort?

ORESTE   Il expire; et nos Grecs irrités
Ont lavé dans son sang ses infidélités.
Je vous l'avais promis; et quoique mon courage
Se fît de ce complot une funeste image,
J'ai couru vers le temple, où nos Grecs dispersés
Se sont jusqu'à l'autel dans la foule glissés.   1500
Pyrrhus m'a reconnu. Mais sans changer de face,
Il semblait que ma vue excitât son audace,
Que tous les Grecs bravés en leur ambassadeur
Dussent de son hymen relever la splendeur.
Enfin, avec transport prenant son diadème,
Sur le front d'Andromaque il l'a posé lui-même :
Je vous donne, a-t-il dit, ma couronne et ma foi,
Andromaque, régnez sur l'Épire et sur moi.
Je voue à votre fils une amitié de père,
J'en atteste les dieux, je le jure à sa mère :   1510

He'll win me – and no danger – at that price.
I give myself and still am not avenged.
Who'll give me justice? Me. Just me alone.
The shrine will echo with their screams of grief.
I'll interrupt their awful ceremony.
If possible, they only will be joined one breath . . .
I'll strike out blindly in a frenzied rage.
The whole world – Orestes even – will be Pyrrhus.   1490
I'll die, but die at least avenged. I shall
Not die alone. Someone will follow me.

[*Orestes enters*

SCENE 3

Orestes, Hermione, Cleone

ORESTES

It's done, my lady, now. You have been served.
Pyrrhus gives up his faithless life to God.

HERMIONE

He's dead . . .

ORESTES   He's dying. Our Greeks were frenzied –
They've washed out all his treachery with his blood.
I promised you his death. Although my mind
Was haunted by the horror of the plot,
I ran towards the temple. Our Greeks had scattered
And slipped up to the altar in the crowds.   1500
Pyrrhus caught sight of me, but did not flinch.
His recklessness seemed fired by seeing me:
That all of Greece was flaunted in its envoy there
And had enhanced the splendour of the rites.
At last, he took his crown ecstatically
And placed it on Andromache himself.
'I give you now,' he said, 'my faith and crown.
Andromache, you reign in Epirus and me.
I swear a father's kindness to your son.
The gods are witness of this oath to you.   1510

Pour tous mes ennemis je déclare les siens,
Et je le reconnais pour le roi des Troyens.
A ces mots, qui du peuple attiraient le suffrage,
Nos Grecs n'ont répondu que par un cri de rage;
L'infidèle s'est vu partout envelopper,
Et je n'ai pu trouver de place pour frapper.
Chacun se disputait la gloire de l'abattre.
Je l'ai vu dans leurs mains quelque temps se débattre,
Tout sanglant à leurs coups vouloir se dérober,
Mais enfin à l'autel il est allé tomber.   1520
Du peuple épouvanté j'ai traversé la presse
Pour venir de ces lieux enlever ma princesse,
Et regagner le port, où bientôt nos amis
Viendront couverts du sang que je vous ai promis.

HERMIONE

Qu'ont-ils fait!

ORESTE   Pardonnez à leur impatience :
Ils ont, je le vois bien, trahi votre vengeance.
Vous vouliez que ma main portât les premiers coups,
Qu'il sentît en mourant qu'il expirait pour vous;
Mais c'est moi dont l'ardeur leur a servi d'exemple :
Je les ai pour vous seule entraînés dans le temple,   1530
Madame, et vous pouvez justement vous flatter
D'une mort que leurs bras n'ont fait qu'exécuter.
Vous seule avez poussé les coups . . .

HERMIONE   Tais-toi, perfide.
Et n'impute qu'à toi ton lâche parricide.
Va faire chez tes Grecs admirer ta fureur,
Va, je la désavoue, et tu me fais horreur.
Barbare, qu'as-tu fait? Avec quelle furie
As-tu tranché le cours d'une si belle vie?
Avez-vous pu, cruels, l'immoler aujourd'hui,
Sans que tout votre sang se soulevât pour lui?   1540
Mais parle : de son sort qui t'a rendu l'arbitre?
Pourquoi l'assassiner? Qu'a-t-il fait? A quel titre?
Qui te l'a dit?

ORESTE   O dieux! Quoi? ne m'avez-vous pas

His enemies I now declare are mine.
I recognise him as the Trojans' king.'
But then these words, at which the people cheered,
Drew from our Greeks a howl of rage.
The traitor was surrounded on all sides.
I couldn't find a place from which to strike.
They fought to have the honour of the blow.
I saw him struggling in their hands awhile,
Trying to hide all bleeding from their blows.
Beside the altar, finally, he fell.   1520
I pushed the horror-stricken crowd aside
To come and take you from this place. We must
Regain the port. Our friends will soon come there,
All covered with the blood I promised you.

HERMIONE

What have they done?

ORESTES   Forgive their hastiness.
They have betrayed your vengeance. I see that.
You wanted me to strike the first death blows,
So that he'd know he died because of you.
I was the one whose zeal, though, guided them.
I drew them to the temple just for you,   1530
My lady. Take rightful pride in a death
Their strength of arms has simply carried out.
Alone you dealt him every blow . . .

HERMIONE   Enough!
You cowardly parricide. You are to blame.
Go flaunt your bravery to the Greeks.
Go. I disown you. Go. You sicken me.
You barbarian . . . what have you done? What madness
Made you cut a glorious life so short?
How could you kill him now . . . you vicious men . . .
And all your blood not rise for him?   1540
Tell me. Who gave you power to choose his fate?
Why murder him? What did he do? What right?
Who told you to?

ORESTES   God, didn't you yourself,

Vous-même, ici, tantôt, ordonné son trépas?

HERMIONE

Ah! fallait-il en croire une amante insensée?
Ne devais-tu pas lire au fond de ma pensée?
Et ne voyais-tu pas dans mes emportements
Que mon cœur démentait ma bouche à tous moments?
Quand je l'aurais voulu, fallait-il y souscrire?
N'as-tu pas dû cent fois te le faire redire,   1550
Toi-même avant le coup me venir consulter,
Y revenir encore, ou plutôt m'éviter?
Que ne me laissais-tu le soin de ma vengeance?
Qui t'amène en des lieux où l'on fuit ta présence?
Voilà de ton amour le détestable fruit :
Tu m'apportais, cruel, le malheur qui te suit.
C'est toi dont l'ambassade, à tous les deux fatale,
L'a fait pour son malheur pencher vers ma rivale.
Nous le verrions encor nous partager ses soins;
Il m'aimerait peut-être, il le feindrait du moins.   1560
Adieu. Tu peux partir. Je demeure en Épire :
Je renonce à la Grèce, à Sparte, à son empire,
A toute ma famille; et c'est assez pour moi,
Traître, qu'elle ait produit un monstre comme toi.

SCÈNE 4

ORESTE [seul]

Que vois-je? Est-ce Hermione? Et que viens-je d'entendre?
Pour qui coule le sang que je viens de répandre?
Je suis, si je l'en crois, un traître, un assassin.
Est-ce Pyrrhus qui meurt? et suis-je Oreste enfin?
Quoi? j'étouffe en mon cœur la raison qui m'éclaire.
J'assassine à regret un roi que je révère,   1570
Je viole en un jour les droits des souverains,
Ceux des ambassadeurs, et tous ceux des humains;
Ceux même des autels, où ma fureur l'assiège :
Je deviens parricide, assassin, sacrilège.

Just here, not long ago, command his death?

HERMIONE

How could a frantic lover be believed?
You should have read my deepest thoughts.
Did you not see in all my rage
My heart belied my words at every turn?
If I had wished it, even, need you obey?
You should have made me say it endlessly,   1550
Have come to seek advice before you struck,
Then come again, or else avoided me.
You should have let me have my own revenge.
What brings you here where you are shunned?
So here's the ghastly outcome of your love.
You've brought the evil following you to me.
It is your embassy that's killed us both,
That made him choose my rival, to his grief.
We might have seen him share his heart.
He might have loved me . . . or pretended to.   1560
Good bye. You can now go. I'll stay in Epirus.
I'll give up Greece, and Sparta – home and all
My family . . . It is enough for me
That it's produced a monster such as you.

[*she leaves*

SCENE 4

ORESTES [*alone*]

What do I see . . . ? Hermione? And hear . . . ?
The blood that I've just spilt flows out for whom?
If she is right, I am a traitor, murderer.
Is Pyrrhus dead? Am I Orestes still?
I've put the light of reason out inside my mind.
I kill unwillingly a king whom I revere.   1570
I violate within one day the rights
Of sovereigns, ambassadors, all humankind –
Even the altars where he was besieged.
I am a parricide, murderer, sacrilege.

Pour qui? pour une ingrate, à qui je le promets,
Qui même, s'il ne meurt, ne me verra jamais,
Dont j'épouse la rage. Et quand je l'ai servie,
Elle me redemande et son sang et sa vie!
Elle l'aime! et je suis un monstre furieux!
Je la vois pour jamais s'éloigner de mes yeux. 1580
Et l'ingrate, en fuyant, me laisse pour salaire
Tous les noms odieux que j'ai pris pour lui plaire!

SCÈNE 5

Oreste, Pylade, Soldats d'Oreste

PYLADE

Il faut partir, Seigneur. Sortons de ce palais,
Ou bien résolvons-nous de n'en sortir jamais.
Nos Grecs pour un moment en défendent la porte;
Tout le peuple assemblé nous poursuit à main-forte;
Aux ordres d'Andromaque ici tout est soumis,
Ils la traitent en reine, et nous comme ennemis.
Andromaque elle-même, à Pyrrhus si rebelle,
Lui rend tous les devoirs d'une veuve fidèle, 1590
Commande qu'on le venge, et peut-être sur nous
Veut venger Troie encore et son premier époux.
Allons. N'attendons pas que l'on nous environne :
Nos Grecs nous rejoindront; et tandis qu'Hermione
Tient encore le peuple autour d'elle arrêté,
Voilà notre chemin, sortons en sûreté.

ORESTE

Non, non, c'est Hermione, amis, que je veux suivre.
A son dernier arrêt je ne puis plus survivre.
Partez : j'ai fait le crime, et je vais l'expier.

PYLADE

Hermione, Seigneur? Il la faut oublier. 1600
Quoi! toujours l'instrument et l'objet de sa rage,
Cherchez-vous chez les morts quelque nouvel outrage?

Who for? That 'lady' whom I promised him,
Who even if he lives won't see me now . . . ?
I wed her rage! And when I'd done her will,
She asks me give her back his life again.
She loves him. And I am monstrous, animal . . .
I see her go for ever from my sight,   1580
And as she runs, she leaves me as reward
Each loathsome name I've earned by pleasing her.
                    [*Pylades enters, with Orestes' soldiers*

SCENE 5

Orestes, Pylades, Orestes' soldiers

PYLADES

My lord, we must set off. Leave this palace;
Or else decide never to try again.
Our Greeks still hold the gates for now,
But mobs are seeking us – they're strongly armed.
Andromache rules everyone who's here.
She is their queen, and we are enemies.
Once she fought the king, but now she gives him
Every respect a faithful widow owes,   1590
Commands he be revenged, and may on us
Wreak vengeance yet for Hector and for Troy.
Let's leave. Don't wait to be surrounded. Quick,
Our Greeks will join us soon. Hermione
Still holds the crowds' astonishment.
Here is the path. Our safety is in flight.

ORESTES

No, it is Hermione I must follow, friends.
I can't survive her last decree. So go.
It was my crime. I will atone for it.

PYLADES

You must forget Hermione, my lord.   1600
You can't still be the means and object of her rage,
Seeking some new affront among the dead?

Et parce qu'elle meurt faut-il que vous mouriez?

ORESTE

Elle meurt? Dieux! qu'entends-je?

PYLADE   Eh quoi? vous l'ignoriez?
En rentrant dans ces lieux nous l'avons rencontrée
Qui courait vers le temple, inquiète, égarée.
Elle a trouvé Pyrrhus porté sur des soldats
Que son sang excitait à venger son trépas.
Sans doute à cet objet sa rage s'est émue.
Mais du haut de la porte enfin nous l'avons vue,   1610
Un poignard à la main, sur Pyrrhus se courber,
Lever les yeux au ciel, se frapper et tomber.

ORESTE

Grâce aux dieux! Mon malheur passe mon espérance.
Oui, je te loue, ô ciel! de ta persévérance.
Appliqué sans relâche au soin de me punir,
Au comble des douleurs tu m'as fait parvenir.
Ta haine a pris plaisir à former ma misère;
J'étais né pour servir d'exemple à ta colère,
Pour être du malheur un modèle accompli.
Hé bien, je meurs content, et mon sort est rempli.   1620
Où sont ces deux amants? Pour couronner ma joie,
Dans leur sang, dans le mien, il faut que je me noie;
L'un et l'autre en mourant je les veux regarder :
Réunissons trois cœurs qui n'ont pu s'accorder.
Mais quelle épaisse nuit tout à coup m'environne?
De quel côté sortir? D'où vient que je frissonne?
Quelle horreur me saisit? Grâce au ciel j'entrevoi.
Dieux! quels ruisseaux de sang coulent autour de moi!

PYLADE

Ah! Seigneur!

ORESTE   Quoi, Pyrrhus, je te rencontre encore?
Trouverai-je partout un rival que j'abhorre?   1630
Percé de tant de coups comment t'es-tu sauvé?
Tiens, tiens, voilà le coup que je t'ai réservé.
Mais que vois-je? A mes yeux Hermione l'embrasse!

Because she's dying, must you die?

ORESTES

She's dying . . . God, what do I hear?

PYLADES   So you don't know?

We met her as we came back to this spot,
Running towards the temple, wild, distraught.
She'd just found Pyrrhus, carried by his guard.
His blood inflamed them to avenge his death.
Her frenzy was so roused to see him so . . .
And then we saw her from our vantage point   1610
Bend over Pyrrhus, dagger in her hand,
And raise her eyes to heaven, stab herself, and fall.

ORESTES

Thanks to the Gods . . . ! I never hoped such grief . . .
The heavens be praised . . . ! such steadfastness
Applied without respite to punish me.
You've made me touch the depths of such despair,
Your hatred savoured making all my pain.
So I was born to illustrate your wrath,
To be the perfect form of wretchedness.
Well then, I die content. My fate's fulfilled.   1620
Where are the lovers now? To crown my joy, I have
To drown myself in blood – in theirs and mine.
So in their death, I want to see them both.
Let's join three hearts that could not be as one . . .
What is this sudden darkness round me now . . . thick dark . . .
I must escape . . . I'm shuddering . . . where from?
The horror seizes me . . . Thank God, I can just glimpse . . .
Great God, what streams of blood race all around.

PYLADES

My lord!

ORESTES   What, Pyrrhus? We meet once more . . . ?
I'll find my hated rival everywhere . . . ?   1630
How are you living . . . pierced with such deep cuts?
Take this . . . this is the blow I kept for you.
What do I see? She kisses him . . . Hermione . . .

Elle vient l'arracher au coup qui le menace?
Dieux, quels affreux regards elle jette sur moi!
Quels démons, quels serpents traîne-t-elle après soi?
Eh bien, filles d'enfer, vos mains sont-elles prêtes?
Pour qui sont ces serpents qui sifflent sur vos têtes?
A qui destinez-vous l'appareil qui vous suit?
Venez-vous m'enlever dans l'éternelle nuit?   1640
Venez, à vos fureurs Oreste s'abandonne.
Mais non, retirez-vous, laissez faire Hermione :
L'ingrate mieux que vous saura me déchirer,
Et je lui porte enfin mon cœur à dévorer.

PYLADE

Il perd le sentiment. Amis, le temps nous presse.
Ménageons les moments que ce transport nous laisse.
Sauvons-le. Nos efforts deviendraient impuissants
S'il reprenait ici sa rage avec ses sens.

She's come to snatch him from my deadly blow.
O God, how terribly she looks at me.
What fiends and snakes does she draw after her?
Daughters of Hades, are you ready now?
Who'll meet those snakes that hiss above your heads?
Your train of followers – who'll meet that fate?
You'll take me off to everlasting night . . . ?   1640
Come then . . . I'm yours. I'm yours – for all your rage.
But no, go back, and leave it to Hermione.
She'll tear me piece by piece more viciously than you.
I bring my heart to her . . . to be devoured at last . . .

PYLADES

He's losing consciousness. The time is vital, friends.
His seizure gives us moments now to try
To save him. Our efforts will be all in vain
If, when he wakes, his madness wakens too.

PHAEDRA

1677

PRÉFACE

Voici encore une tragédie dont le sujet est pris d'Euripide. Quoique j'aie suivi une route un peu différente de celle de cet auteur pour la conduite de l'action, je n'ai pas laissé d'enrichir ma pièce de tout ce qui m'a paru le plus éclatant dans la sienne. Quand je ne lui devrais que la seule idée du caractère de Phèdre, je pourrais dire que je lui dois ce que j'ai peut-être mis de plus raisonnable sur le théâtre. Je ne suis point étonné que ce caractère ait eu un succès si heureux du temps d'Euripide, et qu'il ait encore si bien réussi dans notre siècle, puisqu'il a toutes les qualités qu'Aristote demande dans le héros de la tragédie, et qui sont propres à exciter la compassion et la terreur. En effet, Phèdre n'est ni tout à fait coupable, ni tout à fait innocente. Elle est engagée par sa destinée, et par la colère des dieux dans une passion illégitime dont elle a horreur toute la première. Elle fait tous ses efforts pour la surmonter. Elle aime mieux se laisser mourir que de la déclarer à personne. Et, lorsqu'elle est forcée de la découvrir, elle en parle avec une confusion qui fait bien voir que son crime est plutôt une punition des dieux qu'un mouvement de sa volonté.

J'ai même pris soin de la rendre un peu moins odieuse qu'elle n'est dans les tragédies des Anciens, où elle se résout d'elle-même à accuser Hippolyte. J'ai cru que la calomnie avait quelque chose de trop bas et de trop noir pour la mettre dans la bouche d'une princesse, qui a d'ailleurs des sentiments si nobles et si vertueux. Cette bassesse m'a paru plus convenable à une nourrice, qui pouvait avoir des inclinations plus serviles, et qui néanmoins n'entreprend cette fausse accusation que pour sauver la vie et l'honneur de sa maîtresse. Phèdre n'y donne les mains que parce qu'elle est dans une agitation d'esprit qui la met hors d'elle-même, et elle vient un moment après dans le dessein de justifier l'innocence, et de déclarer la vérité.

PREFACE

Here is another tragedy whose subject is taken from Euripides. Although I have followed a slightly different path from him in terms of plot, I have taken every opportunity to enhance my play with everything that seemed to me most striking in his. Even if I owed him only the idea of Phaedra's character, I could claim that I owed him what is probably the most persuasive play I have written. I am not surprised that this character should have had such a great success in Euripides' day, and that it should still be so successful in our time, since it has all the qualities that Aristotle requires in a tragic hero – that is, the ability to arouse pity and terror. Phaedra is, in fact, neither entirely guilty nor totally innocent. She is involved, through her fate and through the anger of the gods, in a criminal passion, at which she is the very first to be horrified. She makes every effort to overcome it. She would rather die than admit it to anyone. And when she is forced to reveal it, she speaks with such confusion that it is clear her crime is a punishment of the gods, rather than an impulse of her own will.

I have even taken pains to make her rather less odious than in classical tragedies, where she decides on her own to accuse Hippolytus. I felt that that slander was something too low and too foul to be put in the mouth of a princess, whose feelings were otherwise so noble and virtuous. Such lowness seemed to me more appropriate to a nurse, who might have a more slavish attitude, and who would make this false accusation only to save the life and honour of her mistress. Phaedra agrees to it only because she is so disturbed as to be beside herself. She re-appears a moment later to clear the accused and declare the truth.

In Euripides and Seneca, Hippolytus is accused of having actually raped his stepmother: *vim corpus tulit* [he took her by force]. But

Hippolyte est accusé, dans Euripide et dans Sénèque, d'avoir en effet violé sa belle-mère : *vim corpus tulit*. Mais il n'est ici accusé que d'en avoir eu le dessein. J'ai voulu épargner à Thésée une confusion qui l'aurait pu rendre moins agréable aux spectateurs.

Pour ce qui est du personnage d'Hippolyte, j'avais remarqué dans les Anciens qu'on reprochait à Euripide de l'avoir représenté comme un philosophe exempt de toute imperfection. Ce qui faisait que la mort de ce jeune prince causait beaucoup plus d'indignation que de pitié. J'ai cru lui devoir donner quelque faiblesse qui le rendrait un peu coupable envers son père, sans pourtant lui rien ôter de cette grandeur d'âme avec laquelle il épargne l'honneur de Phèdre, et se laisse opprimer sans l'accuser. J'appelle faiblesse la passion qu'il ressent malgré lui pour Aricie, qui est la fille et la sœur des ennemis mortels de son père.

Cette Aricie n'est point un personnage de mon invention. Virgile dit qu'Hippolyte l'épousa et en eut un fils après qu'Esculape l'eut ressuscité. Et j'ai lu encore dans quelques auteurs qu'Hippolyte avait épousé et emmené en Italie une jeune Athénienne de grande naissance, qui s'appelait Aricie, et qui avait donné son nom à une petite ville d'Italie.

Je rapporte ces autorités, parce que je me suis très scrupuleusement attaché à suivre la fable. J'ai même suivi l'histoire de Thésée telle qu'elle est dans Plutarque.

C'est dans cet historien que j'ai trouvé que ce qui avait donné occasion de croire que Thésée fût descendu dans les enfers pour enlever Proserpine, était un voyage que ce prince avait fait en Épire vers la source de l'Achéron, chez un roi dont Pirithous voulait enlever la femme, et qui arreta Thésée prisonnier après avoir fait mourir Pirithous. Ainsi j'ai tâché de conserver la vraisemblance de l'histoire, sans rien perdre des ornements de la fable qui fournit extrêmement à la poésie. Et le bruit de la mort de Thésée, fondé sur ce voyage fabuleux, donne lieu à Phèdre de faire une déclaration d'amour, qui devient une des principales causes de son malheur, et qu'elle n'aurait jamais osé faire tant qu'elle aurait cru que son mari était vivant.

Au reste, je n'ose encore assurer que cette pièce soit en effet la meilleure de mes tragédies. Je laisse aux lecteurs et au temps à décider de son véritable prix. Ce que je puis assurer, ç'est que je n'en ai point fait où la vertu soit plus mise en jour que dans celle-ci.

here he is accused only of having had the intention. I wanted to spare Theseus a mental turmoil which might have made him less sympathetic to the audience.

As far as Hippolytus' character is concerned, I had noticed that in classical times Euripides was criticised for having portrayed him as a philosopher free of all imperfection. The young prince's death, consequently, generated indignation much more than pity. I felt I should give him some weakness that would make him slightly guilty towards his father, without however detracting in any way from that largeness of spirit which lets him spare Phaedra's honour, and be attacked without accusing her. What I call weakness is the passion he feels, despite himself, for Aricia, who is the daughter and sister of his father's deadly enemies.

Aricia is not a character I have invented. Virgil says that Hippolytus married her, and had a son by her, after Aesculapius had brought him back to life. I have also read in some writers that Hippolytus married and took to Italy a young Athenian girl of noble birth, who was called Aricia, and who gave her name to a small Italian town.

I cite these authorities because I have been scrupulous in seeking to follow the classical account. I have even followed the story of Theseus as related in Plutarch.

It was in this historian that I found what gave rise to the belief that Theseus went down to the underworld to abduct Proserpine. It was a journey undertaken in Epirus by the prince towards the source of Acheron, to visit a king whose wife Pirithous wanted to abduct. Having put Pirithous to death, the king kept Theseus prisoner. In this way, I have tried to retain the credibility of the story without losing any of the decorations of the legend, which provide a rich source of poetry. The rumour of Theseus' death, generated by this legendary journey, gives Phaedra the opportunity to confess a love that becomes one of the main reasons for her downfall, and that she would never have dared to speak had she believed her husband was still alive.

For the rest, I do not as yet dare to assert that this play is indeed the best of my tragedies. I leave it to readers and time to decide its true worth. What I can affirm is that in no other play of mine is goodness so clearly shown. The slightest faults are severely punished. The mere thought of crime is regarded with as much horror

Les moindres fautes y sont sévèrement punies. La seule pensée du crime y est regardée avec autant d'horreur que le crime même. Les faiblesses de l'amour y passent pour de vraies faiblesses. Les passions n'y sont présentées aux yeux que pour montrer tout le désordre dont elles sont cause : et le vice y est peint partout avec des couleurs qui en font connaître et haïr la difformité. C'est là proprement le but que tout homme qui travaille pour le public doit se proposer. Et c'est ce que les premiers poètes tragiques avaient en vue sur toute chose. Leur théâtre était une école où la vertu n'était pas moins bien enseignée que dans les écoles des philosophes. Aussi Aristote a bien voulu donner des règles du poème dramatique; et Socrate, le plus sage des philosophes, ne dédaignait pas de mettre la main aux tragédies d'Euripide. Il serait à souhaiter que nos ouvrages fussent aussi solides et aussi pleins d'utiles instructions que ceux de ces poètes. Ce serait peut-être un moyen de réconcilier la tragédie avec quantité de personnes célèbres par leur piété et par leur doctrine, qui l'ont condamnée dans ces derniers temps et qui en jugeraient sans doute plus favorablement, si les auteurs songeaient autant à instruire leurs spectateurs qu'à les divertir, et s'ils suivaient en cela la véritable intention de la tragédie.

as the crime itself. Weaknesses caused by love are treated as genuine weaknesses. Passions are portrayed only to show all the turmoil they cause. Vice is depicted throughout in colours that bring out its ugliness and hatefulness. That is really the aim which everybody working for the public ought to have in mind. It is what the earliest tragedians aimed for above all else. Their theatre was a school where goodness was taught no less well than in the schools of the philosophers. Aristotle was happy to lay down rules for drama, and Socrates, the wisest of philosophers, was not above contributing to Euripides' tragedies. One could wish that modern works were as sound and full of useful teaching as those of these poets. That would perhaps be a way of reconciling to tragedy many people famous for their piety and doctrines, who have recently condemned it. They would no doubt judge it more favourably if writers thought as much about teaching their audiences as amusing them, and thereby followed the real purpose of tragedy.

ACTEURS

THÉSÉE, fils d'Égée, roi d'Athènes

PHÈDRE, femme de Thésée, fille de Minos et de Pasiphaé

HIPPOLYTE, fils de Thésée, et d'Antiope reine des Amazones

ARICIE, princesse du sang royal d'Athènes

ŒNONE, nourrice et confidente de Phèdre

THÉRAMÈNE, gouverneur d'Hippolyte

ISMÈNE, confidente d'Aricie

PANOPE, femme de la suite de Phèdre

Gardes

La scène est à Trézène, ville du Péloponnèse

CAST

THESEUS, son of Aegeus, king of Athens

PHAEDRA, Theseus' wife, daughter of Minos and Pasiphaë

HIPPOLYTUS, son of Theseus and Antiope, queen of the Amazons

ARICIA, princess of the blood royal of Athens

THERAMENES, Hippolytus' tutor

OENONE, Phaedra's nurse and confidante

PANOPE, one of Phaedra's waiting-women

The scene is set in Troezen, a town in the Peloponnese

PHÈDRE

ACTE 1 SCÈNE 1

Hippolyte, Théramène

HIPPOLYTE

Le dessein en est pris, je pars, cher Théramène,
Et quitte le séjour de l'aimable Trézène.
Dans le doute mortel dont je suis agité,
Je commence à rougir de mon oisiveté.
Depuis plus de six mois éloigné de mon père,
J'ignore le destin d'une tête si chère;
J'ignore jusqu'aux lieux qui le peuvent cacher.

THÉRAMÈNE

Et dans quels lieux, Seigneur, l'allez-vous donc chercher?
Déjà pour satisfaire à votre juste crainte,
J'ai couru les deux mers que sépare Corinthe.   10
J'ai demandé Thésée aux peuples de ces bords
Où l'on voit l'Achéron se perdre chez les morts.
J'ai visité l'Élide, et laissant le Ténare,
Passé jusqu'à la mer qui vit tomber Icare.
Sur quel espoir nouveau, dans quels heureux climats
Croyez-vous découvrir la trace de ses pas?
Qui sait même, qui sait si le roi votre père
Veut que de son absence on sache le mystère?
Et si lorsque avec vous nous tremblons pour ses jours,
Tranquille, et nous cachant de nouvelles amours,   20
Ce héros n'attend point qu'une amante abusée . . .

HIPPOLYTE

Cher Théramène, arrête, et respecte Thésée.
De ses jeunes erreurs désormais revenu,
Par un indigne obstacle il n'est point retenu;
Et fixant de ses vœux l'inconstance fatale,
Phèdre depuis longtemps ne craint plus de rivale.
Enfin en le cherchant je suivrai mon devoir,
Et je fuirai ces lieux que je n'ose plus voir.

PHAEDRA

ACT 1 SCENE 1

Hippolytus, Theramenes

HIPPOLYTUS

So, it's decided then. Theramenes,
I have to end this pleasant stay in Troezen.
I'm haunted by my fear about the king.
I am ashamed at all my idleness.
My father has been gone six months or more;
He's dear to me, and yet I do not know his fate
Nor where in all the world he might be now.

THERAMENES

Where would you go, my lord, to look for him?
I've tried to ease your fear. It's merited.
I've scoured the seas that Corinth cuts in two,   10
Asked after Theseus along those shores
Where Acheron flows downwards to the dead.
I've been to Elis, passed by Tenaros,
And sailed the seas where Icarus once fell.
What fresh new hope makes you believe you'll find
Some trace of him in more congenial spots?
Indeed, who knows if the king your father
Wishes the secret for his absence to be known.
While we here worry for his life, might he
Not be at ease, hiding his latest love away,   20
Just waiting to seduce a girl . . .

HIPPOLYTUS

Enough, Theramenes. You owe respect.
He's put the errors of his youth aside.
Those shameful faults no longer weigh him down.
Phaedra has curbed the wanderings of his heart.
She has no fears of any rivals now.
I am in duty bound to look for him.
I have to leave here now. I dare not stay.

THÉRAMÈNE

Hé depuis quand, Seigneur, craignez-vous la présence
De ces paisibles lieux, si chers à votre enfance,   30
Et dont je vous ai vu préférer le séjour
Au tumulte pompeux d'Athène et de la cour?
Quel péril, ou plutôt quel chagrin vous en chasse?

HIPPOLYTE

Cet heureux temps n'est plus. Tout a changé de face
Depuis que sur ces bords les dieux ont envoyé
La fille de Minos et de Pasiphaé.

THÉRAMÈNE

J'entends. De vos douleurs la cause m'est connue,
Phèdre ici vous chagrine, et blesse votre vue.
Dangereuse marâtre, à peine elle vous vit,
Que votre exil d'abord signala son crédit.   40
Mais sa haine sur vous autrefois attachée,
Ou s'est évanouie, ou s'est bien relâchée.
Et d'ailleurs, quels périls vous peut faire courir
Une femme mourante, et qui cherche à mourir?
Phèdre atteinte d'un mal qu'elle s'obstine à taire,
Lasse enfin d'elle-meme, et du jour qui l'éclaire,
Peut-elle contre vous former quelques desseins?

HIPPOLYTE

Sa vaine inimitié n'est pas ce que je crains.
Hippolyte en partant fuit une autre ennemie.
Je fuis, je l'avouerai, cette jeune Aricie,   50
Reste d'un sang fatal conjuré contre nous.

THÉRAMÈNE

Quoi! vous-même, Seigneur, la persécutez-vous?
Jamais l'aimable sœur des cruels Pallantides
Trempa-t-elle aux complots de ses frères perfides?
Et devez-vous haïr ses innocents appas?

HIPPOLYTE

Si je la haïssais, je ne la fuirais pas.

THÉRAMÈNE

Seigneur, m'est-il permis d'expliquer votre fuite?

THERAMENES

But when did you begin, my lord, to fear
This peaceful place? You loved it as a boy.   30
You've liked it better here, I know, than all
The pomp and noise of Athens and the court.
What danger drives you out – or is it grief?

HIPPOLYTUS

Those days of joy have gone. All is now changed
Since the great gods sent Phaedra to these shores,
The child of Minos and Pasiphaë.

THERAMENES

I know. I know the reason for your hurt.
The sight of Phaedra here distresses you.
She was a dangerous stepmother. She'd scarcely seen
Than banished you. That marked her influence.   40
But all the hate that once was fixed on you
Has vanished now, at least has grown much less.
Besides, what threat from her could make you leave,
A dying woman, reaching out to die?
Some sickness has seized hold – she will not say –
She's weary of herself and of the light
Of day. How could she plan to do you harm?

HIPPOLYTUS

It's not her vain hostility I fear.
I go to keep a different enemy away.
Let me confess – I run from young Aricia,   50
Last of that deadly blood-line sworn our foe.

THERAMENES

Oh no, my lord, would you torment her too?
Pallas's sons were cruel, but she was kind.
She never knew about her brothers' plots.
How could you hate the grace of innocence?

HIPPOLYTUS

If I felt hate, I should not run from her.

THERAMENES

Then could I guess the reason for your flight?

Pourriez-vous n'être plus ce superbe Hippolyte,
Implacable ennemi des amoureuses lois,
Et d'un joug que Thésée a subi tant de fois? 60
Vénus, par votre orgueil si longtemps méprisée,
Voudrait-elle à la fin justifier Thésée?
Et vous mettant au rang du reste des mortels,
Vous a-t-elle forcé d'encenser ses autels?
Aimeriez-vous, Seigneur?

HIPPOLYTE   Ami, qu'oses-tu dire?
Toi qui connais mon cœur depuis que je respire,
Des sentiments d'un cœur si fier, si dédaigneux,
Peux-tu me demander le désaveu honteux?
C'est peu qu'avec son lait une mère amazone
M'ait fait sucer encor cet orgueil qui t'étonne. 70
Dans un âge plus mûr moi-même parvenu,
Je me suis applaudi, quand je me suis connu.
Attaché près de moi par un zèle sincère,
Tu me contais alors l'histoire de mon père.
Tu sais combien mon âme attentive à ta voix
S'échauffait aux récits de ses nobles exploits,
Quand tu me dépeignais ce héros intrépide
Consolant les mortels de l'absence d'Alcide,
Les monstres étouffés, et les brigands punis,
Procruste, Cercyon, et Scirron, et Sinnis, 80
Et les os dispersés du géant d'Épidaure,
Et la Crète fumant du sang du Minotaure.
Mais quand tu récitais des faits moins glorieux,
Sa foi partout offerte, et reçue en cent lieux,
Hélène à ses parents dans Sparte dérobée,
Salamine témoin des pleurs de Péribée,
Tant d'autres, dont les noms lui sont même échappés,
Trop crédules esprits que sa flamme a trompés;
Ariane aux rochers contant ses injustices,
Phèdre enlevée enfin sous de meilleurs auspices; 90
Tu sais comme à regret écoutant ce discours,
Je te pressais souvent d'en abréger le cours.
Heureux! si j'avais pu ravir à la mémoire
Cette indigne moitié d'une si belle histoire!

Might you no longer be the proud Hippolytus,
Relentless enemy of all love's laws
And bonds that Theseus bore so many times?   60
You've scorned the power of Venus for so long.
Could she have vindicated him at last,
And made you join the rest of humankind,
Forced you to worship at her shrine?
Might you not be in love?

HIPPOLYTUS   Take care, old friend.
You've known my feelings since I first drew breath.
Don't ask me to deny in shame the pride
And high resolve that's in my heart.
My mother was an Amazon. Her milk
Gave me this vaunted pride. Yet what of that . . .   70
When I grew up, became a man, I too
Endorsed it as my own true self.
Your faithful friendship bound you close to me.
You'd tell me of my father's history.
You knew how much I'd hang upon your words,
Would glow at stories of his marvellous deeds.
You drew for me a Theseus without fear –
Consoling humans for the loss of Hercules –
Who strangled monsters, punished those who'd robbed –
Procrustes, Sciron, Sinis, Cercyon,   80
The bones he scattered of the Epidaurus giant,
And all Crete reeking with the Minotaur's blood.
But other things you told me of – less glorious –
His honour pledged, believed so many times:
Helen in Sparta stolen from her home,
And Salamis, where Periboea wept.
So many more, whose names he then forgot,
Too credulous by far, all duped by him.
Ariadne left crying to the rocks,
And Phaedra kidnapped, though for better ends.   90
You know I heard these tales with pain.
I often urged you cut them short,
Happy to blot out from my memory
The vilest half of such a history.

Et moi-même à mon tour je me verrais lié?
Et les dieux jusque-là m'auraient humilié?
Dans mes lâches soupirs d'autant plus méprisable,
Qu'un long amas d'honneurs rend Thésée excusable,
Qu'aucuns monstres par moi domptés jusqu'aujourd'hui
Ne m'ont acquis le droit de faillir comme lui.   100
Quand même ma fierté pourrait s'être adoucie,
Aurais-je pour vainqueur dû choisir Aricie?
Ne souviendrait-il plus à mes sens égarés,
De l'obstacle éternel qui nous a séparés?
Mon père la réprouve et par des lois sévères
Il défend de donner des neveux à ses frères;
D'une tige coupable il craint un rejeton:
Il veut avec leur sœur ensevelir leur nom,
Et que jusqu'au tombeau soumise à sa tutelle,
Jamais les feux d'hymen ne s'allument pour elle.   110
Dois-je épouser ses droits contre un père irrité?
Donnerai-je l'exemple à la témérité?
Et dans un fol amour ma jeunesse embarquée . . .

THÉRAMÈNE

Ah, Seigneur! si votre heure est une fois marquée,
Le ciel de nos raisons ne sait point s'informer.
Thésée ouvre vos yeux en voulant les fermer,
Et sa haine irritant une flamme rebelle,
Prête à son ennemie une grâce nouvelle.
Enfin d'un chaste amour pourquoi vous effrayer?
S'il a quelque douceur, n'osez-vous l'essayer?   120
En croirez-vous toujours un farouche scrupule?
Craint-on de s'égarer sur les traces d'Hercule?
Quels courages Vénus n'a-t-elle pas domptés!
Vous-même où seriez-vous, vous qui la combattez,
Si toujours Antiope à ses lois opposée
D'une pudique ardeur n'eût brûlé pour Thésée?
Mais que sert d'affecter un superbe discours?
Avouez-le, tout change. Et depuis quelques jours,
On vous voit moins souvent, orgueilleux et sauvage,
Tantôt faire voler un char sur le rivage,   130
Tantôt savant dans l'art par Neptune inventé,

So is it now my turn to be caught up?
The gods would humble me to that extent?
My cowardly cries would bring far more contempt.
Crowded with honours, Theseus is excused.
But no wild monster ever tamed by me   100
Has given me the right to fail like him.
Even suppose my pride were to be quelled,
Would I choose that Aricia should master me?
My wandering senses scarcely could forget
The everlasting obstacle between us both.
My father disapproves of her. Strict laws forbid
Her bearing children to her brothers' line.
He fears the offspring from so false a stock.
He wants to kill their name with hers.
She is his ward till death. He has decreed
The wedding torch shall never light for her.   110
Should I take up her cause, incense the king
And give a lesson in foolhardiness?
I'd launch my youth on reckless love . . . ?

THERAMENES

Ah but my lord – once fate has stamped our hour,
Heaven no longer cares to know our reasonings.
Theseus had hoped to close your eyes, but opened them.
His hate has fanned a rebel fire,
Given his enemy a fresh, new grace.
Besides, why should you fear so chaste a love?
If there is sweetness, why not savour it?   120
You still believe in being scrupulous?
Why fear to follow in the steps of Hercules?
What heart of steel has Venus not made tame?
You fight her; where though would you be yourself
Had not Antiope, who fought her laws,
Still burned for Theseus with a shameless lust?
But what is served by lofty utterance?
Admit it, all is changed. For some days now,
You've been less often seen, in such wild pride,
Racing a chariot at the water's edge,   130
Or showing all your skills in Neptune's art,

Rendre docile au frein un coursier indompté.
Les forêts de nos cris moins souvent retentissent.
Chargés d'un feu secret, vos yeux s'appesantissent.
Il n'en faut point douter, vous aimez, vous brûlez;
Vous périssez d'un mal que vous dissimulez.
La charmante Aricie a-t-elle su vous plaire?

HIPPOLYTE

Théramène, je pars, et vais chercher mon père.

THÉRAMÈNE

Ne verrez-vous point Phèdre avant que de partir,
Seigneur?

HIPPOLYTE   C'est mon dessein, tu peux l'en avertir.   140
Voyons-la, puisque ainsi mon devoir me l'ordonne.
Mais quel nouveau malheur trouble sa chère Œnone?

SCÈNE 2

Hippolyte, Œnone

ŒNONE

Hélas, Seigneur! quel trouble au mien peut être égal?
La reine touche presque à son terme fatal.
En vain à l'observer jour et nuit je m'attache.
Elle meurt dans mes bras d'un mal qu'elle me cache.
Un désordre éternel règne dans son esprit.
Son chagrin inquiet l'arrache de son lit.
Elle veut voir le jour; et sa douleur profonde
M'ordonne toutefois d'écarter tout le monde . . .   150
Elle vient.

HIPPOLYTE   Il suffit, je la laisse en ces lieux
Et ne lui montre point un visage odieux.

Curbing an untamed stallion to the bit.
The woods halloo less often with our cries.
Your eyes are heavy, full of secret fire.
There is no doubt, Love's burning you.
You're suffering from a pain you want to hide.
Has fair Aricia enchanted you?

HIPPOLYTUS

Theramenes, I go to find the king.

THERAMENES

Will you not see Phaedra before you leave,
My lord?

HIPPOLYTUS I mean to, yes. Let her be told.   140
I'll see her soon, since duty says I must.
But there's Oenone. What latest sadness . . . ?

[Oenone enters

SCENE 2

Hippolytus, Oenone, Theramenes

OENONE

My lord, what grief can equal this? The queen
Is all but touching now her hour of death.
I've stayed and watched her day and night in vain;
She's dying in my arms from sickness she won't name.
Some constant turmoil riots in her mind;
A restless sorrow tears her from her bed.
She yearns to see the light. But pain racks her.
She orders me to keep out everyone . . .   150
But here she comes . . .

HIPPOLYTUS   Enough, I must leave now,
So that she does not see a face she loathes.

[*Hippolytus and Theramenes leave. Phaedra enters*

SCÈNE 3

Phèdre, Œnone

PHÈDRE

N'allons point plus avant. Demeurons, chère Œnone.
Je ne me soutiens plus, ma force m'abandonne.
Mes yeux sont éblouis du jour que je revoi,
Et mes genoux tremblants se dérobent sous moi.
Hélas!

                                   [elle s'assied

ŒNONE   Dieux tout-puissants, que nos pleurs vous apaisent!

PHÈDRE

Que ces vains ornements, que ces voiles me pèsent!
Quelle importune main, en formant tous ces nœuds,
A pris soin sur mon front d'assembler mes cheveux?
Tout m'afflige et me nuit, et conspire à me nuire.   160

ŒNONE

Comme on voit tous ses vœux l'un l'autre se détruire!
Vous-même condamnant vos injustes desseins,
Tantôt à vous parer vous excitiez nos mains.
Vous-même rappelant votre force première,
Vous vouliez vous montrer et revoir la lumière;
Vous la voyez, Madame, et prête à vous cacher,
Vous haïssez le jour que vous veniez chercher?

PHÈDRE

Noble et brillant auteur d'une triste famille,
Toi, dont ma mère osait se vanter d'être fille,
Qui peut-être rougis du trouble où tu me vois,   170
Soleil, je te viens voir pour la dernière fois.

ŒNONE

Quoi! vous ne perdrez point cette cruelle envie?
Vous verrai-je toujours, renonçant à la vie,
Faire de votre mort les funestes apprêts?

PHÈDRE

Dieux! que ne suis-je assise à l'ombre des forêts!

SCENE 3

Phaedra, Oenone

PHAEDRA

    Let's not go further, Oenone. Let's rest.
    I can't stand up. I've lost my strength.
    My eyes are dazzled blind by all this light.
    My legs are trembling . . . give way under me.   *[she sits*

OENONE

    May our tears soften you, all-powerful gods.

PHAEDRA

    These silly ornaments, these veils – the weight of them.
    Whose meddling hand has tied up all these knots,
    Arranged my hair so carefully across my brow?   160
    All things distress and hurt. They plot to hurt.

OENONE

    [aside] Her every wish conflicts against the rest.
    [to Phaedra] But you yourself just said your plan was wrong.
    Just now, you urged me decorate your hair.
    You summoned all your old strength up
    And wanted to be shown the light again.
    You see it here; and now you want to hide.
    You hate the daylight that you came to find.

PHAEDRA

    You dazzling founder of this wretched family,
    My mother dared to boast she was your child.   170
    Perhaps you blush to see me so distressed.
    Sun-god, I see you for the final time.

OENONE

    Won't you give up this desperate desire?
    Am I to see you giving up on life,
    Preparing for a mournful, tragic death?

PHAEDRA

    I should be sitting in the forests' shade.

Quand pourrai-je au travers d'une noble poussière,
Suivre de l'œil un char fuyant dans la carrière?

ŒNONE

Quoi, Madame!

PHÈDRE   Insensée, où suis-je? Et qu'ai-je dit?
Où laisse-je égarer mes vœux et mon esprit?   180
Je l'ai perdu. Les dieux m'en ont ravi l'usage.
Œnone, la rougeur me couvre le visage,
Je te laisse trop voir mes honteuses douleurs,
Et mes yeux malgré moi se remplissent de pleurs.

ŒNONE

Ah! s'il vous faut rougir, rougissez d'un silence
Qui de vos maux encore aigrit la violence.
Rebelle à tous nos soins, sourde à tous nos discours,
Voulez-vous sans pitié laisser finir vos jours?
Quelle fureur les borne au milieu de leur course?
Quel charme ou quel poison en a tari la source?   190
Les ombres par trois fois ont obscurci les cieux,
Depuis que le sommeil n'est entré dans vos yeux;
Et le jour a trois fois chassé la nuit obscure,
Depuis que votre corps languit sans nourriture.
A quel affreux dessein vous laissez-vous tenter?
De quel droit sur vous-même osez-vous attenter?
Vous offensez les dieux auteurs de votre vie.
Vous trahissez l'époux à qui la foi vous lie,
Vous trahissez enfin vos enfants malheureux,
Que vous précipitez sous un joug rigoureux.   200
Songez qu'un même jour leur ravira leur mère,
Et rendra l'espérance au fils de l'étrangère,
A ce fier ennemi de vous, de votre sang,
Ce fils qu'une Amazone a porté dans son flanc,
Cet Hippolyte . . .

PHÈDRE   Ah dieux!

ŒNONE   Ce reproche vous touche.

PHÈDRE

Malheureuse, quel nom est sorti de ta bouche?

When will my eyes see through these swirls of dust
And catch a racing chariot in its course . . . ?

OENONE
My lady?

PHAEDRA   I'm mad. Where am I? What have I said?
My reason, my desires - where did they go?   180
They're lost. The gods have taken them away.
My face is flushed, Oenone. So, I've let
You see my shameful grief too much.
I cannot help . . . my eyes fill up with tears.

OENONE
If you must blush, blush for your silence then.
It merely fires the fury of your pain.
You thrust our care aside, you're deaf to all we say –
So you will end your life without concern . . . ?
What madness cuts it short in middle age?
What spell – what poison – has dried up its source?   190
The shades of night have blacked the skies three times
Since your eyes last were overcome by sleep.
The day has driven dark night out three times,
But still your body faints for lack of food.
What terrifying plan tempts you so now?
What right have you to try to kill yourself?
You wrong the gods, the source of all your life,
Betray your husband, whom you wed in faith,
Not least betray your children into grief.
You will force them to such cruel slavery.   200
Remember, the very day their mother dies
Will give fresh hope to the outsider's son,
To that fierce enemy of yours, your blood,
The boy an Amazon bore in her womb,
Hippolytus . . .

PHAEDRA   No, god . . .

OENONE   I make my point . . . ?

PHAEDRA
You wretched woman! What name did you speak?

ŒNONE

Eh bien, votre colère éclate avec raison.
J'aime à vous voir frémir à ce funeste nom.
Vivez donc. Que l'amour, le devoir, vous excite.
Vivez, ne souffrez pas que le fils d'une Scythe,   210
Accablant vos enfants d'un empire odieux,
Commande au plus beau sang de la Grèce et des dieux.
Mais ne différez point, chaque moment vous tue.
Réparez promptement votre force abattue,
Tandis que de vos jours prêts à se consumer,
Le flambeau dure encore, et peut se rallumer

PHÈDRE

J'en ai trop prolongé la coupable durée.

ŒNONE

Quoi! de quelques remords êtes-vous déchirée?
Quel crime a pu produire un trouble si pressant?
Vos mains n'ont point trempé dans le sang innocent?   220

PHÈDRE

Grâces au ciel, mes mains ne sont point criminelles.
Plût aux dieux que mon cœur fût innocent comme elles!

ŒNONE

Et quel affreux projet avez-vous enfanté,
Dont votre cœur encor doive être épouvanté?

PHÈDRE

Je t'en ai dit assez. Épargne-moi le reste.
Je meurs, pour ne point faire un aveu si funeste.

ŒNONE

Mourez donc, et gardez un silence inhumain.
Mais pour fermer vos yeux cherchez une autre main.
Quoiqu'il vous reste à peine une faible lumière,
Mon âme chez les morts descendra la première;   230
Mille chemins ouverts y conduisent toujours,
Et ma juste douleur choisira les plus courts.
Cruelle, quand ma foi vous a-t-elle déçue?
Songez-vous qu'en naissant mes bras vous ont reçue?

OENONE

At last! You burst with anger – justly so.
It's good to see you shudder at his name.
So, live. Let love and duty urge you on.
Live. Don't let a Scythian woman's son   210
Chain up your children in vile slavery
And rule the finest blood of Greece and all
The gods. But don't delay. Each moment kills.
Gather the strength you've lost again at once.
The fire of life is nearly dead. Yet it
Still flickers and can burst alive in flame.

PHAEDRA

I have prolonged my guilty life too much . . .

OENONE

What is this guilt that's tearing you apart?
What crime could ever bring so sharp a pain?
You've never stained your hands with guiltless blood.   220

PHAEDRA

I thank the gods my hands have done no wrong.
Would god my heart were innocent as them.

OENONE

So what vile plan have you conceived
That your whole heart remains still terrified?

PHAEDRA

I've said enough. Spare me the rest.
I'm dying . . . the dreadful secret's safe with me.

OENONE

Then die. Stay silent. It's not natural.
But look for someone else to close your eyes.
The light just flickers for you now, and yet
My soul will go down first to meet the dead.   230
A thousand open roads can take us there.
My grief will choose the shortest way. You are
So cruel. When did I ever break your trust?
I took you in my arms when you were born.

Mon pays, mes enfants, pour vous j'ai tout quitté.
Réserviez-vous ce prix à ma fidélité?

PHÈDRE

Quel fruit espères-tu de tant de violence?
Tu frémiras d'horreur si je romps le silence.

ŒNONE

Et que me direz-vous, qui ne cède, grands dieux!
A l'horreur de vous voir expirer à mes yeux?   240

PHÈDRE

Quand tu sauras mon crime, et le sort qui m'accable,
Je n'en mourrai pas moins, j'en mourrai plus coupable.

ŒNONE

Madame, au nom des pleurs que pour vous j'ai versés,
Par vos faibles genoux que je tiens embrassés,
Délivrez mon esprit de ce funeste doute.

PHÈDRE

Tu le veux. Lève-toi.

ŒNONE   Parlez. Je vous écoute.

PHÈDRE

Ciel! que lui vais-je dire? Et par où commencer?

ŒNONE

Par de vaines frayeurs cessez de m'offenser.

PHÈDRE

O haine de Vénus! ô fatale colère!
Dans quels égarements l'amour jeta ma mère!   250

ŒNONE

Oublions-les, Madame. Et qu'à tout l'avenir
Un silence éternel cache ce souvenir.

PHÈDRE

Ariane, ma sœur, de quel amour blessée,
Vous mourûtes aux bords où vous fûtes laissée?

I left my home, my children – all for you.
Is this the prize you give for faithfulness?

PHAEDRA

Why all this rage? What do you hope to gain?
If I spoke out, you'd shudder in such dread . . .

OENONE

What could you say, great gods, that could be worse   240
Than see you die before my eyes?

PHAEDRA

But if you knew my crime – this hopeless fate –
I should still die, but yet more full of guilt.

OENONE

By all the tears that I have wept for you,
These helpless limbs I hold so close,
You must relieve me from this awful doubt.

PHAEDRA

As you wish. Stand up.

OENONE   Tell me. I'm listening.

PHAEDRA

What can I say to her? Where to begin?

OENONE

Stop terrifying me so needlessly.

PHAEDRA

How Venus hates . . . that deadly rage she has . . .
The frenzy that she threw my mother in . . .   250

OENONE

You must forget. Until the end of time
Eternal silence hide that memory.

PHAEDRA

My sister Ariadne – love wounded you –
They left you dying on an alien shore.

OENONE

Que faites-vous, Madame? Et quel mortel ennui
Contre tout votre sang vous anime aujourd'hui?

PHÈDRE

Puisque Vénus le veut, de ce sang déplorable
Je péris la dernière, et la plus misérable.

OENONE

Aimez-vous?

PHÈDRE   De l'amour j'ai toutes les fureurs.

OENONE

Pour qui?

PHÈDRE   Tu vas ouïr le comble des horreurs.   260
J'aime . . . A ce nom fatal, je tremble, je frissonne.
J'aime . . .

OENONE   Qui?

PHÈDRE   Tu connais ce fils de l'Amazone,
Ce prince si longtemps par moi-même opprimé.

OENONE

Hippolyte! Grands dieux!

PHÈDRE   C'est toi qui l'as nommé.

OENONE

Juste ciel! tout mon sang dans mes veines se glace.
O désespoir! ô crime! ô déplorable race!
Voyage infortuné! rivage malheureux!
Faillait-il approcher de tes bords dangereux!

PHÈDRE

Mon mal vient de plus loin. A peine au fils d'Égée
Sous les lois de l'hymen je m'étais engagée,   270
Mon repos, mon bonheur semblait être affermi,
Athènes me montra mon superbe ennemi.
Je le vis, je rougis, je pâlis à sa vue.
Un trouble s'éleva dans mon âme éperdue;
Mes yeux ne voyaient plus, je ne pouvais parler,

OENONE

What else, my lady? What deadly grieving
Drives you on still to rage against your race?

PHAEDRA

Venus will have it so, and so I'll die,
The last, most wretched member of this tainted line.

OENONE

Are you in love?

PHAEDRA   Its fury burns through me.

OENONE

Who with?

PHAEDRA   Now you will hear the horror to the full.   260
I love . . . the name is death . . . I'm shuddering . . .
I love . . .

OENONE   Who?

PHAEDRA   You know the Amazon woman's son . . .
The young prince I've oppressed so long . . . ?

OENONE

Hippolytus! O god . . .

PHAEDRA   You said his name.

OENONE

Dear god, the blood is frozen is my veins.
Despair . . . the crime . . . this tainted family . . .
It was an ill-starred journey to this tragic land.
Why did I step ashore this dangerous coast?

PHAEDRA

The pain goes further back. I'd scarcely pledged
My marriage vows to Aegus' son –   270
My peace of mind, my happiness, seemed safe, secure –
Then Athens showed my wondrous enemy to me.
I saw him. Blushed. Then paled to look at him.
Some trembling surged. It blurred my mind.
My eyes no longer saw, I couldn't speak.

Je sentis tout mon corps et transir et brûler.
Je reconnus Vénus, et ses feux redoutables,
D'un sang qu'elle poursuit tourments inévitables.
Par des vœux assidus je crus les détourner,
Je lui bâtis un temple, et pris soin de l'orner.   280
De victimes moi-même à toute heure entourée,
Je cherchais dans leurs flancs ma raison égarée.
D'un incurable amour remèdes impuissants!
En vain sur les autels ma main brûlait l'encens.
Quand ma bouche implorait le nom de la déesse,
J'adorais Hippolyte, et le voyant sans cesse,
Même au pied des autels que je faisais fumer,
J'offrais tout à ce dieu, que je n'osais nommer.
Je l'évitais partout. O comble de misère!
Mes yeux le retrouvaient dans les traits de son père.   290
Contre moi-même enfin j'osai me révolter.
J'excitai mon courage à le persécuter.
Pour bannir l'ennemi dont j'étais idolâtre,
J'affectai les chagrins d'une injuste marâtre,
Je pressai son exil, et mes cris éternels
L'arrachèrent du sein et des bras paternels.
Je respirais, Œnone; et depuis son absence,
Mes jours moins agités coulaient dans l'innocence.
Soumise à mon époux, et cachant mes ennuis,
De son fatal hymen je cultivais les fruits.   300
Vaines précautions! cruelle destinée!
Par mon époux lui-même à Trézène amenée
J'ai revu l'ennemi que j'avais éloigné.
Ma blessure trop vive aussitôt a saigné.
Ce n'est plus une ardeur dans mes veines cachée;
C'est Vénus toute entière à sa proie attachée.
J'ai conçu pour mon crime une juste terreur.
J'ai pris la vie en haine, et ma flamme en horreur.
Je voulais en mourant prendre soin de ma gloire,
Et dérober au jour une flamme si noire.   310
Je n'ai pu soutenir tes larmes, tes combats,
Je t'ai tout avoué, je ne m'en repens pas,
Pourvu que de ma mort respectant les approches
Tu ne m'affliges plus par d'injustes reproches,

I felt my body freeze and burn all through.
Then I knew Venus - her appalling fires –
The fated tortures of a race she hounds.
I thought to keep her off by constant prayers;
I built a shrine to her, embellished it with care; 280
Victims were sacrificed at every hour.
I gazed at them in search of my lost mind.
They could not heal. Love was incurable.
My hands burned incense at her shrine in vain.
But even as my lips intoned her name,
I prayed Hippolytus. I saw him everywhere,
Even beside the altars that I kept alight.
I offered to a god I dare not name – the world.
I shunned him everywhere – and yet the worst of all,
I kept on seeing him in Theseus' face. 290
At last I dared to fight myself.
I worked my feelings up to torture him,
To banish now the enemy I adored.
I played the cruel stepmother full of hate.
I urged his exile. My constant pleading
Tore him from his father's arms and heart.
I breathed again, Oenone. With him now gone,
My days flowed by less troubled, free of guilt.
I hid my grief, submitted to my husband's will,
And nursed the children of his fateful bed. 300
Fate is so cruel. Precaution was in vain.
Theseus himself brought me to Troezen's shores.
And so I saw again the man I'd sent away.
The wound was opened, bled again at once,
And now no yearning hidden in the blood.
Venus with all her might clawed at her prey.
I realise the horror of my crime.
My life is cursed, my passion terrible.
I wanted by my death to save my name
And hide so dark a love from light of day. 310
I couldn't bear your tears, your battling.
I've told you everything. I don't regret it now.
Only - please spare me as I start to die.
Don't hurt me now with undeserved reproach.

Et que tes vains secours cessent de rappeler
Un reste de chaleur, tout prêt à s'exhaler.

SCÈNE 4

Phèdre, Œnone, Panope

PANOPE

Je voudrais vous cacher une triste nouvelle,
Madame. Mais il faut que je vous la révèle.
La mort vous a ravi votre invincible époux,
Et ce malheur n'est plus ignoré que de vous.   320

ŒNONE

Panope, que dis-tu?

PANOPE   Que la reine abusée
En vain demande au ciel le retour de Thésée,
Et que par des vaisseaux arrivés dans le port,
Hippolyte son fils vient d'apprendre sa mort.

PHÈDRE

Ciel!

PANOPE   Pour le choix d'un maître Athènes se partage.
Au prince votre fils l'un donne son suffrage,
Madame, et de l'État l'autre oubliant les lois,
Au fils de l'étrangère ose donner sa voix.
On dit même qu'au trône une brigue insolente
Veut placer Aricie, et le sang de Pallante.   330
J'ai cru de ce péril vous devoir avertir.
Déjà même Hippolyte est tout prêt à partir,
Et l'on craint, s'il paraît dans ce nouvel orage,
Qu'il n'entraîne après lui tout un peuple volage.

ŒNONE

Panope, c'est assez. La reine qui t'entend,
Ne négligera point cet avis important.

Your help must stop. It's all in vain. Don't fan
This last faint heat quite ready now to die.

[Panope enters

SCENE 4

Phaedra, Oenone, Panope

PANOPE

My lady? I've such grievous news for you.
I want to hide it. I must though tell you.
Theseus has been torn from you . . . by death . . .
You are the only one who does not know.   320

OENONE

What did you say, Panope? No . . .

PANOPE   The queen
Asks heaven for Theseus' return in vain.
His son Hippolytus has learned his death
From ships arriving in the port.

PHAEDRA

Dear God . . .

PANOPE   For choice of ruler Athens is now split.
One group swears loyalty to the prince your son.
The other now rejects the state's own laws
And dares support the foreign woman's son.
It's even said that devilish plots
Will crown Aricia and the Pallas line.   330
I thought it right to warn you of this threat.
Hippolytus is ready to set sail.
If he appears in this new storm, I fear
He'll draw a fickle people to his side.

OENONE

Enough, Panope. The queen has heard you.
She will not fail to heed this vital news.

[Panope leaves

SCÈNE 5

Phèdre, Œnone

ŒNONE

Madame, je cessais de vous presser de vivre.
Déjà même au tombeau je songeais à vous suivre.
Pour vous en détourner je n'avais plus de voix.
Mais ce nouveau malheur vous prescrit d'autres lois.   340
Votre fortune change et prend une autre face.
Le roi n'est plus, Madame, il faut prendre sa place.
Sa mort vous laisse un fils à qui vous vous devez,
Esclave, s'il vous perd, et roi, si vous vivez.
Sur qui dans son malheur voulez-vous qu'il s'appuie?
Ses larmes n'auront plus de main qui les essuie.
Et ses cris innocents portés jusques aux dieux,
Iront contre sa mère irriter ses aïeux.
Vivez, vous n'avez plus de reproche à vous faire.
Votre flamme devient une flamme ordinaire.   350
Thésée en expirant vient de rompre les nœuds
Qui faisaient tout le crime et l'horreur de vos feux
Hippolyte pour vous devient moins redoutable,
Et vous pouvez le voir sans vous rendre coupable.
Peut-être convaincu de votre aversion
Il va donner un chef à la sédition.
Détrompez son erreur, fléchissez son courage.
Roi de ces bords heureux, Trézène est son partage.
Mais il sait que les lois donnent à votre fils
Les superbes remparts que Minerve a bâtis.   360
Vous avez l'un et l'autre une juste ennemie.
Unissez-vous tous deux pour combattre Aricie.

PHÈDRE

Eh bien! à tes conseils je me laisse entraîner.
Vivons, si vers la vie on peut me ramener,
Et si l'amour d'un fils, en ce moment funeste,
De mes faibles esprits peut ranimer le reste.

SCENE 5

Phaedra, Oenone

OENONE

I'd ceased, my lady, urging you to live.
I'd thought to go with you down to the tomb.
I couldn't say enough to turn you back.
But this new sadness dictates different plans.   340
Your fortune's changed, takes on another face.
The king is dead, and you must take his place.
He leaves a son. Your duty lies with him,
A slave without you; if you live, a king.
On whom should he rely now in his grief?
His tears will not be dried by other hands.
His guiltless cries, borne upward to the gods,
Will bring ancestral anger down on you.
So live. You need accuse yourself no more.
Your love becomes an ordinary love.   350
Theseus has broken by his death the bonds
That made a crime, a horror, of your love.
Hippolytus is less now to be feared.
You now may see him guiltlessly.
If he believes you hate him still, he could
Perhaps become the focus of revolt.
Correct his error. Melt his courage down.
He rules these happy shores, Troezen's his share,
And yet he knows the law gives to your son
The soaring ramparts that Minerva built.   360
You two both have a common enemy:
Unite in strength against Aricia.

PHAEDRA

I'll let myself be drawn to your advice.
I'll live, if I can now be brought to life,
If love for my son in this darkened time
Can fire the dying embers of my soul.

ACTE 2 SCÈNE 1

Aricie, Ismène

ARICIE

Hippolyte demande à me voir en ce lieu?
Hippolyte me cherche, et veut me dire adieu?
Ismène, dis-tu vrai? N'es-tu point abusée?

ISMÈNE

C'est le premier effet de la mort de Thésée.　　　　　370
Préparez-vous, Madame, à voir de tous côtés
Voler vers vous les cœurs par Thésée écartés.
Aricie à la fin de son sort est maîtresse,
Et bientôt à ses pieds verra toute la Grèce.

ARICIE

Ce n'est donc point, Ismène, un bruit mal affermi?
Je cesse d'être esclave, et n'ai plus d'ennemi?

ISMÈNE

Non, Madame, les dieux ne vous sont plus contraires
Et Thésée a rejoint les mânes de vos frères.

ARICIE

Dit-on quelle aventure a terminé ses jours?

ISMÈNE

On sème de sa mort d'incroyables discours.　　　　　380
On dit que ravisseur d'une amante nouvelle
Les flots ont englouti cet époux infidèle.
On dit même, et ce bruit est partout répandu,
Qu'avec Pirithoüs aux enfers descendu
Il a vu le Cocyte et les rivages sombres,
Et s'est montré vivant aux infernales ombres;
Mais qu'il n'a pu sortir de ce triste séjour,
Et repasser les bords qu'on passe sans retour.

ARICIE

Croirai-je qu'un mortel avant sa dernière heure
Peut pénétrer des morts la profonde demeure?　　　　390
Quel charme l'attirait sur ces bords redoutés?

ACT 2 SCENE 1

Aricia, Ismene

ARICIA

Hippolytus has asked to see me here?
Hippolytus now wants to say good-bye?
Is that the truth, Ismene . . . no mistake?

ISMENE

This is the first result of Theseus' death.   370
Prepare to see flying from everywhere
The people Theseus kept away from you.
At last you are the mistress of your fate.
The whole of Greece will soon be at your feet.

ARICIA

It's not an idle rumour then?
I'm not a slave, have no more enemies?

ISMENE

The gods are not against you now, my lady.
Theseus has joined your brothers' ghosts below.

ARICIA

But do they say what exploit caused his death?

ISMENE

Fantastic tales of it are springing up.   380
Some say that while he ravished yet another girl,
The waves engulfed him in his faithlessness.
Others – and this is widely spread – say
That he's gone down to hell with Pirithous,
Seen Cocytus along its dark, sad banks,
Appeared alive before those hellish shades,
But that he cannot leave that mournful place,
Recross the river from which none returns.

ARICIA

But could a living man, before his final hour,
Go deep down to the dwellings of the dead?   390
What charm could draw him to those fearful shores?

ISMÈNE

Thésée est mort, Madame, et vous seule en doutez.
Athènes en gémit, Trézène en est instruite,
Et déjà pour son roi reconnaît Hippolyte.
Phèdre dans ce palais tremblante pour son fils,
De ses amis troublés demande les avis.

ARICIE

Et tu crois que pour moi plus humain que son père
Hippolyte rendra ma chaîne plus légère?
Qu'il plaindra mes malheurs?

ISMÈNE   Madame, je le croi.

ARICIE

L'insensible Hippolyte est-il connu de toi?   400
Sur quel frivole espoir penses-tu qu'il me plaigne,
Et respecte en moi seule un sexe qu'il dédaigne?
Tu vois depuis quel temps il évite nos pas,
Et cherche tous les lieux où nous ne sommes pas.

ISMÈNE

Je sais de ses froideurs tout ce que l'on récite.
Mais j'ai vu près de vous ce superbe Hippolyte.
Et même, en le voyant, le bruit de sa fierté
A redoublé pour lui ma curiosité.
Sa présence à ce bruit n'a point paru répondre.
Dès vos premiers regards je l'ai vu se confondre.   410
Ses yeux, qui vainement voulaient vous éviter,
Déjà pleins de langueur ne pouvaient vous quitter.
Le nom d'amant peut-être offense son courage,
Mais il en a les yeux, s'il n'en a le langage.

ARICIE

Que mon cœur, chère Ismène, écoute avidement
Un discours qui peut-être a peu de fondement!
O toi! qui me connais, te semblait-il croyable
Que le triste jouet d'un sort impitoyable,
Un cœur toujours nourri d'amertume et de pleurs,
Dût connaître l'amour, et ses folles douleurs?   420
Reste du sang d'un roi, noble fils de la terre,

ISMENE

Theseus is dead, my lady. Only you doubt that.
Athens is mourning. Troezen has the news,
Already hails Hippolytus as king.
Here in this palace, Phaedra trembles for her son
And asks her anxious friends for their advice.

ARICIA

You think Hippolytus will be more kind
Than Theseus was to me? Loosen the chains,
Pity my distress?

ISMENE   I do, my lady.

ARICIA

You know Hippolytus? That heart of stone?   400
Why should you think that he will pity me,
Respect in me alone a sex he scorns?
You've seen how long he has avoided me.
He goes to all the places I avoid.

ISMENE

I know what's said about his iciness.
I've seen this haughty man, though, close to you.
As I watched him, the talk of all his pride
Increased my curiosity in him.
His manner did not seem to match the talk.
One glance from you, and he became confused.   410
He tried to shun your gaze – in vain. His eyes
Were very soft, could not be kept off you.
Perhaps the name of lover hurts his pride.
But yet he has the eyes of one, if not the tongue.

ARICIA

How greedily, Ismene, I listen
To all you say, however wrong it is.
You know me well. Could you believe that I –
This sad plaything of unpitying fate,
My heart for ever fed on hurt and tears –
Would ever know the maddening pain of love?   420
Last of a royal line - my father was earth's son –

Je suis seule échappée aux fureurs de la guerre.
J'ai perdu dans la fleur de leur jeune saison
Six frères, quel espoir d'une illustre maison!
Le fer moissonna tout, et la terre humectée
But à regret le sang des neveux d'Érechthée.
Tu sais, depuis leur mort, quelle sévère loi
Défend à tous les Grecs de soupirer pour moi.
On craint que de la sœur les flammes téméraires
Ne raniment un jour la cendre de ses frères.
Mais tu sais bien aussi de quel œil dédaigneux
Je regardais ce soin d'un vainqueur soupçonneux.
Tu sais que de tout temps à l'amour opposée,
Je rendais souvent grâce à l'injuste Thésée
Dont l'heureuse rigueur secondait mes mépris.
Mes yeux alors, mes yeux n'avaient pas vu son fils.
Non que par les yeux seuls lâchement enchantée
J'aime en lui sa beauté, sa grâce tant vantée,
Présents dont la nature a voulu l'honorer,
Qu'il méprise lui-même, et qu'il semble ignorer.
J'aime, je prise en lui de plus nobles richesses,
Les vertus de son père, et non point les faiblesses.
J'aime, je l'avouerai cet orgueil généreux
Qui jamais n'a fléchi sous le joug amoureux.
Phèdre en vain s'honorait des soupirs de Thésée.
Pour moi, je suis plus fière, et fuis la gloire aisée
D'arracher un hommage à mille autres offert
Et d'entrer dans un cœur de toutes parts ouvert.
Mais de faire fléchir un courage inflexible,
De porter la douleur dans une âme insensible,
D'enchaîner un captif de ses fers étonné,
Contre un joug qui lui plaît vainement mutiné;
C'est là ce que je veux, c'est là ce qui m'irrite.
Hercule à désarmer coûtait moins qu'Hippolyte,
Et vaincu plus souvent, et plus tôt surmonté
Préparait moins de gloire aux yeux qui l'ont dompté.
Mais, chère Ismène, hélas! quelle est mon imprudence!
On ne m'opposera que trop de résistance.
Tu m'entendras peut-être, humble dans mon ennui,
Gémir du même orgueil que j'admire aujourd'hui.

430

440

450

460

I have alone escaped the curse of war.
I lost six brothers in the flowering
Of their youth . . . oh the hope my blood-line had for them.
The sword cut down them all. The moistened earth
Was made to drink Erechtheus' nephews' blood.
And since they died, you know how harsh a law
Forbids all Greeks to sympathise with me.
They fear my love could one day challenge them,
Could fire my brothers' ashes into life.   430
And yet you know how scornfully I've viewed
The care of my suspicious conqueror.
You know I was a constant enemy of love.
I used to thank that tyrant Theseus.
His harshness sorted well with my contempt.
But then my eyes . . . I had not seen his son.
It isn't that my eyes have been beguiled
And love him for his handsomeness, his much praised grace.
Those gifts good fortune has bestowed on him,
He despises or is unconscious of.   440
I love, I prize, far nobler wealth in him:
His father's virtues, not his weaknesses.
Let me confess. I love the marvellous pride
That never has been humbled by love's yoke.
Phaedra can boast of Theseus' sighs in vain.
I have more pride. I scorn the easy prize
Of tributes paid to thousands more besides,
Of love that's given out to everyone.
And yet to make a steel-hard courage bend,
To make a heart that has no feelings hurt,   450
To put a startled prisoner in chains
Who fights in vain against a yoke he loves –
It's that I want. That rouses me.
Hercules was often beaten, routed –
That would mean less than with Hippolytus,
Would yield less glory to the eyes that broke him in.
But Ismene, this is all foolishness.
His fierce resistance will be all too strong.
You yet may hear me, humbled by my grief,
Lament the very pride I now admire.   460

Hippolyte aimerait? Par quel bonheur extrême
Aurais-je pu fléchir . . .

ISMÈNE   Vous l'entendrez lui-même.
Il vient à vous.

SCENE 2

Hippolyte, Aricie, Ismène

HIPPOLYTE   Madame, avant que de partir.
J'ai cru de votre sort vous devoir avertir.
Mon père ne vit plus. Ma juste défiance
Présageait les raisons de sa trop longue absence.
La mort seule bornant ses travaux éclatants
Pouvait à l'univers le cacher si longtemps.
Les dieux livrent enfin à la Parque homicide
L'ami, le compagnon, le successeur d'Alcide.   470
Je crois que votre haine, épargnant ses vertus,
Écoute sans regret ces noms qui lui sont dus.
Un espoir adoucit ma tristesse mortelle.
Je puis vous affranchir d'une austère tutelle.
Je révoque des lois dont j'ai plaint la rigueur,
Vous pouvez disposer de vous, de votre cœur.
Et dans cette Trézène, aujourd'hui mon partage,
De mon aïeul Pitthée autrefois l'héritage,
Qui m'a sans balancer reconnu pour son roi,
Je vous laisse aussi libre, et plus libre que moi.   480

ARICIE

Modérez des bontés dont l'excès m'embarrasse.
D'un soin si généreux honorer ma disgrâce,
Seigneur, c'est me ranger, plus que vous ne pensez,
Sous ces austères lois, dont vous me dispensez.

HIPPOLYTE

Du choix d'un successeur Athènes incertaine
Parle de vous, me nomme, et le fils de la reine.

Hippolytus in love? What edge of ecstasy
Would I have touched . . . ?

ISMENE   Hear him himself.

He's coming now.

[*Hippolytus enters*

SCENE 2

Hippolytus, Aricia, Ismene

HIPPOLYTUS   Lady, before I leave,
It's only right that you should know your fate.
My father's dead. I rightly feared
The reasons why he was away so long.
Death could alone have stopped his marvellous deeds
And hidden him from all the world so long.
The gods gave up to murderous fate at last
The friend, companion, heir of Hercules.   470
I hope your hate will spare his qualities
And won't resent the honours that he won.
One hope can soften, though, my grief:
I can release you from his guardianship.
It was too strict. I will revoke his penal laws
Which I deplore. Your life is yours, as is your heart.
And in Troezen here, which is now mine –
My great grandfather Pittheus' legacy –
Which has proclaimed me king with one accord,
I leave you free – much freer than myself.   480

ARICIA
Your kindness is too much. I blush at it.
You treat me now so generously
And tie me – more than you'd believe, my lord –
To those harsh laws from which you've set me free.

HIPPOLYTUS
Athens is uncertain whom to choose as heir.
They talk of you, of me, of the queen's son.

ARICIE

De moi, Seigneur?

HIPPOLYTE   Je sais, sans vouloir me flatter,
Qu'une superbe loi semble me rejeter.
La Grèce me reproche une mère étrangère.
Mais si pour concurrent je n'avais que mon frère,   490
Madame, j'ai sur lui de véritables droits
Que je saurais sauver du caprice des lois.
Un frein plus légitime arrête mon audace.
Je vous cède, ou plutôt je vous rends une place,
Un sceptre, que jadis vos aïeux ont reçu
De ce fameux mortel que la terre a conçu.
L'adoption le mit entre les mains d'Égée.
Athènes par mon père accrue, et protégée,
Reconnut avec joie un roi si généreux,
Et laissa dans l'oubli vos frères malheureux.   500
Athènes dans ses murs maintenant vous rappelle.
Assez elle a gémi d'une longue querelle,
Assez dans ses sillons votre sang englouti
A fait fumer le champ dont il était sorti.
Trézène m'obéit. Les campagnes de Crète
Offrent au fils de Phèdre une riche retraite.
L'Attique est votre bien. Je pars, et vais pour vous
Réunir tous les vœux partagés entre nous.

ARICIE

De tout ce que j'entends étonnée et confuse
Je crains presque, je crains qu'un songe ne m'abuse.   510
Veillé-je? Puis-je croire un semblable dessein?
Quel dieu, Seigneur, quel dieu l'a mis dans votre sein?
Qu'à bon droit votre gloire en tous lieux est semée!
Et que la vérité passe la renommée!
Vous-même en ma faveur vous voulez vous trahir?
N'était-ce pas assez de ne me point haïr?
Et d'avoir si longtemps pu défendre votre âme
De cette inimitié . . .

HIPPOLYTE   Moi, vous haïr, Madame?
Avec quelques couleurs qu'on ait peint ma fierté,

ARICIA

  Of me, my lord?

HIPPOLYTUS   I don't deceive myself.
  I know the rigid law that bars me, so it seems.
  My mother is a foreigner, and Greece
  Objects. But if my only rival were   490
  My stepbrother, I'd take clear precedence
  And would be saved the folly of the law.
  What holds me back is more legitimate.
  I hand or, rather, give you back
  A sceptre that your ancestors received
  From that great man who was the earth's own son.
  Adoption placed it in Aegeus' hands.
  Once Theseus had made Athens great and safe,
  She hailed him as her noble king with joy
  And left your brothers in obscurity.   500
  Now Athens calls you back within her walls.
  This endless feud has made her grieve enough.
  Your family's blood has now been spilled enough.
  The furrowed fields from which it sprang are drenched.
  Troezen is now mine. The lands of Crete
  Will make a rich retreat for Phaedra's son.
  But Attica is yours. I'll set out now
  To unify the votes that still are split.

ARICIA

  All this amazes, troubles me. I fear . . .
  I almost fear . . . a dream's deceiving me.   510
  Am I awake? Can I believe all this?
  My lord, what god inspired you with this plan?
  Your fame is justly spread throughout the world,
  And yet the truth surpasses your renown.
  You would betray yourself to favour me . . . ?
  Ceasing to hate me would have been enough,
  Keeping your heart so long a time
  From old hostilities . . .

HIPPOLYTUS   I, hate you, my lady?
  Whatever has been said about my pride,

Croit-on que dans ses flancs un monstre m'ait porté?   520
Quelles sauvages mœurs, quelle haine endurcie
Pourrait, en vous voyant, n'être point adoucie?
Ai-je pu résister au charme décevant . . .

ARICIE

Quoi, Seigneur?

HIPPOLYTE   Je me suis engagé trop avant.
Je vois que la raison cède à la violence.
Puisque j'ai commencé de rompre le silence,
Madame, il faut poursuivre. Il faut vous informer
D'un secret que mon cœur ne peut plus renfermer.
Vous voyez devant vous un prince déplorable,
D'un téméraire orgueil exemple mémorable.   530
Moi, qui contre l'amour fièrement révolté,
Aux fers de ses captifs ai longtemps insulté,
Qui des faibles mortels déplorant les naufrages,
Pensais toujours du bord contempler les orages,
Asservi maintenant sous la commune loi,
Par quel trouble me vois-je emporté loin de moi!
Un moment a vaincu mon audace imprudente.
Cette âme si superbe est enfin dépendante.
Depuis près de six mois, honteux, désespéré,
Portant partout le trait dont je suis déchiré,   540
Contre vous, contre moi, vainement je m'éprouve.
Présente je vous fuis, absente je vous trouve.
Dans le fond des forêts votre image me suit.
La lumière du jour, les ombres de la nuit
Tout retrace à mes yeux les charmes que j'évite,
Tout vous livre à l'envi le rebelle Hippolyte.
Moi-même pour tout fruit de mes soins superflus,
Maintenant je me cherche et ne me trouve plus.
Mon arc, mes javelots, mon char, tout m'importune.
Je ne me souviens plus des leçons de Neptune.   550
Mes seuls gémissements font retentir les bois,
Et mes coursiers oisifs ont oublié ma voix.
Peut-être le récit d'un amour si sauvage
Vous fait en m'écoutant rougir de votre ouvrage.
D'un cœur qui s'offre à vous quel farouche entretien!

Do you all think some monster gave me birth?   520
What barbarous customs, frozen hate
Would not be melted at the sight of you?
Could I resist the dazzling spell . . .

ARICIA

My lord?

HIPPOLYTUS I've gone too far, I see.
Reason has given way to violence.
And yet . . . I have begun to speak my thoughts.
I must go on. I have to tell
A secret that I can no longer hide.
You see a pitiable prince in front of you,
A haunting illustration of rash pride.   530
I used to be a rebel against love.
I've long despised the chains her captives wore.
I used to mourn the shipwrecks of weak men
And thought to see such storms from safe on shore.
But now I'm subject to the common law,
Swept troubled far away from my true self.
A single moment overcame my pride
And made my strutting mind subservient.
For nearly six whole months – in shame, despair –
I've borne the arrow tearing me apart.   540
I've fought against you and myself in vain.
I shun your presence, seek you when you're gone.
Your image haunts me in the deepest woods.
The light of day, the shadows of the night,
All conjure up the spell from which I run.
Each single thing surrenders me to you.
And the result of all this fruitless care . . . ?
I seek myself and cannot find the man.
My bow, my spears and chariot, all trouble me.
I can't recall the lessons Neptune taught.   550
The woods now echo with my cries alone.
My steeds are idle, do not know my voice.
Perhaps to speak of such a haunted love
Will make you blush to hear what you have done.
I offer you my love so clumsily . . .

Quel étrange captif pour un si beau lien!
Mais l'offrande à vos yeux en doit être plus chère.
Songez que je vous parle une langue étrangère,
Et ne rejetez pas des vœux mal exprimés,
Qu'Hippolyte sans vous n'aurait jamais formés.   560

SCÈNE 3

Hippolyte, Aricie, Théramène

THÉRAMÈNE

Seigneur, la reine vient, et je l'ai devancée.
Elle vous cherche.

HIPPOLYTE   Moi!

THÉRAMÈNE   J'ignore sa pensée,
Mais on vous est venu demander de sa part.
Phèdre veut vous parler avant votre départ.

HIPPOLYTE

Phèdre? Que lui dirai-je? Et que peut-elle attendre . . .

ARICIE

Seigneur, vous ne pouvez refuser de l'entendre.
Quoique trop convaincu de son inimitié,
Vous devez à ses pleurs quelque ombre de pitié.

HIPPOLYTE

Cependant vous sortez. Et je pars. Et j'ignore
Si je n'offense point les charmes que j'adore.   570
J'ignore si ce cœur que je laisse en vos mains . . .

ARICIE

Partez, Prince, et suivez vos généreux desseins.
Rendez de mon pouvoir Athènes tributaire.
J'accepte tous les dons que vous me voulez faire.
Mais cet empire enfin si grand, si glorieux,
N'est pas de vos présents le plus cher à mes yeux.

How strange a prisoner for one so fair . . .
Yet that should make the offering more prized.
Remember that I speak a foreign tongue.
Please, don't reject these graceless words.
I never would have said them but for you.   560

[*Theramenes enters*

SCENE 3

Hippolytus, Aricia, Theramenes, Ismene

THERAMENES

My lord, Phaedra is here. I came ahead.
She wants to speak.

HIPPOLYTUS   With me?

THERAMENES   I don't know why.
Her messenger has come to ask for you.
She has to speak to you before you go.

HIPPOLYTUS

What can I say to her? What can she want?

ARICIA

You cannot say you will not listen now.
However much you know she is your enemy,
You owe some shade of pity for her grief.

HIPPOLYTUS

You go away. Must I too leave not knowing if
I have offended who I most adore?   570
Or if the heart I leave now in your hands . . .

ARICIA

Go now. And follow through your generous plan.
Make Attica pay homage to my power.
I will accept the gifts you've offered me.
Yet this great empire, glorious thought it is,
Is not your dearest present, in my eyes.

[*she and Ismene leave*

SCÈNE 4

Hippolyte, Théramène

HIPPOLYTE

Ami, tout est-il prêt? Mais la reine s'avance.
Va, que pour le départ tout s'arme en diligence.
Fais donner le signal, cours, ordonne, et revien
Me délivrer bientôt d'un fâcheux entretien.　　　　　580

SCÈNE 5

Phèdre, Hippolyte, Œnone

PHÈDRE [*à Œnone*]

Le voici. Vers mon cœur tout mon sang se retire.
J'oublie, en le voyant, ce que je viens lui dire.

ŒNONE

Souvenez-vous d'un fils qui n'espère qu'en vous.

PHÈDRE

On dit qu'un prompt départ vous éloigne de nous,
Seigneur. A vos douleurs je viens joindre mes larmes.
Je vous viens pour un fils expliquer mes alarmes.
Mon fils n'a plus de père, et le jour n'est pas loin
Qui de ma mort encor doit le rendre témoin.
Déjà mille ennemis attaquent son enfance,
Vous seul pouvez contre eux embrasser sa défense.　　　　590
Mais un secret remords agite mes esprits.
Je crains d'avoir fermé votre oreille à ses cris.
Je tremble que sur lui votre juste colère
Ne poursuive bientôt une odieuse mère.

HIPPOLYTE

Madame, je n'ai point des sentiments si bas.

PHÈDRE

Quand vous me haïriez je ne m'en plaindrais pas,
Seigneur. Vous m'avez vue attachée à vous nuire;

SCENE 4

Hippolytus, Theramenes

HIPPOLYTUS

Theramenes, is all now ready? There's the queen.
Go, make everyone prepare to sail at once.
Give them the signal, quick. And hurry back
To save me from an awkward interview.   580

           [*Theramenes leaves. Phaedra and Oenone enter*

SCENE 5

Phaedra, Hippolytus, Oenone

PHAEDRA [*to Oenone, at the back of the stage*]

Oenone, there he is. My heart . . . the blood
Is racing . . . I see him . . . forget my words . . .

OENONE

Think of your son. You are his only hope.

PHAEDRA

They say you leave us very soon, my lord.
I've come to add my tears for what you mourn.
I've come to speak a mother's fears to you.
My son is fatherless; the day is not
Far off when he will see my death as well.
He is a child. A thousand enemies attack,
And you alone can help in his defence.   590
But dark remorseful shadows haunt my mind.
I fear I've made you deaf to all his cries.
I fear your righteous anger at my crimes
Will soon be persecuting him.

HIPPOLYTUS

My feelings, lady, could not sink so low.

PHAEDRA

If you did hate me, I could not complain,
My lord. You've seen me hot to do you harm.

Dans le fond de mon cœur vous ne pouviez pas lire.
A votre inimitié j'ai pris soin de m'offrir.
Aux bords que j'habitais je n'ai pu vous souffrir.   600
En public, en secret, contre vous déclarée,
J'ai voulu par des mers en être séparée.
J'ai même défendu par une expresse loi
Qu'on osât prononcer votre nom devant moi.
Si pourtant à l'offense on mesure la peine,
Si la haine peut seule attirer votre haine,
Jamais femme ne fut plus digne de pitié,
Et moins digne, Seigneur, de votre inimitié.

HIPPOLYTE

Des droits de ses enfants une mère jalouse
Pardonne rarement au fils d'une autre épouse,   610
Madame. Je le sais. Les soupçons importuns
Sont d'un second hymen les fruits les plus communs.
Toute autre aurait pour moi pris les mêmes ombrages,
Et j'en aurais peut-être essuyé plus d'outrages.

PHÈDRE

Ah, Seigneur! que le ciel, j'ose ici l'attester,
De cette loi commune a voulu m'excepter!
Qu'un soin bien différent me trouble, et me dévore!

HIPPOLYTE

Madame, il n'est pas temps de vous troubler encore.
Peut-être votre époux voit encore le jour;
Le ciel peut à nos pleurs accorder son retour.   620
Neptune le protège, et ce dieu tutélaire
Ne sera pas en vain imploré par mon père.

PHÈDRE

On ne voit point deux fois le rivage des morts,
Seigneur. Puisque Thésée a vu les sombres bords,
En vain vous espérez qu'un dieu vous le renvoie,
Et l'avare Achéron ne lâche point sa proie.
Que dis-je? Il n'est point mort, puisqu'il respire en vous.
Toujours devant mes yeux je crois voir mon époux.
Je le vois, je lui parle, et mon cœur . . . Je m'égare,
Seigneur, ma folle ardeur malgré moi se déclare.   630

And yet you could not read my deepest heart.
I've taken pains to nourish your hostility.
I would not have you present where I lived,   600
Opposed you both in public and alone.
I wanted all the seas to keep you far from me.
I even censored, by express decree,
The speaking of your name when I was there.
But if the penalty should match the crime,
If hate alone should draw your hate on me,
No woman is more worthy of your sympathy,
Nor less, my lord, of your hostility.

HIPPOLYTUS

A mother jealous of her children's rights
Seldom forgives another mother's son.   610
I know that well. And troubling suspicions
Are often spawned in second marriages.
Another woman would have felt the same
Distrust, and even made me suffer more.

PHAEDRA

Ah no, my lord. The gods, I can here swear,
Have made me stand outside the common law.
Far different care eats at me, weighs me down.

HIPPOLYTUS

This is no time to hurt you any more:
Theseus perhaps may even yet survive.
The gods may let him back for pity's sake.   620
Neptune will shelter him. His guardian god
Will not be deaf to all my father's prayers.

PHAEDRA

No human visits twice the shores of death,
My lord. Theseus has seen those dark, dark banks.
You hope in vain a god will send him back.
Hungry Acheron does not drop its prey.
And yet, he is not dead. He breathes in you.
I see my husband here . . . before my eyes . . .
I see him, speak to him; my heart . . . I'm lost . . .
This frenzy, passion, bursts in spite of me.   630

HIPPOLYTE

Je vois de votre amour l'effet prodigieux.
Tout mort qu'il est, Thésée est présent à vos yeux.
Toujours de son amour votre âme est embrasée.

PHÈDRE

Oui, Prince, je languis, je brûle pour Thésée,
Je l'aime, non point tel que l'ont vu les enfers,
Volage adorateur de mille objets divers
Qui va du dieu des morts déshonorer la couche;
Mais fidèle, mais fier, et même un peu farouche,
Charmant, jeune, traînant tous les cœurs après soi,
Tel qu'on dépeint nos dieux, ou tel que je vous voi.   640
Il avait votre port, vos yeux, votre langage,
Cette noble pudeur colorait son visage,
Lorsque de notre Crète il traversa les flots,
Digne sujet des vœux des filles de Minos.
Que faisiez-vous alors? Pourquoi sans Hippolyte
Des héros de la Grèce assembla-t-il l'élite?
Pourquoi trop jeune encor ne pûtes-vous alors
Entrer dans le vaisseau qui le mit sur nos bords?
Par vous aurait péri le monstre de la Crète
Malgré tous les détours de sa vaste retraite.   650
Pour en développer l'embarras incertain
Ma sœur du fil fatal eût armé votre main.
Mais non, dans ce dessein je l'aurais devancée.
L'Amour m'en eût d'abord inspiré la pensée.
C'est moi, Prince, c'est moi, dont l'utile secours
Vous eût du Labyrinthe enseigné les détours.
Que de soins m'eut coûtés cette tête charmante!
Un fil n'eût point assez rassuré votre amante.
Compagne du péril qu'il vous fallait chercher,
Moi-même devant vous j'aurais voulu marcher.   660
Et Phèdre au labyrinthe avec vous descendue,
Se serait avec vous retrouvée, ou perdue.

HIPPOLYTE

Dieux! qu'est-ce que j'entends? Madame, oubliez-vous
Que Thésée est mon père, et qu'il est votre époux?

HIPPOLYTUS

   I see the wondrous power of your love.
   Though he is dead, Theseus is here to you.
   Your soul is set on fire still by his love.

PHAEDRA

   Yes, prince, I ache, I burn for Theseus.
   I love him still, but not as he's been seen in hell,
   The fickle worshipper of countless things
   Coming to shame the couch of Hades' god.
   But faithful, proud, even a little shy,
   Charming, and young, the spinner out of hearts,
   As gods are painted . . . as I see you now.   640
   He had your bearing, eyes; he talked like you.
   His face flushed red with modesty
   That time he crossed the seas and came to Crete,
   A fitting man for Minos' daughters' prayers.
   But what were you doing then? Why gather
   All the finest men in Greece, and not Hippolytus?
   Why could you not, for all your youth, have
   Joined the ship that brought him to our shores?
   You would have killed the minotaur of Crete,
   Despite the twists and turns of his great maze.   650
   My sister would have given you the thread
   To find your way through all those tangled paths.
   But no, I would have been in front of her.
   Love would have fired me with the thought at once.
   I would have helped, my lord, I would have taught
   You all the windings of the labyrinth.
   What pain your charm, your face, have cost . . .
   A thread would not have set my heart at rest.
   I would have shared the dangers facing you,
   I would have wanted to go first . . . down, down . . .   660
   And in the labyrinth with you, I would
   Have found my way, or else been doomed.

HIPPOLYTUS

   Dear god, what do I hear? Do you forget
   That Theseus is my father? You're his wife.

PHÈDRE

Et sur quoi jugez-vous que j'en perds la mémoire,
Prince? Aurais-je perdu tout le soin de ma gloire?

HIPPOLYTE

Madame, pardonnez. J'avoue en rougissant,
Que j'accusais à tort un discours innocent.
Ma honte ne peut plus soutenir votre vue,
Et je vais ...

PHÈDRE   Ah! cruel, tu m'as trop entendue.   670
Je t'en ai dit assez pour te tirer d'erreur.
Eh bien, connais donc Phèdre et toute sa fureur.
J'aime. Ne pense pas qu'au moment que je t'aime,
Innocente à mes yeux je m'approuve moi-même,
Ni que du fol amour qui trouble ma raison
Ma lâche complaisance ait nourri le poison.
Objet infortuné des vengeances célestes,
Je m'abhorre encor plus que tu ne me détestes.
Les dieux m'en sont témoins, ces dieux qui dans mon flanc
Ont allumé le feu fatal à tout mon sang,   680
Ces dieux qui se sont fait une gloire cruelle
De séduire le cœur d'une faible mortelle.
Toi-même en ton esprit rappelle le passé.
C'est peu de t'avoir fui, cruel, je t'ai chassé.
J'ai voulu te paraître odieuse, inhumaine.
Pour mieux te résister, j'ai recherché ta haine.
De quoi m'ont profité mes inutiles soins?
Tu me haïssais plus, je ne t'aimais pas moins.
Tes malheurs te prêtaient encor de nouveaux charmes.
J'ai langui, j'ai séché, dans les feux, dans les larmes.   690
Il suffit de tes yeux pour t'en persuader,
Si tes yeux un moment pouvaient me regarder.
Que dis-je? Cet aveu que je te viens de faire,
Cet aveu si honteux, le crois-tu volontaire?
Tremblante pour un fils que je n'osais trahir,
Je te venais prier de ne le point haïr.
Faibles projets d'un cœur trop plein de ce qu'il aime!
Hélas! je ne t'ai pu parler que de toi-même.

PHAEDRA

What makes you think I have forgotten that?
You think I've lost all caring for my name?

HIPPOLYTUS

Forgive me. Look . . . I blush. You spoke in innocence.
I'm sure I misinterpreted your words.
I'm so ashamed . . . I cannot look . . .
I'll go.

PHAEDRA

Don't be so cruel; you understand me all too well.   670
I've said enough to make it clear as day.
You shall know me, in all my wild desires.
I love you. But don't for one moment think
That I believe these feelings to be innocent.
It hasn't been complacency that's fed
The poison of mad love that haunts my mind.
I am the victim of the vengeful gods.
I loathe myself much more than you can hate.
The gods are witness. They kindled the flame
In me that has been death to my whole family.   680
These gods have gloried cruelly in their power
To tempt a feeble human being's heart.
Remember all the past – the ways I tried
To shun you for your cruelty, drove you away.
I tried to seem inhuman to you – vile.
I sought your hate the better to resist.
What good were all these vain attempts?
You hated me the more. I didn't love you less.
Your spell was even stronger as you hurt.
I yearned, dried up inside, in fire and tears.   690
Simply by looking, you would know that's true,
If for one moment you could look at me.
What have I said? Confessed it all to you,
So full of shame. You think I've done this willingly?
I'm trembling for a child I can't betray.
I came to beg you not to hate my son.
How weak a goal when I'm so full of love
I cannot speak of anyone but you.

Venge-toi, punis-moi d'un odieux amour.
Digne fils du héros qui t'a donné le jour,   700
Délivre l'univers d'un monstre qui t'irrite.
La veuve de Thésée ose aimer Hippolyte!
Crois-moi, ce monstre affreux ne doit point t'échapper.
Voilà mon cœur. C'est là que ta main doit frapper.
Impatient déjà d'expier son offense
Au-devant de ton bras je le sens qui s'avance.
Frappe. Ou si tu le crois indigne de tes coups,
Si ta haine m'envie un supplice si doux,
Ou si d'un sang trop vil ta main serait trempée,
Au défaut de ton bras prête-moi ton épée.   710
Donne.

ŒNONE   Que faites-vous, Madame? Justes dieux!
Mais on vient. Évitez des témoins odieux,
Venez, rentrez, fuyez une honte certaine.

SCÈNE 6

Hippolyte, Théramène

THÉRAMÈNE

Est-ce Phèdre qui fuit, ou plutôt qu'on entraîne?
Pourquoi, Seigneur, pourquoi ces marques de douleur?
Je vous vois sans épée, interdit, sans couleur?

HIPPOLYTE

Théramène, fuyons. Ma surprise est extrême.
Je ne puis sans horreur me regarder moi-même.
Phèdre . . . Mais non, grands dieux! qu'en un profond oubli
Cet horrible secret demeure enseveli.   720

THÉRAMÈNE

Si vous voulez partir, la voile est préparée.
Mais Athènes, Seigneur, s'est déjà déclarée;
Ses chefs ont pris les voix de toutes ses tribus.
Votre frère l'emporte, et Phèdre a le dessus.

Have your revenge. Punish this hateful love.
Be worthy of the man who gave you life,   700
And rid the universe of this vile thing.
Theseus' widow dares to love his son!
The awful monster must not get away.
Here is my heart, the spot where you must strike.
I feel it yearning upwards to your arms,
Impatient now to expiate its crime.
Kill me. You think I am too vile to kill . . . ?
Your hate would grudge me such an easy death –
If blood as foul as mine would soil your hands,
If you won't strike, then let me have your sword.   710
Give me it!

OENONE   What are you doing? God.
Someone's coming. We can't have witnesses.
Come, let's go in quick. Hide the disgrace.
           [*Phaedra and Oenone leave. Theramenes enters*

SCENE 6

Hippolytus, Theramenes

THERAMENES

My lord, could that be Phaedra rushing off?
Or dragged away? . . . My lord, you look so ill.
Where is your sword? You're speechless . . . deathly pale.

HIPPOLYTUS

Theramenes, we have to go. I've not the words . . .
I have become a horror to myself.
Phaedra . . . Oh no, great gods, entire forgetfulness
Must keep this secret dark for all eternity.   720

THERAMENES

If you must leave, the ships are all prepared.
But Athens has already cast its vote.
Its leaders have consulted all the tribes;
Your brother carries them. Phaedra has won.

HIPPOLYTE

Phèdre?

THÉRAMÈNE Un héraut chargé des volontés d'Athènes
De l'État en ses mains vient remettre les rênes.
Son fils est roi, Seigneur.

HIPPOLYTE   Dieux, qui la connaissez,
Est-ce donc sa vertu que vous récompensez?

THÉRAMÈNE

Cependant un bruit sourd veut que le roi respire.
On prétend que Thésée a paru dans l'Épire.
Mais moi, qui l'y cherchai, Seigneur, je sais trop bien . . .

730

HIPPOLYTE

N'importe, écoutons tout et ne négligeons rien.
Examinons ce bruit, remontons à sa source.
S'il ne mérite pas d'interrompre ma course,
Partons, et quelque prix qu'il en puisse coûter,
Mettons le sceptre aux mains digne de le porter.

HIPPOLYTUS
  Phaedra?

THERAMENES   A herald authorised by Athens' will
  Has placed the reins of state within her hands.
  Her son is king, my lord.

HIPPOLYTUS   Dear gods, you know
  Her nature. Is it her virtue you reward?

THERAMENES
  But still, vague rumours say the king's alive.
  Theseus, it's claimed, was seen in Epirus.   730
  But I was there in search of him. I know . . .

HIPPOLYTUS
  No matter now. Listen to everything.
  Track all these rumours down now to their source.
  If breaking off my plans is not worthwhile,
  We'll leave; but at whatever cost,
  We'll place the sceptre soon in better hands.

ACTE 3 SCÈNE 1

Phèdre, Œnone

PHÈDRE

Ah! que l'on porte ailleurs les honneurs qu'on m'envoie.
Importune, peux-tu souhaiter qu'on me voie?
De quoi viens-tu flatter mon esprit désolé?
Cache-moi bien plutôt, je n'ai que trop parlé.　　　　　　740
Mes fureurs au dehors ont osé se répandre :
J'ai dit ce que jamais on ne devait entendre.
Ciel! comme il m'écoutait! par combien de détours
L'insensible a longtemps éludé mes discours!
Comme il ne respirait qu'une retraite prompte!
Et combien sa rougeur a redoublé ma honte!
Pourquoi détournais-tu mon funeste dessein?
Hélas! quand son épée allait chercher mon sein,
A-t-il pâli pour moi? Me l'a-t-il arrachée?
Il suffit que ma main l'ait une fois touchée,　　　　　　750
Je l'ai rendue horrible à ses yeux inhumains,
Et ce fer malheureux profanerait ses mains.

ŒNONE

Ainsi dans vos malheurs, ne songeant qu'à vous plaindre,
Vous nourrissez un feu qu'il vous faudrait éteindre.
Ne vaudrait-il pas mieux, digne sang de Minos,
Dans de plus nobles soins chercher votre repos,
Contre un ingrat qui plaît recourir à la fuite,
Régner, et de l'État embrasser la conduite?

PHÈDRE

Moi régner! moi, ranger un État sous ma loi!
Quand ma faible raison ne règne plus sur moi.　　　　　760
Lorsque j'ai de mes sens abandonné l'empire,
Quand sous un joug honteux à peine je respire,
Quand je me meurs!

ŒNONE　　　　　　　　　Fuyez.

PHÈDRE　　　　　　　　　　　　　Je ne le puis quitter.

ACT 3 SCENE 1

Phaedra, Oenone

PHAEDRA

Oh take away these honours that they send.
Stop bothering. You want me to be seen?
How could you hope to soothe my crying heart?
Better to hide me now. I've said too much.   740
My frenzy's dared to spread itself abroad;
I've spoken things that never should be heard.
God! and how he listened . . . How many twists
And turns he made to miss my meaning.
How much he longed to run off there and then.
And how he blushed, to add to all my shame.
Why did you hold me back? I planned to die.
Oh, when his sword was pointed at my breasts,
Did he turn pale for me, snatch it away?
It was enough my hand had touched it once.   750
I'd made it filthy in his eyes.
The wretched sword would soil his hands.

OENONE

You cry and only think of what gives pain.
You fan a fire that ought to be put out.
Your father is king Minos; ought you not
To seek some peace of mind in higher things?
Control this thankless boy who runs away,
And undertake the business of the state.

PHAEDRA

I reign? I rule a people, rule a state,
When I'm too weak to rule myself?   760
When I have lost control of how I feel?
When I am choking at this yoke of shame?
When I am dying?

OENONE   Escape.

PHAEDRA   I cannot leave him.

ŒNONE

Vous l'osâtes bannir, vous n'osez l'éviter.

PHÈDRE

Il n'est plus temps. Il sait mes ardeurs insensées.
De l'austère pudeur les bornes sont passées.
J'ai déclaré ma honte aux yeux de mon vainqueur
Et l'espoir malgré moi s'est glissé dans mon cœur.
Toi-même rappelant ma force défaillante,
Et mon âme déjà sur mes lèvres errante,   770
Par tes conseils flatteurs tu m'as su ranimer,
Tu m'as fait entrevoir que je pouvais l'aimer.

ŒNONE

Hélas! de vos malheurs innocente ou coupable,
De quoi pour vous sauver n'étais-je point capable?
Mais si jamais l'offense irrita vos esprits,
Pouvez-vous d'un superbe oublier les mépris?
Avec quels yeux cruels sa rigueur obstinée
Vous laissait à ses pieds peu s'en faut prosternée!
Que son farouche orgueil le rendait odieux!
Que Phèdre en ce moment n'avait-elle mes yeux!   780

PHÈDRE

Œnone, il peut quitter cet orgueil qui te blesse.
Nourri dans les forêts, il en a la rudesse.
Hippolyte endurci par de sauvages lois
Entend parler d'amour pour la première fois.
Peut-être sa surprise a causé son silence,
Et nos plaintes peut-être ont trop de violence.

ŒNONE

Songez qu'une barbare en son sein l'a formé.

PHÈDRE

Quoique Scythe et barbare, elle a pourtant aimé.

ŒNONE

Il a pour tout le sexe une haine fatale.

PHÈDRE

Je ne me verrai point préférer de rivale.   790

OENONE

You dared to banish him. Dare avoid him.

PHAEDRA

It's all too late. He's seen how mad I am with love.
I've gone beyond all bounds of modesty.
I've voiced my shame to him. He's conquered me.
Despite myself, hope still creeps in my heart.
You summoned up my failing strength yourself,
Just as my soul was hovering on my lips.   770
You stroked me so and brought me back to life.
You let me glimpse that I could worship him.

OENONE

I may be guilty for your pain, or not.
What would I not have done to save your life?
If ever insults, though, offended you,
Can you forget his arrogance?
How cruelly he stared, stiff and severe,
And left you almost prostrate at his feet.
How odious that savage pride he showed.
Why could you not then see him through my eyes?   780

PHAEDRA

He may let go the pride that angers you.
Brought up in forests, he is raw like them.
Some savage laws have hardened him. But now
For the first time he hears us speak of love.
Perhaps surprise has silenced him.
Perhaps we are reproaching him too much.

OENONE

Remember that a savage suckled him.

PHAEDRA

A Scythian savage – and yet she cared.

OENONE

He has a deadly hatred for our sex.

PHAEDRA

I shall then see no rival take my place.   790

Enfin, tous ces conseils ne sont plus de saison,
Sers ma fureur, Œnone, et non point ma raison.
Il oppose à l'amour un cœur inaccessible.
Cherchons pour l'attaquer quelque endroit plus sensible.
Les charmes d'un empire ont paru le toucher.
Athènes l'attirait, il n'a pu s'en cacher.
Déjà de ses vaisseaux la pointe était tournée,
Et la voile flottait aux vents abandonnée.
Va trouver de ma part ce jeune ambitieux,
Œnone. Fais briller la couronne à ses yeux.   800
Qu'il mette sur son front le sacré diadème;
Je ne veux que l'honneur de l'attacher moi-même.
Cédons-lui ce pouvoir que je ne puis garder.
Il instruira mon fils dans l'art de commander.
Peut-être il voudra bien lui tenir lieu de père.
Je mets sous son pouvoir et le fils et la mère.
Pour le fléchir enfin tente tous les moyens.
Tes discours trouveront plus d'accès que les miens.
Presse, pleure, gémis, plains-lui Phèdre mourante,
Ne rougis point de prendre une voix suppliante.   810
Je t'avouerai de tout, je n'espère qu'en toi.
Va, j'attends ton retour pour disposer de moi.

SCÈNE 2

PHÈDRE [seule]

O toi qui vois la honte où je suis descendue,
Implacable Vénus, suis-je assez confondue?
Tu ne saurais plus loin pousser ta cruauté,
Ton triomphe est parfait, tous tes traits ont porté.
Cruelle, si tu veux une gloire nouvelle,
Attaque un ennemi qui te soit plus rebelle.
Hippolyte te fuit, et bravant ton courroux,
Jamais à tes autels n'a fléchi les genoux.   820
Ton nom semble offenser ses superbes oreilles.
Déesse, venge-toi. Nos causes sont pareilles.
Qu'il aime. Mais déjà tu reviens sur tes pas,
Œnone? On me déteste, on ne t'écoute pas.

But all advice from you is much too late.
Help my heart's frenzy, not my reason now.
If he is sealed impervious to love,
We must attack him in a weaker place.
He seemed attracted by the thought of power.
Athens excited him; he couldn't hide that fact.
His ships were turned in that direction,
Their bulging sails all streaming in the wind.
Find this ambitious boy for me, Oenone,
And hold a dazzling crown up to his eyes,   800
A sacred diadem upon his head.
I only want to place it there myself.
I'll yield the power I cannot keep to him.
He'll teach my son the best ways to command.
Perhaps he'll be a father to the boy.
Mother and son I'll give up to his might.
Try every means, in short, to win him round;
He'll listen to your words much more than mine.
Beg him, and cry, and moan. Portray me at death's door.
Don't blush, don't be afraid to plead for me.   810
I'll sanction all you say. You are my only hope.
Go now. I'll wait for you to know my fate.

                              [*Oenone goes*

SCENE 2

PHAEDRA [*alone*]

So then, no pity, Venus, yet? You see the depths
To which I've sunk. Is this now low enough?
You could not be more cruel than this.
You've won completely now: the arrows all struck home.
You want more fame for all your savagery?
Why not take on a man who'll fight you more?
Hippolytus runs from you, braves your rage.
He's never knelt before your shrine.   820
It seems your name offends his scornful ear.
Goddess, have your revenge. Our causes are the same.
Make him love me . . .   [*Oenone enters*
           Oenone, why so quick . . . ?
He hasn't listened to you . . . loathes me still?

SCÈNE 3

Phèdre, Œnone

ŒNONE

Il faut d'un vain amour étouffer la pensée,
Madame. Rappelez votre vertu passée.
Le roi, qu'on a cru mort, va paraître à vos yeux,
Thésée est arrivé. Thésée est en ces lieux.
Le peuple, pour le voir, court et se précipite.
Je sortais par votre ordre, et cherchais Hippolyte,   830
Lorsque jusques au ciel mille cris élancés . . .

PHÈDRE

Mon époux est vivant, Œnone, c'est assez.
J'ai fait l'indigne aveu d'un amour qui l'outrage.
Il vit. Je ne veux pas en savoir davantage.

ŒNONE

Quoi?

PHÈDRE   Je te l'ai prédit, mais tu n'as pas voulu.
Sur mes justes remords tes pleurs ont prévalu.
Je mourais ce matin digne d'être pleurée.
J'ai suivi tes conseils, je meurs déshonorée.

ŒNONE

Vous mourez?

PHÈDRE   Juste ciel! qu'ai-je fait aujourd'hui!
Mon époux va paraître, et son fils avec lui.   840
Je verrai le témoin de ma flamme adultère
Observer de quel front j'ose aborder son père,
Le cœur gros de soupirs, qu'il n'a point écoutés,
L'œil humide de pleurs, par l'ingrat rebutés.
Penses-tu que sensible à l'honneur de Thésée,
Il lui cache l'ardeur dont je suis embrasée?
Laissera-t-il trahir et son père et son roi?
Pourra-t-il contenir l'horreur qu'il a pour moi?
Il se tairait en vain. Je sais mes perfidies,
Œnone, et ne suis point de ces femmes hardies,   850

SCENE 3

Phaedra, Oenone

OENONE

Give up all thoughts of love, my lady, now.
You need to summon up the courage you once had.
You will soon see . . . the king we thought was dead.
Theseus has come. Theseus is here.
The people rush and fling themselves at him.
You ordered me to find Hippolytus,   830
When shouts and cries are thrown up to the skies . . .

PHAEDRA

My husband is alive, Oenone. Enough now . . .
I have confessed a love that fouls his name.
He is alive. I want to hear no more.

OENONE

What?

PHAEDRA   I told you, but you would not hear.
Your tears were stronger than the guilt I felt.
I might have died this morning worthy of those tears.
I followed your advice, and die now in great shame.

OENONE

You die?

PHAEDRA   Dear God, what have I done today?
My husband and his son will soon be here.   840
I'll see the witness to adulterous love
Inspect me as I dare approach the king,
My heart so great with sighs he would not listen to,
My eyes so wet with tears he spurned with scorn.
He's sensitive to Theseus' fame. Will he
Conceal the love ablaze in me from him?
Will he betray his people and his king,
Hold back the loathing that he has for me?
His silence would not help. I know my treachery,
Oenone. I'm not a daring woman   850

Qui goûtant dans le crime une tranquille paix
Ont su se faire un front qui ne rougit jamais.
Je connais mes fureurs, je les rappelle toutes.
Il me semble déjà que ces murs, que ces voûtes,
Vont prendre la parole, et prêts à m'accuser
Attendent mon époux pour le désabuser.
Mourons. De tant d'horreurs qu'un trépas me délivre.
Est-ce un malheur si grand que de cesser de vivre?
La mort aux malheureux ne cause point d'effroi.
Je ne crains que le nom que je laisse après moi.   860
Pour mes tristes enfants quel affreux héritage!
Le sang de Jupiter doit enfler leur courage.
Mais quelque juste orgueil qu'inspire un sang si beau,
Le crime d'une mère est un pesant fardeau.
Je tremble qu'un discours, hélas! trop véritable,
Un jour ne leur reproche une mère coupable,
Je tremble qu'opprimés de ce poids odieux,
L'un ni l'autre jamais n'ose lever les yeux.

ŒNONE

Il n'en faut point douter, je les plains l'un et l'autre.
Jamais crainte ne fut plus juste que la vôtre.   870
Mais à de tels affronts, pourquoi les exposer?
Pourquoi contre vous-même allez-vous déposer?
C'en est fait. On dira que Phèdre trop coupable,
De son époux trahi fuit l'aspect redoutable.
Hippolyte est heureux qu'aux dépens de vos jours,
Vous-même en expirant appuyez ses discours.
A votre accusateur, que pourrai-je répondre?
Je serai devant lui trop facile à confondre.
De son triomphe affreux je le verrai jouir,
Et conter votre honte à qui voudra l'ouïr.   880
Ah! que plutôt du ciel la flamme me dévore!
Mais ne me trompez point, vous est-il cher encore?
De quel œil voyez-vous ce prince audacieux?

PHÈDRE

Je le vois comme un monstre effroyable à mes yeux.

Who finds great peace of mind amid my crimes,
Who feigns a face that never blushes red.
I know my madnesses, recall them all.
Already now, these walls, I think, these vaults
Will start to speak. They're ready to accuse.
They only want my husband here – and then they'll tell.
Please death release me from such horrors now.
Is it so great a hurt to cease to breathe?
Death cannot frighten those who live in pain.
The name I leave behind is all I fear.   860
What dreadful legacy for my poor sons!
The blood of Jupiter should swell their souls;
But yet, whatever pride is felt from blood
So fine, a mother's sin is hard to bear.
I shudder that some words – words all too true –
Will blame them one day for my guilt.
I fear they'll be so crushed by that foul load
That they will never dare to raise their eyes again.

OENONE

No doubt of it. I pity both of them.
Your fears are more than justified.   870
But why expose them to this shame and pain?
And why incriminate yourself? That will prove all.
They'll say that Phaedra was so full of guilt
She fled her wounded husband's eyes in fear.
Hippolytus will thrill at your expense
To see you dead, and so confirm his tale.
Accuse he will – and how can I respond?
I'll be too easily confused in front of him.
I'll see him revelling in his vile success,
Telling your shame to all who want to hear.   880
I'd sooner be destroyed by heaven's fire.
But tell me the truth . . . is he so dear, still?
How do you look upon this daring prince?

PHAEDRA

He is a fearful horror to my eyes.

ŒNONE

Pourquoi donc lui céder une victoire entière?
Vous le craignez . . . Osez l'accuser la première
Du crime dont il peut vous charger aujourd'hui.
Qui vous démentira? Tout parle contre lui.
Son épée en vos mains heureusement laissée,
Votre trouble présent, votre douleur passée,   890
Son père par vos cris dès longtemps prévenu,
Et déjà son exil par vous-même obtenu.

PHÈDRE

Moi, que j'ose opprimer et noircir l'innocence!

ŒNONE

Mon zèle n'a besoin que de votre silence.
Tremblante comme vous, j'en sens quelques remords.
Vous me verriez plus prompte affronter mille morts.
Mais puisque je vous perds sans ce triste remède,
Votre vie est pour moi d'un prix à qui tout cède.
Je parlerai. Thésée aigri par mes avis,
Bornera sa vengeance à l'exil de son fils.   900
Un père en punissant, Madame, est toujours père.
Un supplice léger suffit à sa colère.
Mais le sang innocent dût-il être versé,
Que ne demande point votre honneur menacé?
C'est un trésor trop cher pour oser le commettre.
Quelque loi qu'il vous dicte, il faut vous y soumettre,
Madame, et pour sauver notre honneur combattu,
Il faut immoler tout, et même la vertu.
On vient, je vois Thésée.

PHÈDRE   Ah! je vois Hippolyte.

Dans ses yeux insolents je vois ma perte écrite.   910
Fais ce que tu voudras, je m'abandonne à toi.
Dans le trouble où je suis, je ne puis rien pour moi.

OENONE

Then why allow him total victory?
You're still afraid. Then dare accuse him first
Before he charges you with that same crime.
Who'll contradict? It's all against him now –
He gladly gave his sword to you,
Your anguish now, your past distress,   890
Theseus warned a long time by your cries,
His banishment that you yourself obtained.

PHAEDRA

So am I then to brand a guiltless man?

OENONE

I only need your silence to succeed.
I'm trembling now – like you. I feel remorse.
I'd sooner undergo a thousand deaths.
I'll lose you, though, without this remedy;
I prize your life beyond the world . . .
I'll speak. Theseus will be incensed. He'll curb
His vengeance, though, to banishing his son.   900
A father when he disciplines remains
A father still. A modest punishment will serve
His rage. Even if guiltless blood is shed,
Your honour's threatened, demands that price.
You dare not put so rare a prize at risk.
Whatever it dictates must be obeyed,
My lady. To keep your honour safe,
All – even goodness – must be sacrificed.
Someone is coming. That's Theseus . . .

PHAEDRA   And Hippolytus.

I see my ruin written in his hard   910
Cold eyes. Do what you will. I'm in your hands.
The turmoil that I'm in . . . I cannot help myself . . .

       [*Theseus enters, with Hippolytus and Theramenes*

SCÈNE 4

Thésée, Hippolyte, Phèdre, Œnone, Théramène

THÉSÉE

La fortune à mes yeux cesse d'être opposée,
Madame, et dans vos bras met . . . .

PHÈDRE   Arrêtez, Thésée,
Et ne profanez point des transports si charmants.
Je ne mérite plus ces doux empressements.
Vous êtes offensé. La fortune jalouse
N'a pas en votre absence épargné votre épouse,
Indigne de vous plaire, et de vous approcher,
Je ne dois désormais songer qu'à me cacher.   920

SCÈNE 5

Thésée, Hippolyte, Théramène

THÉSÉE

Quel est l'étrange accueil qu'on fait à votre père,
Mon fils?

HIPPOLYTE   Phèdre peut seule expliquer ce mystère.
Mais si mes vœux ardents vous peuvent émouvoir,
Permettez-moi, Seigneur, de ne la plus revoir,
Souffrez que pour jamais le tremblant Hippolyte
Disparaisse des lieux que votre épouse habite.

THÉSÉE

Vous, mon fils, me quitter?

HIPPOLYTE   Je ne la cherchais pas,
C'est vous qui sur ces bords conduisîtes ses pas.
Vous daignâtes, Seigneur, aux rives de Trézène
Confier en partant Aricie, et la reine.   930
Je fus même chargé du soin de les garder.
Mais quels soins désormais peuvent me retarder?

SCENE 4

Theseus, Hippolytus, Phaedra, Oenone, Theramenes

THESEUS

My fate has turned from darkness now,
My lady. Here in your arms . . .

PHAEDRA   No, Theseus.
Don't desecrate the charm of your delight.
I am no longer worthy of such gentleness.
You have been sinned against. You were away
And jealous fortune did not spare your wife.
I am not fit to please you, or come close.
My only thought now is to hide.   920

[*She leaves with Oenone*

SCENE 5

Theseus, Hippolytus, Theramenes

THESEUS

So why this strangest welcome to me now,
Hippolytus?

HIPPOLYTUS   Phaedra alone can solve the mystery.
But if my burning wishes move you still,
Allow me never to set eyes on her again.
Allow me . . . I'm shaking . . . to disappear
For ever from the places where she is.

THESEUS

You're leaving me?

HIPPOLYTUS   I did not seek her out.
You were the one who brought her to these shores.
And when you left, my lord, you deigned to trust
Aricia and your queen in Troezen.   930
You even placed them both within my care.
But what care now should keep me here?

Assez dans les forêts mon oisive jeunesse
Sur de vils ennemis a montré son adresse.
Ne pourrai-je en fuyant un indigne repos,
D'un sang plus glorieux teindre mes javelots?
Vous n'aviez pas encore atteint l'âge où je touche,
Déjà plus d'un tyran, plus d'un monstre farouche   940
Avait de votre bras senti la pesanteur.
Déjà de l'insolence heureux persécuteur,
Vous aviez des deux mers assuré les rivages,
Le libre voyageur ne craignait plus d'outrages.
Hercule respirant sur le bruit de vos coups,
Déjà de son travail se reposait sur vous.
Et moi, fils inconnu d'un si glorieux père,
Je suis même encor loin des traces de ma mère.
Souffrez que mon courage ose enfin s'occuper.
Souffrez, si quelque monstre a pu vous échapper,
Que j'apporte à vos pieds sa dépouille honorable,
Ou que d'un beau trépas la mémoire durable,   950
Éternisant des jours si noblement finis,
Prouve à tout l'avenir que j'étais votre fils.

THÉSÉE

Que vois-je? Quelle horreur dans ces lieux répandue
Fait fuir devant mes yeux ma famille éperdue?
Si je reviens si craint, et si peu désiré,
O ciel! de ma prison pourquoi m'as-tu tiré?
Je n'avais qu'un ami. Son imprudente flamme
Du tyran de l'Épire allait ravir la femme.
Je servais à regret ses desseins amoureux;
Mais le sort irrité nous aveuglait tous deux.   960
Le tyran m'a surpris sans défense et sans armes.
J'ai vu Pirithoüs, triste objet de mes larmes,
Livré par ce barbare à des monstres cruels,
Qu'il nourrissait du sang des malheureux mortels.
Moi-même il m'enferma dans des cavernes sombres,
Lieux profonds et voisins de l'empire des ombres.
Les dieux, après six mois, enfin m'ont regardé.
J'ai su tromper les yeux de qui j'étais gardé.
D'un perfide ennemi j'ai purgé la nature.

I've wasted youth enough and all my skill
On paltry animals that roam the woods.
It's time to leave this shameful idleness
And stain my javelins with finer blood.
Before you'd reached the age that I am now,
More than one tyrant, one wild beast,   940
Had felt your arm, the strength it had.
You were the scourge of tyranny by then.
You'd made the shorelines of two seas quite safe,
So travellers could roam and fear no harm.
Hercules caught his breath at what you'd done
And handed all his labours on to you.
And I, this glorious father's unknown son,
Am outstripped even by my mother's deeds.
Allow my courage now to find its work.
If some inhuman thing escaped your sword,
Let me throw down its carcass at your feet.
Or let the memory of a glorious death   950
Eternalise a life that ended well
And prove to all the world I was your son.

THESEUS

What's this? What horror has spread through this place
To make my family run from me so distraught?
If I come home so feared, so undesired,
Why, heaven, did you free me from my goal?
I only had one friend. So mad in love,
He tried to steal the wife of Epirus' king.
Reluctantly, I helped him in his scheme.
But fate was angry, blinded both of us.   960
The tyrant-king surprised me – I'd no arms –
And I saw Pirithous, a sight for tears,
Thrown to such beasts by that barbarian,
Who fed them on the blood of tortured men.
He shut me up in stifling, pitch-dark caves,
Deep in the earth, close to the kingdom of the dead.
It was six months before the gods took heed,
And I could trick the eyes that watched me close.
Then I purged nature of a treacherous man

A ses monstres lui-même a servi de pâture.   970
Et lorsque avec transport je pense m'approcher
De tout ce que les dieux m'ont laissé de plus cher;
Que dis-je? Quand mon âme à soi-même rendue
Vient se rassasier d'une si chère vue,
Je n'ai pour tout accueil que des frémissements.
Tout fuit, tout se refuse à mes embrassements.
Et moi-même éprouvant la terreur que j'inspire,
Je voudrais être encor dans les prisons d'Épire.
Parlez. Phèdre se plaint que je suis outragé.
Qui m'a trahi? Pourquoi ne suis-je pas vengé?   980
La Grèce à qui mon bras fut tant de fois utile,
A-t-elle au criminel accordé quelque asile?
Vous ne répondez point. Mon fils, mon propre fils,
Est-il d'intelligence avec mes ennemis?
Entrons. C'est trop garder un doute qui m'accable.
Connaissons à la fois le crime et le coupable.
Que Phèdre explique enfin le trouble où je la voi.

SCÈNE 6

Hippolyte, Théramène

HIPPOLYTE

Où tendait ce discours qui m'a glacé d'effroi?
Phèdre toujours en proie à sa fureur extrême,
Veut-elle s'accuser et se perdre elle-même?   990
Dieux! que dira le roi? Quel funeste poison
L'amour a répandu sur toute sa maison!
Moi-même, plein d'un feu que sa haine réprouve,
Quel il m'a vu jadis, et quel il me retrouve!
De noirs pressentiments viennent m'épouvanter.
Mais l'innocence enfin n'a rien à redouter.
Allons, cherchons ailleurs par quelle heureuse adresse
Je pourrai de mon père émouvoir la tendresse,
Et lui dire un amour qu'il peut vouloir troubler
Mais que tout son pouvoir ne saurait ébranler.   1000

And made him serve as food for his own beasts.   970
And when – with joy – I thought to come back here,
To everything the gods had made most dear –
Where are the words? – my soul was mine again.
I came to feast upon so dear a sight . . .
And then I find my welcome is a shuddering!
You all run off, repulsing my embrace.
I feel myself the horror I inspire.
I'd gladly be back now in my own gaol.
Speak. Phaedra tells of great wrong done to me.
Who has betrayed me? Why aren't I avenged?   980
Has Greece, so often helped by my strong arm,
Now granted sanctuary to the criminal?
You don't reply . . . ? My son, my only son,
Have you had dealings with my enemies?
I must go in. I cannot bear this crushing doubt.
I must know both the crime and criminal.
Phaedra must tell me now what troubles her.

                                                        [*he leaves*

SCENE 6

Hippolytus, Theramenes

HIPPOLYTUS

His words . . . they make me freeze with fear . . .
Phaedra is gripped by wild and utter rage –
Will she accuse herself, destroy her life?   990
Dear God, what will he say? What poison now
Has love spread through this family?
He used to find a passion in me that
His hate condemned. He finds it in me still.
Some dark foreboding terrifies my heart.
Yet nothing, surely, need be feared by innocence.
Come, let's try to find a happier way
To touch my father's tenderness once more.
I'll tell him of a love he may oppose
But which, for all his power, he will not shake.   1000
                                        [*he leaves with Theramenes*

ACTE 4 SCÈNE 1

Thésée, Œnone

THÉSÉE

Ah! qu'est-ce que j'entends? Un traître, un téméraire,
Préparait cet outrage a l'honneur de son pere?
Avec quelle rigueur, Destin, tu me poursuis!
Je ne sais où je vais, je ne sais où je suis.
O tendresse! ô bonté trop mal récompensée!
Projet audacieux! détestable pensée!
Pour parvenir au but de ses noires amours,
L'insolent de la force empruntait le secours.
J'ai reconnu le fer, instrument de sa rage,
Ce fer dont je l'armai pour un plus noble usage. 1010
Tous les liens du sang n'ont pu le retenir!
Et Phèdre différait à le faire punir!
Le silence de Phèdre épargnait le coupable!

ŒNONE

Phèdre épargnait plutôt un père déplorable.
Honteuse du dessein d'un amant furieux,
Et du feu criminel qu'il a pris dans ses yeux,
Phèdre mourait, Seigneur, et sa main meurtrière
Éteignait de ses yeux l'innocente lumière.
J'ai vu lever le bras, j'ai couru la sauver.
Moi seule à votre amour j'ai su la conserver; 1020
Et plaignant à la fois son trouble et vos alarmes,
J'ai servi malgré moi d'interprète à ses larmes.

THÉSÉE

Le perfide! il n'a pu s'empêcher de pâlir.
De crainte en m'abordant je l'ai vu tressaillir.
Je me suis étonné de son peu d'allégresse.
Ses froids embrassements ont glacé ma tendresse.
Mais ce coupable amour dont il est dévoré
Dans Athènes déjà s'était-il déclaré?

ŒNONE

Seigneur, souvenez-vous des plaintes de la reine.

ACT 4 SCENE 1

Theseus, Oenone

THESEUS

My son's a reckless traitor then, Oenone,
Prepared to soil his father's name. That's what I hear.
How harshly, fate, you haunt me still.
I don't know where I am, or where to go.
The tenderness, the kindness repaid so . . .
The boldness of his plan . . . the filthy thoughts . . .
He shamelessly took on the help of force
To gain the object of his dark, dark love.
I recognised the sword he drew on her,
The sword I gave him for a nobler use.   1010
But all those blood-ties could not hold him back.
And Phaedra would put off his punishment?
Her silence would help spare a guilty man?

OENONE

She spared, rather, your wretchedness, my lord.
This lover's raving schemes, the guilt and fire
That burned out in his eyes – she felt such shame . . .
She was dying, my lord. Her murderous hand
Tried to put out the guiltless light of life.
I saw her raise her arm. I ran to rescue her.
I knew, though, how to keep her for your love.   1020
I've pitied both her pain and your alarm.
I've tried to give some reason for her tears.

THESEUS

He has betrayed . . . No wonder he turned pale.
As he came up, I saw him wince with fear.
I was astonished that he showed no joy.
His cold embrace froze all my tenderness.
But had this sinful love that eats him up
Already shown itself in Athens, then?

OENONE

Remember how the queen complained, my lord.

Un amour criminel causa toute sa haine. 1030

THÉSÉE

Et ce feu dans Trézène a donc recommencé?

ŒNONE

Je vous ai dit, Seigneur, tout ce qui s'est passé.
C'est trop laisser la reine à sa douleur mortelle.
Souffrez que je vous quitte et me range auprès d'elle.

SCÈNE 2

Thésée, Hippolyte

THÉSÉE

Ah! le voici. Grands dieux! à ce noble maintien
Quel œil ne serait pas trompé comme le mien?
Faut-il que sur le front d'un profane adultère
Brille de la vertu le sacré caractère?
Et ne devrait-on pas à des signes certains
Reconnaître le cœur des perfides humains? 1040

HIPPOLYTE

Puis-je vous demander quel funeste nuage,
Seigneur, a pu troubler votre auguste visage?
N'osez-vous confier ce secret à ma foi?

THÉSÉE

Perfide, oses-tu bien te montrer devant moi?
Monstre, qu'a trop longtemps épargné le tonnerre,
Reste impur des brigands dont j'ai purgé la terre!
Après que le transport d'un amour plein d'horreur
Jusqu'au lit de ton père a porté sa fureur,
Tu m'oses présenter une tête ennemie,
Tu parais dans des lieux pleins de ton infamie, 1050
Et ne vas pas chercher sous un ciel inconnu
Des pays où mon nom ne soit point parvenu.
Fuis, traître. Ne viens point braver ici ma haine,
Et tenter un courroux que je retiens à peine.

The guilty love gave rise to all her hate.   1030

THESEUS

And here in Troezen, the passion flamed again?

OENONE

My lord, I've told you all I know.
The queen must not be left in deathly grief.
Allow me now to leave and go to her.

[she leaves, as Hippolytus enters

SCENE 2

Theseus, Hippolytus

THESEUS

Ah, there he is. Great god. What eyes would not
Be taken in like mine at such nobility.
Why must a vile adulterer's face shine bright
With all the sacred look of virtuousness?
There should be sure and certain signs
To recognise the hearts of treacherous men.   1040

HIPPOLYTUS

My lord, I have to ask, what deadly cloud
Could cast such shadows on my sovereign's face?
Can't you confide the secret to my trust?

THESEUS

You hypocrite! How dare you come before me now?
You animal . . . the lightning strike's been too long spared.
You foul remains of all the thieves I purged the earth.
Your appetite for gross and filthy lust
Has brought you frenzied to your father's bed –
And you dare show your loathsome face to me . . . ?
You come here steeped in filth and vice.   1050
You haven't sought some foreign sky,
A country where my name has never reached . . . ?
Get out, you traitor. Don't brave my hatred
And tempt a rage I can now scarce restrain.

C'est bien assez pour moi de l'opprobre éternel
D'avoir pu mettre au jour un fils si criminel,
Sans que ta mort encor honteuse à ma mémoire,
De mes nobles travaux vienne souiller la gloire.
Fuis. Et si tu ne veux qu'un châtiment soudain
T'ajoute aux scélérats qu'a punis cette main,   1060
Prends garde que jamais l'astre qui nous éclaire
Ne te voie en ces lieux mettre un pied téméraire.
Fuis, dis-je, et sans retour précipitant tes pas,
De ton horrible aspect purge tous mes États.
Et toi, Neptune, et toi, si jadis mon courage
D'infâmes assassins nettoya ton rivage,
Souviens-toi que pour prix de mes efforts heureux,
Tu promis d'exaucer le premier de mes vœux.
Dans les longues rigueurs d'une prison cruelle
Je n'ai point imploré ta puissance immortelle.   1070
Avare du secours que j'attends de tes soins,
Mes vœux t'ont réservé pour de plus grands besoins.
Je t'implore aujourd'hui. Venge un malheureux père.
J'abandonne ce traître à toute ta colère.
Étouffe dans son sang ses désirs effrontés.
Thésée à tes fureurs connaîtra tes bontés.

HIPPOLYTE

D'un amour criminel Phèdre accuse Hippolyte?
Un tel excès d'horreur rend mon âme interdite;
Tant de coups imprévus m'accablent à la fois
Qu'ils m'ôtent la parole, et m'étouffent la voix.   1080

THÉSÉE

Traître, tu prétendais qu'en un lâche silence,
Phèdre ensevelirait ta brutale insolence.
Il fallait en fuyant ne pas abandonner
Le fer qui dans ses mains aide à te condamner.
Ou plutôt il fallait, comblant ta perfidie,
Lui ravir tout d'un coup la parole et la vie.

HIPPOLYTE

D'un mensonge si noir justement irrité,
Je devrais faire ici parler la vérité,

I share enough of everlasting shame
For having brought so vile a son to life,
Without your death dishonouring my name
And tarnishing the glory of my work.
Get out. You will not care for instant punishment
To add you to the libertines that I have killed.   1060
Make sure the sun that shines on us never
Detects you setting foot in here again.
I said get out. At once. Never come back.
Just cleanse my kingdom of your hideous face.
And Neptune, you – if in the past I dared
To clear vile murderers from off your shores –
Remember the reward for my success:
You swore to grant the chief of my desires.
Through all the tortures of that cruel gaol,
I never called upon your timeless power.   1070
I carefully saved up the help you owed,
Reserved it for much greater need.
I call upon you now. I grieve. Give me revenge.
I hand this traitor over to your wrath.
Drown all his foul desires in his own blood.
I'll recognise your favours by your rage.

HIPPOLYTUS

Phaedra accuses me of sinful love?
The horror is too much . . . my soul is numb.
So many unexpected blows at once . . .
Words fail me. My voice is drowned.   1080

THESEUS

Traitor. You hoped that Phaedra'd be a coward,
Keep quiet about your brutal violence.
You should not, as you fled, have left your sword.
It's in her hands, and helps to prove your guilt.
Better have capped your treachery with one fell blow
And taken speech and life from her.

HIPPOLYTUS

I'm outraged – rightly – at so black a lie.
I ought, my lord, to let the truth speak now

Seigneur. Mais je supprime un secret qui vous touche.
Approuvez le respect qui me ferme la bouche;   1090
Et sans vouloir vous-même augmenter vos ennuis,
Examinez ma vie et songez qui je suis.
Quelques crimes toujours précèdent les grands crimes.
Quiconque a pu franchir les bornes légitimes,
Peut violer enfin les droits les plus sacrés.
Ainsi que la vertu, le crime a ses degrés,
Et jamais on n'a vu la timide innocence
Passer subitement à l'extrême licence.
Un jour seul ne fait point d'un mortel vertueux
Un perfide assassin, un lâche incestueux.   1100
Élevé dans le sein d'une chaste héroïne,
Je n'ai point de son sang démenti l'origine.
Pitthée estimé sage entre tous les humains,
Daigna m'instruire encore au sortir de ses mains.
Je ne veux point me peindre avec trop d'avantage;
Mais si quelque vertu m'est tombée en partage,
Seigneur, je crois surtout avoir fait éclater
La haine des forfaits qu'on ose m'imputer.
C'est par là qu'Hippolyte est connu dans la Grèce.
J'ai poussé la vertu jusques a la rudesse.   1110
On sait de mes chagrins l'inflexible rigueur.
Le jour n'est pas plus pur que le fond de mon cœur
Et l'on veut qu'Hippolyte épris d'un feu profane . . .

THÉSÉE

Oui, c'est ce même orgueil, lâche, qui te condamne.
Je vois de tes froideurs le principe odieux.
Phèdre seule charmait tes impudiques yeux.
Et pour tout autre objet ton âme indifférente
Dédaignait de brûler d'une flamme innocente.

HIPPOLYTE

Non, mon père, ce cœur (c'est trop vous le celer)
N'a point d'un chaste amour dédaigné de brûler.   1120
Je confesse à vos pieds ma véritable offense.
J'aime, j'aime, il est vrai, malgré votre défense.
Aricie à ses lois tient mes vœux asservis;
La fille de Pallante a vaincu votre fils.

But I'll hold back a secret touching you.
Agree now to respect my silences   1090
If you don't want to worsen all your pain.
Look at my life; consider who I am.
Great crimes are always heralded by lesser ones.
Whoever oversteps the bounds of law
Can in the end outrage the holiest rules.
Just as with goodness, crime has its degrees.
Shy innocence has never yet been seen
To change to total licence at a stroke.
A single day can't change an honest man
Into a traitor, killer, lustful coward.   1100
A good, courageous mother brought me up.
I never have betrayed that source of life.
And Pittheus, who's thought the wisest of all men,
Taught me still further when I'd left her care.
I do not want to paint myself as god,
But if some goodness is my heritage,
I think I've shown with blinding force, my lord,
My hatred of the crime that they accuse me of.
That's what my name is known for throughout Greece.
I've held up virtue to the point of boorishness.   1110
I'm known for rigid, grave severity.
Daylight is not more pure than my heart's core,
And yet they want me raptured by unholy love.

THESEUS

It's just this pride, you coward, that damns you now.
I see the reason why you've been so cold.
Phaedra alone could charm your lustful eyes.
For all things else your heart became indifferent,
Refused the warmth of innocent desires.

HIPPOLYTUS

Father, it's far too much to hide the truth from you.
I have not scorned to feel a guiltless love.   1120
I'll tell my true offence – here, at your feet.
Despite your ban, I am indeed in love.
Aricia has captured me quite utterly.
Pallas's daughter holds your son a slave.

Je l'adore, et mon âme à vos ordres rebelle,
Ne peut ni soupirer, ni brûler que pour elle.

THÉSÉE

Tu l'aimes? Ciel! mais non, l'artifice est grossier.
Tu te feins criminel pour te justifier.

HIPPOLYTE

Seigneur, depuis six mois je l'évite, et je l'aime.
Je venais en tremblant vous le dire à vous-même.   1130
Hé quoi? De votre erreur rien ne vous peut tirer?
Par quel affreux serment faut-il vous rassurer?
Que la terre, le ciel, que toute la nature . . .

THÉSÉE

Toujours les scélérats ont recours au parjure.
Cesse, cesse, et m'épargne un importun discours,
Si ta fausse vertu n'a point d'autre secours.

HIPPOLYTE

Elle vous paraît fausse, et pleine d'artifice;
Phèdre au fond de son cœur me rend plus de justice.

THÉSÉE

Ah! que ton impudence excite mon courroux!

HIPPOLYTE

Quel temps à mon exil, quel lieu prescrivez-vous?   1140

THÉSÉE

Fusses-tu par delà les colonnes d'Alcide,
Je me croirais encor trop voisin d'un perfide.

HIPPOLYTE

Chargé du crime affreux dont vous me soupçonnez,
Quels amis me plaindront quand vous m'abandonnez?

THÉSÉE

Va chercher des amis dont l'estime funeste
Honore l'adultère, applaudisse à l'inceste;
Des traîtres, des ingrats sans honneur et sans loi,
Dignes de protéger un méchant tel que toi.

I worship her. In spite of your command,
My soul is all on fire for her alone.

THESEUS

You love her? God, the sham is grosser yet.
You feign a crime to justify yourself.

HIPPOLYTUS

For six months now I've shunned and worshipped her.
I came all fearful here to tell you so.   1130
Will nothing tear you from your fallacies?
What dreadful oath will satisfy you, then?
May earth, the sky, the whole of nature . . .

THESEUS

Foul men have always had recourse to perjury.
Stop, stop. Spare me this self-regarding talk.
Can't your cheap virtue call on other help?

HIPPOLYTUS

It may seem cheap and full of guile to you,
But Phaedra in her heart has been more just.

THESEUS

My anger's boiling at your shamelessness!

HIPPOLYTUS

What period for my exile is prescribed? What place?   1140

THESEUS

Beyond Alcides' pillars far might you sail
And still I'd find your treachery too close.

HIPPOLYTUS

Charged with the crime that you suspect me of,
What friends will mourn if you abandon me?

THESEUS

Then search out friends who value such dark things,
Who clap at incest, cheer adultery:
Betrayers, scum without honour, outside the law,
Fit to protect a vicious man like you.

HIPPOLYTE

Vous me parlez toujours d'inceste et d'adultère!
Je me tais. Cependant Phèdre sort d'une mère,   1150
Phèdre est d'un sang, Seigneur, vous le savez trop bien,
De toutes ces horreurs plus rempli que le mien.

THÉSÉE

Quoi! ta rage à mes veux perd toute retenue?
Pour la dernière fois, ôte-toi de ma vue.
Sors, traître. N'attends pas qu'un père furieux
Te fasse avec opprobre arracher de ces lieux.

SCÈNE 3

THÉSÉE [seul]

Misérable, tu cours à ta perte infaillible.
Neptune, par le fleuve aux dieux mêmes terrible,
M'a donné sa parole, et va l'exécuter.
Un dieu vengeur te suit, tu ne peux l'éviter.   1160
Je t'aimais. Et je sens que malgré ton offense,
Mes entrailles pour toi se troublent par avance.
Mais à te condamner tu m'as trop engagé.
Jamais père en effet fut-il plus outragé?
Justes dieux, qui voyez la douleur qui m'accable,
Ai-je pu mettre au jour un enfant si coupable?

SCÈNE 4

Phèdre, Thésée

PHÈDRE

Seigneur, je viens à vous pleine d'un juste effroi.
Votre voix redoutable a passé jusqu'à moi.
Je crains qu'un prompt effet n'ait suivi la menace.
S'il en est temps encore, épargnez votre race.   1170

HIPPOLYTUS

You harp on incest and adultery.
I will keep quiet. But Phaedra's mother, now . . .   1150
Phaedra is from a race, as well you know,
Fuller in all these horrors than my own.

THESEUS

Has your insanity lost all control?
For the last time, get out — out of my sight.
Get out, you traitor, now, before I start
To tear you from this place in shame.

                       [*Hippolytus leaves*

SCENE 3

THESEUS [*alone*]

Run off, you boy of tears, to certain death.
Along the river dreaded even by the gods,
Neptune gave me his word. It will be kept.
A god of vengeance follows you. You won't escape.   1160
I loved you once. Despite your crime, I feel
My body racked for you and for your fate.
But you have forced me to condemn you now.
What father has been ever so outraged?
O God, you see my overwhelming pain.
Can I have given life to this vile child?

                       [*Phaedra enters*

SCENE 4

Phaedra, Theseus

PHAEDRA

My lord, I've come to you . . . I'm terrified . . .
I've heard the awful things that you have said.
I fear your threat will soon be carried out.
If there is still time left, then spare your son.   1170

Respectez votre sang, j'ose vous en prier.
Sauvez-moi de l'horreur de l'entendre crier;
Ne me préparez point la douleur éternelle
De l'avoir fait répandre à la main paternelle.

THÉSÉE

Non, Madame, en mon sang ma main n'a point trempé.
Mais l'ingrat toutefois ne m'est point échappé.
Une immortelle main de sa perte est chargée.
Neptune me la doit, et vous serez vengée.

PHÈDRE

Neptune vous la doit! quoi! vos vœux irrités . . .

THÉSÉE

Quoi! craignez-vous déjà qu'ils ne soient écoutés?   1180
Joignez-vous bien plutôt à mes vœux légitimes.
Dans toute leur noirceur retracez-moi ses crimes.
Échauffez mes transports trop lents, trop retenus.
Tous ses crimes encor ne vous sont pas connus.
Sa fureur contre vous se répand en injures.
Votre bouche, dit-il, est pleine d'impostures.
Il soutient qu'Aricie a son cœur, a sa foi,
Qu'il l'aime.

PHÈDRE   Quoi, Seigneur!

THÉSÉE   Il l'a dit devant moi.
Mais je sais rejeter un frivole artifice.
Espérons de Neptune une prompte justice.   1190
Je vais moi-même encore au pied de ses autels,
Le presser d'accomplir ses serments immortels.

Respect your flesh and blood, I beg of you.
Don't let me hear the horror of his cries.
Don't lay the everlasting pain on me
Of having made a father let blood flow.

THESEUS

My hands have not been reddened in his blood,
But his obscenity has not gone free.
His death is charged into a god's own hands.
Neptune owes me it. You will be avenged.

PHAEDRA

Neptune owes you it? Have raging prayers from you . . .

THESEUS

Do you already fear they have been heard?   1180
Better you voice the same. They're justified.
Give me the darkest details of his crime.
Stir up my anger – gone too slow and stale –
You do not yet know all his wickedness.
His frenzy has insulted you, your name.
He says your mouth speaks nothing but deceit.
He claims Aricia has won his heart and faith,
That he loves her.

PHAEDRA   My lord . . .

THESEUS   He told me to my face.
But I know how to deal with worthless sham.
I hope that Neptune will judge soon.   1190
I'll go to plead again before his shrine;
I'll urge him to fulfil his binding oath.

                                        [*he leaves*

SCÈNE 5

PHÈDRE [*seule*]

Il sort. Quelle nouvelle a frappé mon oreille?
Quel feu mal étouffé dans mon cœur se réveille?
Quel coup de foudre, ô ciel! et quel funeste avis!
Je volais tout entière au secours de son fils,
Et m'arrachant des bras d'Œnone épouvantée.
Je cédais au remords dont j'étais tourmentée.
Qui sait même où m'allait porter ce repentir?
Peut-être à m'accuser j'aurais pu consentir.   1200
Peut-être, si la voix ne m'eût été coupée,
L'affreuse vérité me serait échappée.
Hippolyte est sensible, et ne sent rien pour moi!
Aricie a son cœur, Aricie a sa foi!
Ah, dieux! lorsqu'à mes vœux l'ingrat inexorable
S'armait d'un œil si fier, d'un front si redoutable,
Je pensais qu'à l'amour son cœur toujours fermé,
Fût contre tout mon sexe également armé.
Une autre cependant a fléchi son audace.
Devant ses yeux cruels une autre a trouvé grâce.   1210
Peut-être a-t-il un cœur facile à s'attendrir.
Je suis le seul objet qu'il ne saurait souffrir.
Et je me chargerais du soin de le défendre!

SCÈNE 6

Phèdre, Œnone

PHÈDRE

Chère Œnone, sais-tu ce que je viens d'apprendre?

ŒNONE

Non. Mais je viens tremblante, à ne vous point mentir.
J'ai pâli du dessein qui vous a fait sortir.
J'ai craint une fureur à vous-même fatale.

SCENE 5

PHAEDRA [*alone*]

He's gone. . . . Such news to burst upon my eyes . . .
What smouldering flame begins to blaze again . . . ?
It's lightning from the sky . . . the deadly news.
I'd run – one thought alone – to save his son.
I'd torn myself from pale Oenone's arms,
Surrendered to the guilt that tortured me.
Who knows how far repentance would have led?
I might have soon accused myself.   1200
Had not the words stuck in my throat, I might
Have let the terrifying truth escape.
And so Hippolytus can feel. But not for me.
Aricia has his heart, his trust . . . Dear God,
The times he was so graceless to my pleas.
He stared with such proud eyes, so stern a face,
I thought his heart for ever closed to love,
Against all women uniformly armed.
And yet another woman breaks his pride,
Finds favour in those callous eyes.   1210
Perhaps he has a heart that can be moved,
And I'm the only thing he cannot stand.
And I took on the task of his defence . . .

[*Oenone enters*

SCENE 6

Phaedra, Oenone

PHAEDRA

Oenone, you know what I have learned?

OENONE

No. And yet I'm trembling, if truth were told.
I paled – went white – to think why you had gone.
I was afraid that you would kill yourself.

PHÈDRE

Œnone, qui l'eût cru? J'avais une rivale.

ŒNONE

Comment?

PHÈDRE   Hippolyte aime, et je n'en puis douter.
Ce farouche ennemi qu'on ne pouvait dompter,   1220
Qu'offensait le respect, qu'importunait la plainte,
Ce tigre, que jamais je n'abordai sans crainte,
Soumis, apprivoisé reconnaît un vainqueur.
Aricie a trouvé le chemin de son cœur.

ŒNONE

Aricie?

PHÈDRE   Ah, douleur non encore éprouvée!
A quel nouveau tourment je me suis réservée!
Tout ce que j'ai souffert, mes craintes, mes transports,
La fureur de mes feux, l'horreur de mes remords,
Et d'un refus cruel l'insupportable injure
N'était qu'un faible essai du tourment que j'endure.   1230
Ils s'aiment! par quel charme ont-ils trompé mes yeux?
Comment se sont-ils vus? Depuis quand? Dans quels lieux?
Tu le savais. Pourquoi me laissais-tu séduire?
De leur furtive ardeur ne pouvais-tu m'instruire?
Les a-t-on vus souvent se parler, se chercher?
Dans le fond des forêts allaient-ils se cacher?
Hélas! ils se voyaient avec pleine licence.
Le ciel de leurs soupirs approuvait l'innocence.
Ils suivaient sans remords leur penchant amoureux.
Tous les jours se levaient clairs et sereins pour eux.   1240
Et moi, triste rebut de la nature entière,
Je me cachais au jour, je fuyais la lumière.
La mort est le seul dieu que j'osais implorer.
J'attendais le moment où j'allais expirer,
Me nourrissant de fiel, de larmes abreuvée;
Encor dans mon malheur de trop près observée,
Je n'osais dans mes pleurs me noyer à loisir,
Je goûtais en tremblant ce funeste plaisir,
Et sous un front serein déguisant mes alarmes,

PHAEDRA
Who would have thought? I have a rival now.

OENONE
What?

PHAEDRA Hippolytus is in love, there is no doubt.
That wild, unconquerable enemy,   1220
Offended by respect, annoyed by tears,
Whom I could never meet without some fear,
Submits, quite tamed, salutes his vanquisher.
Aricia has found the way into his heart.

OENONE
Aricia!

PHAEDRA What deeper sadness can be yet endured . . . ?
What latest torture is reserved for me?
All I've endured – the fears, the ecstasies.
This raging love, the horrors of remorse,
Him saying no, the injury I couldn't bear –
These were mere foretastes of my torment now.   1230
Those two in love? What spell deceived me, then?
How did they see each other? Where? Since when?
You knew. Why did you let me be misled?
You could have told me of their furtive love.
Weren't they seen talking? Looking for each other?
They must have tried to hide deep in the woods . . . ?
Ah, so they met in total liberty . . . ?
Heaven approved their innocent desires.
They walked the ways of love without remorse.
Each day for them dawned cloudless and serene;   1240
And I, rejected by all living things,
Have hidden from the day and shunned the light.
Death was the only god I dared implore.
I waited for the moment I would die.
I fed on gall, I drank my tears. And yet,
My misery was close, so closely watched,
I was not even free to drown in grief.
This deathly pleasure . . . shaking at the taste . . .
I hid my pain behind a calm façade

Il fallait bien souvent me priver de mes larmes. 1250

ŒNONE

Quel fruit recevront-ils de leurs vaines amours?
Ils ne se verront plus.

PHÈDRE   Ils s'aimeront toujours!
Au moment que je parle, ah, mortelle pensée!
Ils bravent la fureur d'une amante insensée.
Malgré ce même exil qui va les écarter,
Ils font mille serments de ne se point quitter.
Non, je ne puis souffrir un bonheur qui m'outrage,
Œnone. Prends pitié de ma jalouse rage.
Il faut perdre Aricie. Il faut de mon époux
Contre un sang odieux réveiller le courroux. 1260
Qu'il ne se borne pas à des peines légères.
Le crime de la sœur passe celui des frères.
Dans mes jaloux transports je le veux implorer.
Que fais-je? Où ma raison se va-t-elle égarer?
Moi jalouse! et Thésée est celui que j'implore!
Mon époux est vivant, et moi je brûle encore!
Pour qui? Quel est le cœur où prétendent mes vœux?
Chaque mot sur mon front fait dresser mes cheveux.
Mes crimes désormais ont comblé la mesure.
Je respire à la fois l'inceste et l'imposture. 1270
Mes homicides mains promptes à me venger,
Dans le sang innocent brûlent de se plonger.
Misérable! et je vis? Et je soutiens la vue
De ce sacré soleil dont je suis descendue?
J'ai pour aïeul le père et le maître des dieux.
Le ciel, tout l'univers est plein de mes aïeux;
Où me cacher? Fuyons dans la nuit infernale.
Mais que dis-je? Mon père y tient l'urne fatale.
Le sort, dit-on, l'a mise en ses sévères mains.
Minos juge aux enfers tous les pâles humains. 1280
Ah! combien frémira son ombre épouvantée,
Lorsqu'il verra sa fille à ses yeux présentée,
Contrainte d'avouer tant de forfaits divers,
Et des crimes peut-être inconnus aux enfers?
Que diras-tu, mon père, à ce spectacle horrible?

And often had to stay without my tears.   1250

OENONE

What can they hope to gain from such a love?
They'll never meet again.

PHAEDRA   They'll always be in love.
Now as I speak – I die to think the thought –
They brave my fury – a queen outraged.
Despite the exile that will sever them,
They swear a thousand oaths never to part.
I cannot bear a joy that racks me so.
Pity my raging jealousy.
Aricia must die. Theseus's rage
Against her odious race must be revived.   1260
A trifling punishment will not suffice.
Her brothers' crimes are far surpassed by hers.
This jealous frenzy . . . I will implore the king . . .
What am I doing? Have I lost my mind?
Me jealous? *I* implore the king?
He's my husband. Still alive . . . yet I burn . . .
Who for? Whose heart holds my desires?
Each word I mouth, my hair stands up on end.
From now my sins will overflow the brim.
I stink of incest and deceit.   1270
These murderous hands, so eager for revenge,
Are burning to be drenched in guiltless blood.
I appal and yet I live. I must still bear the gaze
Of holiness, the sun from which I came.
My ancestor is father, master of the gods.
The sky and all the universe is full of them.
Where can I hide? In darkest, hellish night . . . ?
Useless words . . . my father holds the urn there.
They say fate placed it in his ruthless hands.
Minos is judge in hell of pale humanity.   1280
What shuddering will seize his ghost
To see his daughter stand before his eyes,
Forced to confess so many heinous crimes,
Crimes even unknown, perhaps, in hell.
What, father, will you say to that foul sight?

Je crois voir de ta main tomber l'urne terrible,
Je crois te voir cherchant un supplice nouveau,
Toi-même de ton sang devenir le bourreau.
Pardonne. Un dieu cruel a perdu ta famille.
Reconnais sa vengeance aux fureurs de ta fille.   1290
Hélas! du crime affreux dont la honte me suit,
Jamais mon triste cœur n'a recueilli le fruit.
Jusqu'au dernier soupir de malheurs poursuivie,
Je rends dans les tourments une pénible vie.

ŒNONE

Hé! repoussez, Madame, une injuste terreur!
Regardez d'un autre œil une excusable erreur.
Vous aimez. On ne peut vaincre sa destinée.
Par un charme fatal vous fûtes entraînée.
Est-ce donc un prodige inouï parmi nous?
L'amour n'a-t-il encor triomphé que de vous?   1300
La faiblesse aux humains n'est que trop naturelle.
Mortelle, subissez le sort d'une mortelle.
Vous vous plaignez d'un joug imposé dès longtemps.
Les dieux même, les dieux, de l'Olympe habitants,
Qui d'un bruit si terrible épouvantent les crimes,
Ont brûlé quelquefois de feux illégitimes.

PHÈDRE

Qu'entends-je? Quels conseils ose-t-on me donner?
Ainsi donc jusqu'au bout tu veux m'empoisonner,
Malheureuse! voilà comme tu m'as perdue.
Au jour, que je fuyais, c'est toi qui m'as rendue.   1310
Tes prières m'ont fait oublier mon devoir.
J'évitais Hippolyte, et tu me l'as fait voir.
De quoi te chargeais-tu? Pourquoi ta bouche impie
A-t-elle en l'accusant, osé noircir sa vie?
Il en mourra peut-être, et d'un père insensé
Le sacrilège vœu peut-être est exaucé.
Je ne t'écoute plus. Va-t'en, monstre exécrable.
Va, laisse-moi le soin de mon sort déplorable.
Puisse le juste ciel dignement te payer;
Et puisse ton supplice à jamais effrayer   1320

I see the urn of doom slip from your hands,
I see you seeking out new punishment,
The executioner of your own blood.
Forgive me. Venus now has doomed your race.
You see her vengeance in your daughter's rage.　　　　1290
The shame of hideous crimes pursues me still.
My heart is broken, but never ate the fruit.
The hurt will haunt me to my dying breath.
I place upon the rack a life of pain.

OENONE

You must resist these needless fears.
Your fault might well be seen to have just cause.
You are in love. We cannot master fate.
A fatal magic swept you off your feet.
Is that so new or strange a thing?
Are you the only one to fall in love?　　　　1300
Humanity is all too frail.
You are human. You must accept that fate.
You blame a bondage forged so long ago.
Even the gods who live on Olympus,
Who punish crime so terrifyingly,
Have sometimes burned with wrong desire.

PHAEDRA

You dare to offer this advice to me?
Right to the end you try to poison me,
You awful thing! It's you who's ruined me.
I tried to end my life. You brought me back.　　　　1310
You begged, and I forgot the duty that I had.
I shunned Hippolytus. You made me speak to him.
What have you done? Why did your wicked mouth
Accuse him so and blacken his whole life?
He still may die. His father's outraged
Sacrilegious prayer may still be heard.
I won't listen. You obscenity! Get out.
Get out! Just leave my wretched fate to me.
May heaven be just, reward you properly!
Just let your punishment for ever terrify　　　　1320

Tous ceux qui, comme toi, par de lâches adresses,
Des princes malheureux nourrissent les faiblesses,
Les poussent au penchant où leur cœur est enclin,
Et leur osent du crime aplanir le chemin;
Détestables flatteurs, présent le plus funeste
Que puisse faire aux rois la colère céleste.

ŒNONE [*seule*]

Ah! dieux! pour la servir, j'ai tout fait, tout quitté,
Et j'en reçois ce prix! je l'ai bien mérité.

All those like you who feed so skilfully
The weaknesses of ill-starred kings.
You urge them down the slopes of their desires.
You level out the path to sin for them.
Foul flatterers – the deadliest gift
The anger of the gods can give to kings.   [*she leaves*

OENONE [*alone*]

Dear God, to serve her I left home, did everything . . .
But this is the reward that I deserve . . .

ACTE 5 SCÈNE 1

Hippolyte, Aricie

ARICIE

Quoi! vous pouvez vous taire en ce péril extrême?

Vous laissez dans l'erreur un père qui vous aime?   1330

Cruel, si de mes pleurs méprisant le pouvoir,

Vous consentez sans peine à ne me plus revoir,

Partez, séparez-vous de la triste Aricie.

Mais du moins en partant assurez votre vie.

Défendez votre honneur d'un reproche honteux,

Et forcez votre père à révoquer ses vœux.

Il en est temps encor. Pourquoi, par quel caprice

Laissez-vous le champ libre à votre accusatrice?

Éclaircissez Thésée.

HIPPOLYTE   Hé! que n'ai-je point dit?

Ai-je dû mettre au jour l'opprobre de son lit?   1340

Devais-je, en lui faisant un récit trop sincère,

D'une indigne rougeur couvrir le front d'un père?

Vous seule avez percé ce mystère odieux.

Mon cœur pour s'épancher n'a que vous et les dieux.

Je n'ai pu vous cacher, jugez si je vous aime,

Tout ce que je voulais me cacher à moi-même.

Mais songez sous quel sceau je vous l'ai révélé.

Oubliez, s'il se peut, que je vous ai parlé,

Madame. Et que jamais une bouche si pure

Ne s'ouvre pour conter cette horrible aventure.   1350

Sur l'équité des dieux osons nous confier.

Ils ont trop d'intérêt à me justifier;

Et Phèdre tôt ou tard de son crime punie,

N'en saurait éviter la juste ignominie.

C'est l'unique respect que j'exige de vous.

Je permets tout le reste à mon libre courroux.

Sortez de l'esclavage où vous êtes réduite.

Osez me suivre. Osez accompagner ma fuite.

Arrachez-vous d'un lieu funeste et profané

Où la vertu respire un air empoisonné,   1360

ACT 5 SCENE 1

Hippolytus, Aricia

ARICIA

How can you in this danger still keep quiet?
Your father loves you still. You'll keep him ignorant?   1330
It's cruel to hold my grief so cheap, agree
So easily to never see me more.
Then go. Leave me to all my wretchedness.
But if you go, at least protect your life.
You must defend your name from smears and shame
And force your father to retract his curse.
There is still time. What whim, capriciousness,
Makes you let Phaedra have an open field?
Explain to Theseus.

HIPPOLYTUS   What more is there to say?
Should I have brought the outrage in his bed   1340
To light? Should I have told so frank a tale
And make his face turn scarlet with the shame?
This awful secret you alone now know.
I've opened up my heart to you . . . the gods.
Judge if I love. I couldn't hide from you
Things I would keep secret from myself.
Remember, though – you've sworn to secrecy.
If possible, forget the things I've said.
Your lips are clean. They should not tell
The story of this foul affair.   1350
We must dare trust the justice of the gods.
They have some interest in clearing me.
Sooner or later, Phaedra will receive
The odium her crime deserves. She won't escape.
But this now – this is all I ask of you.
The rest of things can face my rage.
Throw off the slavery that's ground you down.
Dare follow me. Be with me in my flight.
Leave far behind this deadly, obscene place
Where goodness breathes a foul, polluted air.   1360

Profitez pour cacher votre prompte retraite,
De la confusion que ma disgrâce y jette.
Je vous puis de la fuite assurer les moyens,
Vous n'avez jusqu'ici de gardes que les miens,
De puissants défenseurs prendront notre querelle.
Argos nous tend les bras, et Sparte nous appelle;
A nos amis communs portons nos justes cris.
Ne souffrons pas que Phèdre assemblant nos débris
Du trône paternel nous chasse l'un et l'autre,
Et promette à son fils ma dépouille et la vôtre.   1370
L'occasion est belle, il la faut embrasser.
Quelle peur vous retient? Vous semblez balancer?
Votre seul intérêt m'inspire cette audace.
Quand je suis tout de feu, d'où vous vient cette glace?
Sur les pas d'un banni craignez-vous de marcher?

ARICIE

Hélas! qu'un tel exil, Seigneur, me serait cher!
Dans quels ravissements, à votre sort liée
Du reste des mortels je vivrais oubliée!
Mais n'étant point unis par un lien si doux
Me puis-je avec honneur dérober avec vous?   1380
Je sais que sans blesser l'honneur le plus sévère,
Je me puis affranchir des mains de votre père.
Ce n'est point m'arracher du sein de mes parents,
Et la fuite est permise à qui fuit ses tyrans.
Mais vous m'aimez, Seigneur. Et ma gloire alarmée . . .

HIPPOLYTE

Non, non; j'ai trop de soin de votre renommée.
Un plus noble dessein m'amène devant vous.
Fuyez vos ennemis, et suivez votre époux.
Libres dans nos malheurs, puisque le ciel l'ordonne,
Le don de notre foi ne dépend de personne.   1390
L'hymen n'est point toujours entouré de flambeaux.
Aux portes de Trézène, et parmi ces tombeaux,
Des princes de ma race antiques sépultures,
Est un temple sacré formidable aux parjures.
C'est là que les mortels n'osent jurer en vain.
Le perfide y reçoit un châtiment soudain.

We can exploit the turmoil that's been spread
By my disgrace to cover up your flight.
I can make sure that you will get away.
The only guards you have are my own men.
Powerful defenders will support our cause.
Argos holds out its arms, and Sparta calls.
Let's take our rightful claims to friends we share.
Phaedra must not gain profit from our fall –
She'd drive us both far from my father's throne
And give her son what has been stripped from us.   1370
This is our chance. Let's seize it with both hands . . .
What holds you back? You seem to hesitate.
It's only for your sake I urge this plan.
When I am all on fire, why are you ice?
Are you afraid to share an exile's life?

ARICIA

Such banishment, my lord, would be so sweet.
I'd share your life and be in such delight
Forgotten by the rest of humankind.
But we are not yet joined in that dear bond.
How in all honour can I go with you?   1380
I know I can escape your father's hands
And do no harm to honour's strictest codes.
I would not then be breaking family ties;
To flee a tyrant is within the law.
You love me, though, my lord . . . I fear my name . . .

HIPPOLYTUS

No, no. I care too much for your good name.
I've come here with a better plan.
Escape your enemies. Come with me as my wife.
For all the pain that heaven decrees, we're free.
We do not need the world to pledge our faith.   1390
Torches do not light up all marriage vows.
At Troezen's gates, among the tombs,
The ancient vaults for princes of my line,
A sacred temple stands. It's feared by all who lie.
No human dare swear falsely in that place,
For perjurers receive immediate punishment.

Et craignant d'y trouver la mort inévitable,
Le mensonge n'a point de frein plus redoutable.
Là, si vous m'en croyez, d'un amour éternel
Nous irons confirmer le serment solennel.   1400
Nous prendrons à témoin le dieu qu'on y révère.
Nous le prierons tous deux de nous servir de père.
Des dieux les plus sacrés j'attesterai le nom.
Et la chaste Diane, et l'auguste Junon
Et tous les dieux enfin témoins de mes tendresses
Garantiront la foi de mes saintes promesses.

ARICIE

Le roi vient. Fuyez, Prince, et partez promptement.
Pour cacher mon départ je demeure un moment.
Allez, et laissez-moi quelque fidèle guide,
Qui conduise vers vous ma démarche timide.   1410

SCÈNE 2

Thésée, Aricie, Ismène

THÉSÉE

Dieux, éclairez mon trouble, et daignez à mes yeux
Montrer la vérité, que je cherche en ces lieux.

ARICIE

Songe à tout, chère Ismène, et sois prête à la fuite.

SCÈNE 3

Thésée, Aricie

THÉSÉE

Vous changez de couleur, et semblez interdite,
Madame! que faisait Hippolyte en ce lieu?

They face the certainty of death in there.
False oaths have no more dreaded check.
There, if you trust me, we will go and vow
Our solemn oath to everlasting love.   1400
The god who's worshipped there will swear for us.
We'll pray he'll be a father to us both.
I'll call the holiest gods as witnesses.
And chaste Diana, Juno the renowned,
And all the gods that witness my dear love
Will guard the sanctity of what I swear.

ARICIA

The king is coming. Quick. You must go now.
I'll stay a while to cover up my flight.
Go now; but leave me someone I can trust
To take me to you . . . nervously . . .   1410

[Hippolytus leaves. Theseus enters

SCENE 2

Theseus, Aricia, Ismene

THESEUS

O God, lighten this darkness in my soul;
Let my eyes see the truth I'm searching for.

ARICIA

Have everything prepared, Ismene, for our flight.

[Ismene leaves

SCENE 3

Theseus, Aricia

THESEUS

Your colour changes so . . . You seem struck dumb,
My lady. What was Hippolytus doing here?

ARICIE

Seigneur, il me disait un éternel adieu.

THÉSÉE

Vos yeux ont su dompter ce rebelle courage;
Et ses premiers soupirs sont votre heureux ouvrage.

ARICIE

Seigneur, je ne vous puis nier la vérité.
De votre injuste haine il n'a pas hérité.   1420
Il ne me traitait point comme une criminelle.

THÉSÉE

J'entends, il vous jurait une amour éternelle.
Ne vous assurez point sur ce cœur inconstant.
Car à d'autres que vous il en jurait autant.

ARICIE

Lui, Seigneur?

THÉSÉE   Vous deviez le rendre moins volage.
Comment souffriez-vous cet horrible partage?

ARICIE

Et comment souffrez-vous que d'horribles discours
D'une si belle vie osent noircir le cours?
Avez-vous de son cœur si peu de connaissance?
Discernez-vous si mal le crime et l'innocence?   1430
Faut-il qu'à vos yeux seuls un nuage odieux
Dérobe sa vertu qui brille à tous les yeux?
Ah! c'est trop le livrer à des langues perfides.
Cessez. Repentez-vous de vos vœux homicides;
Craignez, Seigneur, craignez que le ciel rigoureux
Ne vous haïsse assez pour exaucer vos vœux.
Souvent dans sa colère il reçoit nos victimes,
Ses présents sont souvent la peine de nos crimes.

THÉSÉE

Non, vous voulez en vain couvrir son attentat.
Votre amour vous aveugle en faveur de l'ingrat.   1440
Mais j'en crois des témoins certains, irréprochables.
J'ai vu, j'ai vu couler des larmes véritables.

ARICIA

He came to say a last goodbye, my lord.

THESEUS

So you have tamed his stubbornness.
The first time that he yearns is due to you.

ARICIA

I can't deny the truth of that, my lord.
Your hate of me was not passed on to him.   1420
He didn't treat me as a criminal.

THESEUS

I understand. He's sworn eternal love.
But don't rely upon that wavering heart.
He's sworn the same to other girls as well.

ARICIA

He what?

THESEUS   You should have made him less disloyal.
How could you bear to be a part of it?

ARICIA

And how could you allow such dreadful smears
To blacken out the honour of his life?
Have you so little knowledge how he feels?
Can you so little tell a crime from innocence?   1430
Must you alone discern this loathsome cloud
Hiding his goodnesses, which shine so bright to all?
I will not give him up to evil tongues.
Stop and repent your murderous prayers.
Fear, my good lord. Fear lest the gods feel harsh,
Hate you enough to grant what you have asked.
They often rage and take our sacrifice.
They often punish us for all our sin.

THESEUS

You try to cover up his crime in vain.
Love makes you blind to all his treachery.   1440
But I have witnesses I trust, beyond reproach.
I've seen real tears . . . real tears have flowed . . .

ARICIE

Prenez garde, Seigneur. Vos invincibles mains
Ont de monstres sans nombre affranchi les humains.
Mais tout n'est pas détruit; et vous en laissez vivre
Un . . . Votre fils, Seigneur, me défend de poursuivre.
Instruite du respect qu'il veut vous conserver,
Je l'affligerais trop, si j'osais achever.
J'imite sa pudeur, et fuis votre présence
Pour n'être pas forcée à rompre le silence.   1450

SCÈNE 4

THÉSÉE [seul]

Quelle est donc sa pensée? Et que cache un discours
Commencé tant de fois, interrompu toujours?
Veulent-ils m'éblouir par une feinte vaine?
Sont-ils d'accord tous deux pour me mettre à la gêne?
Mais moi-même, malgré ma sévère rigueur,
Quelle plaintive voix crie au fond de mon cœur?
Une pitié secrète et m'afflige, et m'étonne.
Une seconde fois interrogeons Œnone.
Je veux de tout le crime être mieux éclairci.
Gardes. Qu'Œnone sorte et vienne seule ici.   1460

SCÈNE 5

Thésée, Panope

PANOPE

J'ignore le projet que la reine médite,
Seigneur. Mais je crains tout du transport qui l'agite.
Un mortel désespoir sur son visage est peint.
La pâleur de la mort est déjà sur son teint.
Déjà de sa présence avec honte chassée
Dans la profonde mer Œnone s'est lancée.
On ne sait point d'où part ce dessein furieux.

ARICIA

Take care, my lord. You're undefeated still.
You've freed mankind from countless murderers,
But all are not destroyed. You've left alive
Just one . . . Your son forbids me speak of it.
I know the reverence he has for you;
I should offend too much were I to tell.
I'll follow his restraint and leave you now
Before I'm forced to make the silence speak.   1450

[*she leaves*

SCENE 4

THESESUS [*alone*]

What does she mean? What lies behind her words?
She starts, then stops, then starts again, then stops.
So what's their aim? To trick and baffle me . . . ?
Have they agreed to put me on the rack . . . ?
For all my harsh severity, I still . . .
What mournful voice cries deep down in my heart?
Some secret pity grieves and harrows me.
Oenone must be questioned once again.
I want to have more light shed on the crime.
Guards, tell her to come here. And by herself.   1460

[*Panope enters*

SCENE 5

Theseus, Panope

PANOPE

I do not know what plan the queen has in her mind,
My lord; and yet I fear the fits that rack her so.
Deadly despair is written on her face,
The ghastliness of death has paled her cheeks.
Oenone has been driven out in shame,
And hurled herself deep down into the sea . . .
We'll never know what caused this awful act.

Et les flots pour jamais l'ont ravie à nos yeux.

THÉSÉE

Qu'entends- je?

PANOPE　　　　　　　　Son trépas n'a point calmé la reine,
Le trouble semble croître en son âme incertaine.　　　　　1470
Quelquefois pour flatter ses secrètes douleurs
Elle prend ses enfants et les baigne de pleurs;
Et soudain renonçant à l'amour maternelle,
Sa main avec horreur les repousse loin d'elle.
Elle porte au hasard ses pas irrésolus.
Son œil tout égaré ne nous reconnaît plus.
Elle a trois fois écrit, et changeant de pensée
Trois fois elle a rompu sa lettre commencée.
Daignez la voir, Seigneur, daignez la secourir.

THÉSÉE

O ciel! Œnone est morte, et Phèdre veut mourir?　　　　1480
Qu'on rappelle mon fils, qu'il vienne se défendre,
Qu'il vienne me parler, je suis prêt de l'entendre.
Ne précipite point tes funestes bienfaits,
Neptune. J'aime mieux n'être exaucé jamais.
J'ai peut-être trop cru des témoins peu fidèles.
Et j'ai trop tôt vers toi levé mes mains cruelles.
Ah! de quel désespoir mes vœux seraient suivis!

SCÈNE 6

Thésée, Théramène

THÉSÉE

Théramène, est-ce toi? Qu'as-tu fait de mon fils?
Je te l'ai confié dès l'âge le plus tendre.
Mais d'où naissent les pleurs que je te vois répandre?　　1490
Que fait mon fils?

The waves have taken her for ever from our sight.

THESEUS

She's drowned . . .

PANOPE   Her dying has not calmed the queen;
The turmoil seems to grow and eat her mind.   1470
Sometimes, as if to ease her secret pain,
She'll hug her children tight, bathe them in tears.
Then suddenly, she turns against her mother's love
And pushes them away in dreadful fear.
She wanders aimlessly, this way then that.
Her eyes are wild, seem not to see us there . . .
Three times she has begun to write, then changed
Her mind, and three times torn the letter up.
Agree to see her now. She must be helped, my lord.

THESEUS

O god . . . Oenone's dead . . . and Phaedra wants to die.   1480
Call back my son. Let him defend himself
And speak to me. I'll listen to him now.
                              [*Panope leaves. Theseus remains alone*
Neptune, don't hurl your deadly gift on him.
Much better to have never heard my prayer . . .
Perhaps I trusted witnesses who lied,
And raised these callous hands to you too soon.
Oh that my prayer should end in such despair . . .
                                          [*Theramenes enters*

SCENE 6

Theramenes, Theseus

THESEUS

Theramenes, it's you? Where is my son?
I trusted him to you while yet a child.
You're crying . . . oh, why weep these tears?   1490
Where is he now?

THÉRAMÈNE   O soins tardifs et superflus!
   Inutile tendresse! Hippolyte n'est plus.

THÉSÉE
   Dieux!

THÉRAMÈNE   J'ai vu des mortels périr le plus aimable,
   Et j'ose dire encor, Seigneur, le moins coupable.

THÉSÉE
   Mon fils n'est plus? Hé quoi! quand je lui tends les bras,
   Les dieux impatients ont hâté son trépas?
   Quel coup me l'a ravi? Quelle foudre soudaine?

THÉRAMÈNE
   A peine nous sortions des portes de Trézène,
   Il était sur son char. Ses gardes affligés
   Imitaient son silence, autour de lui rangés.   1500
   Il suivait tout pensif le chemin de Mycènes.
   Sa main sur ses chevaux laissait flotter les rênes.
   Ses superbes coursiers, qu'on voyait autrefois
   Pleins d'une ardeur si noble obéir à sa voix,
   L'œil morne maintenant et la tête baissée
   Semblaient se conformer à sa triste pensée.
   Un effroyable cri sorti du fond des flots
   Des airs en ce moment a troublé le repos;
   Et du sein de la terre une voix formidable
   Répond en gémissant à ce cri redoutable.   1510
   Jusqu'au fond de nos cœurs notre sang s'est glacé.
   Des coursiers attentifs le crin s'est hérissé.
   Cependant sur le dos de la plaine liquide
   S'élève à gros bouillons une montagne humide.
   L'onde approche, se brise, et vomit à nos yeux
   Parmi des flots d'écume un monstre furieux.
   Son front large est armé de cornes menaçantes,
   Tout son corps est couvert d'écailles jaunissantes.
   Indomptable taureau, dragon impétueux,
   Sa croupe se recourbe en replis tortueux.   1520
   Ses longs mugissements font trembler le rivage.
   Le ciel avec horreur voit ce monstre sauvage,
   La terre s'en émeut, l'air en est infecté,

THERAMENES   You care too late. It's needless now.
The tenderness is useless . . . Hippolytus is dead.

THESEUS

Oh god . . .

THERAMENES   I've seen the best of human beings die . . .
And the most innocent, I dare to say.

THESEUS

My son is gone . . . ? When I would hold him in my arms,
The gods made haste to speed his death? What blow
Has snatched him . . . what sudden thunder . . . ?

THERAMENES

We'd scarcely ridden through the gates of Troezen.
He drove his chariot; his guards, downcast,
Copied his silence as they marched beside.   1500
Lost in thought, he took the Mycenae road,
Letting his horses' reins hang loosely in his hand.
Those splendid stallions, which in times gone by
Obeyed his voice with eagerness and pride,
Now had dulled eyes, their heads bowed down,
As if agreeing with his bitter thoughts.
Then all at once, from deep below the waves,
A ghastly cry shattered the stillness in the air.
From the earth's bowels, another fearful voice
Groaned out aloud to that appalling cry.   1510
Our blood froze to the bottom of our hearts.
The stallions listened, manes all bristling.
And then, along the far edge of the sea,
A liquid mountain rose, a boiling mass.
The surge roared in, broke up and spewed
In front of us a raging monster in the foam.
Its head is massive, armed with fearful horns,
And its whole body sheathed in yellow scales.
An untamed bull, some hell-hound out of mind,
Its crupper rippling into writhing folds.   1520
Its long-drawn bellows rumble down the shore.
The skies look on this monster, horror-struck.
The earth heaves up, the air is poisonous,

Le flot, qui l'apporta, recule épouvanté.
Tout fuit, et sans s'armer d'un courage inutile,
Dans le temple voisin chacun cherche un asile.
Hippolyte lui seul digne fils d'un héros,
Arrête ses coursiers, saisit ses javelots,
Pousse au monstre, et d'un dard lancé d'une main sûre
Il lui fait dans le flanc une large blessure.   1530
De rage et de douleur le monstre bondissant
Vient aux pieds des chevaux tomber en mugissant,
Se roule, et leur présente une gueule enflammée,
Qui les couvre de feu, de sang et de fumée.
La frayeur les emporte, et sourds à cette fois,
Ils ne connaissent plus ni le frein ni la voix;
En efforts impuissants leur maître se consume.
Ils rougissent le mors d'une sanglante écume.
On dit qu'on a vu même en ce désordre affreux
Un dieu qui d'aiguillons pressait leur flanc poudreux.   1540
A travers des rochers la peur les précipite.
L'essieu crie, et se rompt. L'intrépide Hippolyte
Voit voler en éclats tout son char fracassé.
Dans les rênes lui-même, il tombe embarrassé.
Excusez ma douleur. Cette image cruelle
Sera pour moi de pleurs une source éternelle.
J'ai vu, Seigneur, j'ai vu votre malheureux fils
Traîné par les chevaux que sa main a nourris.
Il veut les rappeler, et sa voix les effraie.
Ils courent. Tout son corps n'est bientôt qu'une plaie.   1550
De nos cris douloureux la plaine retentit.
Leur fougue impétueuse enfin se ralentit.
Ils s'arrêtent, non loin de ces tombeaux antiques,
Où des rois ses aïeux sont les froides reliques.
J'y cours en soupirant, et sa garde me suit.
De son généreux sang la trace nous conduit,
Les rochers en sont teints. Les ronces dégouttantes
Portent de ses cheveux les dépouilles sanglantes.
J'arrive, je l'appelle, et me tendant la main
Il ouvre un œil mourant, qu'il referme soudain.   1560
Le ciel, dit-il, m'arrache une innocente vie.
Prends soin après ma mort de la triste Aricie.

The wave that brought it in recoils appalled.
Bravery was useless, would not protect. We fled,
All taking refuge in the temple close at hand.
Hippolytus alone, a hero's son,
Reined in his horses, seized his spears,
Thrust at the monster and, with careful aim,
Made a huge wound there – deep, deep in its side.   1530
The animal writhes up in pain and rage,
Falls roaring at the horses' feet,
Rolls over, coils; its flaming jaws
Spew smoke and blood and fire all over them.
They're terrified, they bolt, they do not hear.
They're no more held by bridles or his voice.
Their master tries and tries but all in vain,
Their bits are reddened with a foam of blood.
In the stampede, some say they even saw
A god digging his spurs into their dusty flanks.   1540
Fear sends them hurtling off across the rocks.
The axle screams and snaps. Hippolytus
Sees his chariot smashed, fly all to bits.
He falls, gets tangled in the reins . . .
Forgive my tears. I cannot bear the sight . . .
The image stays . . . a source of lasting grief.
I watched, my lord, I watched your helpless son
Dragged by the horses that his hands had fed.
He calls to them, but terrifies them more.
They gallop on, his body one huge wound . . .   1550
The plain re-echoes with our cries of grief.
At last, their violent panic eases up;
They stop not far from those ancestral tombs
Where all his forebears rest, the cold remains of kings.
I run there breathless, with his guard behind.
The fresh tracks of his blood show us the way.
The rocks are drenched with it. The dripping thorns
Catch bleeding tufts and shocks of hair.
I reach him, speak his name. He gives his hand,
Opens his dying eyes, then straightway closes them.   1560
He says, 'I'm innocent. The gods, though, take my life.
Take care of poor Aricia when I'm dead.

Cher ami, si mon père un jour désabusé
Plaint le malheur d'un fils faussement accusé,
Pour apaiser mon sang et mon ombre plaintive,
Dis-lui qu'avec douceur il traite sa captive
Qu'il lui rende . . . A ce mot ce héros expiré
N'a laissé dans mes bras qu'un corps défiguré,
Triste objet, où des dieux triomphe la colère,
Et que méconnaîtrait l'œil même de son père.   1570

THÉSÉE

O mon fils! cher espoir que je me suis ravi!
Inexorables dieux, qui m'avez trop servi!
A quels mortels regrets ma vie est réservée!

THÉRAMÈNE

La timide Aricie est alors arrivée.
Elle venait, Seigneur, fuyant votre courroux,
A la face des dieux l'accepter pour époux.
Elle approche. Elle voit l'herbe rouge et fumante.
Elle voit (quel objet pour les yeux d'une amante)
Hippolyte étendu, sans forme et sans couleur.
Elle veut quelque temps douter de son malheur,   1580
Et ne connaissant plus ce héros qu'elle adore,
Elle voit Hippolyte, et le demande encore.
Mais trop sûre à la fin qu'il est devant ses yeux,
Par un triste regard elle accuse les dieux,
Et froide, gémissante, et presque inanimée,
Aux pieds de son amant elle tombe pâmée.
Ismène est auprès d'elle. Ismène toute en pleurs
La rappelle à la vie, ou plutôt aux douleurs.
Et moi, je suis venu, détestant la lumière
Vous dire d'un héros la volonté dernière,   1590
Et m'acquitter, Seigneur, du malheureux emploi,
Dont son cœur expirant s'est reposé sur moi.
Mais j'aperçois venir sa mortelle ennemie.

And if my father ever learns the truth,
Dear friend, and mourns his wretched, slandered son,
To quiet my blood and grieving shade,
Tell him to treat her gently in his care,
To give her back . . . '. Last words. He died, heroically,
And left his mangled corpse all in my arms.
What piteous emblem of the gods' triumphant wrath,
His father, even, would not recognise.   1570

THESEUS

My son . . . I have destroyed my dearest hope.
The gods do not relent; they've served me all too well.
What can my life be now but deathly grief?

THERAMENES

Then nervously, Aricia came near.
She wanted to avoid your rage, my lord,
And marry him before the gods.
She came . . . and saw the reeking, blood-red grass
And there – what kind of sight for loving eyes –
Hippolytus was stretched, disfigured, white . . .
She could not first believe the tragedy;   1580
She didn't recognise the man she loved.
She looked at him, and yet still asked for him.
But finally, convinced that it is him,
She looks in pain, accusing all the gods.
Then cold and moaning, almost without life,
She falls unconscious by her lover's side.
Ismene's there, Ismene all in tears;
She brings her back to life, or more to grief . . .
And I . . . can't bear the sunlight any more . . . I came
To tell you of a hero's final wish.   1590
I've now fulfilled, my lord, the saddest task
That he entrusted to me as he died.
                              [*Phaedra is seen, Panope with her*
But there's his enemy to death. Phaedra.

SCÈNE 7

Thésée, Phèdre, Théramène, Panope, Gardes

THÉSÉE

Eh bien! vous triomphez, et mon fils est sans vie.
Ah que j'ai lieu de craindre! et qu'un cruel soupçon
L'excusant dans mon cœur, m'alarme avec raison!
Mais, Madame, il est mort, prenez votre victime.
Jouissez de sa perte injuste, ou légitime.
Je consens que mes yeux soient toujours abusés,
Je le crois criminel, puisque vous l'accusez.   1600
Son trépas à mes pleurs offre assez de matières,
Sans que j'aille chercher d'odieuses lumières,
Qui ne pouvant le rendre à ma juste douleur,
Peut-être ne feraient qu'accroître mon malheur.
Laissez-moi loin de vous, et loin de ce rivage,
De mon fils déchiré fuir la sanglante image.
Confus, persécuté d'un mortel souvenir,
De l'univers entier je voudrais me bannir.
Tout semble s'élever contre mon injustice.
L'éclat de mon nom même augmente mon supplice.   1610
Moins connu des mortels je me cacherais mieux.
Je hais jusques au soin dont m'honorent les dieux.
Et je m'en vais pleurer leurs faveurs meurtrières,
Sans plus les fatiguer d'inutiles prières.
Quoi qu'ils fissent pour moi, leur funeste bonté
Ne me saurait payer de ce qu'ils m'ont ôté.

PHÈDRE

Non. Thésée, il faut rompre un injuste silence;
Il faut à votre fils rendre son innocence.
Il n'était point coupable.

THÉSÉE   Ah père infortuné!
Et c'est sur votre foi que je l'ai condamné!   1620
Cruelle, pensez-vous être assez excusée . . .

PHÈDRE

Les moments me sont chers, écoutez-moi, Thésée.

SCENE 7

Theseus, Phaedra, Theramenes, Panope, guards

THESEUS

So then, you've won. My son is dead.
What cause I have for fear . . . for rankling doubt
That pardons him but fills me with alarm . . .
My lady, he is dead. Your victim. Take.
Savour his loss, deserved or not.
I am prepared to stay deceived;
Since you've accused him, I believe his guilt.   1600
His death is ample reason for my tears
Without my seeking worse enlightenment.
That could not ease my grief and bring him back,
And might do nothing but increase the pain.
Far from these shores, and far from you, let me
Escape the bloody image of my tortured son.
I'm stunned . . . tormented by this memory of death.
I long for exile from the whole, wide world.
All nature rises up against my crime.
The greatness of my name adds to the pain: 1610
Were I less known, I'd find a better hiding place.
I loathe the honours, even, of the gods.
I'll go away to mourn their murderous gift.
I'll weary them no more with useless prayers.
Whatever they may do to me, no gift
Can ever give me back what I have lost.

PHAEDRA

No, Theseus . . . I must break this silence. It's not just.
I must give back your son his innocence.
He was not guilty . . .

THESEUS   Oh, I am now doomed . . .
It was your word that made me punish him!   1620
The cruelty . . . how will you be forgiven?

PHAEDRA

Each moment's precious to me. Listen, Theseus.

C'est moi qui sur ce fils chaste et respectueux
Osai jeter un œil profane, incestueux.
Le ciel mit dans mon sein une flamme funeste.
La détestable Œnone a conduit tout le reste.
Elle a craint qu'Hippolyte instruit de ma fureur
Ne découvrit un feu qui lui faisait horreur.
La perfide abusant de ma faiblesse extrême,
S'est hâtée à vos yeux de l'accuser lui-même. 1630
Elle s'en est punie, et fuyant mon courroux,
A cherché dans les flots un supplice trop doux.
Le fer aurait déjà tranché ma destinée,
Mais je laissais gémir la vertu soupçonnée.
J'ai voulu, devant vous exposant mes remords,
Par un chemin plus lent descendre chez les morts.
J'ai pris, j'ai fait couler dans mes brûlantes veines
Un poison que Médée apporta dans Athènes.
Déjà jusqu'à mon cœur le venin parvenu
Dans ce cœur expirant jette un froid inconnu; 1640
Déjà je ne vois plus qu'à travers un nuage
Et le ciel, et l'époux que ma présence outrage;
Et la mort à mes yeux dérobant la clarté
Rend au jour, qu'ils souillaient, toute sa pureté.

PANOPE

Elle expire, Seigneur.

THÉSÉE   D'une action si noire
Que ne peut avec elle expirer la mémoire?
Allons de mon erreur, hélas! trop éclaircis
Mêler nos pleurs au sang de mon malheureux fils.
Allons de ce cher fils embrasser ce qui reste,
Expier la fureur d'un vœu que je déteste. 1650
Rendons-lui les honneurs qu'il a trop mérités.
Et pour mieux apaiser ses mânes irrités,
Que malgré les complots d'une injuste famille
Son amante aujourd'hui me tienne lieu de fille.

I was the one who on your pure and honoured son
Dared look with vile, incestuous eyes.
The gods lit up my heart with deadly lust;
Oenone, horribly, did all the rest.
She feared Hippolytus, once told of my mad love,
Would make it public, he would loathe it so.
She broke my trust, exploited my weak state,
And rushed to make him guilty in your sight.   1630
She's found her punishment. She fled my rage
And found too calm a death beneath the waves.
I should by now have perished by the sword.
Suspicion fell on goodness – and I let it grow.
I wanted, though, to tell you my remorse
And go down to the dead a slower way.
I've taken – it's flowing through my veins, on fire -
A poison that Medea brought to Greece.
Already now, it's reached my heart
And spreads out now such cold I never knew.   1640
I see now only through a mist
The heavens and the husband I've defiled.
Death steals the brightness from my eyes,
And gives back daylight . . . all its purity . . .

PANOPE
She is dying, my lord.

THESEUS   Would that the memory
Of this dark deed would die as well.
But come . . . now my mistake is all too clear,
Our tears must mingle in my son's sad blood.
I must embrace his dear remains
And expiate my mad, appalling prayer,   1650
Give him the honour he was surely owed.
And to appease the anger of his soul,
Let his beloved, despite her family's crime,
Become my daughter from this day.

ATHALIAH

1691

PRÉFACE

Tout le monde sait que le royaume de Juda était composé des deux tribus de Juda et de Benjamin, et que les dix autres tribus qui se révoltèrent contre Roboam, composaient le royaume d'Israel. Comme les rois de Juda étaient de la maison de David, et qu'ils avaient dans leur partage la ville et le temple de Jérusalem, tout ce qu'il y avait de prêtres et de lévites se retirèrent auprès d'eux, et leur demeurèrent toujours attachés. Car depuis que le temple de Salomon fut bâti, il n'était plus permis de sacrifier ailleurs, et tous ces autres autels qu'on élevait à Dieu sur des montagnes, appelés par cette raison dans l'Écriture les hauts lieux, ne lui étaient point agréables. Ainsi le culte légitime ne subsistait plus que dans Juda. Les dix tribus, excepté un très petit nombre de personnes, étaient ou idolâtres ou schismatiques.

Au reste ces prêtres et ces lévites faisaient eux-mêmes une tribu fort nombreuse. Ils furent partagés en diverses classes pour servir tour à tour dans le temple, d'un jour de sabbat à l'autre. Les prêtres étaient de la famille d'Aaron, et il n'y avait que ceux de cette famille, lesquels pussent exercer la sacrificature. Les lévites leur étaient subordonnés, et avaient soin entre autres choses du chant, de la préparation des victimes et de la garde du temple. Ce nom de lévite ne laisse pas d'etré donné quelquefois indifféremment à tous ceux de la tribu. Ceux qui étaient en semaine avaient, ainsi que le grand prêtre, leur logement dans les portiques ou galeries dont le temple était environné, et qui faisaient partie du temple même. Tout l'édifice s'appelait en général le lieu saint. Mais on appelait plus particulièrement de ce nom cette partie du temple intérieur où était le chandelier d'or, l'autel des parfums et les tables des pains de proposition. Et cette partie était encore distinguée du Saint des Saints, où etait l'arche, et où le grand prêtre seul avait droit d'entrer

PREFACE

Everyone knows that the kingdom of Judah comprised the two tribes of Judah and Benjamin, and that the ten other tribes who revolted against Rehoboam constituted the kingdom of Israel. As the kings of Judah were from the house of David, and as the town and temple of Jerusalem were part of their territory, all the priests and Levites went back there and remained constantly attached to these places. For, after the temple of Solomon had been built, sacrifices were no longer allowed anywhere else; and all the other altars that were raised to God in the mountains – for that reason called in the Scriptures the high places – were not acceptable to Him. So the legitimate religion survived only in Judah. The ten tribes, apart from a tiny number of people, were either idolaters or schismatics.

Moreover, these priests and Levites themselves made up a very numerous tribe. They were divided into various groups to serve in the temple in turn, from one sabbath to the next. The priests were from the family of Aaron, and only those of this family could perform sacrifices. The Levites were sub-ordinate to them, and were responsible, among other things, for the singing, the preparation of sacrifices, and guarding the temple. However, the name of Levite is sometimes applied indiscriminately to all members of the tribe. Those who were on duty lodged, like the high-priest, in the covered arcades or galleries that surrounded the temple, and that were actually part of it. The whole building was generally called the holy place; but this name was more specifically applied to the part of the inner temple that housed the golden candlestick, the incense altar, and the tables where the show-bread was laid. And this part was distinguished in turn from the Holy of Holies, where the ark was, and which only the high-priest had the

une fois l'année. C'était une tradition assez constante que la montagne sur laquelle le temple fut bâti était la même montagne où Abraham avait autrefois offert en sacrifice son fils Isaac.

J'ai cru devoir expliquer ici ces particularités, afin que ceux à qui l'histoire de l'Ancien Testament ne sera pas assez présente n'en soient point arrêtés en lisant cette tragédie. Elle a pour sujet Joas reconnu et mis sur le trône; et j'aurais dû dans les règles l'intituler Joas. Mais la plupart du monde n'en ayant entendu parler que sous le nom d'Athalie, je n'ai pas jugé à propos de la leur présenter sous un autre titre, puisque d'ailleurs Athalie y joue un personnage si considérable, et que c'est sa mort qui termine la pièce. Voici une partie des principaux événements qui devancèrent cette grande action.

Joram roi de Juda, fils de Josaphat, et le septième roi de la race de David, épousa Athalie fille d'Achab et de Jézabel, qui régnaient en Israël, fameux l'un et l'autre, mais principalement Jézabel, par leurs sanglantes persécutions contre les prophètes. Athalie, non moins impie que sa mère, entraîna bientôt le roi son mari dans l'idolâtrie et fit même construire dans Jérusalem un temple à Baal, qui était le dieu du pays de Tyr et de Sidon, où Jézabel avait pris naissance. Joram, après avoir vu perir par les mains des Arabes et des Philistins tous les princes ses enfants à la réserve d'Ochosias, mourut lui-même misérablement d'une longue maladie qui lui consuma les entrailles. Sa mort funeste n'empêcha pas Ochosias d'imiter son impiété et celle d'Athalie sa mère. Mais ce prince, après avoir régné seulement un an, étant allé rendre visite au roi d'Israël frère d'Athalie, fut enveloppé dans la ruine de la maison d'Achab; et tué par l'ordre de Jéhu, que Dieu avait fait sacrer par ses prophètes, pour régner sur Israël, et pour être le ministre de ses vengeances. Jéhu extermina toute la postérité d'Achab, et fit jeter par les fenêtres Jézabel, qui selon la prédiction d'Elie, fut mangée des chiens dans la vigne de ce même Naboth qu'elle avait fait mourir autrefois pour s'emparer de son héritage. Athalie ayant appris à Jérusalem tous ces massacres, entreprit de son côté d'éteindre entièrement la race royale de David, en faisant mourir tous les enfants d'Ochosias ses petits-fils. Mais heureusement Josabeth sœur d'Ochosias, et fille de Joram, mais d'une autre mère qu'Athalie, étant arrivée lorsqu'on égorgeait les princes ses neveux, elle trouva moyen de dérober du milieu des morts le petit Joas encore à la mamelle, et le confia avec sa nourrice au grand prêtre son mari qui les cacha tous deux dans le

right to enter once a year. There was a fairly continuous tradition that the mountain on which the temple was built was the same as the one on which Abraham had once offered his son Isaac as a sacrifice.

I thought I ought to explain these details here, so that those who are not sufficiently familiar with Old Testament history are not held up in reading the tragedy. Its subject is the recognition of Joash and his restoration to the throne. According to the rules, I should have called it *Joash*. But since most people have only heard of it by the name *Athaliah*, I felt it undesirable to present it with a different title. Besides, Athaliah plays so important a role in it, and the play ends with her death. Here now are some of the major events that led up to this great action.

Joram, king of Judah and son of Jehoshaphat, and the seventh king of the house of David, married Athaliah, the daughter of Ahab and Jezebel who reigned in Israel. Both of them were notorious – especially Jezebel – for their bloody persecution of the prophets. Athaliah was no less ungodly than her mother. She soon dragged her husband into idolatry, and even had a temple to Baal built in Jerusalem. Baal was the god of Tyre and Sidon, where Jezebel was born. Joram saw all the princes, his children, perish at the hands of the Arabs and Philistines – Ahaziah apart – and himself died wretchedly from a long illness that ate up his bowels. His horrible death, though, did not stop Ahaziah following his godlessness and his mother Athaliah's. But having reigned only a year, this prince went to visit the king of Israel, Athaliah's brother, and was caught up in the ruin of the house of Ahab. He was killed on Jehu's orders, whom God had anointed through his prophets to rule over Israel and execute His vengeances. Jehu exterminated all Ahab's posterity, and had Jezebel thrown down from the windows of her palace. As Elijah had foretold, she was eaten by the dogs in Naboth's vineyard – the same Naboth that she had once killed to seize his inheritance. In Jerusalem, Athaliah heard of all these massacres, and decided for her part to exterminate completely the royal line of David by killing all Azariah's children, her grandchildren. But fortunately, Jehoshabeath – who was Azariah's sister and Joram's daughter, though by a different mother than Athaliah – arrived just as her nephews' throats were being cut. She managed to carry little Joash off from amidst the dead. He was still suckling. She entrusted

temple, où l'enfant fut élevé secrètement jusqu'au jour qu'il fut proclamé roi de Juda. L'histoire des *Rois* dit que ce fut la septième année d'après. Mais le texte grec des *Paralipomènes* que Sévère Sulpice a suivi, dit que ce fut la huitième. C'est ce qui m'a autorisé à donner à ce prince neuf à dix ans, pour le mettre déjà en état de répondre aux questions qu'on lui fait.

Je crois ne lui avoir rien fait dire qui soit au-dessus de la portée d'un enfant de cet âge qui a de l'esprit et de la mémoire. Mais quand j'aurais été un peu au-delà, il faut considérer que c'est ici un enfant tout extraordinaire, élevé dans le temple par un grand prêtre, qui le regardant comme l'unique espérance de sa nation, l'avait instruit de bonne heure dans tous les devoirs de la religion et de la royauté. Il n'en était pas de même des enfants des Juifs que de la plupart des nôtres. On leur apprenait les saintes Lettres, non seulement dès qu'ils avaient atteint l'usage de la raison, mais, pour me servir de l'expression de saint Paul, dès la mamelle. Chaque Juif était obligé d'écrire une fois en sa vie de sa propre main le volume de la Loi tout entier. Les rois étaient même obligés de l'écrire deux fois, et il leur était enjoint de l'avoir continuellement devant les yeux. Je puis dire ici que la France voit en la personne d'un prince de huit ans et demi, qui fait aujourd'hui ses plus chères délices, un exemple illustre de ce que peut dans un enfant un heureux naturel aidé d'une excellente éducation, et que si j'avais donné au petit Joas la même vivacité et le même discernement qui brillent dans les reparties de ce jeune prince, on m'aurait accusé avec raison d'avoir péché contre les règles de la vraisemblance.

L'âge de Zacharie fils du grand prêtre, n'étant point marqué, on peut lui supposer si l'on veut deux ou trois ans de plus qu'à Joas.

J'ai suivi l'explication de plusieurs commentateurs fort habiles, qui prouvent par le texte même de l'Écriture, que tous ces soldats à qui Joïada, ou Joad, comme il est appelé dans Josèphe, fit prendre les armes consacrées à Dieu par David, étaient autant de prêtres et de lévites, aussi bien que les cinq centeniers qui les commandaient. En effet, disent ces interprètes, tout devait être saint dans une si sainte action, et aucun profane n'y devait être employé. Il s'y agissait non seulement de conserver le sceptre dans la maison de David, mais encore de conserver à ce grand roi cette suite de descendants dont devait naître le Messie. 'Car ce Messie tant de fois promis comme fils d'Abraham, devait aussi être le fils de David et de tous les rois de

him, with his nurse, to the high-priest, her husband, who hid both
of them in the temple. There, the child was brought up secretly till
the day he was proclaimed king of Judah. The Book of Kings says
that that was seven years afterwards. But the Greek text of the
Book of Chronicles, that Severus Sulpicius followed, says that it
was eight. This is what has allowed me to make Joash nine or ten
years old, so that he would be in a position to answer the questions
he is asked.

I don't think I have made him say anything that is beyond a boy
of that age who is intelligent, and who has a good memory. Even if
I have gone a little too far, it must be borne in mind that he is a quite
exceptional child. He has been brought up in the temple by a high-
priest who sees him as the only hope of his nation, and who has
taught him all the duties of religion and kingship from an early age.
It was not the same with the children of the Jews as it is with most
of ours. They were taught the holy scriptures, not simply when
they were able to use reason, but (to quote Saint Paul's words) at
their mother's breast. Every Jew was obliged, once in his life, to
write out the entire volume of the law in his own hand. Kings were
even obliged to write it out twice, and were ordered to have it
continually before their eyes. I may note at this point that France
sees today, in a prince of eight and a half who is her dearest delight,
a splendid example of what natural talent supported by excellent
education can do in a child. If I had given little Joash the same
vitality and discernment that shine through our young prince's
responses, I should have rightly been accused of having sinned
against the laws of probability.

Since there is no indication about the age of Zechariah, the high
priest's son, we are free to suppose that he is two or three years older
than Joash.

I have followed the explanation of several very learned commentators who prove from the text of the Scripture itself that the
soldiers whom Jehoiada (or Joad as he is called in Josephus) roused
to arms – the arms consecrated to God by David – were all priests
and Levites, as were the five captains who commanded them. As
these interpreters say, everything had to be holy in so holy an
action, and no heathen could be employed in it. It was a question
not merely of keeping the sceptre in the house of David, but of
preserving the line of descendants from that great king, from which

Juda.' De là vient que l'illustre et savant prélat [M. de Meaux] de qui j'ai emprunté ces paroles appelle Joas le précieux reste de la maison de David. Josèphe en parle dans les mêmes termes. Et l'Écriture dit expressément que Dieu n'extermina pas toute la famille de Joram, voulant conserver à David la lampe qu'il lui avait promise. Or cette lampe qu'était-ce autre chose que la lumière qui devait être un jour révélée aux nations?

L'histoire ne spécifie point le jour où Joas fut proclamé. Quelques interprètes veulent que ce fût un jour de fête. J'ai choisi celle de la Pentecôte, qui était l'une des trois grandes fêtes des Juifs. On y célébrait la mémoire de la publication de la loi sur le mont de Sinaï, et on y offrait aussi à Dieu les premiers pains de la nouvelle moisson; ce qui faisait qu'on la nommait encore la fête des prémices. J'ai songé que ces circonstances me fourniraient quelque variété pour les chants du chœur.

Ce chœur est composé de jeunes filles de la tribu de Lévi, et je mets a leur tête une fille que je donne pour sœur à Zacharie. C'est elle qui introduit le chœur chez sa mère. Elle chante avec lui, porte la parole pour lui, et fait enfin les fonctions de ce personnage des anciens chœurs qu'on appelait le coryphée. J'ai aussi essayé d'imiter des Anciens cette continuité d'action qui fait que leur théâtre ne demeure jamais vide; les intervalles des actes n'étant marqués que par des hymnes et par des moralités du chœur, qui ont rapport à ce qui se passe.

On me trouvera peut-être un peu hardi d'avoir osé mettre sur la scène un prophète inspiré de Dieu, et qui prédit l'avenir. Mais j'ai eu la précaution de ne mettre dans sa bouche que des expressions tirées des prophètes mêmes. Quoique l'Écriture ne dise pas en termes exprès que Joïada ait eu l'esprit de prophétie, comme elle le dit de son fils, elle le représente comme un homme tout plein de l'esprit de Dieu. Et d'ailleurs ne paraît-il pas par l'Évangile qu'il a pu prophétiser en qualité de souverain pontife? Je suppose donc qu'il voit en esprit le funeste changement de Joas, qui après trente ans d'un règne fort pieux, s'abandonna aux mauvais conseils des flatteurs, et se souilla du meurtre de Zacharie fils et successeur de ce grand prêtre. Ce meurtre commis dans le temple, fut une des principales causes de la colère de Dieu contre les Juifs, et de tous les malheurs qui leur arrivèrent dans la suite. On prétend même que depuis ce jour-là les réponses de Dieu cessèrent entièrement dans le

the Messiah was to be born. 'The Messiah, so often promised as the son of Abraham, was also to be the son of David and of all the kings of Judah.' It is for this reason that the renowned and learned prelate from whom I have borrowed these words calls Joash the precious survivor of the house of David. Josephus speaks of him in the same terms; and the Scriptures state explicitly that God would not exterminate the entire family of Joram, as He wished to keep alight for David the lamp that He had promised him. What else could this lamp be than the light that was to be revealed one day to the world?

History does not specify on what day Joash was proclaimed. Some commentators argue it was a feast day. I have chosen the Pentecost, which was one of the three great feast days of the Jews. It celebrated the proclamation of the law on Mount Sinai, and God was offered the first loaves from the new harvest, which is why the day is also called the feast of the first-fruits. I felt that these circumstances would help to give me some variety for the songs of the chorus.

The chorus is made up of girls from the tribe of Levi, and I have put at their head a girl I portray as Zechariah's sister. She is the one who introduces the chorus to her mother. She sings with them, speaks for them, in a word acts like the character called *coryphaeus* in classical choruses. I have also tried to copy old writers in their continuity of action, which means their stage is never empty, the intervals between the acts being marked only by the hymns and moral reflections of the chorus, which relate to what is happening.

I may perhaps be thought a little bold to have dared to put on the stage a prophet inspired by God, and who foretells the future. But I have been careful to put in his mouth only expressions taken from the prophets themselves. Although the Bible does not explicitly say that Jehoiada had the gift of prophecy, as it does of his son, it portrays him as a man full of the spirit of God. Besides, does it not seem from the gospel that he could prophesy in his capacity as high-priest? I assume therefore that he can see in his mind's eye the deadly change in Joash who, after thirty years of godly rule, surrenders to the evil advice of flatterers, and defiles himself by the murder of Zechariah, son and successor of the high-priest. This murder, committed in the temple, was one of the main reasons for God's anger against the Jews, and for all the misfortunes that subsequently followed. It is even claimed that, from that day on, God's responses fell entirely silent in the sanctuary. It is this that

sanctuaire. C'est ce qui m'a donné lieu de faire prédire tout de suite à Joad et la destruction du temple et la ruine de Jérusalem. Mais comme les prophètes joignent d'ordinaire les consolations aux menaces, et que d'ailleurs il s'agit de mettre sur le trône un des ancêtres du Messie, j'ai pris occasion de faire entrevoir la venue de ce Consolateur, après lequel tous les anciens justes soupiraient. Cette scène, qui est une espèce d'épisode, amène très naturellement la musique, par la coutume qu'avaient plusieurs prophètes d'entrer dans leurs saints transports au son des instruments. Témoin cette troupe de prophètes, qui vinrent au-devant de Saül avec des harpes et des lyres, qu'on portait devant eux; et témoin Élisée lui-même, qui étant consulté sur l'avenir par le roi de Juda et par le roi d'Israël, dit comme fait ici Joad: *Adducite mihi psaltem.* Ajoutez à cela que cette prophétie sert beaucoup à augmenter le trouble dans la pièce, par la consternation et par les différents mouvements où elle jette le chœur et les principaux acteurs.

gave me grounds for having Jehoiada predict immediately afterwards the destruction of the temple and the ruin of Jerusalem. But,
since the prophets usually add consolation to threats, and since,
besides, the point at issue is putting one of the Messiah's ancestors
on the throne, I have taken the opportunity of giving a glimpse of
the coming of this comforter, for whom all righteous people of
ancient times longed. This scene, which is a kind of episode, very
naturally calls for music, following the custom of several prophets
who went into their holy raptures to the sound of instruments.
Witness the band of prophets who came to Saul with harps and lyres
carried before them. Witness Elisha himself. Asked about the future
by the king of Judah and the king of Israel, he said (as Jehoiada does
here), *Adducite mihi psaltem* [bring me a minstrel]. Furthermore, this
prophecy does much to increase the tension in the play, through
the consternation and the different emotions into which it throws
the chorus and the main actors.

ACTEURS

JOAS, roi de Juda, fils d'Ochosias

ATHALIE, veuve de Joram, aïeule de Joas

JOAD, tautrement Joiada, grand-prêtre

JOSABET, tante de Joas, femme du grand-prêtre

ZACHARIE, fils de Joad et de Josabet.

SALOMITH, sœur de Zacharie

ABNER, l'un des principaux officiers des rois de Juda

AZARIAS, ISMAEL, et les trois autres chefs des prêtres et
    des Lévites

MATHAN, prêtre apostat, sacrificateur de Baal

NABAL, confident de Mathan

AGAR, femme de la suite d'Athalie

Troupe de prêtres et de Lévites

Suite d'Athalie

La Nourrice de Joas

Chœur de jeunes filles de la tribu de Lévi

La scène est dans le temple de Jérusalem, dans un vestibule
de l'appartement du grand-prêtre

CAST

JOASH, king of Judah, son of Ahaziah

ATHALIAH, Joram's widow and Joash's grandmother

JEHOIADA, the high-priest

JEHOSHABEATH, Joash's aunt and wife of the high-priest

ZECHARIAH, the son of Jehoiada and Jehoshabeath

SALOMITH, Zechariah's sister

ABNER, one of the chief officers of the kings of Judah

AZARIAH, ISHMAEL, and the other three leaders of the priests and
  Levites

MATTAN, an apostate, high-priest of Baal

NABAL, Mattan's confidant

HAGAR, waiting-woman to Athaliah

Troop of priests and Levites

Athaliah's attendants

Joash's nurse

Chorus of girls from the tribe of Levi

The scene is set in the temple of Jerusalem, in a hall within the
high-priest's apartments

ATHALIE

ACTE 1 SCÈNE 1

Joad, Abner

ABNER

Oui, je viens dans son temple adorer l'Éternel.
Je viens, selon l'usage antique et solennel,
Célébrer avec vous la fameuse journée
Où sur le mont Sina la loi nous fut donnée.
Que les temps sont changés! Sitôt que de ce jour
La trompette sacrée annonçait le retour,
Du temple, orné partout de festons magnifiques,
Le peuple saint en foule inondait les portiques.
Et tous devant l'autel avec ordre introduits,
De leurs champs dans leurs mains portant les nouveaux fruits, 10
Au Dieu de l'univers consacraient ces prémices.
Les prêtres ne pouvaient, suffire aux sacrifices.
L'audace d'une femme arrêtant ce concours,
En des jours ténébreux a changé ces beaux jours.
D'adorateurs zélés à peine un petit nombre
Ose des premiers temps nous retracer quelque ombre.
Le reste pour son Dieu montre un oubli fatal,
Ou même s'empressant aux autels de Baal,
Se fait initier à ses honteux mystères,
Et blasphème le nom qu'ont invoqué leurs pères.   20
Je tremble qu'Athalie, à ne vous rien cacher,
Vous-même de l'autel vous faisant arracher,
N'achève enfin sur vous ses vengeances funestes,
Et d'un respect forcé ne dépouille les restes.

JOAD

D'où vous vient aujourd'hui ce noir pressentiment?

ABNER

Pensez-vous être saint et juste impunément?
Dès longtemps elle hait cette fermeté rare
Qui rehausse en Joad l'éclat de la tiare.
Dès longtemps votre amour pour la religion

ATHALIAH

ACT 1 SCENE 1

Jehoiada, Abner

ABNER

I come to worship God here in his shrine,
To follow old and solemn ritual
And celebrate that famous day with you,
When holy law was given us on Sinai.
How times have changed. The sacred trumpet then
Had scarcely sounded out the day's return
Than crowds of worshippers streamed through
The temple doors. Garlands were everywhere.
They walked up row by row, up to the shrine,
Bearing the harvest of their fields, first-fruits   10
That they would consecrate to God. The priests
Were all too few to make the sacrifice.
And now a reckless queen has stopped the crowds
And changed those days of joy to darkest night.
A tiny group of faithful worshippers
Dares still keep up some shadow of those days.
The others have forgotten God;
They even crowd around the shrine of Baal.
They've quickly learned his shameful mysteries;
They curse the name their fathers once invoked.   20
I won't disguise my fear . . .   Athaliah
Will have you dragged off from the shrine itself
And so revenge herself on you at last.
The vestiges of forced respect will go.

JEHOIADA

Where does this black foreboding come from now?

ABNER

You think to stay a just and holy man, untouched?
For ages now, she's loathed your rare, unswerving faith
That lends fresh brilliance to your diadem.
For ages now, your love of godly things

Est traité de révolte et de sédition. 30
Du mérite éclatant cette reine jalouse,
Hait surtout Josabet votre fidèle épouse.
Si du grand prêtre Aaron Joad est successeur,
De notre dernier roi Josabet est la sœur.
Mathan d'ailleurs, Mathan, ce prêtre sacrilège,
Plus méchant qu'Athalie, à toute heure l'assiège;
Mathan de nos autels infâme déserteur,
Et de toute vertu zélé persécuteur.
C'est peu que le front ceint d'une mitre étrangère,
Ce lévite à Baal prête son ministère. 40
Ce temple l'importune, et son impiété
Voudrait anéantir le Dieu qu'il a quitté.
Pour vous perdre il n'est point de ressorts qu'il n'invente :
Quelquefois il vous plaint, souvent même il vous vante.
Il affecte pour vous une fausse douceur,
Et par là de son fiel colorant la noirceur,
Tantôt à cette reine il vous peint redoutable,
Tantôt voyant pour l'or sa soif insatiable,
Il lui feint qu'en un lieu que vous seul connaissez,
Vous cachez des trésors par David amassés. 50
Enfin depuis deux jours, la superbe Athalie,
Dans un sombre chagrin paraît ensevelie.
Je l'observais hier, et je voyais ses yeux
Lancer sur le lieu saint des regards furieux;
Comme si dans le fond de ce vaste édifice
Dieu cachait un vengeur armé pour son supplice.
Croyez-moi, plus j'y pense, et moins je puis douter
Que sur vous son courroux ne soit prêt d'éclater,
Et que de Jézabel la fille sanguinaire
Ne vienne attaquer Dieu jusqu'en son sanctuaire. 60

JOAD

Celui qui met un frein à la fureur des flots
Sait aussi des méchants arrêter les complots.
Soumis avec respect à sa volonté sainte,
Je crains Dieu, cher Abner, et n'ai point d'autre crainte.
Cependant je rends grâce au zèle officieux
Qui sur tous mes périls vous fait ouvrir les yeux.

She's treated as disloyalty and revolt.   30
She's envious of any striking grace,
Hates most Jehoshabeath – your faithful wife.
If you succeed our high-priest Aaron now,
Your wife will be our last king's sister then.
And then . . . Mattan. That sacrilegious priest,
Worse than Athaliah, surrounds her day and night.
He's godlessly deserted all our faith
And persecutes what's good so eagerly.
It scarcely matters that he ministers
To Baal, a foreign mitre on his head.   40
This temple troubles him. The heretic
Just wants to crush the God he has renounced.
There's nothing he won't do to ruin you.
Sometimes, he'll pity you; often, he'll praise.
He'll feign some kindly sympathy for you,
And then, to hide the blackness of his gall,
He'll paint you to the queen as dangerous.
Sometimes, seeing her fevered thirst for gold,
He claims that you alone know of the place
Where you've concealed the treasures David left.   50
But for the last two days, Athaliah's pride
Has seemed enshrouded in some dark distress.
I watched her yesterday, and saw her gaze
Upon this sacred spot so furiously –
As if, in this vast building's deepest place,
God hid his vengeance, armed to strike her down.
The more I think of it, the less I doubt
That all her rage will soon explode on you.
The daughter of Jezebel thirsts for blood.
She'll even strike at God inside his sanctuary.   60

JEHOIADA

He who can calm the raging of the seas
Can also foil the plots of wicked men.
I follow and revere his holy will.
I fear my God, Abner, fear God alone.
And yet I'm grateful for the deep concern
That keeps you watchful of the risks I run.

Je vois que l'injustice en secret vous irrite,
Que vous avez encor le cœur israélite.
Le ciel en soit béni. Mais ce secret courroux,
Cette oisive vertu, vous en contentez-vous? 70
La foi qui n'agit point, est-ce une foi sincère?
Huit ans déjà passés, une impie étrangère
Du sceptre de David usurpe tous les droits,
Se baigne impunément dans le sang de nos rois,
Des enfants de son fils détestable homicide,
Et même contre Dieu lève son bras perfide.
Et vous, l'un des soutiens de ce tremblant État,
Vous nourri dans les camps du saint roi Josaphat,
Qui sous son fils Joram commandiez nos armées,
Qui rassurâtes seul nos villes alarmées, 80
Lorsque d'Ochosias le trépas imprévu
Dispersa tout son camp à l'aspect de Jéhu :
Je crains Dieu, dites-vous, sa vérité me touche.
Voici comme ce Dieu vous répond par ma bouche :
Du zèle de ma loi que sert de vous parer?
Par de stériles vœux pensez-vous m'honorer?
Quel fruit me revient-il de tous vos sacrifices?
Ai-je besoin du sang des boucs et des génisses?
Le sang de vos rois crie, et n'est point écouté.
Rompez, rompez tout pacte avec l'impiété. 90
Du milieu de mon peuple exterminez les crimes,
Et vous viendrez alors m'immoler des victimes.

ABNER

Hé que puis-je au milieu de ce peuple abattu?
Benjamin est sans force, et Juda sans vertu.
Le jour qui de leur roi vit éteindre la race
Éteignit tout le feu de leur antique audace.
Dieu même, disent-ils, s'est retiré de nous.
De l'honneur des Hébreux autrefois si jaloux,
Il voit sans intérêt leur grandeur terrassée,
Et sa miséricorde à la fin s'est lassée. 100
On ne voit plus pour nous ses redoutables mains
De merveilles sans nombre effrayer les humains.
L'arche sainte est muette, et ne rend plus d'oracles.

I know injustice wounds you deep inside,
That you are still an Israelite at heart.
May God be praised. But does this inner rage,
This idle goodness, satisfy you now?   70
Can faith that does not act remain sincere?
Eight years ago, a godless foreign queen
Usurped King David's sceptre and his rights.
She's drenched in our kings' blood and goes unpunished still,
Murders most horribly the children of her son.
She even lifts her wicked hand against our God.
And you, a pillar of this tottering state,
Who were brought up in king Jehoshaphat's camp,
Who led our armies when his son was king,
Who reassured our frightened towns alone   80
When Azariah's unexpected death
Scattered his camp as Jehu came in sight –
'I fear God', you say, 'his truth touches me.'
This is God's answer to you, through my lips.
'So why parade a passion for my law?
You think to honour me with barren vows?
What have I gained from all your sacrifice?
Do I have need of goats' and heifers' blood?
Your dead kings' blood cries out, and is not heard.
Break off all covenants with godlessness.   90
And from my people's midst cast out all crime.
Then you will bring me sacrifice indeed.'

ABNER

What can I do with this downtrodden race?
Benjamin has no strength left. Judah no virtue.
The day that saw their line of kings destroyed
Destroyed the fire of all their ancient bravery.
'God has abandoned us,' they say. Our God
Who once was jealous of the Jews' great name
Now sees unmoved our greatness overcome.
His pity is exhausted finally.   100
No longer do we see his powerful hands
Strike terror in mankind by countless miracles.
The sacred ark is dumb, and speaks no oracles.'

JOAD

Et quel temps fut jamais si fertile en miracles?
Quand Dieu par plus d'effets montra-t-il son pouvoir?
Auras-tu donc toujours des yeux pour ne point voir,
Peuple ingrat? Quoi, toujours les plus grandes merveilles
Sans ébranler ton cœur frapperont tes oreilles?
Faut-il, Abner, faut-il vous rappeler le cours
Des prodiges fameux accomplis en nos jours?   110
Des tyrans d'Israël les célèbres disgrâces,
Et Dieu trouvé fidèle en toutes ses menaces;
L'impie Achab détruit, et de son sang trempé
Le champ que par le meurtre il avait usurpé;
Près de ce champ fatal Jézabel immolée,
Sous les pieds des chevaux cette reine foulée;
Dans son sang inhumain les chiens désaltérés,
Et de son corps hideux les membres déchirés;
Des prophètes menteurs la troupe confondue,
Et la flamme du ciel sur l'autel descendue;   120
Élie aux éléments parlant en souverain,
Les cieux par lui fermés et devenus d'airain,
Et la terre trois ans sans pluie et sans rosée;
Les morts se ranimants à la voix d'Élisée;
Reconnaissez, Abner, à ces traits éclatants,
Un Dieu, tel aujourd'hui qu'il fut dans tous les temps.
Il sait quand il lui plaît faire éclater sa gloire,
Et son peuple est toujours présent à sa mémoire.

ABNER

Mais où sont ces honneurs à David tant promis,
Et prédits même encore à Salomon son fils?   130
Hélas! nous espérions que de leur race heureuse
Devait sortir de rois une suite nombreuse,
Que sur toute tribu, sur toute nation,
L'un d'eux établirait sa domination,
Ferait cesser partout la discorde et la guerre,
Et verrait à ses pieds tous les rois de la terre.

JOAD

Aux promesses du ciel pourquoi renoncez-vous?

JEHOIADA

But what age ever saw such miracles?
When did God show his power by greater deeds?
Such cold thanks from a people who have eyes
That will not see. Can all the greatest miracles
Burst on your ears and yet not shake your hearts?
Must I recall those tales for you, Abner –
The famous wonders witnessed in our time?   110
The well-known shame that Israel's tyrants faced –
Our God found faithful in the threats he made.
The godless Ahab killed, the land that he'd
Usurped by murder drenching in his blood.
And, near those fields, queen Jezebel killed too,
Crushed underfoot beneath her horses' hooves.
The dogs went wild, lapped up her monstrous blood,
And tore her twisting body limb from limb.
That troop of lying prophets thunderstruck
As fire from heaven breathed down on the shrine.   120
Elijah's voice, commanding all the elements,
Sealing the heavens, turning them to bronze.
The earth three years with neither rain nor dew,
The dead awakening to Elisha's voice.
In all these wondrous signs, Abner, you see
A God who is today as he has always been.
He can let shine his glory when he wills.
His people are forever in his mind.

ABNER

But where are all the honours promised so
To David, even more to Solomon his son?   130
We used to hope an endless line of kings
Would rise and grow from such a blessed race,
That one of them would gain dominion
Throughout all nations, every tribe –
That he would make all war and discord cease,
And see the earth's great kings fall at his feet.

JEHOIADA

Then why the doubt in heaven's promises?

ABNER

Ce roi fils de David, où le chercherons-nous?
Le ciel même peut-il réparer les ruines
De cet arbre séché jusque dans ses racines? 140
Athalie étouffa l'enfant même au berceau.
Les morts après huit ans, sortent-ils du tombeau?
Ah! si dans sa fureur elle s'était trompée,
Si du sang de nos rois quelque goutte échappée . . .

JOAD

Eh bien? Que feriez-vous?

ABNER

O jour heureux pour moi!
De quelle ardeur j'irais reconnaître mon roi!
Doutez-vous qu'à ses pieds nos tribus empressées . . .
Mais pourquoi me flatter de ces vaines pensées?
Déplorable héritier de ces rois triomphants,
Ochosias restait seul avec ses enfants. 150
Par les traits de Jéhu je vis percer le père,
Vous avez vu les fils massacrés par la mère.

JOAD

Je ne m'explique point. Mais quand l'astre du jour
Aura sur l'horizon fait le tiers de son tour,
Lorsque la troisième heure aux prières rappelle,
Retrouvez-vous au temple avec ce même zèle.
Dieu pourra vous montrer par d'importants bienfaits,
Que sa parole est stable, et ne trompe jamais.
Allez pour ce grand jour il faut que je m'apprête,
Et du temple déjà l'aube blanchit le faîte. 160

ABNER

Quel sera ce bienfait que je ne comprends pas?
L'illustre Josabet porte vers vous ses pas.
Je sors, et vais me joindre à la troupe fidèle
Qu'attire de ce jour la pompe solennelle.

ABNER

David's royal son – where should we look for him?
Can even heaven revive the poor remains
Of this old tree that's withered to the roots?   140
Athaliah smothered the baby at its birth.
Can bodies eight years dead rise from the tomb?
If only in her madness she had been deceived . . .
If just one drop of that child's blood escaped . . .

JEHOIADA

Then you'd have . . . ?

ABNER   I would have kissed the day,
And gone to greet my king in joy.
And at his feet our eager tribes – imagine them . . .
But why delude myself? The thoughts are vain.
The sole successors of these glorious kings
Were tragic Azariah and his sons.   150
I saw the father speared by Jehu's dart.
You saw the mother massacre the sons.

JEHOIADA

I can reveal no more. But when the sun
Has traced a third of its day's course,
And when the third hour calls us all to prayer,
Come back then to the shrine with this same zeal.
And God will show to you by special goodnesses
His word is true. It never will deceive.
Go now. I must prepare for this great day.
Look . . . the temple roof is whitening with the dawn.   160

ABNER

What will this goodness be? I do not understand.
But look, Jehoshabeath comes this way.
I'll go and mingle with the faithful folk
Who've been drawn here by all the ritual.

                    [*he leaves. Jehoshabeath enters*

SCÈNE 2

Joad, Josabet

JOAD

Les temps sont accomplis, Princesse, il faut parler
Et votre heureux larcin ne se peut plus celer.
Des ennemis de Dieu la coupable insolence
Abusant contre lui de ce profond silence,
Accuse trop longtemps ses promesses d'erreur.
Que dis-je? Le succès animant leur fureur,   170
Jusque sur notre autel votre injuste marâtre
Veut offrir à Baal un encens idolâtre.
Montrons ce jeune roi que vos mains ont sauvé,
Sous l'aile du Seigneur dans le temple élevé.
De nos princes hébreux il aura le courage,
Et déjà son esprit a devancé son âge.
Avant que son destin s'explique par ma voix,
Je vais l'offrir au Dieu par qui règnent les rois.
Aussitôt, assemblant nos lévites, nos prêtres,
Je leur déclarerai l'héritier de leurs maîtres.   180

JOSABET

Sait-il déjà son nom et son noble destin?

JOAD

Il ne répond encore qu'au nom d'Éliacin,
Et se croit quelque enfant rejeté par sa mère,
A qui j'ai par pitié daigné servir de père,

JOSABET

Hélas! de quel péril je l'avais su tirer!
Dans quel péril encore est-il prêt de rentrer!

JOAD

Quoi? Déjà votre foi s'affaiblit et s'étonne?

JOSABET

A vos sages conseils, Seigneur, je m'abandonne.
Du jour que j'arrachai cet enfant à la mort,
Je remis en vos mains tout le soin de son sort.   190

SCENE 2

Jehoiada, Jehoshabeath

JEHOIADA

My dearest wife, the time has come to speak.
We can conceal your joyous theft no more.
God's enemies – their guilt and insolence –
Exploit this deepening silence. Far too long
They have accused his promises of deceit.
Still more, success has made them mad.   170
Upon our altar, Athaliah now plans
To offer pagan incense up to Baal.
Let's show the young king whom you've saved
And brought up in the temple in God's care.
He'll have the courage of our Hebrew kings.
He is already wise beyond his years.
Before I speak and tell him of his destiny,
I'll offer him to God, the King of kings.
I'll call our levites, priests, together now,
And then proclaim to them their masters' heir.   180

JEHOSHABEATH

So does he know his name? His destiny?

JEHOIADA

He answers only to Eliacin.
He thinks he is a child his mother has cast out,
That I'm his father out of pity's sake.

JEHOSHABEATH

Oh no, the danger that I saved him from . . .
So what fresh danger does he now confront?

JEHOIADA

You're losing faith already? Wondering?

JEHOSHABEATH

I yield to your wise counsels, then, my lord.
The day I snatched the child from death,
I put his fate entirely in your hands.   190

Même de mon amour craignant la violence,
Autant que je le puis, j'évite sa présence,
De peur qu'en le voyant, quelque trouble indiscret
Ne fasse avec mes pleurs échapper mon secret.
Surtout j'ai cru devoir aux larmes, aux prières,
Consacrer ces trois jours et ces trois nuits entières.
Cependant aujourd'hui puis-je vous demander
Quels amis vous avez prêts à vous seconder?
Abner, le brave Abner viendra-t-il nous défendre?
A-t-il près de son roi fait serment de se rendre?   200

JOAD

Abner, quoiqu'on se pût assurer sur sa foi,
Ne sait pas même encor si nous avons un roi.

JOSABET

Mais à qui de Joas confiez-vous la garde?
Est-ce Obed? Est-ce Ammon que cet honneur regarde?
De mon père sur eux les bienfaits répandus . . .

JOAD

A l'injuste Athalie ils se sont tous vendus.

JOSABET

Qui donc opposez-vous contre ses satellites?

JOAD

Ne vous l'ai-je pas dit? Nos prêtres, nos lévites.

JOSABET

Je sais que près de vous en secret assemblé
Par vos soins prévoyants leur nombre est redoublé;   210
Que pleins d'amour pour vous, d'horreur pour Athalie,
Un serment solennel par avance les lie
A ce fils de David qu'on leur doit révéler.
Mais quelque noble ardeur dont ils puissent brûler,
Peuvent-ils de leur roi venger seuls la querelle?
Pour un si grand ouvrage, est-ce assez de leur zèle?
Doutez-vous qu'Athalie, au premier bruit semé
Qu'un fils d'Ochosias est ici renfermé,
De ses fiers étrangers assemblant les cohortes,

I feared the fierceness of my love. As much
As I could do, I've shunned the boy,
In case I saw him, fussed too much and then
Let out the secret with my tears.
I've spent these last three days and three whole nights
In duty bound, in weeping and in prayer.
But now today, I have to ask what friends
Are ready to support our cause.
Abner is brave – he'll come to our defence?
He's sworn to rally to his king?   200

JEHOIADA

The loyalty of Abner is assured.
He does not know, though, that we have a king.

JEHOSHABEATH

So who will you entrust to guard the boy?
Will Obed have the honour? Or Amnon?
The favours that my father showered on them . . .

JEHOIADA

They've all sold themselves to Athaliah.

JEHOSHABEATH

Then who will stand against her followers?

JEHOIADA

Haven't I said? Our levites, all our priests.

JEHOSHABEATH

I know you've secretly assembled them.
Your foresight has redoubled all their ranks.   210
I know they love you, fear Athaliah,
And that they've made a binding vow to serve
This son of David whom they've yet to know.
But yet, despite this noble, burning zeal,
Can they alone avenge our king's great cause?
Is zeal enough for such an enterprise?
You think Athaliah will catch the merest hint
That Azariah's son is sheltered here,
And won't call in her puffed-up, foreign hordes,

N'environne le temple, et n'en brise les portes?   220
Suffira-t-il contre eux de vos ministres saints,
Qui, levant au Seigneur leurs innocentes mains,
Ne savent que gémir, et prier pour nos crimes,
Et n'ont jamais versé que le sang des victimes?
Peut-être dans leurs bras Joas percé de coups . . .

JOAD

Et comptez-vous pour rien Dieu, qui combat pour nous?
Dieu, qui de l'orphelin protège l'innocence,
Et fait dans la faiblesse éclater sa puissance;
Dieu, qui hait les tyrans, et qui dans Jezraël
Jura d'exterminer Achab et Jezabel;   230
Dieu, qui frappant Joram, le mari de leur fille,
A jusque sur son fils poursuivi leur famille;
Dieu, dont le bras vengeur, pour un temps suspendu,
Sur cette race impie est toujours étendu.

JOSABET

Et c'est sur tous ces rois sa justice sévère,
Que je crains pour le fils de mon malheureux frère.
Qui sait si cet enfant, par leur crime entraîné,
Avec eux en naissant ne fut pas condamné?
Si Dieu le séparant d'une odieuse race,
En faveur de David voudra lui faire grâce?   240
Hélas! l'état horrible où le ciel me l'offrit,
Revient à tout moment effrayer mon esprit.
De princes égorgés la chambre était remplie.
Un poignard à la main, l'implacable Athalie
Au carnage animait ses barbares soldats,
Et poursuivait le cours de ses assassinats.
Joas laissé pour mort frappa soudain ma vue.
Je me figure encor sa nourrice éperdue,
Qui devant les bourreaux s'était jetée en vain
Et faible le tenait renversé sur son sein.   250
Je le pris tout sanglant. En baignant son visage,
Mes pleurs du sentiment lui rendirent l'usage.
Et soit frayeur encore, ou pour me caresser,
De ses bras innocents je me sentis presser.
Grand Dieu! que mon amour ne lui soit point funeste.

Surround the temple and smash down the doors.   220
How could your holy priests resist that force?
They'd raise their guiltless hands to God
And simply mourn and pray for all our sins.
They've shed no blood apart from sacrifice.
But in their arms, perhaps, a Joash pierced by swords . . .

JEHOIADA

So God who fights for us does not now count?
God who protects the orphan's innocence,
Who makes his power shine out among the weak.
God who hates the tyrant, and who in Jezrael
Swore to wipe out Ahab and Jezebel.   230
Who struck their daughter's husband, Joram, down,
And has pursued the family through his son.
Whose vengeful arm, held still now for a time,
Is always stretched above this godless race.

JEHOSHABEATH

It's just such heavy justice to these kings
I fear for my unhappy brother's son.
Who knows if Joash wasn't caught up in their crime
And wasn't damned with them by being born?
Or will God mark him out from all his hated race
And show him mercy now for David's sake?   240
His awful state when heaven showed me him
Keeps flooding back . . . to harrow me – my mind.
The room was full of princes, throats cut out.
Athaliah had a dagger in her hand.
She urged her bestial troops to kill, quite merciless,
And leapt into the butchery herself.
Then suddenly I noticed Joash, left for dead.
I still can see his nurse – distraught –
She'd thrown herself before the murderers in vain
And held him feebly clasped against her breast.   250
I picked him up, all bleeding. I washed his face.
My tears brought back some sense of touch to him.
Whether in fear or else a sign of love,
I felt him press me with his childish hands.
Dear God, don't let my love make for his death.

Du fidèle David, c'est le précieux reste.
Nourri dans ta maison en l'amour de ta loi,
Il ne connaît encor d'autre père que toi.
Sur le point d'attaquer une reine homicide,
A l'aspect du péril si ma foi s'intimide,   260
Si la chair et le sang se troublant aujourd'hui,
Ont trop de part aux pleurs que je répands pour lui,
Conserve l'héritier de tes saintes promesses,
Et ne punis que moi de toutes mes faiblesses.

JOAD

Vos larmes, Josabet, n'ont rien de criminel.
Mais Dieu veut qu'on espère en son soin paternel.
Il ne recherche point, aveugle en sa colère,
Sur le fils qui le craint, l'impiété du père.
Tout ce qui reste encor de fidèles Hébreux
Lui viendront aujourd'hui renouveler leurs vœux.   270
Autant que de David la race est respectée,
Autant de Jézabel la fille est détestée.
Joas les touchera par sa noble pudeur,
Où semble de son sang reluire la splendeur.
Et Dieu par sa voix même appuyant notre exemple,
De plus près à leur cœur parlera dans son temple.
Deux infidèles rois tour à tour l'ont bravé.
Il faut que sur le trône un roi soit élevé,
Qui se souvienne un jour qu'au rang de ses ancêtres,
Dieu l'a fait remonter par la main de ses prêtres,   280
L'a tiré par leur main de l'oubli du tombeau,
Et de David éteint rallumé le flambeau.
Grand Dieu! si tu prévois qu'indigne de sa race,
Il doive de David abandonner la trace;
Qu'il soit comme le fruit en naissant arraché,
Ou qu'un souffle ennemi dans sa fleur a séché.
Mais si ce même enfant, à tes ordres docile,
Doit être à tes desseins un instrument utile;
Fais qu'au juste héritier le sceptre soit remis.
Livre en mes faibles mains ses puissants ennemis;   290
Confonds dans ses conseils une reine cruelle.
Daigne, daigne, mon Dieu, sur Mathan et sur elle
Répandre cet esprit d'imprudence et d'erreur,

He is the precious jewel of David's faith.
Your house has brought him up, taught him your law.
He knows no other father but yourself.
If an attack upon this murderous queen
And sight of danger makes my faith less strong —   260
If flesh and blood are so unnerved today,
Are too much with me in the tears I shed —
Keep safe the heir of all your promises.
For all my weakness, punish me alone.

JEHOIADA

Jehoshabeath — your tears are innocent.
But God our father bids us trust in him.
He isn't blind with rage, trying to wreak
A father's godlessness upon his righteous son.
All those remaining of the faithful Jews
Will come today to swear their vows again.   270
As much as David's line is here revered,
Athaliah is as much abhorred.
Joash will touch them with his modesty;
The glory of his blood shines there again.
God will support us with his voice.
He'll speak out in his temple to their hearts.
Two faithless kings have braved his rage in turn.
But now a king must sit upon the throne
Who will recall how, by his priests' own hands,
The Lord restored him to his ancient place,   280
Preserved him from the grave's oblivion
And so rekindled David's guttering torch.
But if, great God, you think he'll shame his race,
That it's his fate to disown David's ways,
Let him be like the fruit that's picked too young
When violent winds have dried up all the flower.
But if the child obeys your laws,
Becomes the instrument of your design,
Restore the sceptre to its rightful heir.
Put in these weak, old hands his powerful enemies.   290
Upset the counsels of that vicious queen.
Grant me, my God — instil in Mattan and in her
That reckless, blinded arrogance that is

De la chute des rois funeste avant-coureur.
L'heure me presse. Adieu. Des plus saintes familles
Votre fils et sa sœur vous amènent les filles.

SCÈNE 3

Josabet, Zacharie, Salomith, le Chœur

JOSABET

Cher Zacharie, allez, ne vous arrêtez pas,
De votre auguste père accompagnez les pas.
O filles de Lévi, troupe jeune et fidèle,
Que déjà le Seigneur embrase de son zèle,   300
Qui venez si souvent partager mes soupirs,
Enfants, ma seule joie en mes longs déplaisirs;
Ces festons dans vos mains, et ces fleurs sur vos têtes,
Autrefois convenaient à nos pompeuses fêtes.
Mais hélas! en ce temps d'opprobre et de douleurs,
Quelle offrande sied mieux que celle de nos pleurs?
J'entends déjà, j'entends la trompette sacrée,
Et du temple bientôt on permettra l'entrée.
Tandis que je me vais préparer à marcher,
Chantez, louez le Dieu que vous venez chercher.   310

SCÈNE 4

Le Chœur

TOUT LE CHŒUR [*chante*]

Tout l'univers est plein de sa magnificence.
Qu'on l'adore, ce Dieu, qu'on l'invoque à jamais.
Son empire a des temps précédé la naissance.
      Chantons, publions ses bienfaits.

UNE VOIX [*seule*]

      En vain l'injuste violence

The deadly herald of the fall of kings.
The time is short. Goodbye. There, look. Your children bring
The daughters of the holy families.

       [he leaves as Zechariah, Salomith, and the Chorus enter

SCENE 3

Jehoshabeath, Zecharaiah, Salomith, the Chorus

JEHOSHABEATH

Dear Zechariah, go now. Don't delay.
Stay close now with your father in his walk.
Daughters of Levi, young and faithful band –
Our God already lights you with his zeal.   300
You have so often come to share my tears.
You are the only joy in this long pain.
Those garlands in your hands, flowers on your head –
They suited once our glorious festivals.
But in these days of shame and suffering,
What fitter offering than our tears?
But listen . . . there . . . the sacred trumpet sounds.
The temple doors will soon be open now.
I must make ready for the ritual,
So sing and praise the God you've come to find.   310

                        [she leaves

SCENE 4

The Chorus

FULL CHORUS [*sings*]

The whole wide world is his magnificence.
Adore this God and always speak his name.
He ruled before the very birth of time.
Let us proclaim his kindnesses.

FIRST SOLOIST

These unjust, violent men in vain

Au peuple qui le loue, imposerait silence,
      Son nom ne périra jamais.
Le jour annonce au jour sa gloire et sa puissance.
Tout l'univers est plein de sa magnificence.
      Chantons, publions ses bienfaits.   320

TOUT LE CHŒUR [*répète*]

Tout l'univers est plein de sa magnificence.
      Chantons, publions ses bienfaits.

UNE VOIX [*seule*]

    Il donne aux fleurs leur aimable peinture.
      Il fait naître et mûrir les fruits.
      Il leur dispense avec mesure
Et la chaleur des jours, et la fraîcheur des nuits;
Le champ qui les reçut, les rend avec usure.

UNE AUTRE

Il commande au soleil d'animer la nature,
    Et la lumière est un don de ses mains.
      Mais sa loi sainte, sa loi pure   330
Est le plus riche don qu'il ait fait aux humains.

UNE AUTRE

O mont de Sinaï, conserve la mémoire
De ce jour à jamais auguste et renommé,
      Quand sur ton sommet enflammé,
Dans un nuage épais le Seigneur enfermé
Fit luire aux yeux mortels un rayon de sa gloire.
    Dis-nous, pourquoi ces feux et ces éclairs,
Ces torrents de fumée, et ce bruit dans les airs,
      Ces trompettes et ce tonnerre?
Venait-il renverser l'ordre des éléments?   340
      Sur ses antiques fondements
      Venait-il ébranler la terre?

UNE AUTRE

Il venait révéler aux enfants des Hébreux
De ses préceptes saints la lumière immortelle.
      Il venait à ce peuple heureux
Ordonner de l'aimer d'une amour éternelle.

Would silence those who praise our God.
His name will never fade or die.
Day speaks to day his glory and his power.
The whole wide world is his magnificence.
Let us proclaim his kindnesses.   320

FULL CHORUS

The whole wide world is his magnificence.
Let us proclaim his kindnesses.

FIRST SOLOIST

He gives such lovely colours to the flowers.
He makes the fruits give birth and ripens them.
He gives according to their need
The heat of day, the coolness of the night.
The fields then give them back a hundredfold.

SECOND SOLOIST

He bids the sun make nature all alive;
Its light falls as his gift from his own hand.
And yet his law, his pure and holy law,   330
Is far the richest gift he gives to us.

THIRD SOLOIST

Mount Sinai, keep the memory bright
Of that great day until the end of time,
When on the summit, ringed with fire,
Wrapped in a heavy cloud, the Lord let shine
A glorious ray of light on human eyes.
The lightning, all those flames . . . so tell us why . . .
The rushing streams of smoke, the murmurs in the air,
The trumpets, thunderclaps?
Was it to tear apart the order of all things?   340
To shock the earth deep down,
Down to its very core?

FOURTH SOLOIST

He came to show the children of the Jews
The everlasting light of holy law.
He came to bid this blessed race
To love him with a changeless love.

TOUT LE CHŒUR

O divine, ô charmante loi!
O justice, ô bonté suprême!
Que de raisons, quelle douceur extrême
D'engager à ce Dieu son amour et sa foi!   350

UNE VOIX [seule]

D'un joug cruel il sauva nos aïeux,
Les nourrit au désert d'un pain délicieux.
Il nous donne ses lois, il se donne lui-même :
Pour tant de biens il commande qu'on l'aime.

LE CHŒUR

O justice! ô bonté suprême!

LA MÊME VOIX

Des mers pour eux il entrouvrit les eaux,
D'un aride rocher fit sortir des ruisseaux.
Il nous donne ses lois, il se donne lui-même.
Pour tant de biens, il commande qu'on l'aime.

LE CHŒUR

O divine, ô charmante loi!
Que de raisons, quelle douceur extrême   360
D'engager à ce Dieu son amour et sa foi!

UNE AUTRE VOIX [seule]

Vous qui ne connaissez qu'une crainte servile,
Ingrats, un Dieu si bon ne peut-il vous charmer?
Est-il donc à vos cœurs, est-il si difficile
Et si pénible de l'aimer?
L'esclave craint le tyran qui l'outrage.
Mais des enfants l'amour est le partage.
Vous voulez que ce Dieu vous comble de bienfaits,
Et ne l'aimer jamais?   370

TOUT LE CHŒUR

O divine, ô charmante loi!
O justice, ô bonté suprême!
Que de raisons, quelle douceur extrême
D'engager à ce Dieu son amour et sa foi!

FULL CHORUS

Such holy, pleasing law.
Such justice, best of goodnesses.
How very sweet and right it is to pledge
Our love and faithfulness to God.   350

FIRST SOLOIST

He saved our fathers from a cruel yoke
And fed them in the desert sweetest bread.
He gives his laws, he gives himself to us.
He bids us love him for such kindnesses.

FULL CHORUS

Such justice, best of goodnesses.

FIRST SOLOIST

He parted wide the waters of the sea,
Made streams flow forth from barren rocks.
He gives his laws, he gives himself to us.
He bids us love him for such kindnesses.

FULL CHORUS

Such holy, pleasing law.   360
How very sweet and right it is to pledge
Our love and faithfulness to God.

ANOTHER SOLOIST

You who know nothing but a slavish fear,
Cannot so good a God enchant your soul?
How is it in your hearts so difficult,
So hard to give him love?
Slaves cower beneath the tyrant's whip,
But children always share in love.
You want the Lord to lavish kindnesses
And yet not give your love to him?   370

FULL CHORUS

Such holy, pleasing law.
Such justice, best of goodnesses.
How very sweet and right it is to pledge
Our love and faithfulness to God.
                    [*Salomith and the Chorus remain as Jehoshabeath enters*

ACTE 2 SCÈNE 1

Josabet, Salomith, le Chœur

JOSABET

Mes filles, c'est assez; suspendez vos cantiques.
Il est temps de nous joindre aux prières publiques.
Voici notre heure : allons célébrer ce grand jour,
Et devant le Seigneur paraître à notre tour.

SCÈNE 2

Zacharie, Josabet, Salomith, le Chœur

JOSABET

Mais que vois-je? Mon fils, quel sujet vous ramène?
Où courez-vous ainsi tout pâle et hors d'haleine?   380

ZACHARIE

O ma mère!

JOSABET   Eh bien quoi?

ZACHARIE   Le temple est profané.

JOSABET

Comment?

ZACHARIE   Et du Seigneur l'autel abandonné.

JOSABET

Je tremble. Hâtez-vous d'éclaircir votre mère.

ZACHARIE

Déjà, selon la loi, le grand prêtre mon père,
Après avoir au Dieu qui nourrit les humains,
De la moisson nouvelle offert les premiers pains,
Lui présentait encore entre ses mains sanglantes
Des victimes de paix les entrailles fumantes.
Debout à ses côtés le jeune Éliacin,

ACT 2 SCENE I

Jehoshabeath, Salomith, the Chorus

JEHOSHABEATH

Daughters, enough for now. Your songs must end.
It's time for us to join in public prayer.
It's now for us to celebrate this day
And in our turn appear before the Lord.
[*Zechariah rushes in*]

SCENE 2

Jehoshabeath, Zechariah, Salomith, the Chorus

JEHOSHABEATH

But what's all this? Zechariah, why are you back?
Where are you running? You're pale – out of breath.   380

ZECHARIAH

Dear mother . . .

JEHOSHABEATH   What?

ZECHARIAH   The temple . . . sacrilege . . .

JEHOSHABEATH

What?

ZECHARIAH   The Lord's own altar – no-one's there . . .

JEHOSHABEATH

I'm trembling. What has happened? Tell me, quick.

ZECHARIAH

As high-priest, father had observed the law,
And had just offered up the first new harvest loaves
To God who feeds all humankind.
His blood-stained hands were holding up to him
The reeking entrails of the sacrifice.
The young Eliacin stood close to him,

Comme moi, le servait en long habit de lin;   390
Et cependant, du sang de la chair immolée,
Les prêtres arrosaient l'autel et l'assemblée.
Un bruit confus s'élève, et du peuple surpris
Détourne tout à coup les yeux et les esprits.
Une femme . . . Peut-on la nommer sans blasphème?
Une femme . . . C'était Athalie elle-même.

JOSABET

Ciel!

ZACHARIE   Dans un des parvis aux hommes réservé,
Cette femme superbe entre le front levé,
Et se préparait même à passer les limites
De l'enceinte sacrée ouverte aux seuls lévites.   400
Le peuple s'épouvante et fuit de toutes parts.
Mon père . . . Ah, quel courroux animait ses regards!
Moïse à Pharaon parut moins formidable.
Reine, sors, a-t-il dit de ce lieu redoutable,
D'où te bannit ton sexe et ton impiété.
Viens-tu du Dieu vivant braver la majesté?
La reine alors sur lui jetant un œil farouche,
Pour blasphémer sans doute ouvrait déjà la bouche.
J'ignore si de Dieu l'ange se dévoilant,
Est venu lui montrer un glaive étincelant.   410
Mais sa langue en sa bouche à l'instant s'est glacée,
Et toute son audace a paru terrassée.
Ses yeux comme effrayés n'osaient se détourner.
Surtout, Éliacin paraissait l'étonner.

JOSABET

Quoi donc? Éliacin a paru devant elle?

ZACHARIE

Nous regardions tous deux cette reine cruelle,
Et d'une égale horreur nos cœurs étaient frappés.
Mais les prêtres bientôt nous ont enveloppés.
On nous a fait sortir. J'ignore tout le reste,
Et venais vous conter ce désordre funeste.   420

Was serving in his linen robe like me.   390
The priests were sprinkling on the shrine
And worshippers the blood of sacrifice.
And then this noise rose up. The people were amazed.
Their eyes and minds were suddenly caught by
A woman . . . but can I name her and not blaspheme?
A woman, yes . . . it was Athaliah.

JEHOSHABEATH

Dear God . . .

ZECHARIAH   Into a square reserved for men alone
She entered, proud, her head held high.
She would have even crossed the boundaries
Of sacred courts where only priests may go.   400
The people scattered everywhere, quite terrified.
My father, though . . . the rage burned in his eyes.
Moses to Pharaoh must have seemed less terrible.
'Queen,' he shouted, 'leave this place of dread.
Your sex and godlessness both keep you out.
Will you confront the majesty of God?'
The queen looked up at him ferociously,
Opened her mouth to blaspheme certainly . . .
An angel of the Lord may have appeared
And showed a flaming sword – I do not know –   410
Her tongue, though, froze that instant in her mouth
And all her arrogance seemed drained from her.
Her eyes looked terrified. She dared not turn away.
She seemed above all haunted by Eliacin.

JEHOSHABEATH

What! she's seen Eliacin?

ZECHARIAH

We both of us were looking at the queen.
Our hearts were beating fast, quite horrified.
But quick as light, the priests had circled round
And made us leave. What followed I don't know.
I came to tell you of the dreadful scene.   420

JOSABET

Ah! de nos bras sans doute elle vient l'arracher,
Et c'est lui qu'à l'autel sa fureur vient chercher.
Peut-être en ce moment l'objet de tant de larmes . . .
Souviens-toi de David, Dieu qui vois mes alarmes.

SALOMITH

Quel est-il, cet objet des pleurs que vous versez?

ZACHARIE

Les jours d'Éliacin seraient-ils menacés?

SALOMITH

Aurait-il de la reine attiré la colère?

ZACHARIE

Que craint-on d'un enfant sans support, et sans père?

JOSABET

Ah! la voici. Sortons. Il la faut éviter.

SCÈNE 3

Athalie, Agar, Abner, suite d'Athalie

AGAR

Madame, dans ces lieux, pourquoi vous arrêter?   430
Ici tous les objets vous blessent, vous irritent.
Abandonnez ce temple aux prêtres qui l'habitent.
Fuyez tout ce tumulte, et dans votre palais
A vos sens agités venez rendre la paix.

ATHALIE

Non, je ne puis, tu vois mon trouble, et ma faiblesse.
Va, fais dire à Mathan qu'il vienne, qu'il se presse,
Heureuse, si je puis trouver par son secours
Cette paix que je cherche, et qui me fuit toujours!

[elle s'assied

JEHOSHABEATH

She's come to snatch him from our arms, I know.
He is what brought her raging to the shrine.
But even now, the boy I cry for here . . .
Remember David, Lord. You know my fear . . .

SALOMITH

Who is it then? The cause of all these tears?

ZECHARIAH

Eliacin – is he in danger now?

SALOMITH

So is the queen annoyed with him?

ZECHARIAH

Why should she fear a child who's fatherless?

JEHOSHABEATH

Ah, there she is. We must avoid her. Come.

> [*they all leave. Athaliah, Abner, Hagar*
> *and Athaliah's retinue enter*

SCENE 3

Athaliah, Abner, Hagar, Athaliah's retinue

HAGAR

Your majesty . . . why linger any more?   430
Here everything offends and angers you.
So leave this temple to the priests who live in it.
Escape the turmoil. Come to your palace
And find some peace to calm your troubled mind.

ATHALIAH

I cannot leave. You see my helplessness.
Tell Mattan to come here. Make him be quick.
I'd have such joy if he could help me find
The peace I yearn for. It still escapes.

> [*Hagar leaves. She sits*

SCÈNE 4

Athalie, Abner, etc.

ABNER

Madame, pardonnez si j'ose le défendre.
Le zèle de Joad n'a point dû vous surprendre.   440
Du Dieu que nous servons, tel est l'ordre éternel.
Lui-même il nous traça son temple et son autel,
Aux seuls enfants d'Aaron commit ses sacrifices,
Aux lévites marqua leur place et leurs offices,
Et surtout défendit à leur postérité,
Avec tout autre dieu toute société.
Hé quoi! vous de nos rois et la femme et la mère!
Êtes-vous à ce point parmi nous étrangère?
Ignorez-vous nos lois? Et faut-il qu'aujourd'hui . . .
Voici votre Mathan, je vous laisse avec lui.   450

ATHALIE

Votre présence, Abner, est ici nécessaire.
Laissons là de Joad l'audace téméraire,
Et tout ce vain amas de superstitions,
Qui ferment votre temple aux autres nations.
Un sujet plus pressant excite mes alarmes.
Je sais que dès l'enfance élevé dans les armes,
Abner a le cœur noble, et qu'il rend à la fois
Ce qu'il doit à son Dieu, ce qu'il doit à ses rois.
Demeurez.

SCENE 4

Athaliah, Abner, Athaliah's retinue

ABNER

    Forgive me, queen, if I dare speak for him.
    Jehoiada's zeal should not have caused surprise.   440
    This is God's order to the end of time.
    He has marked out his temple and his shrine,
    Entrusted sacrifice to Aaron's sons,
    Assigned the Levites roles and offices,
    Above all ordered their posterity
    Never to follow after other gods.
    You are the wife and mother of our kings,
    You can't have turned a stranger to our ways . . .
    Do you not know our laws? And must you now . . .
    But here's your Mattan. I'll leave you both.   450

ATHALIAH

    Your presence, Abner, is still needed here.
    Forget Jehoiada's rash audacity
    And that vain heap of superstitious faith
    That bars all other nations from your shrine.
    A much more urgent question stirs my fears.
    From childhood you've been reared to fight. I know
    Your heart is loyal. You give what's due to God
    And what is owing to his kings. Stay now.
    Mattan . . . ?

                             [Mattan enters

SCÈNE 5

Mathan, Athalie, Abner, etc.

MATHAN   Grande reine, est-ce ici votre place?
Quel trouble vous agite, et quel effroi vous glace?   460
Parmi vos ennemis que venez-vous chercher?
De ce temple profane osez-vous approcher?
Avez-vous dépouillé cette haine si vive . . .

ATHALIE
Prêtez-moi l'un et l'autre une oreille attentive.
Je ne veux point ici rappeler le passé,
Ni vous rendre raison du sang que j'ai versé.
Ce que j'ai fait, Abner, j'ai cru le devoir faire.
Je ne prends point pour juge un peuple téméraire.
Quoi que son insolence ait osé publier,
Le ciel même a pris soin de me justifier.   470
Sur d'éclatants succès ma puissance établie
A fait jusqu'aux deux mers respecter Athalie.
Par moi Jérusalem goûte un calme profond.
Le Jourdain ne voit plus l'Arabe vagabond,
Ni l'altier Philistin, par d'éternels ravages,
Comme au temps de vos rois, désoler ses rivages,
Le Syrien me traite et de reine et de sœur,
Enfin de ma maison le perfide oppresseur,
Qui devait jusqu'à moi pousser sa barbarie,
Jéhu le fier Jéhu tremble dans Samarie.   480
De toutes parts pressé par un puissant voisin
Que j'ai su soulever contre cet assassin,
Il me laisse en ces lieux souveraine maîtresse.
Je jouissais en paix du fruit de ma sagesse.
Mais un trouble importun vient depuis quelques jours
De mes prospérités interrompre le cours.
Un songe (me devrais-je inquiéter d'un songe?)
Entretient dans mon cœur un chagrin qui le ronge.
Je l'évite partout, partout il me poursuit.
C'était pendant l'horreur d'une profonde nuit.   490
Ma mère Jézabel devant moi s'est montrée,

SCENE 5

Mattan, Athaliah, Abner, Athaliah's retinue

MATTAN   Great queen, is this the place for you?
  What care can trouble you, terror chill your heart?   460
  What do you look for here among your enemies?
  You dare come near this god-forsaken shrine?
  Have you forgotten all that violent hate?

ATHALIAH

  Listen, both of you. Listen carefully.
  I do not mean to summon up the past
  Nor yet to justify the blood that I have shed.
  What I have done, Abner, I thought I had to do.
  I will not have a reckless mob as judge,
  Whatever insults they may dare to shout.
  I have been justified by heaven itself.   470
  I've built my power on brilliant victories.
  My name commands respect from sea to sea.
  Through me, Jerusalem enjoys a lasting peace.
  The Jordan sees its banks laid waste no more
  By wandering Arabs or proud Philistines
  In constant raids, as in your old kings' time.
  I'm held by Syria as a sister, as a queen.
  And last – that lawless traitor to my house,
  Who would have forced his barbarousness on me –
  Jehu, proud Jehu, trembles in Samaria.   480
  The murderer's beset on every side
  By powerful neighbours I've stirred up.
  He leaves me sovereign mistress here.
  The fruits of statecraft savoured so in peace . . .
  But now for several days, a haunting care
  Has stolen in upon my happiness.
  A dream – should I be troubled by a dream? –
  Keeps up this gnawing worry in my heart.
  I put it out of mind. It haunts me still.
  During the horror of a black, black night,   490
  My mother Jezebel appeared to me,

Comme au jour de sa mort pompeusement parée.
Ses malheurs n'avaient point abattu sa fierté.
Même elle avait encor cet éclat emprunté,
Dont elle eut soin de peindre et d'orner son visage,
Pour réparer des ans l'irréparable outrage.
Tremble, m'a-t-elle dit, fille digne de moi.
Le cruel Dieu des Juifs l'emporte aussi sur toi.
Je te plains de tomber dans ses mains redoutables,
Ma fille. En achevant ces mots épouvantables,   500
Son ombre vers mon lit a paru se baisser.
Et moi, je lui tendais les mains pour l'embrasser.
Mais je n'ai plus trouvé qu'un horrible mélange
D'os et de chairs meurtris, et traînés dans la fange,
Des lambeaux pleins de sang, et des membres affreux,
Que des chiens dévorants se disputaient entre eux.

ABNER

Grand Dieu!

ATHALIE   Dans ce désordre à mes yeux se présente
Un jeune enfant couvert d'une robe éclatante,
Tels qu'on voit des Hébreux les prêtres revêtus.
Sa vue a ranimé mes esprits abattus.   510
Mais lorsque revenant de mon trouble funeste,
J'admirais sa douceur, son air noble et modeste,
J'ai senti tout à coup un homicide acier
Que le traître en mon sein a plongé tout entier.
De tant d'objets divers le bizarre assemblage
Peut-être du hasard vous paraît un ouvrage.
Moi-même quelque temps honteuse de ma peur
Je l'ai pris pour l'effet d'une sombre vapeur.
Mais de ce souvenir mon âme possédée
A deux fois en dormant revu la même idée.   520
Deux fois mes tristes yeux se sont vu retracer
Ce même enfant toujours tout prêt à me percer.
Lasse enfin des horreurs dont j'étais poursuivie
J'allais prier Baal de veiller sur ma vie,
Et chercher du repos au pied de ses autels.
Que ne peut la frayeur sur l'esprit des mortels!
Dans le temple des Juifs un instinct m'a poussée,

Grandly arrayed as on the day she died.
All her misfortunes had not crushed her pride.
Her looks still had that borrowed sheen
With which she painted and adorned her face
To hide the unrelenting ravages of time.
'Tremble,' she said, 'true daughter that you are.
The cruel Jewish God will beat you too.
You'll fall – I pity you – into his dreadful hands,
My daughter.' As she said those terrifying words,   500
Her ghost appeared to bend over my bed.
I reached out with my hands to kiss her face
And found them clutching at a loathsome mess
Of bones and putrid flesh dragged through the mud,
And blood-soaked rags and hideous, shattered limbs
That ravenous dogs tore from each other's jaws.

ABNER
Dear God . . .

ATHALIAH   Then in the turmoil there appeared
A young boy covered in a dazzling robe
Like those in which the Hebrew priests are seen.
The sight of him restored my broken mind.   510
I was recovering from that dead despair
And wondering at his gentle modesty,
When all at once I felt a murderous blade
He'd treacherously plunged into my heart.
This mixture of such strange and different things
May seem to be the work of chance to you.
I was ashamed for some time of my fear;
I thought it came from darkest fantasy.
And yet my mind was haunted by the memory.
Twice as I've slept, I've had the dream again.   520
Twice now my harrowed eyes have seen this boy.
And always he's about to stab at me.
I grew so weary of these awful fears,
I was about to pray to Baal to guard my life
And find some peace upon his altar steps.
What terror cannot do inside the mind . . .
And yet some instinct drove me to the Jews' own shrine.

Et d'apaiser leur Dieu j'ai conçu la pensée.
J'ai cru que des présents calmeraient son courroux,
Que ce Dieu, quel qu'il soit, en deviendrait plus doux.   530
Pontife de Baal, excusez ma faiblesse.
J'entre. Le peuple fuit. Le sacrifice cesse.
Le grand prêtre vers moi s'avance avec fureur.
Pendant qu'il me parlait, ô surprise! ô terreur!
J'ai vu ce même enfant dont je suis menacée,
Tel qu'un songe effrayant l'a peint à ma pensée.
Je l'ai vu. Son même air, son même habit de lin,
Sa démarche, ses yeux, et tous ses traits enfin.
C'est lui-même. Il marchait à côté du grand prêtre.
Mais bientôt à ma vue on l'a fait disparaître.   540
Voilà quel trouble ici m'oblige à m'arrêter,
Et sur quoi j'ai voulu tous deux vous consulter.
Que présage, Mathan, ce prodige incroyable?

MATHAN

Ce songe, et ce rapport, tout me semble effroyable.

ATHALIE

Mais cet enfant fatal, Abner, vous l'avez vu.
Quel est-il? De quel sang? Et de quelle tribu?

ABNER

Deux enfants à l'autel prêtaient leur ministère.
L'un est fils de Joad, Josabet est sa mère.
L'autre m'est inconnu.

MATHAN   Pourquoi délibérer?
De tous les deux, Madame, il se faut assurer.   550
Vous savez pour Joad mes égards, mes mesures,
Que je ne cherche point à venger mes injures,
Que la seule équité règne en tous mes avis.
Mais lui-même après tout, fût-ce son propre fils,
Voudrait-il un moment laisser vivre un coupable?

ABNER

De quel crime un enfant peut-il être capable?

MATHAN

Le ciel nous le fait voir un poignard à la main.

I thought I might appease their God.
I thought that presents might assuage his rage,
Whatever God he was, and he'd be kind.   530
High priest of Baal, forgive my weakness there.
I entered. People fled. The sacrifice was stopped.
The chief priest came raging up to me
And as he screamed . . . I shook in fear . . .
I saw the very boy who'd threatened me
Just as I'd seen him in that awful dream.
I saw him there – same look, same linen robe,
His walk, his eyes, his features all the same.
It was the boy. Walking beside the priest.
But in a trice they made him disappear.   540
You see the turmoil now that keeps me here.
That's why I wanted to consult you both.
What, Mattan, does this awful omen mean?

MATTAN

The dream and what you've said are full of fear.

ATHALIAH

Abner, this deadly child, you've seen him too.
What is he like? What is his race, his tribe?

ABNER

Two boys were serving at the shrine. One was
Jehoiada's son. His mother is Jehoshabeath.
I do not know the other boy.

MATTAN   Why hesitate?
My queen, you must detain them both. You know   550
Jehoiada has my due respect.
I do not seek revenge for injuries.
Justice alone determines my advice.
Would he himself desire a guilty life
To be one moment spared, even his only son's?

ABNER

But what crime can a child be guilty of?

MATTAN

Heaven has shown him, dagger in his hand.

Le ciel est juste et sage et ne fait rien en vain.
Que cherchez-vous de plus?

ABNER   Mais sur la foi d'un songe

Dans le sang d'un enfant voulez-vous qu'on se plonge?   560
Vous ne savez encor de quel père il est né,
Quel il est.

MATHAN   On le craint, tout est examiné.
A d'illustres parents s'il doit son origine,
La splendeur de son sort doit hâter sa ruine.
Dans le vulgaire obscur si le sort l'a placé,
Qu'importe qu'au hasard un sang vil soit versé?
Est-ce aux rois à garder cette lente justice?
Leur sûreté souvent dépend d'un prompt supplice.
N'allons point les gêner d'un soin embarrassant.
Dès qu'on leur est suspect on n'est plus innocent.   570

ABNER

Hé quoi, Mathan? D'un prêtre est-ce là le langage?
Moi, nourri dans la guerre aux horreurs du carnage,
Des vengeances des rois ministre rigoureux,
C'est moi qui prête ici ma voix au malheureux.
Et vous, qui lui devez des entrailles de père,
Vous, ministre de paix dans les temps de colère,
Couvrant d'un zèle faux votre ressentiment,
Le sang à votre gré coule trop lentement?
Vous m'avez commandé de vous parler sans feinte,
Madame. Quel est donc ce grand sujet de crainte?   580
Un songe, un faible enfant, que votre œil prévenu
Peut-être sans raison croit avoir reconnu.

ATHALIE

Je le veux croire, Abner; je puis m'être trompée.
Peut-être un songe vain m'a trop préoccupée.
Eh bien! il faut revoir cet enfant de plus près,
Il en faut à loisir examiner les traits.
Qu'on les fasse tous deux paraître en ma présence.

ABNER

Je crains . . .

Heaven is wise and just, does naught in vain.
What more to ask?

ABNER   But yet to trust a dream . . .
   To drench ourselves in children's blood for that . . .   560
   You don't know even who his father is,
   Or who he is.

MATTAN   He's feared. That is enough.
   If he's from family of honoured name,
   His glorious rank should hasten on his death.
   If fate has put him in the common throng,
   What matter lowly blood is spilt by chance?
   Is such slow, cautious justice fit for kings?
   Their safety often rests on swift despatch.
   We should not hinder them by being scrupulous.
   Whoever they suspect is from that time condemned.   570

ABNER

   Is this, Mattan, the language of a priest?
   I've been brought up in all the carnages of war,
   The strict executor of kings' revenge,
   And yet it's me who pleads the poor child's cause.
   And you who owe a father's love to him –
   A minister of peace in angry times –
   You hide resentment with this hollow zeal.
   Too slowly for your liking does blood flow.
   You ordered me, Athaliah, to speak my mind.
   So what is then this massive cause for fear?   580
   A dream? A little boy that you'd prejudged
   And thought mistakenly you recognised?

ATHALIAH

   That may well be. I could have been deceived.
   Perhaps I've been obsessed by empty dreams.
   Then I must see this boy much closer to.
   I must have time to look, to gaze on him.
   Let them be brought before me, both of them.

ABNER

   I fear –

ATHALIE   Manquerait-on pour moi de complaisance?
De ce refus bizarre où seraient les raisons?
Il pourrait me jeter en d'étranges soupçons.   590
Que Josabet, vous dis-je, ou Joad les amène.
Je puis, quand je voudrai, parler en souveraine.
Vos prêtres, je veux bien, Abner, vous l'avouer,
Des bontés d'Athalie ont lieu de se louer.
Je sais sur ma conduite et contre ma puissance
Jusqu'où de leurs discours ils portent la licence.
Ils vivent cependant, et leur temple est debout.
Mais je sens que bientôt ma douceur est à bout.
Que Joad mette un frein à son zèle sauvage,
Et ne m'irrite point par un second outrage.   600
Allez.

SCÈNE 6

Athalie, Mathan, etc.

MATHAN   Enfin je puis parler en liberté.
Je puis dans tout son jour mettre la vérité.
Quelque monstre naissant dans ce temple s'élève,
Reine. N'attendez pas que le nuage crève.
Abner chez le grand prêtre a devancé le jour.
Pour le sang de ses rois vous savez son amour.
Et qui sait si Joad ne veut point en leur place
Substituer l'enfant dont le ciel vous menace,
Soit son fils, soit quelque autre . . .

ATHALIE   Oui, vous m'ouvrez les yeux.
Je commence à voir clair dans cet avis des cieux.   610
Mais je veux de mon doute être débarrassée.
Un enfant est peu propre à trahir sa pensée.
Souvent d'un grand dessein un mot nous fait juger.
Laissez-moi, cher Mathan, le voir, l'interroger.
Vous cependant allez, et sans jeter d'alarmes,
A tous mes Tyriens faites prendre les armes.

ATHALIAH　　　You will not fail to do my will . . . ?
　What reasons could there be for saying no?
　You might inspire the strangest doubts in me . . . 　　　590
　Jehoshabeath, Jehoiada, brings them here.
　I can when I so wish speak as a queen.
　Let me be frank, Abner. Your priests have cause
　Enough to recognise my kindnesses.
　I know the lengths to which they've spoken out
　Against my conduct and my power.
　And yet they live. Their temple's standing still.
　But soon, I think, my patience quite runs out . . .
　Jehoiada should curb his zeal
　And not provoke me with a fresh affront. 　　　　　600
　Go.

　　　　　　　　　　　　　　　　　　　　　[*Abner leaves*

SCENE 6

Athaliah, Mattan, Athaliah's retinue

MATTAN　　　So now I can speak out at last,
　Reveal the pure, unvarnished truth.
　Some monster in this shrine is being born.
　Oh queen, don't wait until the storm bursts forth.
　Abner was with Jehoiada before the dawn.
　You know how much he loves his line of kings.
　Perhaps he wants to put now in their place
　The boy with whom the heavens threaten you.
　Either his son, or else some . . .

ATHALIAH　　　　　　　　　　You open my eyes.
　I now begin to see what heaven warns. 　　　　　610
　But still I must be rid of all my doubts.
　A child is little used to hide his thoughts.
　One word will often tell a grand design.
　Let me, dear Mattan, see and question him.
　Meanwhile, you go. Raise no alarm.
　Just see my Tyrian soldiers have their arms.
　　　　　　[*Mattan leaves. Jehoshabeath and Abner enter, together
　　　　　　　　with Joash, Zechariah and Salomith. Two Levites,
　　　　　　　　　the Chorus and Athaliah's retinue also enter*

SCÈNE 7

Joas, Josabet, Athalie, Zacharie, Abner, Salomith,
deux Lévites, le Chœur, etc.

JOSABET [*aux deux Lévites*]

O vous, sur ces enfants si chers, si précieux,
Ministres du Seigneur, ayez toujours les yeux.

ABNER [*à Josabet*]

Princesse, assurez-vous, je les prends sous ma garde.

ATHALIE

O ciel! plus j'examine et plus je le regarde,   620
C'est lui. D'horreur encor tous mes sens sont saisis.
Épouse de Joad, est-ce là votre fils?

JOSABET

Qui? Lui, Madame?

ATHALIE   Lui.

JOSABET   Je ne suis point sa mère.
Voilà mon fils.

ATHALIE   Et vous, quel est donc votre père?
Jeune enfant, répondez.

JOSABET   Le ciel jusqu'aujourd'hui . . .

ATHALIE

Pourquoi vous pressez-vous de répondre pour lui?
C'est à lui de parler.

JOSABET   Dans un âge si tendre
Quel éclaircissement en pouvez-vous attendre?

ATHALIE

Cet âge est innocent. Son ingénuité
N'altère point encor la simple vérité.   630
Laissez-le s'expliquer sur tout ce qui le touche.

JOSABET [*tout bas*]

Daigne mettre, grand Dieu, ta sagesse en sa bouche.

SCENE 7

Joash, Jehoshabeath, Athaliah, Zachariah, Abner, Salomith,
two Levites, the chorus, Athaliah's retinue

JEHOSHABEATH [*to the two Levites*]
    Oh ministers of God, keep careful watch
    On these two boys. They're very dear to us.

ABNER [*to Jehoshabeath*]
    Be reassured. I'll take good care of them.

ATHALIAH
    Dear God, the more I look, the more I gaze . . .   620
    It's him. New horror . . . seizes . . . grips my mind.
    Jehoshabeath, is this your son?

JEHOSHABEATH
    Who, him?

ATHALIAH   Yes, him.

JEHOSHABEATH   He's not my child.
    [*she points to Zachariah*] That is my son.

ATHALIAH [*to Joash*]   So who then is your father?
    Tell me, little boy.

JEHOSHABEATH   Until today the heavens . . .

ATHALIAH
    Why hurry to reply for him so fast?
    It's up to him to speak.

JEHOSHABEATH   But he's so young.
    What explanation can you hope to have?

ATHALIAH
    He's at the age of innocence – naive.
    He won't distort the simple truth.   630
    So let him talk about what touches him.

JEHOSHABEATH [*aside, quietly*]
    Dear Lord, please place your wisdom on his lips.

ATHALIE

Comment vous nommez-vous?

JOAS   J'ai nom Éliacin.

ATHALIE

Votre père?

JOAS   Je suis, dit-on, un orphelin,
Entre les bras de Dieu jeté dès ma naissance,
Et qui de mes parents n'eus jamais connaissance.

ATHALIE

Vous êtes sans parents?

JOAS   Ils m'ont abandonné.

ATHALIE

Comment? Et depuis quand?

JOAS   Depuis que je suis né.

ATHALIE

Ne sait-on pas au moins quel pays est le vôtre?

JOAS

Ce temple est mon pays, je n'en connais point d'autre.   640

ATHALIE

Où dit-on que le sort vous a fait rencontrer?

JOAS

Parmi des loups cruels prêts à me dévorer.

ATHALIE

Qui vous mit dans ce temple?

JOAS   Une femme inconnue,
Qui ne dit point son nom, et qu'on n'a point revue.

ATHALIE

Mais de vos premiers ans quelles mains ont pris soin?

JOAS

Dieu laissa-t-il jamais ses enfants au besoin?

ATHALIAH

What is your name?

JOASH   Eliacin.

ATHALIAH

Your father?

JOASH   I'm an orphan, so they say –
Thrown on God's mercy since my birth.
I've never known just who my parents were.

ATHALIAH

You have no parents?

JOASH   They abandoned me.

ATHALIAH

So how? Since when?

JOASH   Since I was born.

ATHALIAH

But don't you know what country you are from?

JOASH

This temple is my home. I have no other one.   640

ATHALIAH

Where do they say they found you first of all?

JOASH

With cruel wolves about to eat me up.

ATHALIAH

Who brought you to this shrine?

JOASH   A lady . . . I don't know.
She didn't say her name. I haven't seen her since.

ATHALIAH

When you were very small, who cared for you?

JOASH

But does God ever let his children want?

Aux petits des oiseaux il donne leur pâture,
Et sa bonté s'étend sur toute la nature.
Tous les jours je l'invoque et, d'un soin paternel,
Il me nourrit des dons offerts sur son autel.   650

ATHALIE

Quel prodige nouveau me trouble et m'embarrasse?
La douceur de sa voix, son enfance, sa grâce
Font insensiblement à mon inimitié
Succéder . . . Je serais sensible à la pitié?

ABNER

Madame, voilà donc cet ennemi terrible.
De vos songes menteurs l'imposture est visible,
A moins que la pitié qui semble vous troubler
Ne soit ce coup fatal qui vous faisait trembler.

ATHALIE [à Joas et à Josabet]

Vous sortez?

JOSABET   Vous avez entendu sa fortune.

Sa présence à la fin pourrait être importune.   660

ATHALIE

Non. Revenez. Quel est tous les jours votre emploi?

JOAS

J'adore le Seigneur. On m'explique sa loi.
Dans son livre divin on m'apprend à la lire,
Et déjà de ma main je commence à l'écrire.

ATHALIE

Que vous dit cette loi?

JOAS   Que Dieu veut être aimé;

Qu'il venge tôt ou tard son saint nom blasphémé;
Qu'il est le défenseur de l'orphelin timide;
Qu'il résiste au superbe, et punit l'homicide.

ATHALIE

J'entends. Mais tout ce peuple enfermé dans ce lieu,
A quoi s'occupe-t-il?

He gives the little birds their daily bread.
His goodness stretches out to all the world.
So every day I pray to him. His father's care
Gives me my food, gifts offered at his shrine.   650

ATHALIAH

Another miracle to trouble me . . . ?
The sweetness of his voice, his childish grace,
Make hatred imperceptibly give way
To . . . Can I be feeling pity now?

ABNER

So this boy is the fearful enemy?
Your dreams have lied. It's clear they're false –
Unless the deadly blow that made you shake
Was not this sense of pity haunting you.

ATHALIAH [*to Joash and Jehoshabeath*]
You're leaving?

JEHOSHABEATH   You've heard his story. He might
Be bothersome if he stayed longer now.   660

ATHALIAH

Come back . . . What do you do, then, every day?

JOASH

I worship God. I'm taught his laws. I'm taught
How I can read them in his holy book.
I've started now to write them out myself.

ATHALIAH

What does it say, this law?

JOASH   That God wants love.
If we blaspheme his name, he'll be avenged.
That he'll protect us orphans, who are weak.
That he'll put down the proud, and punish murderers.

ATHALIAH

I see. But all the people shut up here,
What do they do?

JOAS   Il loue, il bénit Dieu.   670

ATHALIE

Dieu veut-il qu'à toute heure on prie, on le contemple?

JOAS

Tout profane exercice est banni de son temple.

ATHALIE

Quels sont donc vos plaisirs?

JOAS   Quelquefois à l'autel,
Je présente au grand prêtre ou l'encens ou le sel.
J'entends chanter de Dieu les grandeurs infinies.
Je vois l'ordre pompeux de ses cérémonies.

ATHALIE

Hé quoi? Vous n'avez point de passe-temps plus doux?
Je plains le triste sort d'un enfant tel que vous.
Venez dans mon palais, vous y verrez ma gloire.

JOAS

Moi des bienfaits de Dieu je perdrais la mémoire?   680

ATHALIE

Non, je ne vous veux pas contraindre à l'oublier.

JOAS

Vous ne le priez point.

ATHALIE   Vous pourrez le prier.

JOAS

Je verrais cependant en invoquer un autre?

ATHALIE

J'ai mon dieu que je sers. Vous servirez le vôtre.
Ce sont deux puissants dieux.

JOAS   Il faut craindre le mien,
Lui seul est Dieu, Madame, et le vôtre n'est rien.

ATHALIE

Les plaisirs près de moi vous chercheront en foule.

JOASH   They praise and bless the Lord.   670

ATHALIAH

Does God want prayer and contemplation all the time?

JOASH

All pagan things are banished from the shrine.

ATHALIAH

What do you like to do?

JOASH   Sometimes I give
Some salt or incense to the high priest at the shrine.
I hear God's boundless greatness sung aloud.
I see the solemn order of his rites.

ATHALIAH

But don't you have some nicer ways to pass the time?
I'd pity any boy like you so harsh a life.
Come to my palace. See the wonders there.

JOASH

But I'd forget God's kindnesses.   680

ATHALIAH

I'd never force you to forget.

JOASH

But you don't pray to him.

ATHALIAH   Yet you could pray.

JOASH

I'd see you praying to another god.

ATHALIAH

I'd serve my god, and you'd serve yours.
They both are powerful gods.

JOASH   Mine must be feared.
He is the only God. Yours is nothing.

ATHALIAH

You'd so enjoy yourself were you with me.

JOAS

Le bonheur des méchants comme un torrent s'écoule.

ATHALIE

Ces méchants, qui sont-ils?

JOSABET   Hé, Madame! excusez
Un enfant . . .

ATHALIE [à Josabet]   J'aime à voir comme vous l'instruisez.   690
Enfin, Éliacin, vous avez su me plaire.
Vous n'êtes point sans doute un enfant ordinaire.
Vous voyez, je suis reine, et n'ai point d'héritier.
Laissez là cet habit, quittez ce vil métier.
Je veux vous faire part de toutes mes richesses.
Essayez dès ce jour l'effet de mes promesses.
A ma table, partout, à mes côtés assis,
Je prétends vous traiter comme mon propre fils.

JOAS

Comme votre fils?

ATHALIE   Oui. Vous vous taisez?

JOAS   Quel père
Je quitterais! et pour . . .

ATHALIE   Eh bien?

JOAS   Pour quelle mère?   700

ATHALIE [à Josabet]

Sa mémoire est fidèle, et dans tout ce qu'il dit
De vous et de Joad je reconnais l'esprit.
Voilà comme infectant cette simple jeunesse
Vous employez tous deux le calme où je vous laisse.
Vous cultivez déjà leur haine et leur fureur.
Vous ne leur prononcez mon nom qu'avec horreur.

JOSABET

Peut-on de nos malheurs leur dérober l'histoire?
Tout l'univers les sait. Vous-même en faites gloire.

JOASH

The joy of wicked men flows past like streams.

ATHALIAH

Who are the wicked, then?

JEHOSHABEATH   Oh queen, forgive
A child . . .

ATHALIAH [*to Jehoshabeath*]   I like the way you've taught the boy.
Eliacin, I'm very pleased with you.
It's clear you are no ordinary child.
You see, I'm queen, and yet I have no heir.
Take off that robe. Give up these paltry tasks.
I want you now to share in all my wealth.
This very day, you test my promises.
At table, everywhere, sit close to me.
I mean to treat you as my own dear son.

JOASH

Your son?

ATHALIAH   Yes, why . . . you do not speak.

JOASH   But what
A father I should leave, for . . .

ATHALIAH   For?

JOASH   . . . what a mother.   700

ATHALIAH

His memory is good. In all he says,
I recognise Jehoiada's hand and yours.
So this is how you poison trusting youth
And put the peace I left you with to use . . .
You foster both their hatred and their rage.
Only with horror do you speak my name.

JEHOSHABEATH

How can we hide the story of our grief?
The whole world knows. You boast of it yourself.

ATHALIE

Oui, ma juste fureur, et j'en fais vanité,
A vengé mes parents sur ma postérité.   710
J'aurais vu massacrer et mon père, et mon frère,
Du haut de son palais précipiter ma mère,
Et dans un même jour égorger à la fois,
Quel spectacle d'horreur! quatre-vingts fils de rois?
Et pourquoi? Pour venger je ne sais quels prophètes,
Dont elle avait puni les fureurs indiscrètes,
Et moi reine sans cœur, fille sans amitié,
Esclave d'une lâche et frivole pitié,
Je n'aurais pas du moins à cette aveugle rage
Rendu meurtre pour meurtre, outrage pour outrage,   720
Et de votre David traité tous les neveux,
Comme on traitait d'Achab les restes malheureux?
Où serais-je aujourd'hui, si domptant ma faiblesse
Je n'eusse d'une mère étouffé la tendresse,
Si de mon propre sang ma main versant des flots
N'eût par ce coup hardi réprimé vos complots?
Enfin de votre Dieu l'implacable vengeance
Entre nos deux maisons rompit toute alliance.
David m'est en horreur, et les fils de ce roi
Quoique nés de mon sang, sont étrangers pour moi.   730

JOSABET

Tout vous a réussi? Que Dieu voie, et nous juge.

ATHALIE

Ce Dieu depuis longtemps votre unique refuge,
Que deviendra l'effet de ses prédictions?
Qu'il vous donne ce roi promis aux nations,
Cet enfant de David, votre espoir, votre attente . . .
Mais nous nous reverrons. Adieu, je sors contente,
J'ai voulu voir, j'ai vu.

ABNER [à Josabet]   Je vous l'avais promis,
Je vous rends le dépôt que vous m'avez commis.

ATHALIAH

I have good cause for rage – I'm proud of it –
I have avenged my parents' death on all my race . . .   710
I saw my father and my brother killed,
My mother hurled down from the palace walls;
Within one day, some eighty sons of kings,
Their throats slit out . . . The horror . . . in that sight . . .
And why? So that some obscure prophets then,
Whose raging fury she had curbed, might be avenged?
And me – a loveless daughter, heartless queen,
A slave to pity, like a shallow coward –
Should I have not paid back this blinding rage
At least with crime for crime, and death for death,   720
And treated all your David's race just as
You treated Ahab's wretched sons.
Where would I be today if I'd been tamed
And not choked back a mother's tenderness?
If I'd not poured my son's own blood in streams
And not killed off your plots at one fell stroke?
So then, the ruthless vengeance of your God
Broke every friendly pact that we had made.
I shudder so at David's name . . . His royal sons
Are of my blood. But they are strangers now.   730

JEHOSHABEATH

You've had success. But God will see and judge.

ATHALIAH

This God – he's been your refuge for so long –
What will become of all his prophecies?
So let him give the world this promised king,
This David's son, for whom you wait in hope.
We'll meet again. Goodbye. I leave content.
I wished to see. And I have seen.   [*she leaves*

ABNER [*to Jehoshabeath*]   I promised you.
And now I'll give you back what I was trusted with.

SCÈNE 8

Joad, Josabet, Joas, Zacharie, Abner,
Salomith, Lévites, le Chœur

JOSABET [*à Joad*]

Avez-vous entendu cette superbe reine,
Seigneur?

JOAD   J'entendais tout, et plaignais votre peine.   740
Ces lévites et moi prêts à vous secourir
Nous étions avec vous résolus de périr.
[*à Joas, en l'embrassant*]
Que Dieu veille sur vous, enfant dont le courage
Vient de rendre à son nom ce noble témoignage.
Je reconnais, Abner, ce service important.
Souvenez-vous de l'heure où Joad vous attend.
Et nous, dont cette femme impie et meurtrière
A souillé les regards et troublé la prière,
Rentrons, et qu'un sang pur par mes mains épanché
Lave jusques au marbre où ses pas ont touché.   750

SCÈNE 9

Le Chœur

UNE DES FILLES DU CHŒUR

Quel astre à nos yeux vient de luire?
Quel sera quelque jour cet enfant merveilleux?
Il brave le faste orgueilleux,
Et ne se laisse point séduire
A tous ses attraits périlleux.

UNE AUTRE

Pendant que du dieu d'Athalie
Chacun court encenser l'autel,
Un enfant courageux publie
Que Dieu lui seul est éternel,

SCENE 8

Jehoiada, Jehoshabeath, Joash, Zechariah,
Abner, Salomith, Levites, the Chorus

JEHOSHABEATH [*to Jehoiada*]

So did you hear this puffed-up queen, my lord?

JEHOIADA

I heard it all. I pitied all your pain.   740
These Levites at my side were all prepared
To help. We were resolved to die with you.
[*to Joash, embracing him*]
May God watch over you. Your courage, child,
Has borne a noble witness to his name.
Abner, I thank you for the help you gave.
I will expect you. Don't forget the time.
And us – we've had our eyes defiled, our prayers
Disturbed all by this godless, murderous queen –
Let us go in. And let the pure blood I have shed
Wash even the marble that her feet have touched.   750
                    [*they all leave apart from the Chorus*

SCENE 9

The Chorus

ONE OF THE CHORUS

What star has newly gleamed on us?
What will this wondrous child grow up to be?
For he defies her pride and all its show
And will not be seduced
By all its dangerous spells.

A SECOND

While crowds rush up to worship at
The shrine of Baal, her god,
A brave young boy declares
That God alone endures.

Et parle comme un autre Élie   760
Devant cette autre Jézabel.

UNE AUTRE

Qui nous révélera ta naissance secrète,
Cher enfant? Es-tu fils de quelque saint prophète?

UNE AUTRE

Ainsi l'on vit l'aimable Samuel
     Croître à l'ombre du tabernacle.
Il devint des Hébreux l'espérance et l'oracle.
Puisses-tu, comme lui, consoler Israël!

UNE AUTRE [*chante*]

     O bienheureux mille fois
     L'enfant que le Seigneur aime,
       Qui de bonne heure entend sa voix,   770
Et que ce Dieu daigne instruire lui-même!
   Loin du monde élevé, de tous les dons des cieux
     Il est orné dès sa naissance;
   Et du méchant l'abord contagieux
     N'altère point son innocence.

TOUT LE CHŒUR

     Heureuse, heureuse l'enfance
Que le Seigneur instruit et prend sous sa défense!

LA MÊME VOIX [*seule*]

     Tel en un secret vallon
     Sur le bord d'une onde pure
     Croît à l'abri de l'aquilon   780
     Un jeune lis, l'amour de la nature.
   Loin du monde élevé, de tous les dons des cieux
     Il est orné dès sa naissance;
   Et du méchant l'abord contagieux
     N'altère point son innocence.

TOUT LE CHŒUR

     Heureux, heureux mille fois
L'enfant que le Seigneur rend docile à ses lois!

He speaks now in Elijah's voice   760
Before this second Jezebel.

A THIRD

Who will reveal your secret birth to us,
Dear child? Are you some holy prophet's son?

A FOURTH

Sweet Samuel was seen as he grew up
Within the tabernacle's shade
To be the Hebrews' hope and guide.
May you, like him, wipe Israel's tears away.

A FIFTH [*singing*]

He's blessed a thousand times,
The child who's loved by God,
Who early hears his voice   770
And who is taught by him.
Brought up beyond the world, he's graced
With all of heaven's gifts from birth.
The plagues of those who sin
Can never taint his innocence.

FULL CHORUS

The greatest joy is with that child
Whom God instructs and will defend.

THE FIFTH [*alone*]

Just as in a secret vale
Beside a crystal stream,
A budding lily, nature's dearest love,   780
Grows sheltered from the cold north wind.
Brought up beyond the world, he's graced
With all of heaven's gifts from birth.
The plagues of those who sin
Can never taint his innocence.

FULL CHORUS

He's blessed a thousand times,
The child whom God makes humble to his law.

UNE VOIX [*seule*]

        Mon Dieu, qu'une vertu naissante
Parmi tant de périls marche à pas incertains!
Qu'une âme qui te cherche et veut être innocente,   790
        Trouve d'obstacle à ses desseins!
        Que d'ennemis lui font la guerre!
      Où se peuvent cacher tes saints?
      Les pécheurs couvrent la terre.

UNE AUTRE

  O palais de David, et sa chère cité,
  Mont fameux, que Dieu même a longtemps habité,
  Comment as-tu du ciel attiré la colère?
  Sion, chère Sion, que dis-tu quand tu vois
        Une impie étrangère
      Assise, hélas! au trône de tes rois?   800

TOUT LE CHŒUR

  Sion, chère Sion, que dis-tu quand tu vois
        Une impie étrangère
      Assise, hélas! au trône de tes rois?

LA MÊME VOIX [*continue*]

      Au lieu des cantiques charmants
  Où David t'exprimait ses saints ravissements,
  Et bénissait son Dieu, son Seigneur, et son père;
  Sion, chère Sion, que dis-tu quand tu vois
      Louer le dieu de l'impie étrangère,
  Et blasphémer le nom qu'ont adoré tes rois?

UNE VOIX [*seule*]

  Combien de temps, Seigneur, combien de temps encore   810
  Verrons-nous contre toi les méchants s'élever?
  Jusque dans ton saint temple ils viennent te braver.
  Ils traitent d'insensé le peuple qui t'adore.
  Combien de temps, Seigneur, combien de temps encore
  Verrons-nous contre toi les méchants s'élever?

UNE AUTRE

  Que vous sert, disent-ils, cette vertu sauvage?
      De tant de plaisirs si doux

A SOLOIST

O Lord, that goodness from its birth
Should through such danger walk unsure.
That souls that yearn for you, that would be pure,   790
Are checked in their desire.
How many enemies make war on them.
Where can your saints then hide?
The men of sin possess the earth.

ANOTHER SOLOIST

Palace of David, city that he loved,
The famous mount where God himself has lived,
How have you drawn down heaven's rage?
Beloved Zion, what have you to say?
You see this godless foreigner —
Her seated now upon your royal throne.   800

FULL CHORUS

Beloved Zion, what have you to say?
You see this godless foreigner —
Her seated now upon your royal throne.

THE SAME SOLOIST [*continues*]

Instead of those enchanting songs
That David sang to you in purest joy,
Blessing his God, his father and his lord,
Beloved Zion, what have you to say?
You see them praise this godless foreigner's Lord,
Blaspheme the name your kings adored.

A SOLOIST

How long, O Lord, how long must we still see   810
The men of evil rise against your law?
They challenge you in your own holy shrine.
They call us mad, all we who worship you.
How long, O Lord, how long must we still see
The men of evil rise against your law?

ANOTHER SOLOIST

What good has outcast virtue done,
They ask. Why run away from all

Pourquoi fuyez-vous l'usage?
Votre Dieu ne fait rien pour vous.

UNE AUTRE

Rions, chantons dit cette troupe impie;   820
De fleurs en fleurs, de plaisirs en plaisirs,
     Promenons nos désirs.
Sur l'avenir insensé qui se fie.
De nos ans passagers le nombre est incertain.
Hâtons-nous aujourd'hui de jouir de la vie,
     Qui sait si nous serons demain!

TOUT LE CHŒUR

Qu'ils pleurent, ô mon Dieu, qu'ils frémissent de crainte
   Ces malheureux, qui de ta cité sainte
   Ne verront point l'éternelle splendeur.
C'est à nous de chanter, nous à qui tu révèles   830
     Tes clartés immortelles;
C'est à nous de chanter tes dons et ta grandeur.

UNE VOIX [seule]

De tous ces vains plaisirs où leur âme se plonge,
Que leur restera-t-il? Ce qui reste d'un songe
     Dont on a reconnu l'erreur.
   A leur réveil, ô réveil plein d'horreur!
     Pendant que le pauvre à ta table
Goûtera de ta paix la douceur ineffable,
Ils boiront dans la coupe affreuse, inépuisable,
Que tu présenteras au jour de ta fureur   840
     A toute la race coupable.

TOUT LE CHŒUR

     O réveil plein d'horreur!
     O songe peu durable!
     O dangereuse erreur!

These pleasures . . . sweet to taste?
Your God does nothing for you now.

ANOTHER SOLOIST

Let's sing and dance, say all this godless crowd.   820
Desire can flit
From flower to flower, one pleasure to the next.
To trust the future is insanity.
We do not know how long we'll live,
So let's enjoy life now, today.
Who knows if we'll be here tomorrow.

FULL CHORUS

Then let them weep, dear God, and shake with fear,
Those wretched sinners who will never see
Your holy city's everlasting light.
It is for us to sing, to whom you have revealed   830
The brightness of eternal life.
It is for us to sing your gifts and majesty.

ANOTHER SOLOIST

What will remain of all those vain delights
In which they drown their souls? Only a dream,
Whose falseness they will recognise
When they wake up – a waking terrified . . .
And while the poor man at your feast
Will taste such sweetness in your peace,
They'll drink that fearful, overflowing cup
That you will give upon the day of wrath   840
To all the guilty race.

FULL CHORUS

Such wakening full of dread,
A dream that vanishes,
What dangerous mistake . . .
                          [*the Chorus remain as Mattan and Nabal enter*

ACTE 3 SCÈNE 1

Mathan, Nabal, le Chœur

MATHAN

Jeunes filles, allez. Qu'on dise à Josabet
Que Mathan veut ici lui parler en secret.

UNE DES FILLES DU CHŒUR

Mathan! O Dieu du ciel, puisses-tu le confondre.

NABAL

Hé quoi? Tout se disperse et fuit sans vous répondre?

MATHAN

Approchons.

SCÈNE 2

Zacharie, Mathan, Nabal

ZACHARIE   Téméraire, où voulez-vous passer?
Au-delà de ce lieu gardez-vous d'avancer.   850
C'est des ministres saints la demeure sacrée.
Les lois à tout profane en défendent l'entrée.
Qui cherchez-vous? Mon père en ce jour solennel
De l'idolâtre impur fuit l'aspect criminel,
Et devant le Seigneur maintenant prosternée
Ma mère en ce devoir craint d'être détournée.

MATHAN

Mon fils, nous attendrons, cessez de vous troubler.
C'est votre illustre mère à qui je veux parler.
Je viens ici chargé d'un ordre de la reine.

ACT 3 SCENE 1

Mattan, Nabal, the Chorus

MATTAN

Young girls, go now and tell Jehoshabeath
That Mattan wants to talk to her alone.

ONE OF THE GIRLS

Mattan . . . ! Dear Lord in heaven, grind him to dust.

NABAL

They scatter – look – run off without a word.

MATTAN

So let's go in.

[the Chorus leaves. Zechariah enters

SCENE 2

Zechariah, Mattan, Nabal

ZECHARIAH   Stop. Where are you going?
Be careful now. Don't come beyond this point.   850
The holy ministers of God live here.
The godless are forbidden here by law.
You look for who . . . ? My father on this holy day
Avoids the sight of foul idolaters.
My mother's worshipping before her God.
She fears all interruptions to her prayers.

MATTAN

My son, we'll wait. Don't be concerned.
It is your mother that I want to see.
I've come here with an order from the queen.

[Zechariah leaves

SCÈNE 3

Mathan, Nabal

NABAL

Leurs enfants ont déjà leur audace hautaine.   860
Mais que veut Athalie en cette occasion?
D'où naît dans ses conseils cette confusion?
Par l'insolent Joad ce matin offensée,
Et d'un enfant fatal en songe menacée,
Elle allait immoler Joad à son courroux,
Et dans ce temple enfin placer Baal et vous.
Vous m'en aviez déjà confié votre joie,
Et j'espérais ma part d'une si riche proie.
Qui fait changer ainsi ses vœux irrésolus?

MATHAN

Ami, depuis deux jours je ne la connais plus.   870
Ce n'est plus cette reine éclairée, intrépide,
Élevée au-dessus de son sexe timide,
Qui d'abord accablait ses ennemis surpris,
Et d'un instant perdu connaissait tout le prix.
La peur d'un vain remords trouble cette grande âme,
Elle flotte, elle hésite, en un mot elle est femme.
J'avais tantôt rempli d'amertume et de fiel
Son cœur déjà saisi des menaces du ciel.
Elle-même à mes soins confiant sa vengeance
M'avait dit d'assembler sa garde en diligence.   880
Mais soit que cet enfant devant elle amené,
De ses parents, dit-on, rebut infortuné,
Eût d'un songe effrayant diminué l'alarme,
Soit qu'elle eût même en lui vu je ne sais quel charme,
J'ai trouvé son courroux chancelant, incertain,
Et déjà remettant sa vengeance à demain.
Tous ses projets semblaient l'un l'autre se détruire.
Du sort de cet enfant je me suis fait instruire,
Ai-je dit; on commence à vanter ses aïeux.
Joad de temps en temps le montre aux factieux,   890
Le fait attendre aux Juifs comme un autre Moïse,

SCENE 3

Mattan, Nabal

NABAL

Even their children have this haughty air . . .   860
What does Athaliah want to do?
How is it that her plans are so confused?
Jehoiada's pride has not pleased her,
A deadly child has threatened her in dreams –
She was about to sacrifice the priest in rage
And then place Baal and you inside this shrine.
You had already told me of your joy,
And I had hopes to share so rich a prey.
What makes her shift and change like this?

MATTAN

These last two days she has not been herself.   870
She is no more that bold, clear-sighted queen
Who towered above her timid female sex,
Who overwhelmed her startled enemies
And knew how much it cost to let the moment pass.
Fear of some vain remorse infects her mind.
She drifts and hesitates. Becomes a girl.
I'd filled her heart with poisonous bitterness –
She was already stunned by heaven's threats –
She'd trusted to my charge all her revenge,
Had told me urgently to call her guards.   880
Whether the boy they brought in front of her –
They say his parents had abandoned him –
Then made the terror of her nightmare fade,
Whether she saw a certain charm in him,
I found her rage uncertain, wavering.
She put off vengeance to another day
And all her plans seemed warring with themselves.
'I've found out now about this young boy's fate,'
I said to her. 'His ancestry is boasted of.
Jehoiada shows him off to those   890
Who criticise, and uses lying oracles

Et d'oracles menteurs s'appuie et s'autorise.
Ces mots ont fait monter la rougeur sur son front.
Jamais mensonge heureux n'eût un effet si prompt.
Est-ce à moi de languir dans cette incertitude?
Sortons, a-t-elle dit, sortons d'inquiétude.
Vous-même à Josabet prononcez cet arrêt.
Les feux vont s'allumer, et le fer est tout prêt.
Rien ne peut de leur temple empêcher le ravage,
Si je n'ai de leur foi cet enfant pour otage.   900

NABAL

Eh bien! pour un enfant qu'ils ne connaissent pas,
Que le hasard peut-être a jeté dans leurs bras,
Voudront-ils que leur temple, enseveli sous l'herbe . . .

MATHAN

Ah! de tous les mortels connais le plus superbe.
Plutôt que dans mes mains par Joad soit livré
Un enfant qu'à son Dieu Joad a consacré,
Tu lui verras subir la mort la plus terrible.
D'ailleurs pour cet enfant leur attache est visible.
Si j'ai bien de la reine entendu le récit,
Joad sur sa naissance en sait plus qu'il ne dit.   910
Quel qu'il soit, je prévois qu'il leur sera funeste.
Ils le refuseront. Je prends sur moi le reste.
Et j'espère qu'enfin de ce temple odieux
Et la flamme et le fer vont délivrer mes yeux.

NABAL

Qui peut vous inspirer une haine si forte?
Est-ce que de Baal le zèle vous transporte?
Pour moi, vous le savez, descendu d'Ismaël,
Je ne sers ni Baal, ni le dieu d'Israël.

MATHAN

Ami, peux-tu penser que d'un zèle frivole
Je me laisse aveugler pour une vaine idole,   920
Pour un fragile bois, que malgré mon secours
Les vers sur son autel consument tous les jours?
Né ministre du Dieu qu'en ce temple on adore,
Peut-être que Mathan le servirait encore,

To make the Jews expect another Moses.'
The words brought blushes to her face at once.
There never was a lie that worked so fast.
'Must I waste time in such uncertainty?'
She said. 'Enough of this anxiety.
You tell Jehoshabeath of this decree.
The fires will now be lit, the swords unsheathed.
Nothing can save their temples from the torch
Unless I have this child as hostage for their word.'   900

NABAL

So . . . will they for a child they do not know,
Whom chance perhaps has thrown into their arms,
Will they allow the grass to wreathe their shrine . . . ?

MATTAN

Ah, but recognise the proudest man alive.
Before Jehoiada will give a child
He's consecrated to his God to me,
You'll see him face the cruellest death.
Their great attachment to the boy is clear.
If I have understood the queen aright,
The priest knows more about him than he says.   910
Whoever he may be, he'll be their death.
They won't surrender him. I'll do the rest,
And hope that fire and sword will rid my eyes
Of all that odious shrine at last.

NABAL

What can inspire so deep a hate in you?
Is it the passion that you feel for Baal?
I am from Ishmael's line, as well you know.
I do not serve the god of Israel nor Baal.

MATTAN

You can't suppose, my friend, I'd blind myself
With wild zeal for an idol? For a piece   920
Of rotten wood that worms eat every day
Upon the shrine, in spite of me? The God
Who's worshipped here – I was his minister.
I'd still be serving him, perhaps,

Si l'amour des grandeurs, la soif de commander,
Avec son joug étroit pouvaient s'accommoder.
Qu'est-il besoin, Nabal, qu'à tes yeux je rappelle
De Joad et de moi la fameuse querelle,
Quand j'osai contre lui disputer l'encensoir,
Mes brigues, mes combats, mes pleurs, mon désespoir?   930
Vaincu par lui, j'entrai dans une autre carrière,
Et mon âme à la cour s'attacha toute entière.
J'approchai par degrés de l'oreille des rois,
Et bientôt en oracle on érigea ma voix.
J'étudiai leur cœur, je flattai leurs caprices,
Je leur semai de fleurs les bords des précipices.
Près de leurs passions rien ne me fut sacré.
De mesure et de poids je changeais à leur gré.
Autant que de Joad l'inflexible rudesse
De leur superbe oreille offensait la mollesse,   940
Autant je les charmais par ma dextérité,
Dérobant à leurs yeux la triste vérité,
Prêtant à leurs fureurs des couleurs favorables,
Et prodigue surtout du sang des misérables.
Enfin au dieu nouveau qu'elle avait introduit
Par les mains d'Athalie un temple fut construit.
Jérusalem pleura de se voir profanée.
Des enfants de Lévi la troupe consternée
En poussa vers le ciel des hurlements affreux.
Moi seul, donnant l'exemple aux timides Hébreux,   950
Déserteur de leur loi, j'approuvai l'entreprise,
Et par là de Baal méritai la prêtrise.
Par là je me rendis terrible à mon rival,
Je ceignis la tiare, et marchai son égal.
Toutefois, je l'avoue, en ce comble de gloire,
Du Dieu que j'ai quitté l'importune mémoire
Jette encore en mon âme un reste de terreur.
Et c'est ce qui redouble et nourrit ma fureur.
Heureux! si sur son temple achevant ma vengeance,
Je puis convaincre enfin sa haine d'impuissance,   960
Et parmi le débris, le ravage, et les morts,
A force d'attentats perdre tous mes remords.
Mais voici Josabet.

If love of power, the thirst to be obeyed,
Could once have yielded to his narrow yoke.
There is no need, Nabal, to tell you of
My famous quarrel with Jehoiada, when
I dared to fight him for the censer's prize.
The intrigues, struggles, tears . . . and the despair.　930
He won. So I took up another path
And gave myself completely to the court.
I slowly came to have the ear of kings,
And soon my words became an oracle.
I read their hearts. I flattered every whim.
I sowed the edge of the abyss with flowers.
Nothing was sacred but their yearning blood.
I changed my principles to suit their taste.
Jehoiada's stern austerity
Grated upon their proud and honeyed ears　940
While I enthralled them with my skill.
I hid the painful truth from all their eyes.
I gave their lusts a rosy hue,
Especially their lavish way with victims' blood.
At last, Athaliah had a temple built
To the new god that she had introduced.
Jerusalem wept so to see itself blasphemed.
In consternation, Levi's children hurled
Such terrifying cries to heaven above.
I gave the timorous Jews some guidance, though.　950
I'd left their faith, and I approved the enterprise.
And so I earned the right to be Baal's priest.
I struck such terror in my rival's heart.
I wore a crown, and walked alongside him.
But I'll confess . . . bathed in this glory . . . yet
The haunting memory of the God I've left
Still casts a lingering terror on my soul.
This is what feeds and stokes the fire in me.
My joy will be to wreak revenge upon
His shrine and prove his hate has lost its power –　960
Among the wreckage, ravage, and the dead,
Lose all remorse by force of violence.
I see Jehoshabeath . . .

[*Jehoshabeath enters*

SCÈNE 4

Josabet, Mathan, Nabal

MATHAN   Envoyé par la reine
Pour rétablir le calme et dissiper la haine,
Princesse, en qui le ciel mit un esprit si doux,
Ne vous étonnez pas si je m'adresse à vous.
Un bruit, que j'ai pourtant soupçonné de mensonge,
Appuyant les avis qu'elle a reçus en songe,
Sur Joad accusé de dangereux complots,
Allait de sa colère attirer tous les flots.   970
Je ne veux point ici vous vanter mes services.
De Joad contre moi je sais les injustices.
Mais il faut à l'offense opposer les bienfaits.
Enfin je viens chargé de paroles de paix.
Vivez, solennisez vos fêtes sans ombrage.
De votre obéissance elle ne veut qu'un gage.
C'est, pour l'en détourner j'ai fait ce que j'ai pu,
Cet enfant sans parents, qu'elle dit qu'elle a vu.

JOSABET
Éliacin!

MATHAN   J'en ai pour elle quelque honte :
D'un vain songe peut-être elle fait trop de compte;   980
Mais vous vous déclarez ses mortels ennemis,
Si cet enfant sur l'heure en mes mains n'est remis.
La reine impatiente attend votre réponse.

JOSABET
Et voilà de sa part la paix qu'on nous annonce!

MATHAN
Pourriez-vous un moment douter de l'accepter?
D'un peu de complaisance, est-ce trop l'acheter?

JOSABET
J'admirais si Mathan dépouillant l'artifice,
Avait pu de son cœur surmonter l'injustice,
Et si de tant de maux le funeste inventeur,

SCENE 4

Jehoshabeath, Mattan, Nabal

MATTAN   The queen has sent me here,
To break down hate and re-establish peace.
Heaven has given you so sweet a soul,
You cannot be surprised I turn to you.
Some rumour – I suspect it is a lie –
Has backed up warnings she's received in dreams
About Jehoiada. He's charged with dangerous plots.
The floodtide of her rage is streaming out.   970
I do not want to boast about my services.
Jehoiada has not been fair to me.
But we must pay back evil acts with good.
And so I come to you with words of peace.
Live. Celebrate your feastdays as you will.
She wants one pledge alone of your obedience.
That is – I did my best to put her off –
That is the orphan boy she says she saw.

JEHOSHABEATH

Eliacin?

MATTAN   I am ashamed for her.
She makes too much, perhaps, of idle dreams.   980
But you'll confirm yourselves as deadly enemies
Unless you give this child to me at once.
She is impatient, waits for your reply.

JEHOSHABEATH

Is this the peace she sends you to announce?

MATTAN

Accept it. Don't hesitate a moment.
A small compliance – is that too high a price?

JEHOSHABEATH

I wondered if you'd shaken off your guile
And overcome your innate wickedness –
If after doing so much deadly harm,

De quelque ombre de bien pouvait être l'auteur.   990

MATHAN

De quoi vous plaignez-vous? Vient-on avec furie
Arracher de vos bras votre fils Zacharie?
Quel est cet autre enfant si cher à votre amour?
Ce grand attachement me surprend à mon tour.
Est-ce un trésor pour vous si précieux, si rare?
Est-ce un libérateur que le ciel vous prépare?
Songez-y. Vos refus pourraient me confirmer
Un bruit sourd que déjà l'on commence à semer.

JOSABET

Quel bruit?

MATHAN   Que cet enfant vient d'illustre origine,
Qu'à quelque grand projet votre époux le destine.   1000

JOSABET

Et Mathan par ce bruit qui flatte sa fureur . . .

MATHAN

Princesse, c'est à vous à me tirer d'erreur.
Je sais que du mensonge implacable ennemie,
Josabet livrerait même sa propre vie,
S'il fallait que sa vie à sa sincérité
Coûtât le moindre mot contre la vérité.
Du sort de cet enfant on n'a donc nulle trace?
Une profonde nuit enveloppe sa race?
Et vous-même ignorez de quels parents issu,
De quelles mains Joad en ses bras l'a reçu?   1010
Parlez, je vous écoute, et suis prêt de vous croire.
Au Dieu que vous servez, Princesse, rendez gloire.

JOSABET

Méchant, c'est bien à vous d'oser ainsi nommer
Un Dieu que votre bouche enseigne à blasphémer.
Sa vérité par vous peut-elle être attestée,
Vous, malheureux, assis dans la chaire empestée
Où le mensonge règne et répand son poison,
Vous, nourri dans la fourbe et dans la trahison?

You could create the slightest touch of good.   990

MATTAN

Why the complaining? Do I come in rage
To snatch your Zechariah from your arms?
Who is this other boy you hold so dear?
Such strong attachment makes me curious too.
Is he so rare a treasure for you both?
The saviour heaven promised you?
Think carefully. If you say no, you may confirm
A rumour that's already noised abroad.

JEHOSHABEATH

What rumour?

MATTAN   That the boy's of noble birth,
And that your husband has great plans for him.   1000

JEHOSHABEATH

And so this rumour's pandered to your rage . . .

MATTAN

It is for you to show me I am wrong.
I know you hate all lies, implacably –
That you'd give up your very life
If life and honesty would cost
A single syllable against the truth.
So there's no trace of where the boy comes from?
An utter darkness shrouds his birth?
You don't know who his parents were? The hands
That gave him up into your husband's arms?   1010
Speak. I'm listening. I'm ready to believe.
Do honour, princess, to the God you serve.

JEHOSHABEATH

You vicious priest. How dare you name a God
Whom you have taught your hearers to blaspheme?
How could his truth be known through you –
Sitting there in a seat of plague
Where lying reigns and spreads its poison round –
Who've fed on guile and treachery?

                                        [*Jehoiada enters*

SCÈNE 5

Joad, Josabet, Mathan, Nabal

JOAD

Où suis-je? De Baal ne vois-je pas le prêtre?
Quoi! fille de David, vous parlez à ce traître?   1020
Vous souffrez qu'il vous parle? Et vous ne craignez pas
Que du fond de l'abîme entr'ouvert sous ses pas,
Il ne sorte à l'instant des feux qui vous embrasent,
Ou qu'en tombant sur lui ces murs ne vous écrasent?
Que veut-il? De quel front cet ennemi de Dieu
Vient-il infecter l'air qu'on respire en ce lieu?

MATHAN

On reconnaît Joad à cette violence.
Toutefois il devrait montrer plus de prudence,
Respecter une reine, et ne pas outrager
Celui que de son ordre elle a daigné charger.   1030

JOAD

Eh bien, que nous fait-elle annoncer de sinistre?
Quel sera l'ordre affreux qu'apporte un tel ministre?

MATHAN

J'ai fait à Josabet savoir sa volonté.

JOAD

Sors donc de devant moi, monstre d'impiété.
De toutes les horreurs, va, comble la mesure.
Dieu s'apprête à te joindre à la race parjure,
Abiron et Dathan, Doëg, Achitophel,
Les chiens, à qui son bras a livré Jézabel,
Attendant que sur toi sa fureur se déploie,
Déjà sont à ta porte et demandent leur proie.   1040

MATHAN [*il se trouble*]

Avant la fin du jour . . . on verra qui de nous . . .
Doit . . . Mais sortons, Nabal.

NABAL   Où vous égarez-vous?

SCENE 5

Jehoiada, Jehoshabeath, Mattan, Nabal

JEHOIADA

Where am I? No . . . is that Baal's priest?
Jehoshabeath, you're talking to that traitor?   1020
You let him speak to you? Aren't you afraid
That sheets of flame will burn you up at once
From the deep hell that opens at his feet?
That all these walls will fall and crush you both?
What does he want, this enemy of God?
Why has he come to foul the air we breathe?

MATTAN

How like Jehoiada all this rage . . .
You ought to show more judgment at the least.
You should respect a queen, and not insult
The man she's charged with her commands.   1030

JEHOIADA

So then, what evil news does she now send?
What ghastly orders do you . . . priest . . . bring?

MATTAN

I've told your wife of what the queen has willed.

JEHOIADA

Then get out from my sight, you foul, black thing.
Let all your horror pour down over us.
God will now put you in the race of perjurers –
Abiram, Dathan, Doeg, Achitophel.
The dogs to whom he threw down Jezebel
Just wait until his rage descends on you.
They're at your door now, slavering for their prey.   1040

MATTAN [*troubled*]

Before the day has passed . . . we'll see which one of us
Will . . . Let's leave, Nabal.

NABAL   You seem quite lost . . .

De vos sens étonnés, quel désordre s'empare?
Voilà votre chemin.

SCÈNE 6

Joad, Josabet

JOSABET   L'orage se déclare.
Athalie en fureur demande Éliacin.
Déjà de sa naissance et de votre dessein
On commence, Seigneur, à percer le mystère.
Peu s'en faut que Mathan ne m'ait nommé son père.

JOAD

Au perfide Mathan qui l'aurait révélé?
Votre trouble à Mathan n'a-t-il point trop parlé?   1050

JOSABET

J'ai fait ce que j'ai pu pour m'en rendre maîtresse.
Cependant, croyez-moi, Seigneur, le péril presse.
Réservons cet enfant pour un temps plus heureux.
Tandis que les méchants délibèrent entre eux,
Avant qu'on l'environne, avant qu'on nous l'arrache,
Une seconde fois souffrez que je le cache.
Les portes, les chemins lui sont encore ouverts.
Faut-il le transporter aux plus affreux déserts?
Je suis prête. Je sais une secrète issue
Par où, sans qu'on le voie, et sans être aperçue,   1060
De Cédron avec lui traversant le torrent,
J'irai dans le désert, où jadis en pleurant,
Et cherchant comme nous son salut dans la fuite,
David d'un fils rebelle évita la poursuite.
Je craindrai moins pour lui les lions, et les ours . . .
Mais pourquoi de Jéhu refuser le secours?
Je vous ouvre peut-être un avis salutaire.
Faisons de ce trésor Jéhu dépositaire.
On peut dans ses États le conduire aujourd'hui,
Et le chemin est court qui mène jusqu'à lui.   1070

What wildness stuns your senses now?
This is the way.

[they leave

SCENE 6

Jehoiada, Jehoshabeath

JEHOSHABEATH   The storm's about to break.
Athaliah rages, will have Eliacin.
Already now, the mystery of his birth
And all your plans are being brought to light.
Mattan came close to saying who his father was.

JEHOIADA

Who could have told that traitor then?
Did your confusion not reveal too much?   1050

JEHOSHABEATH

I tried my utmost to remain composed.
You must believe me, though – the danger's close.
We must protect the boy for happier times.
The wicked plot among themselves.
Before they circle round, snatch him away.
Let me now hide him for a second time.
The gates and roads are open to him still.
Should he taken to the desert wastes?
I am prepared. I know a secret way –
We won't be noticed, seen at all –   1060
We'll cross the torrent Cedron hand in hand
And reach the desert where king David wept.
He looked for safety in his flight – like us –
In order to escape his rebel son.
And so, I'm less afraid of lions and bears . . .
Yet why refuse the help that Jehu gives?
Let me suggest a useful plan for us.
Why not make Jehu guardian of the boy?
He could be taken to his states today.
The journey there does not take long.   1070

Jéhu n'a point un cœur farouche, inexorable,
De David à ses yeux le nom est favorable.
Hélas! est-il un roi si dur et si cruel,
A moins qu'il n'eut pour mère une autre Jézabel,
Qui d'un tel suppliant ne plaignît l'infortune?
Sa cause à tous les rois n'est-elle pas commune?

JOAD

Quels timides conseils m'osez-vous suggérer?
En l'appui de Jéhu pourriez-vous espérer?

JOSABET

Dieu défend-il tout soin et toute prévoyance?
Ne l'offense-t-on point par trop de confiance?   1080
A ses desseins sacrés employant les humains,
N'a-t-il pas de Jéhu lui-même armé les mains?

JOAD

Jéhu, qu'avait choisi sa sagesse profonde,
Jéhu, sur qui je vois que votre espoir se fonde,
D'un oubli trop ingrat a payé ses bienfaits.
Jéhu laisse d'Achab l'affreuse fille en paix,
Suit des rois d'Israël les profanes exemples,
Du vil dieu de l'Égypte a conservé les temples.
Jéhu sur les hauts lieux enfin osant offrir
Un téméraire encens que Dieu ne peut souffrir,   1090
N'a pour servir sa cause et venger ses injures,
Ni le cœur assez droit, ni les mains assez pures.
Non, non, c'est à Dieu seul qu'il nous faut attacher.
Montrons Éliacin, et loin de le cacher,
Que du bandeau royal sa tête soit ornée.
Je veux même avancer l'heure déterminée,
Avant que de Mathan le complot soit formé.

Jehu's not fierce of heart, inexorable.
The name of David's pleasing to his ear.
There could not be so harsh and cruel a king,
Unless his mother were another Jezebel,
Who would not pity such a supplicant.
Is not his cause the cause that all kings share?

JEHOIADA

What timid counsel dare you offer me?
You think to place your trust in Jehu's help?

JEHOSHABEATH

Does God forbid all forethought and concern?
Don't we offend by so much confidence?   1080
He uses humans for his sacred ends.
So didn't he put arms in Jehu's hands?

JEHOIADA

Jehu was chosen in God's own wisdom.
I see you place your trust in him, but he's
Repaid his benefits in cruel forgetfulness.
He leaves the feared Athaliah in peace,
Follows the godless paths of Israel's kings
And leaves the shrines of Egypt's gods untouched.
He dares to offer in the highest shrine
A blasphemous incense God cannot abide.   1090
His heart's not true. His hands aren't pure enough
To serve God's cause and take revenge for wrong.
No, no. We must hold fast to God alone.
We must not hide but show Eliacin,
Place on his head the royal diadem.
I'll even now advance the destined hour
Before Mattan can finalise his plot.

            [*Azariah enters, followed by the Chorus and several Levites*

SCÈNE 7

Joad, Josabet, Azarias, suivi du Chœur et de plusieurs Lévites.

JOAD

Eh bien, Azarias, le temple est-il fermé?

AZARIAS

J'en ai fait devant moi fermer toutes les portes.

JOAD

N'y reste-t-il que vous, et vos saintes cohortes?   1100

AZARIAS

De ses parvis sacrés j'ai deux fois fait le tour.
Tout a fui. Tous se sont séparés sans retour,
Misérable troupeau qu'a dispersé la crainte,
Et Dieu n'est plus servi que dans la tribu sainte.
Depuis qu'à Pharaon ce peuple est échappé,
Une égale terreur ne l'avait point frappé.

JOAD

Peuple lâche en effet, et né pour l'esclavage,
Hardi contre Dieu seul! Poursuivons notre ouvrage.
Mais qui retient encor ces enfants parmi nous?

UNE DES FILLES DU CHŒUR

Hé! pourrions-nous, Seigneur, nous séparer de vous?   1110
Dans le temple de Dieu sommes-nous étrangères?
Vous avez près de vous nos pères et nos frères.

UNE AUTRE

Hélas! si pour venger l'opprobre d'Israël,
Nos mains ne peuvent pas, comme autrefois Jahel,
Des ennemis de Dieu percer la tête impie,
Nous lui pouvons du moins immoler notre vie.
Quand vos bras combattront pour son temple attaqué,
Par nos larmes du moins il peut être invoqué.

JOAD

Voilà donc quels vengeurs s'arment pour ta querelle,
Des prêtres, des enfants, ô Sagesse éternelle!   1120

SCENE 7

Jehoiada, Jehoshabeath, Azarias

JEHOIADA

So, Azariah, is the temple closed?

AZARIAH

I saw the doors locked up myself.

JEHOIADA

The holy priests and you are all who're left?   1100

AZARIAH

I've twice gone round the sacred courts.
The people all ran off. They won't be back.
A wretched flock of sheep scattered by fear.
Only the holy priesthood now serve God.
Terror like this last struck the Jews
When they escaped from Pharaoh's hands.

JEHOIADA

A race of cowards indeed, and born for slavery.
Bold against God alone. Our work, though, must go on.
And yet these children . . . who keeps them here?

ONE OF THE MAIDENS OF THE CHORUS

How could we part from you, my Lord? Are we   1110
Now strangers in the temple of our God?
Our fathers, brothers – all are at your side.

ANOTHER MAIDEN

If to avenge the shame of Israel,
Our hands can't pierce, as Jael did of old,
The wicked hands of all God's enemies,
We can at least give up our lives to him.
So when you fight to save his shrine from harm,
We can at least invoke him with our tears.

JEHOIADA

Wisdom beyond all time . . . you see the troops
Who arm themselves for you? Children and priests.   1120

Mais si tu les soutiens, qui peut les ébranler?
Du tombeau quand tu veux tu sais nous rappeler.
Tu frappes, et guéris. Tu perds et ressuscites.
Ils ne s'assurent point en leurs propres mérites,
Mais en ton nom sur eux invoqué tant de fois
En tes serments jurés au plus saint de leurs rois,
En ce temple où tu fais ta demeure sacrée,
Et qui doit du soleil égaler la durée.
Mais d'où vient que mon cœur frémit d'un saint effroi?
Est-ce l'Esprit divin qui s'empare de moi?   1130
C'est lui-même. Il m'échauffe, il parle. Mes yeux s'ouvrent,
Et les siècles obscurs devant moi se découvrent.
Lévites, de vos sons prêtez-moi les accords,
Et de ses mouvements secondez les transports.

LE CHŒUR [*chante au son de toute la symphonie des instruments*]

    Que du Seigneur la voix se fasse entendre,
    Et qu'à nos cœurs son oracle divin
        Soit ce qu'à l'herbe tendre
    Est au printemps la fraîcheur du matin.

JOAD

Cieux, écoutez ma voix. Terre, prête l'oreille.
Ne dis plus, ô Jacob, que ton Seigneur sommeille!   1140
Pécheurs, disparaissez : le Seigneur se réveille.

        [*ici recommence la symphonie,
        et Joad aussitôt reprend la parole*

Comment en un plomb vil l'or pur s'est-il changé?
Quel est dans le lieu saint ce pontife égorgé?
Pleure, Jérusalem, pleure, cité perfide!
Des prophètes divins malheureuse homicide.
De son amour pour toi ton Dieu s'est dépouillé.
Ton encens à ses yeux est un encens souillé.
    Où menez-vous ces enfants, et ces femmes?
Le Seigneur a détruit la reine des cités.
Ses prêtres sont captifs, ses rois sont rejetés.   1150
Dieu ne veut plus qu'on vienne à ses solennités.
Temple, renverse-toi, cèdres, jetez des flammes.
    Jérusalem, objet de ma douleur,
Quelle main en ce jour t'a ravi tous tes charmes?

But who will shake them if you're by their side?
If you should wish, you could recall us from the tomb.
You strike and cure, you kill and bring to life.
They cannot be secure in their own worthiness
But in your name, invoked so many times,
In oaths you swore to their most holy kings,
And in this temple where your sacred dwelling is
And which will last for ever like the sun.
Yet why the holy dread that shakes my heart . . . ?
Is this God's spirit seizing me? It is.   1130
He makes me warm. He speaks to me. My eyes
Now see the unborn centuries unfold.
Levites, give me your music's harmonies
To voice this movement's ecstasy.

THE CHORUS [*sings to the accompaniment of the whole orchestra*]
So let the voice of God be heard,
And let his holy word upon our hearts
Be as the freshness of the dawn
Upon new grass in spring.

JEHOIADA
Heaven, hear my voice. Listen, earth.
Jacob, no longer say your God sleeps on.   1140
Sinners, fly from our sight. The Lord awakes.
[*Here the orchestra begins afresh, and Jehoiada
at once begins to speak again*]
How is pure gold transformed to common lead?
Who is the priest who's killed in this most holy place?
Weep, weep, Jerusalem – city of treachery –
The tragic murderer of prophets of the Lord.
Your God has torn his love for you away.
Your incense in his eyes is now obscene.
These women, children here – where are they being led?
The Lord has laid the queen of cities low,
Its kings rejected, and its priests in chains.   1150
God now wants no-one at his festivals.
Temple, collapse; and cedar tree, spurt flame.
I grieve for you, Jerusalem.
Whose hands have ravaged all your charm this day?

Qui changera mes yeux en deux sources de larmes
                    Pour pleurer ton malheur?

AZARIAS

O saint temple!

JOSABET   O David!

LE CHŒUR   Dieu de Sion, rappelle,
Rappelle en sa faveur tes antiques bontés.

                    [la symphonie recommence encore,
                    et Joad un moment après l'interrompt

JOAD

                    Quelle Jérusalem nouvelle
Sort du fond du désert brillante de clartés,   1160
Et porte sur le front une marque immortelle?
                    Peuples de la terre, chantez.
Jérusalem renaît plus charmante, et plus belle.
                    D'où lui viennent de tous côtés
Ces enfants qu'en son sein elle n'a point portés?
Lève, Jérusalem, lève ta tête altière.
Regarde tous ces rois de ta gloire étonnés;
Les rois des nations devant toi prosternés,
                    De tes pieds baisent la poussière.
Les peuples à l'envi marchent à ta lumière.   1170
Heureux! qui pour Sion d'une sainte ferveur
                    Sentira son âme embrasée.
                    Cieux, répandez votre rosée,
            Et que la terre enfante son Sauveur.

JOSABET

Hélas! d'où nous viendra cette insigne faveur,
Si les rois de qui doit descendre ce Sauveur . . . .

JOAD

Préparez, Josabet, le riche diadème,
Que sur son front sacré David porta lui-même.
[aux Lévites]
Et vous, pour vous armer, suivez-moi dans ces lieux
Où se garde caché, loin des profanes yeux,   1180
Ce formidable amas de lances et d'épées,

Who'll make my eyes two springs of tears
To weep your tragedy?

AZARIAS

Oh holy temple . . .

JEHOSHABEATH   David . . .

CHORUS   God of Zion,
Recall your ancient kindnesses to it.
[*the orchestra begins again. After a moment,
Jehoiada interrupts it*]

JEHOIADA

What new Jerusalem arises now
From desert wastes, ablaze with light,   1160
And bears an everlasting seal upon her brow?
Sing, peoples of the earth.
Jerusalem is born again more brilliant, lovelier.
Where do they come from now on every side,
These children whom she did not bear?
Lift up, Jerusalem, lift up your head.
See all these kings astonished by your fame.
The kings of nations now bow down to you
And kiss the dust from off your feet.
The nations vie to walk within your light.   1170
Happy all those who feel their souls ablaze
With Zion's holy zeal.
Heaven, now shed your dew, and let the earth
Give its redeemer birth.

JEHOSHABEATH

How can this special favour come to us
If all the kings from whom the Saviour descends . . .

JEHOIADA

Jehoshabeath, prepare the diadem
That David wore upon his brow.
[*to the Levites*]
And Levites, now be armed – come, follow me
To where lies hidden, far from godless eyes,   1180
A fearful arsenal of swords and spears

Qui du sang philistin jadis furent trempées,
Et que David vainqueur, d'ans et d'honneurs chargé,
Fit consacrer au Dieu qui l'avait protégé.
Peut-on les employer pour un plus noble usage?
Venez, je veux moi-même en faire le partage.

SCÈNE 8

Salomith, le Chœur

SALOMITH

Que de craintes, mes sœurs, que de troubles mortels!
    Dieu tout-puissant, sont-ce là les prémices,
       Les parfums et les sacrifices
Qu'on devait en ce jour offrir sur tes autels?   1190

UNE FILLE DU CHŒUR

       Quel spectacle à nos yeux timides!
       Qui l'eût cru, qu'on dût voir jamais
Les glaives meurtriers, les lances homicides,
       Briller dans la maison de paix?

UNE AUTRE

D'où vient que, pour son Dieu pleine d'indifférence,
Jérusalem se tait en ce pressant danger?
       D'où vient, mes sœurs, que pour nous protéger,
Le brave Abner au moins ne rompt pas le silence?

SALOMITH

Hélas! dans une cour, où l'on n'a d'autres lois
       Que la force et la violence,   1200
       Où les honneurs et les emplois
Sont le prix d'une aveugle et basse obéissance,
       Ma sœur, pour la triste innocence,
       Qui voudrait élever la voix?

UNE AUTRE

       Dans ce péril, dans ce désordre extrême,
Pour qui prépare-t-on le sacré diadème?

That once were drenched with blood of Philistines.
Victorious David, crowned with years,
Had consecrated them to God his saviour.
Could they be put to nobler use?
Come, I'll share the weapons out myself.

> [*They all leave apart from Salomith and the Chorus*

SCENE 8

Salomith, the Chorus

SALOMITH

This fear, my sisters, all these deathly cries.
Are these, almighty God, the first-fruits,
The scents and sacrifice
That should be placed upon your shrine today?   1190

ONE OF THE MAIDENS OF THE CHORUS

This is an awful sight for guiltless eyes.
Who would have thought that we would ever see
Such deadly swords and murderous spears
Gleam brilliant in this house of peace?

ANOTHER MAIDEN

Now all these dangers press, how can Jerusalem
Stay silent, indifferent to its God?
Sisters, why at least, to guard us all,
Does Abner fail to speak? He has great heart.

SALOMITH

In courts that have no other laws
But force and violence,   1200
Office and honours are
The prize for blind and crawling deference.
Sisters, who will speak up
For mourning innocence?

ANOTHER MAIDEN

In this danger – all this turmoil –
For whom do they prepare the sacred diadem?

SALOMITH

> Le Seigneur a daigné parler,
> Mais ce qu'à son prophète il vient de révéler,
> > Qui pourra nous le faire entendre?
> > S'arme-t-il pour nous défendre?
> > S'arme-t-il pour nous accabler?   1210

TOUT LE CHŒUR CHANTE

> O promesse! ô menace! ô ténébreux mystère!
> Que de maux, que de biens sont prédits tour à tour!
> > Comment peut-on avec tant de colère
> > Accorder tant d'amour?

UNE VOIX [*seule*]

> Sion ne sera plus. Une flamme cruelle
> > Détruira tous ses ornements.

UNE AUTRE VOIX

> Dieu protège Sion. Elle a pour fondements
> > Sa parole éternelle.

LA PREMIÈRE

> Je vois tout son éclat disparaître à mes yeux.   1220

LA SECONDE

> Je vois de toutes parts sa clarté répandue.

LA PREMIÈRE

> Dans un gouffre profond Sion est descendue.

LA SECONDE

> > Sion a son front dans les cieux.

LA PREMIÈRE

> Quel triste abaissement!

LA SECONDE

> > Quelle immortelle gloire!

LA PREMIÈRE

> Que de cris de douleur!

LA SECONDE

> > Que de chants de victoire!

SALOMITH

The Lord has deigned to speak.
But to his prophet what has he revealed?
Who can explain to us?
Does he now arm to shield us all? 1210
Or does he arm to crush us down?

THE WHOLE CHORUS [*sings*]

Both promises and threats. The darkest mystery.
The ills and blessings prophesied in turn.
How can such rage be reconciled
With so much love?

A SINGLE VOICE

Zion will be no more. A cruel fire
Will burn its beauties to the ground.

ANOTHER VOICE

Zion God will protect. It rests so deeply now
Upon his everlasting word.

THE FIRST VOICE

I see its brilliance fade before my eyes. 1220

THE SECOND VOICE

I see its light spread everywhere.

THE FIRST VOICE

Zion now plunges down a bottomless pit.

THE SECOND VOICE

The head of Zion towers up to the skies.

THE FIRST VOICE

The depth of her disgrace.

THE SECOND VOICE   A glory without end.

THE FIRST VOICE

Those cries of agony.

THE SECOND VOICE   Those songs of victory.

UNE TROISIÈME

Cessons de nous troubler. Notre Dieu quelque jour
            Dévoilera ce grand mystère.

TOUTES TROIS

            Révérons sa colère;
        Espérons en son amour.

UNE AUTRE

                    D'un cœur qui t'aime,   1230
        Mon Dieu, qui peut troubler la paix?
    Il cherche en tout ta volonté suprême,
            Et ne se cherche jamais.
        Sur la terre, dans le ciel même,
Est-il d'autre bonheur que la tranquille paix
                    D'un cœur qui t'aime?

A THIRD VOICE

> We should not be disturbed. One day, our God
> Will tear aside the veil of this great mystery.

ALL THREE VOICES

> We must revere his wrath,
> And trust his love.

ANOTHER VOICE

> My God, who can disturb the peace   1230
> Of one whose heart is turned to you?
> It seeks your highest will in everything
> And never seeks itself.
> On earth, in heaven itself,
> Can any joy surpass that sweetest peace
> Of hearts that love the Lord?

> > [*Salomith and the Chorus remain as Joash,*
> > *Jehoshabeath, Zechariah and a Levite enter*

ACTE 4 SCÈNE 1

Joas, Josabet, Zacharie, Salomith, un Lévite, le Chœur

SALOMITH

D'un pas majestueux, à côté de ma mère,
Le jeune Éliacin s'avance avec mon frère.
Dans ces voiles, mes sœurs, que portent-ils tous deux?
Quel est ce glaive enfin qui marche devant eux?   1240

JOSABET [*à Zacharie*]

Mon fils, avec respect posez sur cette table
De notre sainte loi le livre redoutable.
Et vous aussi posez, aimable Éliacin,
Cet auguste bandeau près du livre divin.
Lévite, il faut placer, Joad ainsi l'ordonne,
Le glaive de David auprès de sa couronne.

JOAS

Princesse, quel est donc ce spectacle nouveau?
Pourquoi ce livre saint, ce glaive, ce bandeau?
Depuis que le Seigneur m'a reçu dans son temple,
D'un semblable appareil je n'ai point vu d'exemple.   1250

JOSABET

Tous vos doutes mon fils, bientôt s'éclairciront.

JOAS

Vous voulez essayer ce bandeau sur mon front?
Ah! Princesse, gardez d'en profaner la gloire.
Du roi qui l'a porté respectez la mémoire.
Un malheureux enfant aux ours abandonné . . .

JOSABET [*lui essayant le diadème*]

Laissez, mon fils, je fais ce qui m'est ordonné.

JOAS

Mais j'entends les sanglots sortir de votre bouche!
Princesse, vous pleurez! Quelle pitié vous touche?
Est-ce qu'en holocauste aujourd'hui présenté,
Je dois, comme autrefois la fille de Jephté,   1260

ACT 4 SCENE I

Joash, Jehoshabeath, Zechariah, Salomith, a Levite, the Chorus

SALOMITH

    Here comes Eliacin – my brother too.
    He walks majestically, my mother by his side.
    What do they carry, sisters, in those veils?
    What is the sword that's borne in front of them?   1240

JEHOSHABEATH [*to Zechariah*]

    My son, place on this table carefully
    The dreaded book of all our holy law.
    And you too, dear Eliacin, place by
    The sacred book this wondrous diadem.
    Levite, Jehoiada orders you to put
    The sword of David there beside his crown.

JOASH

    Princess, this spectacle . . . it's strange to me.
    Why bring the holy book, the sword, the diadem?
    Since God received me in his temple here,
    I've never seen a scene like this.   1250

JEHOSHABEATH

    My son, your doubts will soon be cleared away.

JOASH

    You want to try this diadem upon my head?
    Take care we don't profane its holiness.
    We must respect the king who wore it once,
    That little boy they gave up to the bears . . .

JEHOSHABEATH [*trying the diadem on him*]

    Let me, my son. I must do what I'm told.

JOASH

    There's sobbing in your voice, though. I can tell.
    You're crying, yes. What is it moves you so?
    Is it because I'm like a sacrifice today?
    Like Jephthah's daughter, all dressed up   1260

Du Seigneur par ma mort apaiser la colère?
Hélas! un fils n'a rien qui ne soit à son père.

JOSABET

    Voici qui vous dira les volontés des cieux.
    Ne craignez rien. Et nous, sortons tous de ces lieux.

SCÈNE 2

Joad, Joas

JOAS [*courant dans les bras du grand-prêtre*]
    Mon père!

JOAD   Eh bien, mon fils?

JOAS   Qu'est-ce donc qu'on prépare?

JOAD

    Il est juste, mon fils, que je vous le déclare.
    Il faut que vous soyez instruit, même avant tous,
    Des grands desseins de Dieu sur son peuple et sur vous.
    Armez-vous d'un courage et d'une foi nouvelle.
    Il est temps de montrer cette ardeur et ce zèle,   1270
    Qu'au fond de votre cœur mes soins ont cultivés,
    Et de payer à Dieu ce que vous lui devez.
    Sentez-vous cette noble et généreuse envie?

JOAS

    Je me sens prêt, s'il veut, de lui donner ma vie.

JOAD

    On vous a lu souvent l'histoire de nos rois.
    Vous souvient-il mon fils, quelles étroites lois
    Doit s'imposer un roi digne du diadème?

JOAS

    Un roi sage, ainsi Dieu l'a prononcé lui-même,
    Sur la richesse et l'or ne met point son appui,
    Craint le Seigneur son Dieu, sans cesse a devant lui   1280

To quell God's rage by my own death?
A father can demand the world from his own son.

JEHOSHABEATH

Here is the man who'll tell you heaven's will.
Don't be afraid. The rest of us will go.

[*all leave apart from Joash, as Jehoiada enters*

SCENE 2

Joash, Jehoiada

JOASH [*running to the high-priest's arms*]
Father.

JEHOIADA   And so, my son?

JOASH   What is all this?

JEHOIADA

It's only right, my son, that I should say.
You must be told, before them all,
Of God's great plan for you and for his race.
You must be armed with courage and new faith.
Now is the time to show that burning zeal   1270
I've taken care to plant deep in your heart,
And pay to God all that you owe to him.
So do you feel such generous desire?

JOASH

I'm ready, if he wants, to give my life.

JEHOIADA

You've often heard the story of our kings.
Do you recall, my son, to what strict laws
A king fit to be crowned must hold himself?

JOASH

A king who's wise – so God himself has said –
Does not rely on riches or on gold.
He fears the Lord his God; and keeps in front of him   1280

Ses préceptes, ses lois, ses jugements sévères,
Et d'injustes fardeaux n'accable point ses frères.

JOAD

Mais, sur l'un de ces rois s'il fallait vous régler,
A qui choisiriez-vous, mon fils, de ressembler?

JOAS

David, pour le Seigneur plein d'un amour fidèle,
Me paraît des grands rois le plus parfait modèle.

JOAD

Ainsi dans leurs excès vous n'imiteriez pas
L'infidèle Joram, l'impie Ochosias?

JOAS

O mon père!

JOAD   Achevez, dites, que vous en semble?

JOAS

Puisse périr comme eux quiconque leur ressemble.   1290
Mon père, en quel état vous vois-je devant moi?

JOAD [se prosternant à ses pieds]

Je vous rends le respect que je dois à mon roi.
De votre aïeul David, Joas, rendez-vous digne.

JOAS

Joas? Moi?

JOAD   Vous saurez par quelle grâce insigne,
D'une mère en fureur Dieu trompant le dessein,
Quand déjà son poignard était dans votre sein,
Vous choisit, vous sauva du milieu du carnage.
Vous n'êtes pas encore échappé de sa rage.
Avec la même ardeur qu'elle voulut jadis
Perdre en vous le dernier des enfants de son fils,   1300
A vous faire périr sa cruauté s'attache,
Et vous poursuit encor sous le nom qui vous cache.
Mais sous vos étendards j'ai déjà su ranger
Un peuple obéissant et prompt à vous venger.

His precepts, sternest judgments, and his laws.
He doesn't weigh his brothers down with unjust loads.

JEHOIADA

But if you had to mould yourself on one
Of them, who would you choose to be like most?

JOASH

David was full of faithful love for God.
He seems the best example of a king.

JEHOIADA

And so you would not follow faithlessness
And evil then, like Joram, Ahaziah . . . ?

JOASH

Father . . .

JEHOIADA   Go on. Say what you feel.

JOASH

Whoever is like them should lose his life.   1290
                    [*Jehoiada throws himself at his feet*
Father, why do you fall before my feet?

JEHOIADA

This is the reverence I owe my king.
Be worthy of David, your forefather.

JOASH

Me?

JEHOIADA   You'll learn by what a special grace
God thwarted mad Athaliah's design.
Her dagger was already in your heart,
But he chose you, and rescued you from death.
You haven't yet escaped her rage.
With the same passion that she tried to kill
Her son's last child in you, she cruelly   1300
Stays obsessed that you shall die. She still
Pursues you now, despite your altered name.
Under your banner, though, I have drawn up
A faithful people ready for revenge.

Entrez, généreux chefs des familles sacrées,
Du ministère saint tour à tour honorées.

SCÈNE 3

Joas, Joad, Azaries, Ismael,
et les trois autres chefs des Lévites

JOAD [*continue*]

Roi, voilà vos vengeurs contre vos ennemis.
Prêtres, voilà le roi que je vous ai promis.

AZARIAS

Quoi, c'est Éliacin?

ISMAEL   Quoi, cet enfant aimable . . .

JOAD

Est des rois de Juda l'héritier véritable,   1310
Dernier né des enfants du triste Ochosias,
Nourri, vous le savez, sous le nom de Joas.
De cette fleur si tendre et sitôt moissonnée,
Tout Juda, comme vous, plaignant la destinée,
Avec ses frères morts le crut enveloppé.
Du perfide couteau comme eux il fut frappé.
Mais Dieu d'un coup mortel sut détourner l'atteinte,
Conserva dans son cœur la chaleur presque éteinte,
Permit que des bourreaux trompant l'œil vigilant,
Josabet dans son sein l'emportât tout sanglant,   1320
Et n'ayant de son vol que moi seul pour complice,
Dans le temple cachât l'enfant et la nourrice.

JOAS

Hélas! de tant d'amour et de tant de bienfaits,
Mon père, quel moyen de m'acquitter jamais?

JOAD

Gardez pour d'autres temps cette reconnaissance.
Voilà donc votre roi, votre unique espérance.

Heads of the sacred families, who hold
The holy ministry in turn, come forward now.
    [*Azariah, Ishmael, and the three other chiefs of the Levites, enter*

SCENE 3

Joash, Jehoiada, Azarias, Ishmael,
and the three other chiefs of the Levites.

JEHOIADA

These will avenge you on your enemies.
Priests, here is the king I promised you.

AZARIAH

Eliacin?

ISHMAEL   This lovely child . . . ?

JEHOIADA

. . . Is the true heir of all of Judah's kings,   1310
The last-born child of sad Ahaziah,
Brought up as Joash, as you know.
All Judah mourned like you the fate
Of this frail flower cut down so soon.
You thought that he had shared his brothers' deaths.
A traitor's knife struck him like them,
But God then warded off the deadly blow
And kept a trace of warmth still in his heart.
He let my wife elude the murderers,
Carry him off all bleeding on her breast.   1320
I was accomplice to the theft alone
And in the temple hid both nurse and child.

JOASH

Father, how can I ever pay you back
For so much love, so many benefits?

JEHOIADA

Keep all your thanks now for another time.
Here then is your new king, your only hope.

J'ai pris soin jusqu'ici de vous le conserver,
Ministres du Seigneur, c'est à vous d'achever.
Bientôt de Jézabel la fille meurtrière
Instruite que Joas voit encor la lumière,   1330
Dans l'horreur du tombeau viendra le replonger.
Déjà sans le connaître elle veut l'égorger.
Prêtres saints, c'est à vous de prévenir sa rage.
Il faut finir des Juifs le honteux esclavage,
Venger vos princes morts, relever votre loi,
Et faire aux deux tribus reconnaître leur roi.
L'entreprise sans doute est grande et périlleuse.
J'attaque sur son trône une reine orgueilleuse,
Qui voit sous ses drapeaux marcher un camp nombreux
De hardis étrangers, d'infidèles Hébreux.   1340
Mais ma force est au Dieu dont l'intérêt me guide.
Songez qu'en cet enfant tout Israël réside.
Déjà ce Dieu vengeur commence à la troubler.
Déjà trompant ses soins j'ai su vous rassembler.
Elle nous croit ici sans armes, sans défense.
Couronnons, proclamons Joas en diligence.
De là, du nouveau prince intrépides soldats,
Marchons en invoquant l'arbitre des combats,
Et réveillant la foi dans les cœurs endormie,
Jusque dans son palais cherchons notre ennemie.   1350
Et quels cœurs si plongés dans un lâche sommeil,
Nous voyant avancer dans ce saint appareil,
Ne s'empresseront pas à suivre notre exemple?
Un roi que Dieu lui-même a nourri dans son temple,
Le successeur d'Aaron de ses prêtres suivi,
Conduisant au combat les enfants de Lévi
Et dans ces mêmes mains des peuples révérées,
Les armes au Seigneur par David consacrées?
Dieu sur ses ennemis répandra sa terreur.
Dans l'infidèle sang baignez-vous sans horreur.   1360
Frappez et Tyriens, et même Israélites.
Ne descendez-vous pas de ces fameux lévites
Qui lorsque au dieu du Nil le volage Israël
Rendit dans le désert un culte criminel,
De leurs plus chers parents saintement homicides,

I've carefully protected him for you till now.
The last act is for you, the ministers of God.
Quite soon, the murderous queen Athaliah
Will learn that Joash here is still alive. 1330
She'll come to plunge him back into the tomb.
Already now, not knowing him, she wants his throat.
God's holy priests, you must forestall her rage.
The shameful slavery of the Jews must end.
Avenge your princes' deaths, restore your law,
And force both tribes to recognise their king.
No doubt, the task is great and perilous.
I now attack a puffed up queen upon her throne.
Beneath her banners march a countless horde
Of brazen foreigners and turncoat Jews. 1340
But God is all my strength. His interest, my guide.
Remember. In this child all Israel lives.
Already our avenging God begins
To trouble her. I've brought you here in spite of her.
She thinks we have no arms, and no defence.
Let us proclaim and crown young Joash now.
Then, valiant soldiers of our new-found prince,
Let's march and call upon the Lord of Battles' name.
Let's kindle faith again in slumbering hearts,
And in her palace seek our enemy. 1350
What hearts so plunged in cowardly sleep
Will see us march out in this holy band
And not run up at once to follow us?
A king raised in his shrine by God himself,
Aaron's successor, followed by his priests,
Leading the sons of Levi on to war,
And in their hands, the arms revered by all
That David consecrated to the Lord.
God will spread terror on his enemies.
Bathe bravely in the blood of infidels. 1360
Strike at the Tyrians, even the Israelites.
Are not your forebears those famed Levites who,
While fickle Israel in the wilderness
Worshipped the Nile's own god so sinfully,
Murdered their dearest family in holy zeal

Consacrèrent leurs mains dans le sang des perfides,
Et par ce noble exploit vous acquirent l'honneur
D'être seuls employés aux autels du Seigneur?
Mais je vois que déjà vous brûlez de me suivre.
Jurez donc, avant tout, sur cet auguste livre,   1370
A ce roi que le ciel vous redonne aujourd'hui,
De vivre, de combattre, et de mourir pour lui.

AZARIAS

Oui, nous jurons ici pour nous, pour tous nos frères,
De rétablir Joas au trône de ses pères,
De ne poser le fer entre nos mains remis,
Qu'après l'avoir vengé de tous ses ennemis.
Si quelque transgresseur enfreint cette promesse,
Qu'il éprouve, grand Dieu, ta fureur vengeresse :
Qu'avec lui, ses enfants de ton partage exclus,
Soient au rang de ces morts que tu ne connais plus!   1380

JOAD

Et vous à cette loi, votre règle éternelle,
Roi, ne jurez-vous pas d'être toujours fidèle?

JOAS

Pourrais-je à cette loi ne pas me conformer?

JOAD

O mon fils, de ce nom j'ose encor vous nommer,
Souffrez cette tendresse, et pardonnez aux larmes
Que m'arrachent pour vous de trop justes alarmes.
Loin du trône nourri, de ce fatal honneur,
Hélas! vous ignorez le charme empoisonneur.
De l'absolu pouvoir vous ignorez l'ivresse,
Et des lâches flatteurs la voix enchanteresse.   1390
Bientôt ils vous diront que les plus saintes lois,
Maîtresses du vil peuple obéissent aux rois;
Qu'un roi n'a d'autre frein que sa volonté même;
Qu'il doit immoler tout à sa grandeur suprême;
Qu'aux larmes, au travail le peuple est condamné,
Et d'un sceptre de fer veut être gouverné;
Que s'il n'est opprimé, tôt ou tard il opprime.
Ainsi de piège en piège et d'abîme en abîme,

And sanctified their hands in traitors' blood?
By such a noble act, they won for you the right
To serve the altars of the Lord alone.
Yet even now, I see, you burn to follow me.
Then swear upon this holy book, before all else,   1370
To this young king whom God today gives back
To you – to live and fight and die for him.

AZARIAH

We swear for all our brothers and ourselves
To set King Joash on his fathers' throne,
And not lay down the arms that we now bear
Until he's been revenged on all his enemies.
If anyone should fail to keep this pledge,
Let him, great God, feel your avenging wrath.
Let him, his children, lose their heritage,
Be like the dead whom you no longer know.   1380

JEHOIADA

And you, my king, will swear your constant faith
To this great law, your everlasting rule?

JOASH

How could I not be guided by that law?

JEHOIADA

My son – I still dare call you by that name –
Bear with my tenderness. Forgive the tears
That my just cares for you force from me now.
You've been brought up far from the throne. You do not know
The poisoning magic of its deadly spell.
How boundless power intoxicates, or how
The soothing voice of flatterers beguiles.   1390
Soon they will tell you that the holiest laws,
Which rule the common throng, must bow to kings.
That kings are held back only by their will,
That to their greatness everything must yield,
That people are condemned to tears and toil
And must be governed by a rod of iron.
If not held down, they will themselves oppress.
And so from snare to snare, from pit to pit,

Corrompant de vos mœurs l'aimable pureté,
Ils vous feront enfin haïr la vérité,   1400
Vous peindront la vertu sous une affreuse image.
Hélas! ils ont des rois égaré le plus sage.
Promettez sur ce livre et devant ces témoins,
Que Dieu fera toujours le premier de vos soins,
Que, sévère aux méchants, et des bons le refuge,
Entre le pauvre et vous vous prendrez Dieu pour juge;
Vous souvenant, mon fils, que caché sous ce lin,
Comme eux vous fûtes pauvre, et comme eux orphelin.

JOAS

Je promets d'observer ce que la loi m'ordonne.
Mon Dieu, punissez-moi, si je vous abandonne.   1410

JOAD

Venez, de l'huile sainte il faut vous consacrer.
Paraissez, Josabet, vous pouvez vous montrer.

SCÈNE 4

Joas, Joad, Josabet, Zacharie,
Azarias, etc., Salomith, le Chœur.

JOSABET [*embrassant Joas*]

O Roi, fils de David!

JOAS   O mon unique mère!
Venez, cher Zacharie, embrasser votre frère.

JOSABET [*à Zacharie*]

Aux pieds de votre roi prosternez-vous, mon fils.

JOAD [*pendant qu'ils s'embrassent*]

Enfants, ainsi toujours puissiez-vous être unis!

JOSABET [*à Joas*]

Vous savez donc quel sang vous a donné la vie?

They'll foul the lovely pureness of your ways;
They'll paint you goodness with a hideous face   1400
And in the end will make you hate the truth.
The best of kings have been depraved by them.
Swear on this book, before these witnesses,
That God will always be your first concern;
That you will scourge the wicked and protect the good,
That you'll take God as judge between the poor and you.
Remember once that in this linen coat,
Like them, you were an orphan – like them, poor.

JOASH

I swear to follow what the law commands.
Punish me, God, if I abandon you.   1410

JEHOIADA

You must be hallowed now with holy oil.
Come in, Jehoshabeath. You may appear.
                    [*Jehoshabeath and Zechariah enter,*
                    together with Salomith and the Chorus.

SCENE 4

Joash, Jehoiada, Jehoshabeath, Zechariah, Salomith, Azarias,
Ishmael, the three other chiefs of the Levites, the Chorus

JEHOSHABEATH [*embracing Joash*]
    My king. The son of David.

JOASH   You are my mother then . . .
    Embrace your brother, Zechariah. Come.

JEHOSHABEATH [*to Zechariah*]
    My son, bow down before your new king now.
                    [*Zechariah falls at Joash's feet*

JEHOIADA [*while they embrace*]
    My children, may you always be as one.

JEHOSHABEATH [*to Joash*]
    So do you know the blood that gave you life?

JOAS

Et je sais quelle main sans vous me l'eût ravie.

JOSABET

De votre nom, Joas, je puis donc vous nommer.

JOAS

Joas ne cessera jamais de vous aimer. 1420

LE CHŒUR

Quoi, c'est la . . . .

JOSABET   C'est Joas.

JOAD   Écoutons ce lévite.

SCÈNE 5

Joas, Josabet, Joad etc. Un Lévite.

UN LÉVITE

J'ignore contre Dieu quel projet on médite,
Mais l'airain menaçant frémit de toutes parts.
On voit luire des feux parmi des étendards.
Et sans doute Athalie assemble son armée.
Déjà même au secours toute voie est fermée.
Déjà le sacré mont où le temple est bâti
D'insolents Tyriens est partout investi.
L'un d'eux en blasphémant, vient de nous faire entendre
Qu'Abner est dans les fers, et ne peut nous défendre. 1430

JOSABET [*à Joas*]

Cher enfant, que le ciel en vain m'avait rendu,
Hélas! pour vous sauver j'ai fait ce que j'ai pu.
Dieu ne se souvient plus de David votre père.

JOAD [*à Josabet*]

Quoi! vous ne craignez pas d'attirer sa colère
Sur vous et sur ce roi si cher à votre amour?
Et quand Dieu de vos bras l'arrachant sans retour,

JOASH

And who too would have killed me but for you.

JEHOSHABEATH

Then I can call you, Joash, by your name.

JOASH

I'll never stop from loving you.   1420

THE CHORUS

What's that?

JEHOSHABEATH   Joash.

JEHOIADA   A Levite. Quick. Report.

[*a Levite enters*

SCENE 5

Joash, Jehoiada, Jehoshabeath, etc., a Levite

A LEVITE

There is some plot against the Lord – I don't know what –
But threatening bronze blares out on every side.
Amid the banners burn the glow of fires.
I'm sure Athaliah has drawn her army up.
All paths to help have been already closed.
The sacred hill on which the temple stands
Is now besieged by sneering Tyrians.
One cursed our God and said that Abner now
Is held in chains. He cannot help us now.   1430

JEHOSHABEATH [*to Joash*]

Dear son, God gave you back to me in vain.
I have done all I could to save your life.
God has forgotten your father, David.

JEHOIADA [*to Jehoshabeath*]

Aren't you afraid to draw his anger down
On you, and on this king so dear to you?
Even if God took him for ever from your arms

Voudrait que de David la maison fût éteinte;
N'êtes-vous pas ici sur la montagne sainte,
Où le père des Juifs sur son fils innocent
Leva sans murmurer un bras obéissant,   1440
Et mit sur un bûcher ce fruit de sa vieillesse,
Laissant à Dieu le soin d'accomplir sa promesse,
Et lui sacrifiant avec ce fils aimé,
Tout l'espoir de sa race en lui seul renfermé?
Amis, partageons-nous. Qu'Ismaël en sa garde,
Prenne tout le côté que l'orient regarde.
Vous, le côté de l'ourse, et vous, de l'occident.
Vous, le midi. Qu'aucun par un zèle imprudent,
Découvrant mes desseins, soit prêtre, soit lévite,
Ne sorte avant le temps et ne se précipite,   1450
Et que chacun enfin d'un même esprit poussé,
Garde en mourant le poste où je l'aurai placé.
L'ennemi nous regarde en son aveugle rage
Comme de vils troupeaux réservés au carnage,
Et croit ne rencontrer que désordre et qu'effroi.
Qu'Azarias partout accompagne le roi.
[à Joas] Venez, cher rejeton d'une vaillante race,
Remplir vos défenseurs d'une nouvelle audace.
Venez du diadème à leurs yeux vous couvrir,
Et périssez du moins en roi, s'il faut périr.   1460
Suivez-le, Josabet.
         [à un lévite] Vous, donnez-moi ces armes.
Enfants, offrez à Dieu vos innocentes larmes.

And willed the overthrow of David's house,
Aren't we now standing on the sacred heights
Where Abraham raised up his steadfast hands
Above his guiltless son without complaint.   1440
He laid the fruit of his old age upon the pyre,
Left it to God to keep his promises.
In this loved son, he sacrificed to him
The last surviving hope of his own line.
Friends, we must split up. Ishmael, you guard
The whole side facing to the east.
You, take the north. And you the west. You guard
The south. And no-one now in careless haste
Reveal my plan, Levite or priest.
You must not rush out before it's time.   1450
Each man must be moved by the one same mind,
Guard to the death the place I've given him.
The enemy is watching us in blinding rage,
Like some poor cattle waiting to be killed.
They think they'll find us fearful and confused.
Azariah, stay close to Joash constantly.
[*to Joash*] Joash, you are the heir of this brave race.
Fill with new daring those defending you.
Put on your diadem before their eyes.
Die as a king at least, if you must die.   1460
Stay with him, Jehoshabeath.
[*to a Levite*] Levite, give me those arms.
Children, offer to God your guiltless tears.
                 [*all leave apart from Salomith and the Chorus*

SCÈNE 6

Salomith, le Chœur

TOUT LE CHŒUR [*chante*]

> Partez, enfants d'Aaron, partez.
> Jamais plus illustre querelle
> De vos aïeux n'arma le zèle.
> Partez, enfants d'Aaron, partez.
> C'est votre roi, c'est Dieu, pour qui vous combattez.

UNE VOIX [*seule*]

> Où sont les traits que tu lances,
> Grand Dieu, dans ton juste courroux?
> N'es-tu plus le Dieu jaloux?　　　　　　1470
> N'es-tu plus le Dieu des vengeances?

UNE AUTRE

> Où sont, Dieu de Jacob, tes antiques bontés?
> Dans l'horreur qui nous environne,
> N'entends-tu que la voix de nos iniquités?
> N'es-tu plus le Dieu qui pardonne?

TOUT LE CHŒUR

> Où sont, Dieu de Jacob, tes antiques bontés?

UNE VOIX [*seule*]

> C'est à toi que dans cette guerre
> Les flèches des méchants prétendent s'adresser.
> Faisons, disent-ils, cesser
> Les fêtes de Dieu sur la terre;　　　　　1480
> De son joug importun délivrons les mortels.
> Massacrons tous ses saints. Renversons ses autels.
> Que de son nom, que de sa gloire
> Il ne reste plus de mémoire;
> Que ni lui, ni son Christ ne règnent plus sur nous.

TOUT LE CHŒUR

> Où sont les traits que tu lances,
> Grand Dieu, dans ton juste courroux?

SCENE 6

Salomith, the Chorus

WHOLE CHORUS [*sings*]

Sons of Aaron, go forth now.
A greater cause has never
Steeled your forebears' zeal.
Sons of Aaron, go forth now.
It is your king, your God, for whom you fight.

FIRST VOICE [*alone*]

Where are the thunderbolts you hurl,
Great God, in your just wrath?
Are you a jealous God no more?   1470
No more the God of vengeances?

ANOTHER VOICE

Where, God of Jacob, is your kindness shown of old?
In all the horror round us now,
Do you hear nothing but the sound of sin?
Are you no more a God who pardons us?

WHOLE CHORUS

Where, God of Jacob, is your kindness shown of old?

ANOTHER VOICE [*alone*]

It is at you that, in this war,
The arrows of the wicked aim.
'Let us now end,' they say,
'God's festivals on earth.   1480
Let us deliver humans from his weary yoke,
Slaughter his saints, smash down his shrines,
And of his name and glory
Blot out all trace,
That neither he nor Christ reign over us.'

WHOLE CHORUS

Where are the thunderbolts you hurl,
Great God, in your just wrath?

N'es-tu plus le Dieu jaloux?
N'es-tu plus le Dieu des vengeances?

UNE VOIX [*seule*]

Triste reste de nos rois, 1490
Chère et dernière fleur d'une tige si belle,
Hélas! sous le couteau d'une mère cruelle
Te verrons-nous tomber une seconde fois?
Prince aimable, dis-nous si quelque ange au berceau
Contre tes assassins prit soin de te défendre;
Ou si dans la nuit du tombeau
La voix du Dieu vivant a ranimé ta cendre.

UNE AUTRE

D'un père et d'un aïeul contre toi révoltés,
Grand Dieu, les attentats lui sont-ils imputés?
Est-ce que sans retour ta pitié l'abandonne? 1500

LE CHŒUR

Où sont, Dieu de Jacob, tes antiques bontés?
N'es-tu plus le Dieu qui pardonne?

UNE DES FILLES DE CHŒUR [*sans chanter*]

Chères sœurs, n'entendez-vous pas
Des cruels Tyriens la trompette qui sonne?

SALOMITH

J'entends même les cris des barbares soldats,
Et d'horreur j'en frissonne.
Courons, fuyons, retirons-nous
A l'ombre salutaire
Du redoutable sanctuaire.

Are you a jealous God no more?
No more the God of vengeances?

A VOICE [*alone*]

Sad heir of all our kings,   1490
The last dear blossom of so fair a stem,
Are we to see you fall a second time
Beneath a cruel mother's knife?
Tell us, sweet prince, was there some angel at your crib
Who cared to save you from your murderers?
Or in the darkness of the tomb,
Did God's own living voice bring back your life?

ANOTHER VOICE

His father's and his forebears' sins – great God,
Must their revolt be visited on him?
So has your mercy left him now for ever more?   1500

CHORUS

Where, God of Jacob, is your kindness shown of old?
Are you no more a God who pardons us?

ONE OF THE MAIDENS [*speaking*]

Dear sisters, can't you hear
The Tyrians' awful trumpet sound?

SALOMITH

I even hear the blood-filled soldiers' cry
And shudder all with fear.
Run quickly. Hide away
In the safe shadows
Of the feared sanctuary.

> [*Salomith and the Chorus remain, as Zechariah enters*

ACTE 5 SCÈNE 1

Zacharie, Salomith, le Chœur

SALOMITH

Cher Zacharie, eh bien? Que nous apprenez-vous?   1510

ZACHARIE

Redoublez au Seigneur votre ardente prière.
Peut-être nous touchons à notre heure dernière.
Pour l'horrible combat, ma sœur, l'ordre est donné.

SALOMITH

Que fait Joas?

ZACHARIE   Joas vient d'être couronné.
Le grand prêtre a sur lui répandu l'huile sainte.
O ciel! dans tous les yeux quelle joie était peinte
A l'aspect de ce roi racheté du tombeau!
Ma sœur, on voit encor la marque du couteau.
On voit paraître aussi sa fidèle nourrice,
Qui cachée en un coin de ce vaste édifice   1520
Gardait ce cher dépôt, et n'avait de ses soins
Que les yeux de ma mère, et que Dieu pour témoins.
Nos lévites pleuraient de joie et de tendresse
Et mêlaient leurs sanglots à leurs cris d'allégresse.
Lui parmi ces transports, affable, et sans orgueil,
A l'un tendait la main, flattait l'autre de l'œil,
Jurait de se régler par leurs avis sincères,
Et les appelait tous ses pères ou ses frères.

SALOMITH

Ce secret au dehors est-il aussi semé?

ZACHARIE

Ce secret dans le temple est encor renfermé.   1530
Des enfants de Lévi la troupe partagée
Dans un profond silence aux portes s'est rangée.
Tous doivent à la fois précipiter leurs pas,
Et crier pour signal : Vive le roi Joas!
Mais mon père défend que le roi se hasarde,

ACT 5 SCENE I

Zechariah, Salomith, the Chorus.

SALOMITH

So Zechariah, what can you report?   1510

ZECHARIAH

Strengthen, cry out, your heartfelt prayers to God.
Our final hour may well be close to us.
The order has been given for the awful fight.

SALOMITH

And Joash?

ZECHARIAH   He's just been crowned.
The high priest has anointed him with oil.
O heaven . . . what joy lit up in every eye
To see this king delivered from the dead.
You still could see the marks the knife had made.
His faithful nurse has also now appeared.
She'd hid herself deep down in this great house,   1520
Guarding the treasure given to her care,
God and my mother her sole witnesses.
Our Levites wept for tender, loving joy,
Mingling their sobs with gladness in their cries.
Amid this joy, he stood – charming, no pride –
Shook hands with one, smiled then at another,
Swore to be guided by their true advice,
And called each one his father or his friend.

SALOMITH

So has the secret now been spread outside?

ZECHARIAH

It's still been kept within the temple's bounds.   1530
The sons of Levi have been split in groups
And stand in total silence at the doors.
They must rush forward at a single stroke
And shout the signal then, 'Long live the king!'
Father will not allow the king to risk himself.

Et veut qu'Azarias demeure pour sa garde.
Cependant Athalie un poignard à la main
Rit des faibles remparts de nos portes d'airain.
Pour les rompre, elle attend les fatales machines,
Et ne respire enfin que sang et que ruines.   1540
Quelques prêtres, ma sœur, ont d'abord proposé
Qu'en un lieu souterrain par nos pères creusé
On renfermât du moins notre arche précieuse.
O crainte, a dit mon père, indigne, injurieuse!
L'arche, qui fit tomber tant de superbes tours,
Et força le Jourdain de rebrousser son cours,
Des dieux des nations tant de fois triomphante,
Fuirait donc à l'aspect d'une femme insolente?
Ma mère auprès du roi, dans un trouble mortel,
L'œil tantôt sur ce prince, et tantôt vers l'autel,   1550
Muette, et succombant sous le poids des alarmes,
Aux yeux les plus cruels arracherait des larmes.
Le roi de temps en temps la presse entre ses bras,
La flatte . . . Chères sœurs, suivez toutes mes pas.
Et s'il faut aujourd'hui que notre roi périsse,
Allons, qu'un même sort avec lui nous unisse.

SALOMITH

Quelle insolente main frappe à coups redoublés?
Qui fait courir ainsi ces lévites troublés?
Quelle précaution leur fait cacher leurs armes?
Le temple est-il forcé?

ZACHARIE   Dissipez vos alarmes.   1560
Dieu nous envoie Abner.

He's told Azariah to stay as guard.
Meanwhile, Athaliah, a dagger in her hand,
Mocks the weak ramparts of our doors of bronze.
She waits for her machines of death to smash
Them down. She's breathing ruin and our blood.   1540
Some priests had first of all proposed
To hide our sacred ark at least, deep in
Some hollow that our fathers had dug out.
'The fear's unworthy, cheap,' my father said,
'The ark that has brought down so many towers
And forced the Jordan to retrace its course,
So often conqueror of foreign gods,
Must it now flee a woman's arrogance?'
My mother, near the king, in deadly fear
With one eye on her boy, one on the shrine,   1550
Was dumb. But then she broke beneath the weight of cares
And would have drawn tears from the cruellest eyes.
From time to time, the king hugged her so close
To comfort her . . . Dear sisters, follow me.
If our king must be killed today, then come
And let us join him in the selfsame fate.

SALOMITH

What tyrant's hand knocks harder at the door?
Why do these Levites run about confused?
They hide their arms. Why the precaution?
So has the shrine been forced?

ZECHARIAH   Don't be afraid.   1560
Abner's been sent. By God.

> [*Jehoiada, Jehoshabeath, Abner,*
> *Ishmael and two Levites enter*

SCÈNE 2

Abner, Joad, Josabet, Zacherie, Salomith,
Ismael, deux Lévites, etc.

JOAD   En croirai-je mes yeux,
Cher Abner? Quel chemin a pu jusqu'en ces lieux
Vous conduire au travers d'un camp qui nous assiège?
On disait que d'Achab la fille sacrilège
Avait, pour assurer ses projets inhumains,
Chargé d'indignes fers vos généreuses mains.

ABNER

Oui, Seigneur, elle a craint mon zèle et mon courage.
Mais c'est le moindre prix que me gardait sa rage.
Dans l'horreur d'un cachot par son ordre enfermé,
J'attendais que le temple en cendre consumé,   1570
De tant de flots de sang non encore assouvie
Elle vînt m'affranchir d'une importune vie,
Et retrancher des jours qu'aurait dû mille fois
Terminer la douleur de survivre à mes rois.

JOAD

Par quel miracle a-t-on obtenu votre grâce?

ABNER

Dieu dans ce cœur cruel sait seul ce qui se passe.
Elle m'a fait venir, et d'un air égaré,
Tu vois de mes soldats tout ce temple entouré,
Dit-elle. Un feu vengeur va le réduire en cendre,
Et ton Dieu contre moi ne le saurait défendre.   1580
Ses prêtres toutefois, mais il faut se hâter,
A deux conditions peuvent se racheter :
Qu'avec Éliacin on mette en ma puissance
Un trésor, dont je sais qu'ils ont la connaissance,
Par votre roi David autrefois amassé,
Sous le sceau du secret au grand prêtre laissé.
Va, dis-leur qu'à ce prix je leur permets de vivre.

JOAD

Quel conseil, cher Abner, croyez-vous qu'on doit suivre?

SCENE 2

Jehoiada, Jehoshabeath, Zechariah, Salomith, Abner,
Ishmael, two Levites, the Chorus

JEHOIADA   Can I believe my eyes?
Dear Abner . . . What path could bring you here
Across the enemy camp besieging us?
Ahab's accursed daughter – they said she'd
Weighed these goodly hands with shameful irons,
To be assured of her inhuman plans.

ABNER

She feared my courage and my zeal, my lord.
But that's the least her rage reserved for me.
She ordered me imprisoned in the darkest cell.
I waited till the temple had been burnt to ash.   1570
Still unassuaged by all those seas of blood,
She came to free me from the pain of life
That should have been cut short a thousand times
From grief at living longer than my kings.

JEHOIADA

What miracle obtained your pardon, then?

ABNER

God knows alone what happened in that cruel heart.
She sent for me. She said distractedly,
'You see that temple circled by my troops.
Avenging swords will crush it into dust.
Your God can't save it from me now.   1580
But still his priests – if you make haste –
Can make amends on two conditions:
I want Eliacin. And in my hands I want
The treasure that I'm sure they know about.
It was amassed by your king David once,
Left with the high priest, sworn to secrecy.
Go, tell them, at this price I'll let him live.

JEHOIADA

So what course should we take? What do you think?

ABNER

Et tout l'or de David, s'il est vrai qu'en effet
Vous gardiez de David quelque trésor secret,　　　　　1590
Et tout ce que des mains de cette reine avare
Vous avez pu sauver et de riche et de rare,
Donnez-le. Voulez-vous que d'impurs assassins
Viennent briser l'autel, brûler les chérubins,
Et portant sur notre arche une main téméraire,
De votre propre sang souiller le sanctuaire?

JOAD

Mais siérait-il, Abner, à des cœurs généreux
De livrer au supplice un enfant malheureux,
Un enfant, que Dieu même à ma garde confie,
Et de nous racheter aux dépens de sa vie?　　　　　1600

ABNER

Hélas! Dieu voit mon cœur. Plût à ce Dieu puissant
Qu'Athalie oubliât un enfant innocent,
Et que du sang d'Abner sa cruauté contente
Crût calmer par ma mort le ciel qui la tourmente!
Mais que peuvent pour lui vos inutiles soins?
Quand vous périrez tous en périra-t-il moins?
Dieu vous ordonne-t-il de tenter l'impossible?
Pour obéir aux lois d'un tyran inflexible,
Moïse par sa mère au Nil abandonné,
Se vit, presque en naissant, à périr condamné;　　　1610
Mais Dieu le conservant contre toute espérance,
Fit par le tyran même élever son enfance.
Qui sait ce qu'il réserve à votre Éliacin,
Et si lui préparant un semblable destin,
Il n'a point de pitié déjà rendu capable
De nos malheureux rois l'homicide implacable?
Du moins, et Josabet, comme moi, l'a pu voir,
Tantôt à son aspect je l'ai vu s'émouvoir.
J'ai vu de son courroux tomber la violence.
Princesse, en ce péril, vous gardez le silence?　　　1620
Hé quoi? Pour un enfant qui vous est étranger,
Souffrez-vous que sans fruit Joad laisse égorger
Vous, son fils, tout ce peuple, et que le feu dévore

ÁBNER

All David's gold – if it is true indeed
You've kept some secret treasure of the king –   1590
And all that's rich and rare that you have saved
From the grasp of this avaricious queen,
Give her it. You want foul murderers
To smash the altar, burn the cherubim,
To smear their reckless hands upon the ark
And foul the sanctuary with your own blood?

JEHOIADA

But Abner, is it right that virtuous men
Should send a poor, unhappy boy to death –
A boy whom God himself entrusted to my care –
To buy our ransom with his life?   1600

ABNER

God sees my heart. Would that his power would make
Athaliah forget this guiltless child,
Her cruelty rest content with my own life,
And so placate the heaven that tortures her.
What can your vain concern, though, do for him?
When you all perish, will he die the less?
Is God not ordering you a hopeless task?
Once – to obey a tyrant's callous laws –
Moses was left beside the river Nile,
And was condemned to death almost at birth.   1610
But God protected him, against all hope,
And made the tyrant bring him up himself.
Who knows what God may do for your Eliacin?
He may prepare a matching fate for him.
He may yet touch the murderess of our
Unhappy kings with tears of sympathy.
At least – Jehoshabeath saw it too –
She has been moved at seeing him.
I saw the violence of her rage die down.
Jehoshabeath, there's danger and you do not speak.   1620
So for a child who is a stranger here,
You'll let Jehoiada waste the lives
Of you, his son, these priests, and let the fire

Le seul lieu sur la terre où Dieu veut qu'on l'adore?
Que feriez-vous de plus, si des rois vos aïeux
Ce jeune enfant était un reste précieux?

JOSABET [*tout bas à Joad*]

Pour le sang de ses rois vous voyez sa tendresse.
Que ne lui parlez-vous?

JOAD   Il n'est pas temps, Princesse.

ABNER

Le temps est cher, Seigneur, plus que vous ne pensez.
Tandis qu'à me répondre ici vous balancez,   1630
Mathan près d'Athalie étincelant de rage
Demande le signal, et presse le carnage.
Faut-il que je me jette à vos sacrés genoux?
Au nom du lieu si saint, qui n'est ouvert qu'à vous,
Lieu terrible, où de Dieu la majesté repose,
Quelque dure que soit la loi qu'on vous impose,
De ce coup imprévu songeons à nous parer.
Donnez-moi seulement le temps de respirer.
Demain, dès cette nuit, je prendrai des mesures
Pour assurer le temple, et venger ses injures.   1640
Mais je vois que mes pleurs et que mes vains discours
Pour vous persuader sont un faible secours.
Votre austère vertu n'en peut être frappée.
Eh bien! trouvez-moi donc quelque arme, quelque épée
Et qu'aux portes du temple où l'ennemi m'attend,
Abner puisse du moins mourir en combattant.

JOAD

Je me rends. Vous m'ouvrez un avis que j'embrasse.
De tant de maux, Abner, détournons la menace.
Il est vrai, de David un trésor est resté.
La garde en fut commise à ma fidélité.   1650
C'était des tristes Juifs l'espérance dernière,
Que mes soins vigilants cachaient à la lumière.
Mais puisqu'à votre reine il faut le découvrir,
Je vais la contenter, nos portes vont s'ouvrir.
De ses plus braves chefs qu'elle entre accompagnée
Mais de nos saints autels qu'elle tienne éloignée

Burn down the only place on earth where God
Desires to be adored? Would you do more
If this boy were the final jewel of all your kings?

JEHOSHABEATH [*aside to Jehoiada*]

You see his deep devotion to his kings.
Why not speak out?

JEHOIADA   It's not yet time.

ABNER

The time's much later than you think, my lord.
While you here hesitate in your reply,   1630
Mattan is with Athaliah, white with rage,
Begging her word to start the massacre.
So must I throw myself before your feet?
By that most holy place where only you
May go, the fearful home of God's own majesty –
However harsh these terms may seem to you,
We must ward off this unexpected blow.
Just give me time to catch my breath.
Tomorrow – no, tonight – I will take steps
To make the temple safe, avenge the sacrilege.   1640
But I can see that tears and argument
Help little in persuading you.
Your cast-iron virtue won't be moved by them.
So find some weapon for me then, some sword.
The enemy is waiting at the temple doors –
I can at least die there a soldier's death.

JEHOIADA

I give in . . . I'll take the course that you propose.
We must fend off the threat of so much harm.
It's true that David's treasure is still here.
It was entrusted to my faithful care –   1650
The final hope of all the suffering Jews.
I hid it carefully from light of day.
But since it must be shown now to your queen,
I'll satisfy her. Our doors will open.
Let her come in with all her bravest chiefs.
She'll keep the mindless fury of a mob

D'un ramas d'étrangers l'indiscrète fureur.
Du pillage du temple épargnez-moi l'horreur.
Des prêtres, des enfants lui feraient-ils quelque ombre?
De sa suite avec vous qu'elle règle le nombre.   1660
Et quant à cet enfant si craint, si redouté,
De votre cœur, Abner, je connais l'équité.
Je vous veux devant elle expliquer sa naissance.
Vous verrez s'il le faut remettre en sa puissance,
Et je vous ferai juge entre Athalie et lui.

ABNER

Ah! je le prends déjà, Seigneur, sous mon appui.
Ne craignez rien. Je cours vers celle qui m'envoie.

SCÈNE 3
Joad, Josabet, Ismaël, Zacharie, etc.

JOAD

Grand Dieu, voici ton heure, on t'amène ta proie.
Ismaël, écoutez.
[*il lui parle à l'oreille*]

JOSABET   Puissant maître des cieux,
Remets-lui le bandeau dont tu couvris ses yeux,   1670
Lorsque lui dérobant tout le fruit de son crime,
Tu cachas dans mon sein cette tendre victime.

JOAD

Allez, sage Ismaël, ne perdez point de temps.
Suivez de point en point ces ordres importants.
Surtout, qu'à son entrée, et que sur son passage,
Tout d'un calme profond lui présente l'image.
Vous, enfants, préparez un trône pour Joas.
Qu'il s'avance suivi de nos sacrés soldats.
Faites venir aussi sa fidèle nourrice,
Princesse, et de vos pleurs que la source tarisse.   1680
[*A un lévite*]
Vous dès que cette reine, ivre d'un fol orgueil

Of foreigners, though, from our holy shrine.
Spare me the horror of the temple sacked.
Would children give offence to her, or priests?
She must agree with you the number that she brings.　　1660
As for this boy, so feared and dreaded here,
I know you are a just and righteous man.
I will explain his birth to you in front of her.
You'll see if he should then be given up to her.
I'll make you judge between Athaliah and him.

ABNER

I'll take him now, my lord, into my care.
Don't be afraid. I'll hurry back to her.

[he leaves

SCENE 3

*Jehoiada, Jehoshabeath, Zechariah, Salomith, Ishmael,
two Levites, the Chorus*

JEHOIADA

Great God, here is your hour. Your prey comes here.
Listen, Ishmael.
[he whispers to him]

JEHOSHABEATH　　　　Great lord of heaven,
Put back the blindfold on her eyes. With it,　　　1670
You hid the harmless victim at my breast
And stole the whole fruit of her crime from her.

JEHOIADA

So go, Ishmael. There's no time now to lose.
Follow these crucial orders point by point.
Above all – as she comes in and makes her way –
The sight she sees must be of total calm.
You children, prepare a throne for Joash.
He must walk forth and lead his priestly soldiers on.
His faithful nurse must come forth too.
And no more crying now, Jehoshabeath.　　　1680
[to a Levite] Levite . . . this queen is drunk with maddened pride.

De la porte du temple aura passé le seuil,
Qu'elle ne pourra plus retourner en arrière,
Prenez soin qu'à l'instant la trompette guerrière
Dans le camp ennemi jette un subit effroi.
Appelez tout le peuple au secours de son roi.
Et faites retentir jusques à son oreille
De Joas conservé l'étonnante merveille.
Il vient.

SCÈNE 4

Joas, Joad, Josabet, troupes de Prêtres et de Lévites, etc.

JOAD [*continue*]   Lévites saints, prêtres de notre Dieu,
Partout, sans vous montrer, environnez ce lieu,   1690
Et laissant à mes soins gouverner votre zèle,
Pour paraître attendez que ma voix vous appelle.
[*ils se cachent tous*]
Roi, je crois qu'à vos vœux cet espoir est permis,
Venez voir à vos pieds tomber vos ennemis.
Celle dont la fureur poursuivit votre enfance
Vers ces lieux à grands pas pour vous perdre s'avance.
Mais ne la craignez point. Songez qu'autour de vous
L'ange exterminateur est debout avec nous.
Montez sur votre trône, et . . . Mais la porte s'ouvre,
Permettez un moment que ce voile vous couvre.   1700
[*il tire un rideau*]
Vous changez de couleur, Princesse?

JOSABET   Ah! sans pâlir
Puis-je voir d'assassins le temple se remplir?
Quoi! ne voyez-vous pas quelle nombreuse escorte . . .

JOAD

Je vois que du saint temple on referme la porte.
Tout est en sûreté.

The moment she has crossed the temple doors
And has no chance of going back again,
Make sure that blaring trumpets sound at once
And terrorise the enemy off-guard.
Call all the people to their king's support.
Just keep for ever ringing in their ears
The wondrous miracle that Joash lives.
He's here.

> [*Ishmael leaves. Priests, Levites and Joash enter*

SCENE 4

Jehoiada, Jehoshabeath, Joash, priests, Levites, etc.

JEHOIADA [*continues*]   You holy Levites, priests of God,
Surround this place, but do not show yourselves.   1690
All passion now must be controlled by me.
Wait till I tell you to appear.
[*they all hide*]
My king – I think you may now hope for this –
Come, see your enemies fall at your feet.
The queen whose rage has haunted you throughout
Your youth, is striding here to kill you now.
Don't be afraid of her. Remember, all around,
The angel of the Lord stands guarding us.
Sit on the throne up there . . . the door, it's opening . . .
I'll draw this curtain down in front of you.   1700
[*he draws a curtain*]
Jehoshabeath, you're white . . .

JEHOSHABEATH
Should I see killers in this shrine and not
Turn white? You see how many she has brought . . . ?

JEHOIADA
I see the temple door is closing now.
All is secure.

> [*Athaliah enters with her attendants,*
> *together with Abner*

SCÈNE 5

Athalie, Joas, caché derrière le rideau, Joad, Josabet,
Abner, suite d'Athalie

ATHALIE [à *Joad*]   Te voilà, séducteur,

De ligues, de complots pernicieux auteur,

Qui dans le trouble seul a mis tes espérances,

Éternel ennemi des suprêmes puissances.

En l'appui de ton Dieu tu t'étais reposé.

De ton espoir frivole es-tu désabusé?   1710

Il laisse en mon pouvoir et son temple et ta vie.

Je devrais sur l'autel où ta main sacrifie

Te . . . Mais du prix qu'on m'offre il faut me contenter.

Ce que tu m'as promis songe à l'exécuter.

Cet enfant, ce trésor, qu'il faut qu'on me remette,

Où sont-ils?

JOAD   Sur-le-champ tu seras satisfaite.

Je te les vais montrer l'un et l'autre à la fois.

[*le rideau se tire*]

Paraissez, cher enfant, digne sang de nos rois.

Connais-tu l'héritier du plus saint des monarques,

Reine? De ton poignard connais du moins ces marques.   1720

Voilà ton roi, ton fils, le fils d'Ochosias.

Peuples, et vous Abner, reconnaissez Joas.

ABNER

Ciel!

ATHALIE [à *Joad*]   Perfide!

JOAD   Vois-tu cette Juive fidèle

Dont tu sais bien qu'alors il suçait la mamelle?

Il fut par Josabet à ta rage enlevé.

Ce temple le reçut, et Dieu l'a conservé.

Des trésors de David voilà ce qui me reste.

ATHALIE

Ta fourbe à cet enfant, traître, sera funeste.

D'un fantôme odieux, soldats, délivrez-moi.

SCENE 5

Athaliah, Joash hidden behind the curtain, Jehoiada, Jehoshabeath,
Abner, Athaliah's attendants

ATHALIAH [*to Jehoiada*]   So there you are, you scum,
    You vicious seed of secret pacts and plots.
    You hoped there would be chaos – nothing less –
    The lasting enemy of total power.
    You placed reliance in your God's support.
    What futile hope. So are you disabused?   1710
    He's left your life and temple in my power.
    So on the altar where you sacrifice,
    I ought . . . But I will take the prize that's offered me.
    What you promised me – turn your mind to that,
    This boy, the treasure that you will give up,
    Where are they?

JEHOIADA   I'll satisfy you straight away.
    I'll show you both of them together. Now.
    [*the curtain is drawn back*]
    Dear child, stand forth, the true blood of our kings.
    So do you know our holiest monarch's heir?
    You'll know at least the marks your dagger left.   1720
    Here is your king, and Ahaziah's son.
    Do homage now to Joash, Abner, all of you.

ABNER

    God.

ATHALIAH [*to Jehoiada*]   Traitor.

JEHOIADA   You see this faithful nurse
    Whose teats he was then sucking, as you know?
    Jehoshabeath saved him from your rage.
    This temple took him in, and God looked after him.
    All David's treasures – this is what remains.

ATHALIAH

    Your treachery will be this young boy's death.
    Soldiers – so save me from this loathsome ghost.

JOAD

Soldats du Dieu vivant défendez votre roi.　　　　　1730
[*ici le fond du théâtre s'ouvre. On voit le dedans du temple,
et les Lévites armés sortent de tous côtés sur la scène*]

ATHALIE

Où suis-je? O trahison! ô reine infortunée!
D'armes et d'ennemis je suis environnée.

JOAD

Tes yeux cherchent en vain, tu ne peux échapper,
Et Dieu de toutes parts a su t'envelopper.
Ce Dieu que tu bravais en nos mains t'a livrée.
Rends-lui compte du sang dont tu t'es enivrée.

ATHALIE

Quoi? La peur a glacé mes indignes soldats?
Lâche Abner, dans quel piège as-tu conduit mes pas?

ABNER

Reine, Dieu m'est témoin . . . .

ATHALIE　　　　　　　　　　　Laisse là ton Dieu, traître,
Et venge-moi.

ABNER [*se jetant aux pieds de Joas*]
　　　　　　　Sur qui? Sur Joas! sur mon maître!　　　1740

ATHALIE

Lui Joas? Lui ton roi? Songez, méchants, songez
Que mes armes encor vous tiennent assiégés.
J'entends à haute voix tout mon camp qui m'appelle.
On vient à mon secours. Tremblez, troupe rebelle.

JEHOIADA

    Troops of the living God, defend your king.   1730
    [*the back of the stage opens, to show the inside of the temple.*
    Armed Levites emerge from all sides on to the stage]

ATHALIAH

    Where am I? It's treason . . . I am ill-starred . . .
    I am surrounded quite by arms and enemies.

JEHOIADA

    You look around in vain. You can't escape.
    Our God has closed you in on every side.
    The God you fought against has given you to us.
    You're drunk on blood – account to him for that.

ATHALIAH

    So fear has chilled my worthless soldiers' hearts.
    Abner, you coward. You've trapped me here.

ABNER

    Queen, God is my witness . . .

ATHALIAH   Forget your God!
    Give me revenge!

ABNER [*throwing himself at Joash's feet*]
              On who? Joash? my king?   1740

ATHALIAH

    Joash? Your king? Think, traitors, think –
    My armies hold you here besieged.
    I hear my soldiers calling for me now.
    They've come to rescue me. You rebels, tremble now!
                         [*Ishmael comes back*

SCÈNE 6

Ismaël, Joas, Joad, Athalie, etc.

ISMAEL [à Joad]

Seigneur, le temple est libre et n'a plus d'ennemis.
L'étranger est en fuite, et le Juif est soumis.
Comme le vent dans l'air dissipe la fumée,
La voix du Tout-Puissant a chassé cette armée.
Nos lévites, du haut de nos sacrés parvis,
D'Ochosias au peuple ont annoncé le fils,   1750
Ont conté son enfance au glaive dérobée,
Et la fille d'Achab dans le piège tombée.
Partout en même temps la trompette a sonné.
Et ses sons, et leurs cris dans son camp étonné
Ont répandu le trouble et la terreur subite,
Dont Gédéon frappa le fier Madianite.
Les Tyriens, jetant armes et boucliers,
Ont par divers chemins disparu les premiers.
Quelques Juifs éperdus ont aussi pris la fuite.
Mais de Dieu sur Joas admirant la conduite   1760
Le reste à haute voix s'est pour lui déclaré.
Enfin d'un même esprit tout le peuple inspiré,
Femmes, vieillards, enfants, s'embrassant avec joie,
Bénissent le Seigneur, et celui qu'il envoie.
Tous chantent de David le fils ressuscité.
Baal est en horreur dans la sainte cité.
De son temple profane on a brisé les portes.
Mathan est égorgé.

ATHALIE   Dieu des Juifs, tu l'emportes!
Oui, c'est Joas, je cherche en vain à me tromper.
Je reconnais l'endroit où je le fis frapper.   1770
Je vois d'Ochosias et le port et le geste.
Tout me retrace enfin un sang que je déteste.
David, David triomphe, Achab seul est détruit.
Impitoyable Dieu, toi seul as tout conduit.
C'est toi, qui me flattant d'une vengeance aisée,
M'as vingt fois en un jour à moi-même opposée,

SCENE 6

Ishmael, Joash, Jehoiada, Athaliah, etc.

ISHMAEL [*to Jehoiada*]
  My lord, the temple's cleared. The enemy has gone.
  The foreigners run off, the Jews submit.
  Her army has been driven off by God's own voice
  As smoke is scattered in the air by wind.
  Our Levites from the sacred courts on high
  Have now proclaimed to all Joash as king.   1750
  They've told his childhood rescue from the sword,
  And Ahab's daughter fallen in the trap.
  The trumpets sounded everywhere at once.
  The blasts, the enemy's astounded cries,
  Spread forth the chaos and the sudden fear
  That Gideon hurled upon the Midianites.
  The Tyrians threw their arms and shields aside
  And disappeared the first by various paths.
  Some panic-stricken Jews took flight as well.
  But all the rest have gazed in awe at God's   1760
  Great plan, and cried aloud for Joash as their king.
  In short, the people speak now with a single mind.
  Women, old men and children joyously embrace
  And bless the Lord, and him the Lord has sent.
  All sing of David's son brought back to life.
  In this our holy city, Baal is loathed.
  His obscene temple's doors are smashed.
  Mattan's throat is cut.

ATHALIAH   God of the Jews, you've won.
  It's Joash, yes. I can't deceive myself.
  I recognise the spot I had him stabbed.   1770
  It's Azariah's bearing, gestures, looks.
  All conjures up a blood that I detest.
  And David triumphs. Ahab is destroyed.
  You pitiless God! Alone, you fashioned this.
  You flattered me with sweet revenge, set me
  Against myself a score of times a day,

Tantôt pour un enfant excitant mes remords,
Tantôt m'éblouissant de tes riches trésors,
Que j'ai craint de livrer aux flammes, au pillage
Qu'il règne donc ce fils, ton soin et ton ouvrage;   1780
Et que pour signaler son empire nouveau
On lui fasse en mon sein enfoncer le couteau.
Voici ce qu'en mourant lui souhaite sa mère.
Que dis-je souhaiter? Je me flatte, j'espère,
Qu'indocile à ton joug, fatigué de ta loi,
Fidèle au sang d'Achab, qu'il a reçu de moi,
Conforme à son aïeul, à son père semblable,
On verra de David l'héritier détestable
Abolir tes honneurs, profaner ton autel,
Et venger Athalie, Achab, et Jézabel.   1790

JOAD

Qu'à l'instant hors du temple elle soit emmenée;
Et que la sainteté n'en soit point profanée.
Allez, sacrés vengeurs de vos princes meurtris,
De leur sang par sa mort faire cesser les cris.
Si quelque audacieux embrasse sa querelle,
Qu'à la fureur du glaive on le livre avec elle.

SCÈNE 7

Joas, Joad, Josabet, Abner, etc.

JOAS

Dieu, qui voyez mon trouble et mon affliction,
Détournez loin de moi sa malédiction,
Et ne souffrez jamais qu'elle soit accomplie.
Faites que Joas meure, avant qu'il vous oublie.   1800

JOAD [*aux Lévites*]

Appelez tout le peuple, et montrons-lui son roi,
Qu'il lui vienne en ses mains renouveler sa foi.
Roi, prêtres, peuple, allons, pleins de reconnaissance,
De Jacob avec Dieu confirmer l'alliance,

Arousing my remorse now for a child,
Now dazzling me with riches and with gold
I feared to pillage, throw into the flames.
Then let him reign, this son, your handiwork;   1780
And as a sign of his new power, tell him
To plunge his knife deep in my heart.
His dying mother wishes this for him.
Wishes, did I say? I'm proud to hope
He'll not endure your chains – your laws will tire –
That he'll keep faith with Ahab's blood in me,
That like his grandfather, his father too,
He will be seen as David's loathsome heir
Who'll crush your honour, desecrate your shrine,
And so avenge Athaliah, Ahab, Jezebel.   1790

JEHOIADA

Drag her outside the temple's bounds at once
So that its sanctity is not profaned.
Sacred avengers of your murdered kings,
Go, quiet the mourning of their blood with her own death.
And any man who dares take up her cause,
Deliver to the fury of the sword with her.

                [*Athaliah is dragged away by the priests and Levites*

SCENE 7

Joash, Jehoiada, Jehoshabeath, Abner, etc.

JOASH

My god, you see my deeply troubled heart,
Turn all her evil words far, far away
From me. Don't let them ever come to pass.
If ever I forget you, let me die.   1800

JEHOIADA [*to the Levites*]

Call all the people. Let them see their king.
Let them renew their homage to his throne.
King, priests, people – let us affirm with thanks
The covenant that Jacob made with God.

Et saintement confus de nos égarements,
Nous rengager à lui par de nouveaux serments.
Abner, auprès du roi reprenez votre place.
Eh bien? de cette impie a-t-on puni l'audace?

SCÈNE 8

Un Lévite, Joas, Joad, etc.

LE LÉVITE

Le fer a de sa vie expié les horreurs.
Jérusalem longtemps en proie à ses fureurs,
De son joug odieux à la fin soulagée,
Avec joie en son sang la regarde plongée.

JOAD

Par cette fin terrible, et due à ses forfaits,
Apprenez, roi des Juifs, et n'oubliez jamais
Que les rois dans le ciel ont un juge sévère,
L'innocence un vengeur, et l'orphelin un père.

1810

We are ashamed that we have strayed,
And bind ourselves to him with renewed vows.
Abner, take up your place again beside the king.

> [*Abner sits beside Joash*

SCENE 8

A Levite, Joash, Jehoiada, etc.

JEHOIADA [*to the Levite*]

So, have you punished now that godless queen?

THE LEVITE

The sword has purged the horror of her life.
So long a prey to all her rage, Jerusalem   1810
Is freed at last from hateful slavery,
And sees with joy her lying in her blood.

JEHOIADA

From this black end, which all her crimes deserved,
Be warned, King of the Jews. Never forget
That in God's heaven, kings have a testing judge,
The child is safe, the orphan finds a home.

GLOSSARY

Racine frequently alludes to classical and biblical figures, as well as places, in the three plays presented here. The main references are summarised below. Cross-references are italicised.

Aaron: the older brother of Moses, gifted as a speaker and prophet. As the first high-priest, he created the most important priestly class, the 'sons of Aaron'.

Abiram: a little-known character, the son of Eliab, who with his brother Dathan joined in rebellion against Moses. He was swallowed up by the earth as punishment.

Acheron: derived from the Greek word for 'affliction', the river Acheron, into which the *Cocytus* flowed, was one of the four main rivers of the underworld. To cross it, Charon the ferryman had to be paid. Its source above ground was in the mountains of Epirus in north-west Greece.

Achilles: the son of Peleus and Thetis, who was destined to win immortal fame at *Troy* and to die doing so. He killed *Hector* in single combat beneath the walls of the city, but was himself killed by an arrow shot by either Apollo or Paris into his vulnerable heel. Pyrrhus was his son.

Achitophel: a treacherous adviser to King David and later his rebel son Absalom. He hanged himself once his treachery was discovered.

Aegeus: king of Athens, and father of Theseus.

Agamemnon: husband to Clytemnestra and father of Orestes, he sought to sacrifice his own daughter, Iphigenia, to appease the gods. In revenge, Clytemnestra murdered him in his bath.

Ahab: husband of *Jezebel* and father to Athaliah. He recognised the rights of religions and gods other than the Jewish; hence his condemnation by Hebrew prophets and priesthood.

Alcide: another name for *Hercules*. Alcide's pillars, which were one of the limits of the known ancient world, are today's Straits of Gibraltar.

Amazon[s]: a mythical race of female warriors, renowned for their prowess as fighters and haters of men.

Amnon: a biblical name for an imaginary character, similar to *Obed*.

Antiope: a famous Amazon, abducted by Theseus, by whom she bore Hippolytus.

Argos: a city in the Peloponnese, just south of *Mycenae*.

Ariadne: the daughter of *Minos*, and Phaedra's sister. She fell in love with Theseus, for whom she provided the ball of thread to lead him safely out of the Labyrinth after he had killed the Minotaur. She was taken but then abandoned on the island of Naxos by Theseus, who preferred her sister Phaedra.

Ark, the: the chest of wood overlaid with gold containing the tablets of God's law. It was placed in the holiest part of the sanctuary.

Astyanax: Hector's son, who was saved from death by his mother Andromache pretending that another child was him.

Attica: the region surrounding Athens.

Azariah: two people bear this name: first, the son of *Ahab* and *Jezebel* who maintained the idolatrous traditions of his father; second, the son of Athaliah and father of Joash.

Baal: a collective name given by the Hebrews to numerous pagan gods.

Benjamin: the youngest son of Jacob. The tribe of Benjamin was one of the smallest, and with the tribe of Judah, made up the kingdom of Judah.

Cassandra: daughter of the Trojan King Priam, she was given the gift of foretelling the future by Apollo. But he took from her at the same time the power of persuasion, so that she remained destined for ever not to be believed.

Cedron: the Cedron is a fast-flowing steep-sided stream, its valley separating Jerusalem from the Mount of Olives. Beyond it is the wilderness between Jerusalem and Jericho.

Celadon: the hero of Honoré d'Urfé's *L'Astrée*, who became a symbol of the constant lover.

Cercyon: an Arcadian fighter and bandit, he forced travellers to wrestle with him, and killed the vanquished. He was in turn killed by Theseus.

Cocytus: the river of lamentation, which flowed into the *Acheron*, and became one of the rivers of the underworld.

Corinth: the town and isthmus separating the Ionian and the Aegean seas.

Dathan: like his brother *Abiram*, a character little known apart from his rebellion against Moses. Like Abiram, he was swallowed up by the earth as punishment.

David: chosen by God to replace Saul, he became, despite his faults, the greatest of all Hebrew kings, and founded the dynasty that bears his name. He reigned for forty years. He brought the *Ark* to Jerusalem, and was the father of Solomon.

Diana: a goddess associated particularly with light, mountains and woods. She was the Roman form of the Greek Artemis, who was similarly identified with hunting, and also with chastity.

Doeg: following Saul's command, he massacred eighty-five Hebrew priests in revenge for their alliance with *King David*.

Elijah: the Hebrew prophet who challenged the followers of *Baal* to invoke their god for fire at a sacrifice, at the same time as he prayed for the same. They were killed upon their failure.

Elis: a province of Greece on the western shore of the Peloponnese.

Elisha: prophet and disciple of Elijah, he brought a young boy back to life, one of many miracles and cures he is credited with.

Epidaurus: the giant of Epidaurus was Peripetes, who clubbed passing travellers to death for their flesh. He was killed by Theseus.

Epirus: the north-western region of Greece.

Erechtheus: found as an abandoned child by Athene, who protected him, Erechtheus became king of Athens, and introduced the solemn cult of Athena to the city.

Gideon: one of the Hebrew judges, he saved Israel from the Midianites, a hostile tribe, by terrifying them with the sound of his army's trumpets, making it seem much larger than it was.

Hades: the underworld. The god of Hades was Pluto, whose wife, Persephone, Theseus was thought to have gone down to the underworld to abduct. The daughters of Hades were the Erinyes or Furies, who exacted vengeance on murderers.

Hector: son of *King Priam*, and husband of Andromache, he was supreme commander of the Trojan army, and inflicted numerous defeats upon the Greeks until he was killed by *Achilles* outside the walls of Troy. His son was Astyanax.

Hecuba: wife of *Priam*, and mother of *Hector*.

Helen: the daughter of Leda and Zeus or Tyndareus. Renowned for her beauty, she was abducted by Theseus, but was returned and married Menelaus. Later, Paris fell in love with her, and also abducted her, an act that precipitated the Trojan war.

Hercules: famed for his physical strength and endurance, he undertook the twelve labours in order to atone for the crime of mistakenly killing his family. After the labours, he went on to many further feats and achievements, and was finally admitted to the gods' home on Mount Olympus as an immortal. See also *Alcide*.

Icarus: imprisoned with his father Daedalus in the Labyrinth on Crete, he escaped by making wings fixed with wax. In his rashness, though, he flew too close to the sun, the wax melted, and he fell into the sea that now bears his name.

Ilium: another name for *Troy*.

Ishmael: son of Abraham. Ishmael's descendants, forming numerous Arab tribes, were however later classed among Israel's enemies, and there were frequent wars between them.

Jacob: the son of Isaac and Rebecca, he obtained his father's blessing by deception, thereby depriving his brother Esau of his birthright. He was given the name Israel, a name later applied to the twelve tribes who were descended from his twelve sons. His name also became synonymous with the entire Hebrew people.

Jehoshapat: the fourth king of *Judah*, who reigned from 870-848 BC. His son was *Joram*.

Jehu: chosen by God through Elisha to avenge his enemies, he destroyed the worshippers of *Baal*, but nonetheless finally fell to temptation and sin. He had become king of Israel by usurping the throne and killing *Joram*, *Jezebel* and their family.

Jepthah: he sacrificed his daughter to honour a promise made to God, in order to secure victory over the Ammonites, enemies of his people.

Jerusalem: capital city of the Hebrews, founded by *David*, where *Solomon* built the temple. The new Jerusalem is the Church, as recorded in the Apocalypse.

Jezebel: the wife of *Ahab* and mother of Athaliah. She was responsible for the death of Naboth, and was in turn killed by *Jehu*, as foretold by *Elijah*.

Jezrael: a town in the kingdom of Israel, close to the capital *Samaria*.

Joram: two people bear this name: first, the king of Israel who was the second son of *Ahab* and *Jezebel*; second, the king of *Judah*, who reigned from 848-841 BC, and who married Athaliah. His father was *Jehoshapat*.

Jordan: the river that flows into the Sea of Galilee, and then southwards into the Dead Sea.

Judah: *Jacob*'s fourth son, who gave his name to the tribe descended from him. The kingdom of Judah stood in opposition to the kingdom of Israel, after the schism.

Juno: the sister of *Jupiter*, and one of the greatest of the gods, she was goddess of light and of childbirth.

Jupiter: the greatest of the Roman gods, associated with light, creativity and heavenly phenomena, as well as the just protector of city and state.

Levi: *Jacob*'s third son, who gave his name to the tribe of Levites descended from him.

Medea: renowned for her skills as a magician, she helped Jason seize the Golden Fleece and lived with him for ten years before he abandoned her. She cut the throats of the children she had had by him, and fled to Athens.

Menelaus: the Greek king, husband of *Helen*, whose abduction by Paris caused the Trojan War. She was returned to him and reconciled after the fall of Troy.

Midianites: one of the Arab tribes often at war with the Jews. They were defeated by *Gideon*.

Minerva: another name for Athene, who had been born out of Zeus' skull. She was goddess of wisdom, and became the chief protector of Athens.

Minos: One of the three sons of Zeus and Europa, he was king of Crete, and married *Pasiphaë*, who conceived the *Minotaur*. Renowned for his wisdom and justice, he became judge of the dead in the Underworld.

Minotaur: a monster with a human body and bull's head, born to *Pasiphaë* after she had conceived a passion for a bull. Feeding only on human flesh, provided every year by adolescents from Athens, the Minotaur was imprisoned in the Labyrinth constructed by *Daedalus*. He was finally killed by Theseus.

Moses: one the greatest figures of the Hebrew people, hidden as a baby in the bulrushes and brought up by Pharaoh's daughter. He was called by God to be the saviour of Israel, and led its people safely through the Red Sea. He received the ten commandments from God on Mount *Sinai*, as well as instructions for making the *Ark*. Upon his death at a great age, he was succeeeded by *Joshua*.

Mycenae: a city in the Peloponnese, some twenty miles south of Corinth, renowned for its grandeur and luxury.

Neptune: Roman god of the sea, corresponding to the Greek Poseidon, who was the son of Cronos and the brother of Zeus. His favourite animal was the horse, which he taught human beings to train. He was guardian god to Theseus.

Nile: the great river of Egypt, where *Moses* was found by Pharaoh's daughter.

Obed: like *Amnon*, a biblical name for an imaginary person.

Olympus: the mountain rising from the shores of the Aegean Sea to over 9,000 feet, famed as the home of the Gods.

Pallas: the brother of *Aegeus*, whose sons, the Pallantids, tried to take power from Aegeus when he failed to produce a successor. Some fifty in number, they were killed by Theseus. Pallas' daughter was Aricia.

Pasiphaë: wife of *Minos*, and mother of Phaedra, she also bore the *Minotaur* after conceiving a passion for a bull.

Periboea: after having been abducted and then abandoned by Theseus, she married Telamon, king of Salamis.

Pharaoh: the generic title given to the kings of Egypt.

Philistines: the Jews' long-time enemies, fought against by Samson and *David* especially.

Phrygia: a country in north-western Asia Minor.

Pirithous: close friend of Theseus, with whom he had a number of adventures, including a battle against the *Amazons* and the abduction of the young *Helen*.

Pittheus: Theseus' grandfather, who founded the city of Troezen. He was renowed for his wisdom.

Polyxena: the daughter of *Priam* and *Hecuba*. She had been betrothed to Achilles, but he had died before their marriage. Her throat was cut by Pyrrhus.

Priam: king of Troy, father to *Hector* and Paris.

Procrustes: a famed giant who forced his captives on to a bed of iron, stretching them if they were too short, and cutting off their limbs if they were too long. Theseus made him undergo the same treatment.

Salamis: a town and island in the Saronic Gulf, about fifteen miles west of Athens.

Samaria: capital of the kingdom of Israel.

Samuel: judge of the Hebrews. Pledged to the service of God from childhood, he consecrated Saul and then *David* as kings.

Sciron: a legendary bandit who forced travellers to wash his feet. When they bent down to do so, he would kick them over a cliff into the sea, where they were devoured by a monstrous turtle. He was killed by Theseus.

Scythians: a nomadic tribe known for its cruelty and savagery.

Sinai: the mountain on which God gave *Moses* the ten commandments.

Sinis: a legendary bandit who tied his victims to the branches of sprung pine-trees, which he then released. Theseus forced him to undergo the same torture.

Solomon: son of King *David*, renowned for his wisdom and justice.

Sparta: the capital city of Lacedaemon, the home of *Menelaus*.

Syria: a reference to Hazael, king of Syria, who wrought destruction over a vast part of Israel. Heavy tributes had to be paid by both *Jehu* and Joash.

Tenaros: a promontory on the southern coast of the Peloponnese, corresponding to today's Cape Matapan.

Troezen: a town by the Aegean sea in the eastern Peloponnese.

Troy: also called Ilium, Troy was a rich, well-fortified city on the coast of Asia Minor near the Hellespont, the western narrows of the waterway from the Black Sea to the Aegean. After the death of *Hector*, it fell to the Achaeans under *Achilles*.

Tyrian soldiers: from Tyre, a major seaport and trading centre on the Eastern Mediterranean coast. Its wealth and beauty were corrupted by its prince, who was denounced by Ezekiel.

Ulysses: the Latin form of Odysseus, and symbol of the eternal wanderer who confronted many dangers.

Venus: the goddess of love, known to the Greeks as Aphrodite. Aphrodite is the daughter of Zeus and Dione.

Zion: the name of the citadel that dominated all of Jerusalem, and on whose hill stood the temple. The name soon became symbolic for the Holy City.